Us and Them

DAVID BERREBY

Us and Them

Understanding Your Tribal Mind

HUTCHINSON
LONDON

Published by Hutchinson in 2006

1 3 5 7 9 10 8 6 4 2

First published in 2005 in the United States by Little, Brown and Company

Hutchinson
Random House, 20 Vauxhall Bridge Road,
London SW1V 2SA

Random House Australia (Pty) Limited
20 Alfred Street, Milsons Point, Sydney,
New South Wales 2061, Australia

Random House New Zealand Limited
18 Poland Road, Glenfield,
Auckland 10, New Zealand

Random House South Africa (Pty) Limited
Isle of Houghton, Corner of Boundary Road & Carse O'Gowrie,
Houghton 2198, South Africa

The Random House Group Limited Reg. No. 954009
www.randomhouse.co.uk

A CIP catalogue record for this book is available from the British Library

ISBN 0 09 180111 7

Papers used by Random House are natural,
recyclable products made from wood grown in sustainable forests;
the manufacturing processes conform to the environmental
regulations of the country of origin

Printed and bound in Great Britain by
William Clowes Ltd, Beccles, Suffolk

For Beverly

We found several sick and famished Indians, who begged hard for mercy and for food. It hurt my feelings; but the understanding was that all were to be killed. So we did the work.

—SETTLER, OREGON, 1857

Keiko was not one of our kind but nonetheless he was still one of us.

—VETERINARY CHAPLAIN,
SPEAKING AT THE FUNERAL OF KEIKO,
A KILLER WHALE, OREGON, 2003

Contents

Us and Them

Introduction

There are chemicals in coffee, but you don't need a chemist to make a cup. In the same way, brain cells are firing when you love your country, or religion, or culture, but you don't need to know neuroscience to be a patriot.

Still, chemistry has its uses. It's a way of understanding the world that explains much more than routines for kettles and coffee filters. The sciences of mind and brain have their uses too. They offer a new way to look at love of country, of culture, of religion (and at hatred too) — a way that explains more than our day-to-day rules of thumb. These sciences can offer promising answers to the central question of our time: Why can't we all get along? Why, instead, do people live, and die, in nations, races, ethnic groups, religious traditions, and ideologies that mark some as part of Us and others as Them?

The news offers up variations on this problem every morning: Why did these people starve rather than eat food that is not "what we eat"? Why do those people feel ashamed of conduct by "their" soldiers — soldiers they never met, in a place they never saw? Why would that crowd set fire to a religious school because of a crime committed by other believers in that religion who had never seen the place? Why did these people burn expensive, cherished possessions after learning they might have been used in the rites of some *other* kind of people? Old, familiar rules of thumb for making sense of the world offer up old answers: It's their culture. It's in their blood. It's a part of their history. It's just human nature.

These commonsense answers don't explain much. They come in two flavors, both of them platitudinous and vague. One is wonderment: How good and noble is the human soul, to make a man willing to die to save his people. The other is despair: How evil is human nature, which lets a man kill a harmless baby only because it belongs to its parents' tribe.

The sciences of mind and brain can do better than this. They've already begun to explain how and why people think and feel in tribes, and why all of us are capable of *both* tribal good and tribal evil. Those sciences are succeeding, as all the sciences have, by overthrowing commonsense rules of thumb. In other words, scientists today are studying race, ethnicity, nationalism, and other tribalisms, but their results don't confirm what we like to believe about those concepts.

After all, chemistry, the linguist Noam Chomsky has pointed out, has nothing to do with my opinion about how the hot water in my mug turns into tea. Similarly, Francisco Gil-White, an anthropologist at the University of Pennsylvania who studies ethnicity, has written: "It does not matter to me what truck-drivers or lawyers etc. usually mean by 'ethnic group.'" We may feel sure we know what we mean when we talk of races and nations and cultures; we may think we know what we're doing when we classify a stranger and then use that category to understand him. But from a scientific point of view, we don't always know what we're talking about.

For example, it's only common sense that a young person studying for the ministry would prove charitable and kindly. In other words, a person who shows X trait (studying to be a pastor) is a Y kind of human being (a religious person), and those people do Z (behave with charity).

An experiment by the psychologists John M. Darley and C. Dan Batson once tested this assumption. All the participants were students at Princeton Theological Seminary. They were told they had to walk over to another part of the campus and give a talk. Some learned they had just enough minutes left to get to the other building; others had plenty of time; people in the third group were told they were already late.

On the way, each student encountered a stranger, slumped on the ground and in obvious trouble. The real point of the experiment was this moment of choice: Help, or walk on by?

Only one in ten of the rushed students stopped to assist the "victim." But more than 40 percent of the moderate-hurry students stopped, and six in ten of the students with plenty of time did too. It made no difference that all were future ministers, nor did their different philosophies and religious convictions (indicated by questionnaires they'd filled out) predict what they'd do. It didn't even make a difference that half of them were about to give their talk on the parable of the Good Samaritan. The only reliable predictor was how much time pressure they felt.

More recently, psychologists at New York University found that people's altruistic impulses are quite sensitive to subtler differences in their experience. As part of a longer questionnaire, some of their study participants had to list the qualities of comic-book superheroes. Others were asked specifically about Superman. Later on, when they were asked to volunteer for community service, the people who'd thought about superheroes offered much more time than the people who thought about Superman. Thinking about an outstanding *particular* person apparently made people feel they could not measure up — or didn't have to. Thinking about a *kind* of person who is altruistic and good apparently made people act a bit more like that themselves. (That's one way thinking about *kinds* of persons appears to have a different effect than thinking about individuals.)

These studies show how everyday common sense is different from disciplined, rigorous, and systematic methods for posing and answering questions. Sometimes what you're *sure* you know is not what's really going on. Common sense says you see people as they really are, and that you classify them according to true and real categories, like race, religion, and nation, or like occupation, personality type, and age group. But the real causes and effects that work on the mind are likely different from what folk wisdom says. Specifically, these two studies hint that it isn't just *what* you are that causes you to think, feel, and do things; it's *where* you are — what you see happening around you and how you must relate to it.

We see this clearly when we're thinking about ourselves, not others. After all, we tend to explain our own behavior by circumstances. It's our understanding of *other* people that leans on categories. I slept in because of a hard workday. You overslept because of your Mediterranean culture (or because your generation are slackers, or because you're gay and flighty). This is the perceptual difference that Lee D. Ross, a social psychologist, has called the "fundamental attribution error" — too much stress on supposedly unchanging traits to explain others' behavior, too little on situation. One way you can tell it's an error is that you'd never apply such crude generalizations to yourself.

Many, if not most, psychologists are reluctant to go the whole route with this evidence and posit that character types like *aggressive* or *neurotic* are created by circumstance. We see a person in the same surroundings day after day and conclude that his actions come from some unchangeable, unshakable core of his being. So we believe in permanent traits, and support a vast industry to define and measure and detect humankind categories like "extrovert" and "introvert," or "conscientious" and "sensation-seeking." (There are several widely used scales, all of which posit a basic five or six personality traits for everyone.)

But if that person's actions depend on his surroundings, not his core, then we should not be surprised to see him act differently when his surroundings change. That's the position of Walter Mischel, the Columbia psychologist whose work over the past three decades has forced psychologists to take another look at their notions of permanent traits. As he once said, "Someone who cheats on an arithmetic test might not cheat on a spelling test."

One of the most famous demonstrations of circumstances changing behavior took place in the early 1970s at Stanford University. There, the psychologist Philip Zimbardo and his colleagues divided a group of male college students into "guards" and "prisoners" in a simulated jail. In less than a week, the men had changed their behavior to fit their new categories. The "prisoners" sank into despair and helpless rage. Some talked about committing crimes. The "guards" looked down on their former fellow-students in the prison uniforms, and a third of the guards actually abused their charges.

We believe in character traits because, for many people, surroundings don't change much and the belief lets us make good predictions.

But changes in context do happen, and a family's shy brother turns out to be the ham of the high school play; the swaggering athlete becomes shy and awkward in the wedding party.

What is true about our hunches about personality types and occupations is true as well of our beliefs about other categories for human beings — cultures, nations, ethnic groups, races, religions, castes, and political affiliations, to name a few types. Our intuitions may be good enough for day-to-day life, but they don't square with what scientists are learning about how brain and mind work.

So the arrival of mind science will change ancient arguments about race, ethnicity, religion, nation, and other tribal identities. Science brings to those arguments an unfamiliar way of understanding the world. It's a fundamental difference, which I was taught, actually, when I was ten years old, though it took me thirty more years to realize what I had learned.

It began with a very simple experiment. All it needed was a stove, a pot, some water, and a ten-year-old boy. The boy, who was me, knew how it was going to turn out and wanted to get it over with.

Pour water from the tap into the pot, said the homework assignment. Note whether it's cloudy or clear. Then boil the water. Note any changes you see. Come to school on Monday with your report.

Ten minutes, tops, I figured. The water came out cloudy from the tap. After it sat for a few minutes it was clear. Once it was boiling, I knew, it would be cloudy again. How did I know? That's not a question you ask about self-evident truth. And so I poured, and looked, and noted. Cloudy. Then I put the pot on the stove, and lit a burner. My mother watched, mildly interested in the protocol and very interested in fire prevention.

The water boiled. I looked. Then things got difficult.

The boiling water was clear. Very clear, clear as air, annoyingly, inescapably clear. Something was wrong.

So I did it all again. Same results. I got water from the bathroom tap. I changed pots. I did the procedure again. And again. My mother, a morning person, went to bed. I am a night owl. I poured. I looked. I boiled. Over and over and over. What was wrong with this water? It was 1:00 or 2:00 A.M. when I finally got the point and learned the real lesson.

The problem wasn't the water, or the pot, or the stove. The problem was in my head. My absolute, confident certainty that heat made water go cloudy was not ever going to be confirmed by this little experiment. I now had a choice: Trust my knowledge, of which I had been so sure at dinnertime. Or trust my method for finding out what was real. I had to trust my *method*.

The uniquely scientific point I'd learned, then, was definitely not the sense that I had found "the answer." Religious people know that feeling too, and so do political fanatics, Civil War reenactors, and people who read mystery novels. Many nonscientific activities offer the satisfaction of working out an answer from principles; many experiences can leave me feeling that I know the truth. Many scientists do remark on a feeling of rightness and inevitability when work goes well. But so do novelists.

Nor was the key point that I had learned to respect the facts. I had, but that's not unique to science either. Almost every human activity, from accounting to writing operas to buying groceries, demands that you relate the thoughts between your ears to known facts. To be brought up short by reality is not science; it's just life. What made this a *science* lesson was the long time I spent not feeling certainty and not knowing facts — when the only thing I knew for sure was that I did not know what to think.

In most walks of life, it's the ultimate answer that's cherished. You're expected to stick by your Truth, and the questioning stage that got you there is dark and difficult. It is an endurance test that you shudder to enter and are glad to leave. Uncertainty is work. Certainty is the payoff.

Science is different. In science, uncertainty is the payoff. Every scientist I've met enjoys explaining something, but few want to explain *everything*. If anybody ever does, after all, the joys of science will end. For scientists, the fun part is figuring out the right question, devising a way to address it, and seeing what happens next. To do it right, they know, they must remind themselves — whatever they may have read, or been taught, or hope to find, or feel is right because they did the calculations or they have a hunch — that in their work they are waiting to see what will happen, because they *don't know*. Not knowing isn't a problem. It's the goal.

As Robert M. Sapolsky, the biologist and essayist, puts it, "For every question answered, a dozen newer ones are generated. And they are usually far more puzzling, more challenging than the prior problems. . . . [T]he purpose of science is not to cure us of our sense of mystery and wonder, but to constantly reinvent and reinvigorate it."

That practice takes mental discipline, but it's a mental discipline at odds with what people do when they're thinking nonscientifically. There, most often, you fight against doubt. If you think that maybe your God does not exist, or your nation's cause is unjust, then you wrestle with your thoughts, trying not to let them mar your behavior. In science, though, your faith in the outcome is beside the point. What matters — what you strive to get right, and what gets you judged by your peers — is your means of answering the question: experimental procedures, conferences, journals, and the other practices that make up science. What scientists hold to over time are the standards for doing it right. Not today's theory, which must inevitably be replaced by tomorrow's.

Eternal truth, unfailing truth, truth that cannot be doubted, is not what science is for. In this, science is not a different kind of work from other occupations that require decisions and commitments based on incomplete knowledge — lines of work that include medicine, law, politics, and journalism. Scientists do not deal in final answers, guaranteed for all time. They deal in probabilities about the relationship of one observation to another. Are human activities a cause of global warming? Likely. Does cigarette smoking cause cancer? Very likely. Will the sun rise tomorrow? Very, very likely. The most accurate reply to a question in science is that answer X has some probability of being right and that we can be some percent sure that this is correct. Both probability and that percentage of assurance can get really close to 100 but they never attain it. If a problem can't be framed for this kind of answer — X percent probability, to a Y percent degree of confidence — then it probably isn't a scientific question in the first place.

Does heating cloudy tap water make it go clear? Also very likely. At least in Manhattan when I was ten years old. Does the same prediction hold in Seattle and in Sri Lanka? Are my definitions of *heat* and *cloudy* and *clear* good enough for the job? Is this even the right question to be asking about water? Surely, scientists would say, more research is needed. Unless they would say, as often they do, oh, no one works on that anymore. Other questions have come along.

Doing science means accepting that truths are temporary — the best we can do now, until more is learned. So when creationists say that evolution is just a theory, they're missing the point. *All* scientific knowledge is "just theory," destined to be replaced. Creation myths don't belong in science class precisely because they're supposed to be the final, unchanging truth about the universe, and science doesn't deal in that sort of knowledge.

The historian and physicist Peter Galison once put it this way: "Most physicists think equations suggest there's something out there. But that those equations are true forever? Most physicists don't think that. If they found something that was true forever, they'd probably be disappointed."

For the past five centuries, science has been encroaching on areas of life once dominated by plain common sense. Common sense said the sun moves around the earth; not so, said Galileo and company. Common sense tells you that unguided accidents can't design a complicated biological machine like an eye. Wrong, say evolutionary biologists. Eyes need no design; in fact, they have evolved many separate times out of whatever parts could serve. Common sense says that time moves at the same rate everywhere. Not so, says relativity theory.

It's part of the job of science to explain why you can't trust what you are sure you know, and then to give you today's best picture of what's really happening. That picture is sure to change, but today's version is useful right now. Truth and certainty and fact are not matters that endure forever. For knowledge to increase, they must be subject to the useful discipline of doubt.

If you had kept up with the latest science over the past century, for instance, you would have learned that Albert Einstein once considered the cosmological constant in his theory of the universe to be his "greatest blunder" — but in this decade, the cosmological constant may be back. You would have learned early in the last century that continents don't drift around the surface of the globe — until geologists decided that they do. You might have toured the natural history museum and admired the skeleton of brontosaurus, until the day paleontologists canceled brontosaurus and arranged the bones in a new shape, under a new name, according to a better picture.

In basic biology, you would also have been told that women and other female mammals are born with all the eggs they will have in life, because the body doesn't make more. But in 2004, researchers announced that this may not be true. In the early part of the last decade, your doctor might have prescribed a bone marrow transplant for your cancer; by decade's end, doctors decided those transplants don't do much good. You might have shunned protein and fat in your diet and eaten a lot of carbohydrates — the path to good health, according to nutritionists' ideas of the 1980s. Now you're told too many carbs will fatten you up and kill you.

A few more examples: If you're middle-aged today, you learned in basic biology that most parts of the adult human brain can't grow new cells — but in the 1990s scientists came up with experiments that indicate that, in fact, adult brains can and do. You would also have been taught that human beings have a larger proportion of their brains devoted to the frontal cortex, the apparent seat of thinking and planning, than do chimpanzees or monkeys. In 2004, though, a comparative study found that this proportion is the same in the brains of all twenty-five primate species examined.

All this revising does not mean there is anything wrong. Rather, this is science working as it should. Today's theory will be replaced by tomorrow's, and everyone knows it. That, by the way, is why science can't be the basis of a religion or a political creed. We want our gods, and our rights and obligations, to be good forever. But scientists must doubt, check, reexamine, and reconceive their work. Science *changes.*

Once scientists get hold of a subject, then, it has left the realm of absolute certainty. So biology, the science of life, is different from "folk biology," the set of beliefs everyone has about living things, just as psychology, the science of mind, is different from folk psychology, the commonsense notions everyone uses to explain why people do things. Once you learn your folk biology and folk psychology in childhood, it appears, you count on them for the rest of your life.

They don't question themselves. Science does. That is what makes it such a force for political and cultural upheaval.

That disturbing force is not supported by industries and governments for its own sake. There is a payoff — one that, at the level of technology, almost everyone happily takes. As the evolutionary theorist Richard Dawkins notes, even fundamentalist creationists trust the worldview of science with their lives whenever they take a plane to meet other fundamentalists. Though no scientific theory will endure forever, each breakthrough affords people power to make things happen. When a theory evaporates, it's usually replaced by one that can do more, not less.

Us and Them describes another one of science's assaults on certainty. Just as a chemist doesn't care how we make tea, so, increasingly, psychologists, neuroscientists, and anthropologists are letting go of supposedly obvious truths about nationalism, religion, and race. Those notions are being subjected to the discipline of doubt.

You could see this undermining of common sense about how people are as a threat. But a lot of common sense has proved, in other times and places, to be both blind and cruel. In North America, common sense once included the idea that slavery was a natural state of affairs, that women should not vote, and that only heterosexuals were worthy of respect. Good riddance to all that. Longstanding miseries can't be cured until the overthrow of the certainties that support them.

Defending common sense, the English novelist and essayist G. K. Chesterton once compared change in human affairs to an unpainted fence. The white fence post soon becomes black, he wrote, unless someone keeps painting it the same color. A person of orthodox beliefs is out there with a brush, restoring the fence to its ideal state.

Science, as Chesterton saw, is inherently, inescapably antiorthodox (whatever your orthodoxy might be). Science has to wonder, What happens if the fence isn't white? Maybe it's worth finding out. A scientist wouldn't let the fence rot for the hell of it, but if she could create a controlled situation in which the fence's decay would teach her something, then she'd do it. That's the definition of an experiment — a situation that has been carefully managed to make sure that you can learn from the unexpected. The experimenter is waiting to be surprised (ideally, waiting with precise, controlled instruments to make sure the surprise isn't wasted). If you know exactly what will happen, you aren't doing an experiment. You're doing a drill.

Bringing science to the conversation about race, ethnicity, religion, nationalism, and the rest of the human kinds, then, means changing how we view them. It means giving up certainties. For the moment, many of us are still arguing about whether races are real. About whether, objectively speaking, my tribe's diet is healthier than yours. About whether people at the top of society's heap have better brains, or better genes, or better cultures than the rest of us. Soon these arguments will seem as quaint as medieval counts of angels dancing on the head of a pin. When science comes to look at the tribal mind, it will not use familiar categories and ask old questions.

That's a little disorienting. But, as I discovered late one night in the kitchen, not every certainty is worth preserving.

One

"That's Our Biggest Difference"

All good people agree,
And all good people say,
All nice people, like Us, are We
And every one else is They.

— RUDYARD KIPLING, "A FRIEND OF THE FAMILY"

Scientists, when they turn their attention to people, usually talk about the entire human race or about the individual human being. Those are two faces of the same idea. Truth about all is truth about each; a theory about the mind or morality applies to everyone who ever lived, as well as to you in particular. Either perspective yields big explanations, which make many predictions to test and suggest many experiments. It's where researchers like to be — working on "the" genome, or "the" brain, or "the" self.

They aren't nearly as comfortable with the categories in between one person and all people — the ones that researchers, like everyone else, use when they're off duty, away from their work. Categories like Americans and Iranians, Muslims and Christians, blacks and whites, men and women, southerners and northerners, doctors and lawyers, gays and straights, soccer moms and NASCAR dads, outgoing people and shy types, smart ones and lucky ones. Those — and all other labels that define more than one person but fewer than all — are what

I (following the philosopher Ian Hacking and the psychological anthropologist Lawrence A. Hirschfeld) call "human kinds."

Human kinds, whose memberships fall between All and One, map a much more variegated world than that one-size-fits-all label *Homo sapiens.* Some human kinds are types, like cranky old men and plumbers. Others are cultures, like Basques and Thais. Some are old and populous, like the category Japanese or Jain; others are small-scale and recent, like "former graduate students of Steven Pinker."

Some human kinds even include nonhumans. Your family, for example, might include a dog or a cat for which you feel more and do more than you do for faraway people. And human kinds may also enfold nonliving things — like flags, sacred books, and graves — that are revered and protected as if they too had lives to live and lose.

Human kinds are infinitely divisible: examine one, and you find inside it subcategories and, inside those, still more. For example, military veterans are a distinct kind of person from those who did not serve; Navy vets are distinct from other services; those who served in the brown-shoe navy (its aviation-related services) are distinct from the black-shoe navy (other ships), and among the black-shoe vets submariners are their own tribe, and so on and on. Some human kinds, we are told from a very early age, we were born into — families, races, ethnic groups, religions, and nations. Other kinds are based on bodies: male and female, athletic or disabled. There are other kinds that other people put us into, like nerd or jock, Bible-thumper or Godless secular humanist. There are the kinds we join by passing special tests, like doctor or accountant. And the ones we join to make a living, like pizza guy or copyeditor. There are happenstance human kinds, like "women in the ladies' room on the 8:15 ferry." There are others we sign ourselves into by conviction, like the National Rifle Association or the Democratic Party, and some we join because we think we must to survive — like gangs, militias, and secret societies.

Some human kinds make sense only because members see and depend on each other every day, like the soldiers in a combat unit. Others consist of people who never meet, like the millions of fellow citizens those soldiers defend. In other words, human kinds serve so many different needs, there is no single recipe for making one. Parentage makes a person a Brahmin, training makes her a soldier, sending in dues makes her a member of a religious congregation. She can convert to Islam, but not to Chineseness; she can marry into Protestantism, not into liberalism.

Why is all this variety possible? That's not a question that can be answered by looking at the political, economic, or cultural aspects of human kinds, as important as those aspects are. The issue is not what human kinds are in the *world,* but what they are in the *mind* — not how we tell Tamils and Seventh-Day Adventists and fans of Manchester United from their fellow human beings, but why we want to.

After all, other creatures get along fine without dividing themselves into such tribes. With one important exception, for instance, humanity's close relative the chimpanzee goes through life quite well solving only problems about Everychimp and problems about My Friend and Cousin, the one with the long face and the limp — chimps in general and individuals. Yet a human who went through life like that would not know what "our kind" of food is, or enjoy "our kind" of music, or know what "we do" when someone dies. Such a person, lacking any sense of family tradition, religious history, patriotism, or cultural pride, would not live a fully human life. Human-kind thinking is an absolute requirement for being human.

Which brings up the dark side: people are killed for nothing more than their membership in the "wrong" tribes. Many times in the past few years, young men who were polite and thoughtful to members of their own sort, who loved their mothers and listened to their fathers and cared for their children, set out to kill other people's mothers and fathers and children without a qualm — in New York City on September 11, 2001; in Beslan, Russia, on September 1, 2004; in Nazi-ruled Europe in the 1930s and 1940s. More examples could fill every page of this book. Throughout history, killers have worked with zeal because they believed their victims were not of the same kind as the people they cared about, the people who mattered. No wonder people both cherish and fear the power of tribal thinking. No wonder they want to understand it.

Many people today find themselves struggling, again and again, with a difficult question: Who is "our side"? In the days after the September 11 attacks, the prime minister of Italy spoke of the superiority of Christian civilization and was immediately denounced by his allies; two religious leaders in the United States tried to claim that abortionists and civil libertarians did not belong in the new alliance against terror because they made God angry. The president of the United States, though he was a political ally, rebuked the clergymen. The new antiterror coalition of nations could not make war on Islam because they had millions of Muslim citizens. Was it, then, a coalition of democracies? The most important frontline ally in the ensuing war was Pakistan, a dictatorship. Obviously, sides in the current conflict were *chosen;* they aren't a matter of "natural" or inevitable divisions. Today it is clear as never before that human kinds — those categories we use to explain human acts on every scale, from a morning walk ("Why were those men wearing turbans?") to all of history ("Is war inevitable?") — don't depend on what people *are,* but on what people *believe.*

That's the difference between human tribes and the boundaries animals observe. Many creatures, from mice and pigeons to lions and dolphins, know a member of "our group" from a stranger. All these creatures have been well studied in the past few decades, and the pattern is clear: fights *within* the group are limited and tend not to get out of hand, but fights *between* groups end in deaths. This in-group restraint, as the psychiatrist and author Jonathan Shay has said, gave rise to the widely believed myth that animals don't kill their own kind. In fact many animals — lions, gorillas, chimpanzees, hyenas — are happy to kill their own. The victim just can't be a member of their little band.

Animals, though, don't make *decisions* about who is "in" and who is "out." A dog guards her puppies because they are kin, and members of her human family because they are friends. But no dog quits her humans because they have converted to Catholicism or put a peace sign on the lawn.

People can and will make that sort of change, because people, unlike animals, make choices based on signs — crosses, uniforms, peace signs, oaths, and other indicators of a particular human kind. Animals have kin and animals have friends, but only human beings trust *symbols* to tell who is kin and who is a friend.

One August night in New York City in 1997, for example, the crucial symbol was a tiny piece of metal. A white cop beat up a black man he had arrested. Later, both men were in the bathroom of the police station, where the officer spotted a tiny crucifix that his victim wore around his neck. That was enough to make the cop put away one map of human kinds and take up another — instead of police against suspect, or white against black, he now saw two fellow Christians. The officer said he too believed in Jesus, and apologized.

In Sovu, Rwanda, on May 6, 1994, the symbol was a bit of cloth. That day, Tutsi refugees sought escape from bands of Hutus in Sovu's convent. The mother superior, Sister Gertrude, called in the Hutu militia. Hundreds of the Tutsi were shot, hacked, or burned to death. But Sister Gertrude did not turn over the convent's Tutsi nuns. Their veils protected them. Seeing this, a nineteen-year-old woman named Aline, the niece of a nun, begged for a veil. Sister Gertrude refused.

Seven years later, she was convicted in Belgium of war crimes. Among the witnesses was the murdered niece's mother. "My daughter was killed because of a little piece of cloth," she said. If humans are, as the neuroscientist Terence Deacon puts it, the "symbolic species," then human kinds are among those features that reveal our uniqueness. A symbolic strip of cloth — its presence saving you from a pack of rampaging killers, its absence marking you as the kind to kill — is something only *Homo sapiens* creates.

But a symbol, like that nun's veil, is meaningless unless it is understood. If the murderers had thought it was *just* a bit of cloth, for example, they would have killed all the Tutsi who wore it. Any activity that depends on symbols can't be understood without taking into account the human minds that use those symbols. Imagine trying to get by in Kinyarwanda, the language shared by Hutu and Tutsi, by treating it only as a system of sounds — wavelengths and acoustic properties. You wouldn't get far until you accepted that these sounds *meant* something, and found someone to explain what those meanings were.

In the same way, human kinds can't be understood objectively, as a collection of facts about blood types, skull shapes, average ages, preferred brands, and so on. Those facts seen from the outside can never tell what the human kind *means*. That meaning is made inside the heads of people who believe in it.

Scientists who study a pack of macaque monkeys can predict who gets along with whom. Knowing which animals are relatives and which are allies lets an observer explain the fights and frolics very well. But "objective" knowledge of human kinds does not. Sister Gertrude was a Hutu, so you would not be surprised if she had sent all the Tutsi in the convent to death. Yet she was also a nun, so it's not a surprise that she saved fellow *nuns* even though they were Tutsi. She was also a Christian; it would be admirable and understandable if she had stood, on religious principles, against the killing of any human being.

The important point is that *any* of these alternatives is possible. Mindless facts — who is a Tutsi, who is a Hutu, who has a veil, who lacks one — cannot predict what people will do. Human beings are unusually alike, compared to most species. We're also, each of us, unique. From those two facts, it follows that measurable, objective differences will always exist between *any* two groupings of people, and that any two groups, no matter how different, will be the same on many other measures. It will always be possible to find differences between this race and that one, this nation and those, people with this gene versus people without it. But not one of those facts will tell why you divided people into the human kinds you chose to analyze.

People who look at the traits of the kinds themselves, then, are posing the wrong questions. Do American Jews have higher average scores on certain academic tests than other Americans? Do African American marrieds have sex more often than others? Are Hispanics more likely to attend church? Maybe so, maybe not; but people don't start with data and then divide the world into Jews, African Americans, and Hispanics. It's the other way around. First we believe in those human kinds, and then, because we believe, we gather the data. To understand this aspect of ourselves, we don't need any more facts about human kinds. We need facts about human *minds*.

One way to find those facts is to study human kinds as if they were rules for *thinking* — methods of sorting out perceptions. You see a woman caring for her child and class her as a mother; you see a white-haired, stooped man and class him as an old person. That's a psychologist's approach. On the other hand, sociologists and anthropologists have looked at human kinds as rules for *behavior* — methods of knowing what people are supposed to do. In the right circum-stances, knowing that someone is in the navy, or a doctor, or a de-vout Christian, tells you what he's likely to do, and how you should act in your turn. That knowledge serves as a bulwark against the force of ever-changing circumstances. Feeling hurried or stressed makes people less likely to help another person, but a reminder of their duties as members of a human kind can make them turn back. A military uniform, a Hippocratic oath, a bracelet that asks Chris-tians "what would Jesus do?" — such tokens of membership make our actions more consistent than they would otherwise be. They re-mind us to look beyond the emotions of right here, right now, and act as members should. The navy is supposed to defend the nation, doctors to heal the sick, Christians to be Christlike, no matter what.

So these human kinds offer the joy of belonging to something larger than the little self; they let us thrill to a feeling of existence across centuries and continents, of being alive so long as "we," our kind, endure. The first type of human kind is a category based on traits ("white hair equals old person," for example). The second type is based on obligations ("Soldiers must serve the nation"). An insti-tution of this second sort, we sense, must act consistently, even if in-dividual members fail it. That's what defines human kinds of this second type: the things people do to belong.

That consistency makes it easy to think of this sort of human kind as if it were a person itself — a being with thoughts, plans, and feel-ings of its own. Nations have moods, schools have spirits, and a con-gregation can repent. You can say the navy has decided to seek more recruits next year. It's harder to come up with a sentence about how the world's mothers have decided to act.

Nonetheless, these two viewpoints — human kinds as categories and human kinds as entities that happen to be made of people — are looking at one phenomenon. All human kinds have aspects of both, though the proportions can change over time. Half a century ago in North America, "homosexual" was mostly a category for people. To-day in many Western nations, gays and lesbians are seen as an entity that wants, hopes, decides, and votes. On the other hand, the Nor-wegian community of New York City used to be an entity, with neighborhoods, clubs, and churches that helped organize people's lives. "Norwegians" made up a thing made *of* people. Today New York's Norwegians, despite annual parades, are mostly members of a category *for* people.

Underlying our myriad human kinds, then, is a fundamental unity. It is reflected in the way people blur distinctions. Most people don't blink at the much-used phrase "moderate Hutus," for example, even though "moderate" and "militant" describe political convictions and the Hutu are an ethnic group. Yes, it's birth that makes you a Brahmin, but it takes training to live as one; yes, you must sign up for army service, but many a son and grandson of military officers has enlisted because he felt "born to it." You become an employee of a corporation to make a living, but you can come to feel a familylike love for the place — like those Apple Computer employees who were said to bleed in the six colors of the company logo.

In fact, people speak about all human kinds with one language; something said about one can be said about any other. For example, when the American political commentator Paul Begala interviewed a prominent congressman, J. C. Watts, for a television program in 2002, he began: "Let me say, I'm a liberal. You're a conservative. That's not our biggest difference. I'm white, you're black, that's not our biggest difference. I'm a Texas Longhorn and you're an Oklahoma Sooner, and . . ."

"That's our biggest difference," Watts said.

"That's the biggest," Begala replied. "That's bigger than anything else."

It wasn't, of course. Banter about college football was, in fact, a demonstration that there was a way in which they were *not* different. They were getting in sync, establishing that there is a human kind to which they both belong: powerful Washington guy. (For men of this tribe, as the journalist Nicholas Lemann noted, sports joshing is a way to signal that "membership in a community of important people trumps the enmity the system forces them to act out.") Notice, though, what made the conversation possible: the way politics, race, and sports fandom can be talked about as if they were the same.

Why should these different human kinds, with their different purposes and histories, feel equivalent? One reason is that they share mental processes. Your ability to think of people as "German" partly depends on your general ability to categorize *anything* — to divide a flood of perceptions into birds and trees, gears and Gummi bears, hip-hop on the radio and grapes in a bowl on the table. Pigeonholes for people get some of their qualities from the mental equipment that makes pigeonholes for everything.

Categories of all sorts help explain what's happened and predict what will come next. Human kinds help predict what *people* will do, and there too they draw from a general capacity to find causes and patterns. "Today is cloudy and humid" is information that licenses you to predict that it might rain. Similarly, "He is a graduate of the University of Oklahoma" is a piece of information that lets you predict a stranger likely will follow the Sooners through football season.

You also use human kinds to understand yourself. That means they must link to the brain's systems for monitoring the body, both inside and outside of your conscious awareness. "I feel tired and achy because I have been working hard" is a statement that combines your mind's reports on your mood and bodily state with memories and thoughts about cause and effect. "I get my self-reliance from my pioneer ancestors" is the same kind of multiprocess report, which relates your sense of yourself to your knowledge of cause and effect.

There are other ways in which thoughts and feelings about human kinds must involve a general-purpose mental machine, applied to the particular problem of understanding others. For example, people tend to treat nonhuman things as if they were human. We say cancer is a cruel disease, as if cancer had a personality; we yell at the crashed computer, as if it decided to ruin our file. Whether or not it can be true, we assume that things happen as the result of thoughts and moods in the minds of other beings. When people do the same thing to a tribe, as when they say, "America is arrogant," or "Buddhists are gentle," they're applying this general-purpose habit to human kinds.

The mind also is equipped with a predisposition to understand other people and to get along with them. We attach this ability to team up with others to our sense of human kinds. We decide that someone is trustworthy not because we know him but because "he's a Mormon" or "she's a surgeon." There, too, we're applying a general habit to the special realm of human kinds.

So it's not too surprising that football fandom and race and nationality and religion can be talked about with the same words. These
human-kind perceptions have different fates in society, but they
come from shared pathways in the mind.

Yet that doesn't explain why people, unlike other creatures, have
such elaborate categories for one another. Robins are a kind of bird,
and Christians are a kind of person, and so those two concepts must
share categorizing processes in the brain. But the category "Christians" also taps emotions and thoughts that don't arise when classing
birds. It's likely, then, that there's a second major reason all human
kinds feel alike: they draw on a *special* piece of the mind, which is
dedicated only to them.

What might this special human-kind maker be like? One safe bet
is this: it is not based on the rules of logic. It works outside of awareness, according to rules of its own. It is not at all like the rigorous
study of causes and effects that people call science.

After all, much of what people say about human kinds is, as a matter of measurable fact and logic, meaningless. A soccer fan says, "We
have a good chance of getting to the playoffs," but he'll have no
effect on the matches, because he isn't on the team. A corporate
spokesman says, "We're sorry that our product was defective," though
he had nothing to do with making or marketing it. An African American preacher says, "We came to this continent as slaves," yet neither
he nor anyone he knows was ever in shackles. A devout Shiite weeps
and flagellates himself in grief on the tenth of Muharram for the
death of Imam Hussein at Karbala; but that martyrdom took place
more than thirteen hundred years ago, in the year 680 C.E., and no
one alive today could have seen it.

These nonliteral ways of saying "we" aren't logical, but obviously
they aren't meaningless. People understand them, and distinguish them
from nonsense. That means people use *some* set of rules to decide
that a sentence like "We Americans fought a war with Spain" is
comprehensible, while "We left-handed folk are a generous people"
is twaddle. These aren't the rules of science, but so what? They do
different work for the mind and heart.

Language, though, has its own rules, which don't respect this distinction. Grammar doesn't reveal when we're speaking logically and when we're speaking — often with the same words — in the special code of human kinds. So we're inclined to think the same word means the same thing all the time. That hunch is wrong.

The way it's wrong reminds me of the story of an awkward lunch in 1944 where the British prime minister, Winston Churchill, met Mr. Berlin.

Isaiah Berlin, the philosopher and historian, had been serving as a diplomat in New York and Washington. Churchill had been impressed with his work. He asked: "Berlin, what do you think is your most important piece you've done for us lately?"

A little hesitantly, his guest replied: "'White Christmas.'" He was the wrong Mr. Berlin — Irving, the songwriter, not Isaiah, the polymath. In that instance, one word — Berlin — certainly did *not* mean one thing. Human-kind words often exhibit this variability. Just as a screwdriver in the toolbox is different from the screwdriver you order from a bartender, so "we" in a sentence like "We Americans beat Spain in a war" is different from the "we" in "We Americans number about 290 million."

One of those two meanings — we the citizens of the United States, as defined by law, who are alive today — fits into the framework of science. It describes physical objects that can be measured. The other idea — we Americans, including people who no longer exist because they died a century ago; we Americans, including people who did not experience the war — comes out of different rules for defining *we*.

If human kinds have their own rules, separate from those of logic or human institutions, and if those rules operate outside of our awareness, then the scientific study of human-kind beliefs will have some weird implications. For one thing, trivial, meaningless, ephemeral human kinds — if they meet the requirements of the hidden rules — could make and unmake people's lives with the same force as the human kinds we respect, like religions, nations, and ethnicities.

It's a strange idea. Could human kinds like "*Star Trek* fan" and "Porsche owner" ever weigh as heavy in a human heart as a religious tradition, with all its culture and moral seriousness? If that were so, then history would afford examples of oddball academic ideas that turned into the basis for mass murder; it would include instances of people changing their lives, even killing and dying, for sports teams or handkerchiefs.

Most peculiar. Yet this has happened throughout history. That too is part of the evidence that human kinds have a separate realm in the mind.

In the nineteenth century, linguists and anthropologists took a Sanskrit word for *noble* and turned it into a term to describe a family of ancient languages. So the human kind called "Aryans" was born. Languages were all it referred to, wrote the German scholar Max Müller: "I have declared again and again that if I say Aryas, I mean neither blood nor bones, nor hair, nor skull." Nonetheless, as Müller's protest shows, this academic term quickly took on tribal trappings. A few decades later, reinforced by other newly created human kinds, like National Socialist and "expert" on Jewish matters — assigned by law to every government office under Hitler — Aryan was a life-and-death human kind. Nowadays, in the form of gangs like the Aryan Brotherhood in American prisons, it continues to be a category that gets people killed.

In 1969 Honduras and El Salvador went to war over a soccer match. Today gangs of "soccer hooligans" shadow games in Europe, where they maim and occasionally kill each other in the name of their teams. A study of such violence in Holland in the 1990s found that these soccer tribes were racially mixed and drew poor, working-class, and higher-income men. In other words, members' devotion to their teams wasn't a stand-in for some supposedly more serious loyalty to class or race. The human kind for which they risked their lives was the soccer gang.

As sports wars go, these recent instances are unremarkable compared to combat between "fans of the green team in the chariot race" versus "fans of the blue." The fighting over those two kinds of person spanned centuries in the Byzantine Empire, as the opposed groupings grew into political, cultural, and organized-crime institutions. One of these outbreaks of mass violence, at Constantinople in 532 C.E., killed thirty thousand people.

A human kind need not acquire tribal myths, as "Aryan" did, nor gather people under team colors, as sports fans do. Banal, practical human kinds have also been made fatal. One way to be targeted during the Cambodian genocide of 1975–79, for example, was to be the kind of person who wears eyeglasses.

This was not because the country's traditional human kinds were forgotten. The Yale historian Ben Kiernan has documented how the Khmer Rouge's genocidal policies hit — and were intended to hit — Vietnamese, Chinese, and Cham people harder than Cambodian Khmers. Nonetheless, more than 1 million Khmer perished out of approximately 1.7 million people killed in this atrocity; being Khmer was not in itself enough to protect anyone. To be spared, one had to be the *right sort* of Khmer. To wear glasses was to show the sign of being the wrong sort — a person who had received an education under the old regime. A happenstance human kind became a means to sort the living from the doomed.

Many don't want to believe people kill, or die, for a mere mental pigeonhole. So they turn to the other levels of explanation: wars over soccer games and chariots must "really" have been about other, respectably economic and political matters.

Certainly soccer wars and chariot races did not blot out Salvadoran thoughts or Byzantine schemes. But people belong to many human kinds at once; he who is proudly Dutch in many circumstances may nonetheless die fighting other Dutchmen, in the name of Rotterdam's team. In that moment, in that place, it is not nation or race that determines who is murdered, but soccer fandom. In that moment, it's the warrior's belief that counts. An economist may find causes for mob violence that the mob never heard of; the fact remains that the people killing and dying in ancient Antioch were talking chariots, not economics.

So kind-mindedness is not "really" something else in disguise. It is itself — the mind's guide for understanding anyone we do not know personally, for seeing our place in the human world, and for judging our actions. This human-kind psychology is a source, not just a consequence, of institutions: national governments, religious authorities, promoters of ethnic, racial, class, or gender pride. We care about today's political tribes only because these entities have learned how to speak to the human-kind faculty in its language.

Speaking the right human-kind language, you can make *any* happenstance collection of people feel tribal, even one like "women on the 8:15 ferry." In fact, in 2003 a documentary filmmaker made a movie about just that group — women who spent their morning commute together chatting, putting on makeup, and relaxing in the ladies' room of the 8:15 Staten Island Ferry. When the film came out, the women told reporters their membership in that particular human kind meant a lot to them. And their earliest response to the filmmaker had been to wonder who this outsider was and why she was hanging out in their territory.

Then, too, even a trivial human kind, defined by nothing more consequential than what people buy, can call up the intense emotions supposedly reserved for the serious tribes. That's what happened to one owner of a Porsche 911 sports car after he learned that the company had started to make sport utility vehicles. "Every SUV I've seen is driven by some soccer mom on her cellphone," he told a reporter. "I hate these people, and that Porsche would throw me into that category made me speechless. Just speechless."

Speechless! Kind-mindedness can be downright embarrassing. It lacks gravitas. It goes its own way. That's a good reason for scientists to shun the whole business. Who wants to be yelled at for supposedly equating race and religion with soccer hooligans and Porsche owners?

And yelling there will be. Aside from being messy conceptually, human kinds are sticky, emotionally. There's no place to stand outside of them, to look on them without feeling. All people are members of human kinds, and so whenever human kinds are the subject, the conversation feels personal. Reading the news in the morning, we're pained to learn that studies show "our people" are fat, or do poorly on math tests, or don't spend enough time with their children. We're proud and pleased when our athletes win at the Olympics, or when we read that our troops acted nobly. We're scared when we learn about a human kind that threatens ours. Presented with any list of human kinds — in a newspaper article, on a Web site, on a restaurant place mat with the Chinese zodiac printed on it — always, inescapably, a part of us wonders: Which one fits *me?* Am I metro or retro? Gobbler or nibbler? Snake or horse? Human-kind thoughts are impossible to separate from your feelings about yourself.

Some scientists' distaste for human kinds as a research subject may come from a desire to avoid thoughtless, factless passion. They want to stay within the framework of science, confining themselves to matters their methods can address. Outside that realm, many feel, science can't venture, and scientists shouldn't. As the great physicist Richard Feynman said, "A scientist looking at a non-scientific problem is just as dumb as the next guy."

And what could be less like science than talk of race and nation and religion, family and sexual identity and sports — veined as it always is with vague words and strong emotions? Human kinds are gnarly, demanding, and perplexing, like intimate life. If a human kind matters, people will talk of it as if it were a family: the "brothers and sisters" of houses of worship, union halls, and political rallies; the "children of God" of the preachers; the "brothers" who went through war, or college, or prison together; the friendly office with the family atmosphere.

This doesn't mean, of course, that we think of such groupings as literal families, or that we wish they were. If you call your sexual partner "baby," it doesn't indicate you'd rather have sex with an infant. But it is an expression of something everyone learns as groups sort themselves on the playgrounds of early childhood: being part of a human kind, or excluded from one, can alter your life.

Such consequential changes, wrought by being in a human kind, can be conscious and deliberate, as it is for Christians who ask themselves, "What would Jesus do?" Sometimes, though, the effects of human-kind thinking take place outside awareness. In one experiment, for example, Asian American women students at Harvard who were reminded that they were Asian did better on a math test than Asian American women who were reminded that they were women. Math may be the most rational of activities, but it's apparently not free of the sort of human-kind thinking that tells you women aren't so good at it, while Asians are. This does not mean that all human kinds *make* you change; it does mean that they have that potential, and being a human being, you know it.

Professionally, as I've mentioned, many scientists want nothing to do with such an emotional and conceptual swamp. Human-kind categories are fine for life outside the lab — sure, set up a committee to attract more minorities into our field; yes, let us try to make our nation a leader in stem-cell research. But nations, minorities, creeds, professions, as an object of scientific research? Leave that to colleagues with a screw loose or, worse, to cranks and journalists.

This is not to say that scientists are less tribal than anyone else. The passions of Us and Them affect them too. In fact, feelings about nation, religion, culture, tradition, and other human kinds have helped to motivate scientific work, as they have helped to motivate almost all organized activities, for good and for ill, from Olympic athletics to mass murder.

For example, modern neuroscience rests on the successes of the great Spanish anatomist Santiago Ramón y Cajal, who finished publishing his masterpiece on the brain and nervous system in 1904. In another example of the ever-changing character of scientific knowledge, Cajal's work ended a long debate about whether the human brain consisted of distinct cells at all. He championed the neuron doctrine — that the brain, like every other organ, was made up of millions of distinct cells, the neurons. (Nowadays the brain is described as neurons and glial cells, but the central argument, which Cajal won, was that it was not organized differently from the rest of the body.)

When the book was published, Spain had just lost a war to the United States, and that unscientific fact was much on the author's mind.

"Above all," Cajal wrote in his autobiography, "I wanted my book to be — please excuse the presumption — a trophy to be laid at the feet of our prostrate national science and an offering of fervent devotion by a Spaniard to his scorned country." Clearly, Cajal valued his fervent devotion. Yet he did not study patriotic neurons or Spanish neurons, but all neurons. He saw brain cells as a scientist, but apparently he saw his book about cells as a patriot.

Well, as the cognitive scientist George Lakoff of the University of California at Berkeley has put it, ask different questions, you get different answers. The rules of patriotism and the rules of the lab aren't the same. The best way to live with different systems of rules is not to try to fit them together, because they don't align. It's quite enough work to keep clear about how each system is different from the others.

On the one hand, philosophy and psychology, at least in the West, have largely focused on the individual soul. In these fields there was never as great an interest in how people came to believe in mass entities, like nations, religious communities, and social classes. For instance, Sigmund Freud's interpretation of "group psychology" stresses the fears and frustrations of the unconscious mind, which, he held, is formed in early childhood. By this light, today's experience is far less important than the earliest days of one's life. Armies, churches (Freud's examples) as well as race, religion, nationality, and all the other "groups" are turned into fodder for the psychoanalytic apparatus that explores your dreams and your attitude toward masturbation.

So, for example, a contemporary Freudian, the psychoanalyst and writer Elisabeth Young-Bruehl, argues that racism "exemplifies hysterical prejudice, by which I mean a prejudice that a person uses unconsciously to appoint a group to act out in the world forbidden sexual and sexually aggressive desires that the person has repressed."

While psychology shunned the tribal aspect of human kinds, the traditional political and cultural disciplines haven't wanted to address the individual mind. If your work involves comparing Spanish and German culture, you wouldn't want to confuse the issue by looking into what makes a person feel more Spanish or less, in the course of a week, and what made her forget her Spanishness and think of herself instead as a Madrileno last Tuesday night. Ignoring individual psychology and variety, this mass approach yields theories for analyzing collective action, for instance, to explain why France conquered much of Europe in the early nineteenth century.

Yet it was not France that fought wars, literally. It was people who considered themselves French and who considered Frenchness important enough to fight for and die for — or, at least, who considered it a sensible enough concept that they did not rebel when they were organized to fight in its name. If psychology seems to neglect the fact that people see themselves as more than individuals, history seems to ignore the fact that individuality does matter. The mind sciences now offer a way across this chasm — methods for describing how collective human kinds and individual human minds depend on one another.

Today, perhaps for the first time in human history, large masses of people recognize that human kinds are made, not discovered. Globalization is showing people that "our side" is determined by beliefs, not facts. It's now obvious that human-kind violence belongs to no one religion, nation, race, culture, or political ideology; it's equally obvious that a "good man" at home can be a torturer at work and that supposedly ancient hatreds can disappear, even as supposedly peaceful societies can turn genocidal. All of this has led to a hunger for new ways to think about human kinds.

Meanwhile, the politics of science — or rather, the way science is used in politics — creates a different kind of pressure for new ideas. The prestige of science around the world is so great that almost everyone wants to get some on his side. Science has been invoked for claims that melanin makes black people more intelligent. Science has been invoked to support the opposite claim too: that black people have smaller skulls than whites and therefore must be *less* intelligent. Science has been called in to support the idea that some people are "genetically programmed" to be hostile to Croatia.

If scientists don't come up with a good science of human kinds, it's clear they'll be stuck with a bad one — claims about racial, ethnic, national, and religious superiority supposedly "proven" by biology. Much as mind scientists might have preferred those fine abstractions, Everyone and The Individual, the problem of human kinds is not going to wait.

So the moment for new ideas has arrived. Despite a certain discomfort with the subject, mind science is working on kind-mindedness. The work takes place on a level of explanation above the isolated individual but below the abstract sphere of nations and cultures. It's being made at the intersection of neuroscience, psychology, philosophy of mind, and anthropology, where kind-mindedness, once a mystery, has become a problem that science can address.

Two

"There Are Few Questions
More Curious Than This"

In the spring of 2004, the Republican Party of Illinois found itself with a problem. Its nominee in the upcoming election for the U.S. Senate, Jack Ryan, had been severely embarrassed by revelations about his sexual tastes contained in five-year-old divorce papers. It was bad news for a party that had already been tarnished by corruption charges two years earlier against the state's Republican governor, George Ryan (who was no relation).

Jack Ryan dropped out of the race. One party official, discussing its search for a replacement, told reporters, "We're just not going to ever nominate a guy named Ryan again."

You know he was kidding. No one would say in earnest that unrelated people, who happen to share a name, will all be tarnished politicians. The hidden rules of human kinds tell you to reject the thought. If you want to understand those rules, then, the question is: *How* do you know that?

Imagine, for instance, that the two Ryans *were* relatives. Refusing to nominate another person from the same family might or might not be unfair, but it doesn't feel absurd. Maybe there's a family problem, after all. So part of the grammar of human kinds says some categories, like family connection, tell a lot about their members. Others, like a shared name, are not informative. We don't have to think about this distinction. The mind observes the rule without any conscious thought.

Your first hunch might be to say that this rule is founded in objective fact. There are accidental human kinds, like people who have the same last name, and then there are "real" human kinds, like the Ryan family — or the Dar al Islam, the worldwide community of Muslims, or the nation of Senegal. Accidental human kinds tell you nothing about the people who have been thrown into them, then, but the "real" kinds tell a lot. That's reassuring. But it cannot be right.

Consider a human kind in whose meaning people certainly have confidence: France. Most of us would say that French people and French culture have persisted for ages. Yet it is hard to say what, exactly, has done this persisting.

Millions of today's French people trace their roots to recent ancestors who lived far from their country (including, for example, the nation's interior minister and potential future president Nicolas Sarkozy, whose father's family, until his generation, was Hungarian). So the common ground of Frenchness is not in DNA. Nor can the essence be linked to territory: Until a few hundred years ago, nations were not politically important human kinds. In premodern Europe, as one historian has written, rulers were "kings of peoples, not of regions. A king of the Goths was king of the Goths whether they were settled on the shores of the Baltic, the Black Sea, or the Bay of Biscay. . . . A kingdom was composed of people who recognized a certain royal family as their royal family, just as a kin-group was composed of people who recognized the founders of a certain family as their common ancestors."

Then, too, the French language of, say, 1431, is not spoken today. That's a fact about language change of which medieval writers were well aware. As Dante noticed in the fourteenth century, "if those who died a thousand years ago were to return to their cities, they would believe that these had been occupied by some foreign people, because the language would be at variance with their own." And what the world knows as French cuisine didn't exist then, either. In fact, all the indicators that identify a human kind are different now

than they were in the century when Joan of Arc fought for her sovereign's kingdom. If she could return to her cities, would this religious
warrior feel solidarity with the church-shunning, marriage-avoiding,
war-hating people she likely would meet? Not probable. So when
we say that France has endured — "the same soul which spans the
generations, constantly rejuvenating but always the same," as one
French writer put it — what, exactly, are we talking about?

"There are few questions more curious than this," wrote the Enlightenment philosopher David Hume, in a prescient essay on "national characters." Because he wrote more than 250 years ago, his
descriptions of "nations" now exemplify the problem: "We have
reason to expect greater wit and gaiety in a Frenchman than in a
Spaniard . . . and an Englishman will naturally be supposed more
knowledgeable than a Dane." Then, too, everyone knew that Spaniards
and Chinese manifest "gravity and serious deportment," quite unlike
those merry French, Egyptians, and Persians.

Anticipating, as he often did, more recent thinkers, Hume noted
that peoples who live near each other without mixing often show
extremes of difference. His illustration was the integrity, gravity, and
bravery of the Turks, another serious people, versus the deceit, lev-
ity, and cowardice of the Greeks.

None of this — serious Spaniards, solemn Turks, cowardly Greeks,
laugh-a-minute Persians, dumb Danes — rings true today. Hume
foresaw that. "The manners of a people," he wrote, "change very
considerably from one age to another." Reaching for an explanation,
he uncharacteristically threw up his hands. The change must be
caused "either by great alterations in their government, by the mix-
tures of new people, or by that inconstancy, to which all human affairs are subject."

That frustrating mutability is the root of the Joan of Arc problem:
How can all signs of Frenchness change over the centuries, while
Frenchness stays, somehow, the same? This was the real mystery, Hume
saw, even though many thought the problem was elsewhere. Though
he made short work of their mistakes, every one of the errors he
identified is still common today.

For one thing, Hume wrote, uneducated people expected every

single Dane or Frenchman to display the traits that defined Denmark and France, but that was an error. "Men of sense condemn these undistinguishing judgments," he wrote. They recognized that "some particular qualities are more frequently to be met among one people than among their neighbors." (His example was the then well-known "fact" that the Swiss are more honest than the Irish.) You're more likely to be cheated in Ireland than in Switzerland, Hume thought, but still there are forthright Irishmen and sneaky Swiss. Human kinds aren't logical definitions. They're statements about probability.

Another common mistake, Hume saw, was to think differences among peoples were based on physical facts about them — their climate, or body types, or the food they ate. After all, nations change even when their physical environment does not, and people are often different from their ancestors, as children are from parents. (The Enlightenment English admired the ancient Greeks, for instance, while thinking the contemporary ones were less impressive than those somber Turks.) But the more important reason that the traits of human kinds could not derive from physical causes, Hume noted, was that many of these groupings were scattered all over the earth, experiencing different environments, yet all displaying their defining traits.

After all, there is nothing special about nations as a basis for organizing human kinds. That was why in his essay on differences among countries Hume also ponders what we would now call races ("Negroes," he was "apt to suspect," were "naturally inferior to the whites"), and ethnic groups (like the Jews, who, he wrote, are prone to fraud, or the Armenians, who are uncommonly honest). A line of work, too, produces a reliable human kind, no matter where in the world those people are. For example, soldiers (whom Hume rather liked) are different everywhere from priests (whom he didn't like at all).

Hume also saw the absurdity of claiming that people come together, get along, and cooperate because they are "the same." People are the same on some measures but different on others, and it is never hard to find ways in which any two human beings are exactly alike and other ways in which the same two are different. As the American psychologist Kurt Lewin once pointed out, any mother is

more similar in many ways to other mothers than she is to her partner or their child, yet those similarities don't matter in defining a
family.

Hundreds of years before they were conducted, then, Hume had
foretold the flaw in surveys that show people marry, befriend, and
live near others "like themselves." Often, life works the other way
around: instead of looking for people like you and joining their
team, you join a team and then decide its members are like you.

"The human mind," Hume wrote,

> is of a very imitative nature; nor is it possible for any set of men to
> converse often together, without acquiring a similitude of manners,
> and communicating to each other their vices as well as their virtues.
> The propensity to company and society is strong in all rational crea-
> tures; and the same disposition which gives us this propensity, makes
> us enter deeply into each other's sentiments, and causes like passions
> and inclinations to run, as it were, by contagion, through the whole
> club or knot of companions.

Such a club or knot might be a nation, but it could also be
some other grouping. Soldiers and priests got their traits by training,
which shows that beliefs alone were sufficient to change people's
behavior. As examples, Hume cited elite military units in armies,
which were drawn from the mass of men, yet made each member
into a superior soldier: "Having once entertained the notion that
they were the best troops in the service, this very opinion really made
them such."

Hume also perceived that even the human kinds we call nations
and races were not fixed by definition or physical circumstances. And
what he observed in those cases is also true of ethnic groups, religions, and other human kinds. These, too, come into or pass out of
existence, in ways that don't depend on the physical facts about the
people they depict. In fact, all human kinds have a life-cycle.

Less than a century ago, some newborn babies suffered from a
condition called status thymicolymphaticus — an enlargement of the
thymus gland in the throat, which could cause the infant to choke
and die. To prevent what we now call sudden infant death syndrome,
the era's best doctors knew to shrink those oversized glands. They

turned, as they usually do, with confidence and enthusiasm, to the latest technology: radiation. From the 1920s until the 1950s, thousands of infants in industrialized nations had their throats irradiated to shrink their thymus glands.

But status thymicolymphaticus did not account for sudden infant death syndrome, whose cause remains a subject of investigation today. It was all a mistake — a mistake whose origin wasn't in the science of the human body, but in the way society is organized, and how that organization causes people to think about one another.

Medical students and medical textbooks had gotten their notions of a normal thymus gland from dissections of bodies left to science. Then, as now, people were repelled by the idea of dissection, and so almost all the bodies that served to teach anatomy came from people whose relatives had no choice. The "normal" thymus glands of the schools and textbooks all came from people without power and without money. They came from poor people.

As it turns out, poor people in industrialized nations have exceptionally small thymuses. Robert M. Sapolsky, a biologist at Stanford University who has documented and described the rise and fall of status thymicolymphaticus, has explained why.

Being at the bottom of a society is, in our modern parlance, stressful. Sapolsky is among the scientists who have shown just how stress hormones, when overused, will shrivel important parts of both body and brain — including the thymus gland, which is an important part of the immune system. Those supposedly large thymus glands of dead newborns were actually typical, but medical students were used to seeing the abnormally *small* glands of the poor. The occasional affluent corpse in autopsies only served to confirm the impression that big thymus glands are rare.

Meanwhile, lower lifelong stress also led the well-off to die with smaller adrenal glands than did the poor — less travail over a lifetime meant less adrenaline required. That led to another erroneous category, idiopathic adrenal atrophy, for people with supposedly shrunken adrenals.

There's no scandal here. This is science at work. Its categories for human beings are subject to change. In 1901, for example, the journal *Nature* informed its readers that the latest research from the Yale

Psychological Laboratory had shown how "nervous persons, in train-ing for the development of strength, require light practice, and phleg-matic persons require vigorous practice. The phlegmatic type of temperament is apparently characterized by the presence of much reserve energy of muscle and nerve cell. The nervous type has less reserve energy but a greater ability to use the energy at hand."

In the twenty-first century, what has happened to those kinds of human being, the phlegmatic and the nervous? They're no longer on science's map of human types. Abandoned by researchers, they have become unofficial. You might call a coworker phlegmatic, but doc-tors don't prescribe pills for phlegmatism.

The life-cycle of concepts about people — birth, life, and death — continues today. Some seventy years after the Yale report, for in-stance, scientists proposed a different kind of person and said this type was at higher risk than the rest of us for heart trouble. This was the Type A personality — impatient, self-critical, and hostile, unlike those mellow Type Bs. Even as it entered the speech of ordinary people in the 1980s, though, this idea was fading out of the medical journals where it began. As a predictor of heart attacks, it has been something of a bust, so that by the early 1990s, many researchers had decided that the Type A–Type B distinction is, as one put it, a "false trail that should be abandoned." A major review in the mid-1990s concluded that Type A traits were not that tightly linked with anger or aggression on the one hand nor with heart attacks on the other. There did seem to be some meaningful connection between heart disease and scores on psychological tests for overall hostility, but the effect was so small that many in the field have concluded the link is medically useless.

In other words, Type A, as an official, medical category, is on its way to joining phlegmatic and nervous on the heap of canceled kinds. As with phlegmatic and nervous types, the label lives on in day-to-day talk, as "common sense" absorbs the prestigious jargon of aca-demia. But for scientists, the category is fading: in mid-2004, I searched the PubMed database for clinical trials performed between 1985 and 1991 that mentioned the Type A concept. I found fifty-eight. Be-tween 1992 and 2004, the number was zero.

More recently, neuroscientists who use imaging technology to study the human brain — positron emission tomography, the PET scan, and nuclear magnetic resonance imaging, or MRI — have been working to repair a similar artifact of history. As the MIT anthropologist Joseph Dumit has pointed out, the first generation of PET studies focused on white, male, right-handed subjects. Only in the last decade have imagers stopped working with a picture of the "normal" human brain that was really the picture of a right-handed white guy's.

These human kinds — status thymicolymphaticus, idiopathic adrenal atrophy, phlegmatic and nervous, Type A and Type B, the "normal" brain as white and male — share a historical pattern. They arose, they convinced, and then they fell away. Yet these concepts weren't just talk. When they were believed in, they had consequences. All that irradiating of babies' thymuses, Sapolsky notes, also zapped their nearby thyroid glands. That caused thousands of thyroid cancers. But however many lives these concepts changed, however well they convinced people, they weren't immortal. The day came when no one believed in them anymore.

The objective facts, though, did not disappear. People with less patience than their neighbors, or smaller thymuses, weren't massacred or magically transformed. They were simply *recategorized*. That's part of the life-cycle of concepts about human beings.

That cycle is most obvious with categories that have a written history, from birth in a scientific paper to rejection in another paper, decades later. But the same life-cycle also governs other human kinds, the ones that have emotional as well as intellectual impact: cultures, ethnic groups, nations, races, religions, cults, castes, political movements.

Just as people have ceased to believe in phlegmatics in medicine, so they no longer see Vikings, Visigoths, and Aztecs; Mithraists and Pelagian Christians; coloreds and octaroons. None of these kinds of person was wiped out, either. They, too, were recategorized — sometimes by their choice, sometimes from force imposed by others, and usually by a combination of both.

People see this clearly, as long as the subject is not their own convictions about race, religion, or nation. It's easy, if not polite, to scoff at *other* people's myths and traditions. Alien nations, other tribes, other religions — they refuse to eat the perfectly good things we eat; they won't let their kids do the perfectly healthy things that ours do; they talk funny and their history is a childish fantasy. Of course, such ideas can change. But us? Our tradition? That's different. The foods we avoid are unhealthy; we raise our kids right; our dialect is beautiful. And our noble history? All true!

Americans don't have to look far to see that their definitions of human kinds have changed with the years. People from Ireland, for example, were not considered white by most nineteenth-century Americans. Their descendants are. And it would be a mistake to think this shifting of the lines is peculiarly modern or peculiarly American. It has taken place throughout history.

Since the 1400s, French villages recognized a distinct human kind, with all the signs of what we would now call a people. They were called *cagots.* Spread throughout the southwest of France and along its western coasts, they lived separately from other people, at the edge of towns and villages. They entered churches by separate entrances, and they could not touch an ordinary Christian, much less marry one. They were confined to a few occupations, mostly to do with woodworking. Folklore declared that you could tell them apart from regular folk by their pallor, their unusual height, or (one source reports) by the way their ears were shaped. Cagots lived apart, married apart, worked apart, and according to their neighbors, looked different. They were as clearly separate a people in their time as were the Jews of France (and they, like the Jews, were required to wear an identifying mark on their clothes). Centuries later, the term *ethnic group* was coined to describe people with a distinct way of life and clothing, a story of shared history and ancestry, and a strong tendency to marry only among themselves. The cagots would have fit the definition. But by then, they no longer existed.

A trace of them survives in French in the word *cagoterie,* meaning a gaucheness or stupidity. The cagots had been oppressed, by law before the French Revolution and by custom afterward, but they were never massacred. They too simply were recategorized.

Lest this give the impression that this European example is extraordinary, let's look at one other vanished tribe, from a different part of the world. Traditional Korean society also included outcasts, the *paekchong,* who, like the cagots, lived apart from the rest of society and worked in special occupations — butchery, leatherworking, shoemaking, and related trades.

Paekchong and prejudice against them were alive in the memories of Koreans fifty years ago, even though the legal status had been abolished in 1894. It took the upheavals of Japanese occupation and war over the last century to erase the paekchong category. Today the paekchong, as a separate kind of Korean, no longer exist. They have, as one scholar wrote in 1974, "vanished almost without a trace into the mainstream of Korean society."

Human kinds, as I've said, arise, have their day, and fade, then, whatever their origins. The ones by which we organize our politics — ethnic groups, nations, religions, races — aren't different, in that way, from the human kinds invented by researchers, like Type A personalities and phlegmatic people.

Histories of human kinds can take many paths. A human *kind* may persist, even when the traits that define it don't. We still believe in human kinds called Danes and Englishmen, but we no longer naturally expect that Englishmen know more than Danes. In other cases, the *traits* of a human kind will persist, though the kind itself vanishes from our minds. For example, the same physical features that define Italian Americans in the early twenty-first century as "white people" marked their immigrant ancestors as nonwhite.

There's a third possibility: sometimes trait *and* tribe survive, but the connection between them breaks. Tattoos, for instance, were studied as a sign of "deviance" in the United States of the 1960s. Today, in the same country, tattoos are normal. Tattoos and deviants are still around, in other words, but Americans no longer link one to the other.

These constant changes make human kinds unusual among the categories we use to get through life. Set aside their emotional intensity. Even considered as thoughts — "cognition," in research-speak — human kinds are odd.

Any category is a kind of decision to treat individuals in a group as if they were all the same, which saves your time and attention for other things. Instead of looking closely at every single flying, feathered creature in a yard, for example, you can simply tell yourself, "There are birds in the yard."

Human kinds certainly do that for you. They answer questions when you have no time or inclination to get to know every individual person involved in your problem. A good example, coined by the American social psychologist Solomon Asch in the 1960s, is a flying wedge of police. It would be edifying to learn each officer's name and find out which ones loved the job and which ones planned to go to law school, but, at the moment, it is much more practical to tell yourself: "The police are running toward me with clubs." That category gets you quickly to the safest response: Run!

But human kinds don't work *exactly* as do natural kinds, like birds, or manufactured kinds, like billy clubs. The defining traits of birds always include feathers and they always will. Yet the defining traits of cagots no longer add up to a kind. Meanwhile, "French person" is still a human kind, but few of the traits that made the list in 1400 need be on it today.

The reason for this flexibility is that there is no necessary link between the traits that tell us who belongs in a human kind and what that kind is all about. In fact, the traits we use to define the human kinds — the way people look and sound — often have nothing to do with the behavior we expect of them.

Many Americans, who tend to believe Asians are good at math, decide who is Asian by skin color, hair, eye shape, and sometimes accent and language. Yet no one thinks having a particular skin tone or accent *causes* a person to be good at math. Between the traits we can see and the actions we expect, there is a link we can't perceive directly. So how do we know it is there? Hume was right. There are few questions more curious.

All this would be work for philosophers of knowledge, if only it were merely curious. But the human kinds in which we and our neighbors believe have power over us, defining the shape of our lives. It begins before you're born, when nationality, religion, race, class, caste, and other such categories determine how well your mother fared in pregnancy. It doesn't end until you're near death, judging what *kind* of person you were. This of course assumes you manage to live a full life — without being killed for your membership in a particular tribe, religion, race, class, or nation.

Human-kind beliefs matter, as Hume saw, because they make people do things. Human-kind awareness drives you to do better — to be a good Muslim, a good citizen, or a good father, because you see the gap between the kind of person you can imagine and what you are. Yet the same sort of belief can lead you to decide that certain human kinds are not worthy of respect, or honesty, or even of life. Human-kind thinking has no necessary moral direction. It can spur the prick of conscience that makes your soul fly upward. It can be a message of inescapable hatred that nails your heart into the earth.

Human kinds involve what researchers call "hot cognition" — they're bound up in emotions and actions. We can consider human kinds as abstract, disembodied thoughts, but only by ignoring their essential nature. They aren't just mental activities the mind dreamed up, like chess or prime numbers. Human kinds are thoughts that cause — and are caused by — emotions and actions. They exist to make us act.

Know that I am an American, and you will expect me to behave according to your idea of what Americans are like. You'll act accordingly. And when *I* know that I am an American, I feel that there are things I should do and things I should have — the right things for my kind. Knowing what kind of person you are is the way you measure the value of your life and its choices. It tells you what you must have and must not, what you must do and must not do.

Your definition may not agree with other members of your kind. You might, for example, be a male who thinks you aren't a real man unless you have children; next door might be another member of the male kind who feels a proper man gives all to his work, never mind family life. Yet inevitably, both do agree on this: there is a kind of person in this world who belongs to a category called "men" and, being a member, you must either be a good one or live your days in anguish.

This is the power of the human-kind map — the reason a human being can be harmed, as an animal cannot, by having his head shaved and his children raised to eat food he shuns. The map of human kinds tells us what *and* who we are.

Our reliance on this map makes most of us easy targets for advertisers. Your conscious mind may know they're just trying to sell you stuff, yet their messages still make you feel, often outside awareness, that the right kind of person, *your* kind, are all sporting iPods or driving SUV's. Doing this often involves inventing a tribe of people to which you supposedly always belonged — the tribe of cool people who, say, wear Tommy Hilfiger. In every sense of the word, people buy these images, despite knowing, elsewhere in a part of the mind that doesn't care about belonging, that they're contrived.

The map of human kinds is knit together with your sense of well-being — with *feeling* right — and with your sense of morality — with *doing* right. Both right and wrong conduct depend on the kind of people the conduct involves. Most people believe it's wrong to kill other human beings — unless they are enemy soldiers, or vile criminals justly condemned to death. Even the ethics of killing, then, depends on how we classify the victims, how we place them on the mental map of human kinds.

This is not to claim that people feel moral obligations only to their own kind, and not to outsiders. The mind is subtler than that. It does not keep ethics like a favorite track on a hard drive, to play the same way every time. Instead, it decides a hundred times a day what is right and wrong to do to other people, which depends on what kinds of people are involved. Ever felt anxious that you're not a good mother? Or said some act — burning the flag, torturing prisoners — was "un-American"? You were referring to the map of human kinds to place yourself.

That act makes for strong emotions. We want other mothers to be good to their children, even if we never meet them; we want soldiers of our nation to behave decently, even if we'll never know what they did. We want to feel good about our human kinds and, through them, ourselves.

Families, ethnicities, religions, nations, civic groups, and any other sort of tribe you care about are made of these feelings. So are the tribes you hate, or think you hate — those people you would not want to share your dinner or your neighborhood with. When you understand your own kind–mindedness, then, you don't just see yourself more clearly; you also see how ethnicities, nations, and all the other kinds can come to be. And you start to ask what it is about the mind that makes us see these human kinds, and believe in them, and fight about them.

Three

Counting and Measuring

Victor: I'm glad I'm normal.
Amanda: What an odd thing to be glad about. Why?

— NOEL COWARD, PRIVATE LIVES

Sir Francis Galton, the Victorian polymath, believed the mysteries of human kinds could be solved, as would all mysteries, by objective measurements and calculations.

A surprising amount of life as we now live it traces back to this faith. Internet retailers suggest you buy a video to go with your new book, and supermarkets put beer near diapers, because merchants track how often one purchase is associated with another. This sort of research is now so well developed that an expert can look at your answers to a few questions and make an excellent guess about what brand of razor blades you buy. Today's many methods for figuring out how strongly zip codes and razor purchases tie together all descend from the first. It was created by Galton, in work on the relationship between the length of people's forearms and the size of their heads. From that, he derived general principles for determining how much two measurements are related — their correlation.

If you don't pay for the beer and diapers, and get arrested, you'll be fingerprinted — another fruit of Galton's talent for practical measurements and publicity. (He did not invent the fingerprint, but he

· 46 ·

perfected the system and got Scotland Yard to adopt it.) Then, as a newly minted crime statistic, you'll be fodder for claims that law-breaking is "in the genes." Galton again: he believed heredity was the key to human behavior. Ever practical, he proposed methods of tracking "the same" genes in different lives by studying identical twins. That idea continues to drive research today.

In pursuit of ways to measure the precise attributes of great scientists, Galton was also one of the first researchers to use that now-ubiquitous tool, the questionnaire. He sent one to his cousin Charles Darwin, making him one of the first human beings to experience questionnaire fatigue. Apparently exasperated by all the items, each demanding an answer that fit on some scale of measurement, Darwin wrote back: "I have filled up the answers as well as I could, but it is simply impossible for me to estimate the degrees."

Galton published the results of that survey in a book whose title he seems to have taken from Shakespeare's Prospero, the magus of *The Tempest,* who calls his slave Caliban "a devil, a born devil, on whose nature nurture can never stick." More than a century later, despite wide unease with the way those terms misrepresent biology, scientists still debate human behavior in Galton's terms: nature versus nurture.

In the 1870s, he launched a project for sussing out true human kinds: "the portrait of a type." He would photograph many members of a group of people, one after another, sitting in the same position in the same spot, on the same photographic plate. Light would etch their shared features again and again on the plate, but any individual details — a mole here, a crooked nose there — would blur out. Only their shared traits would show up in the finished image.

It worked, with careful tinkering (often with photos of photos). For example, Galton was able to produce two portraits that, he said, summed up the faces of all Victorian criminals. "In one, the features are broad and massive, like those of Henry VIII, but with a much smaller brain. The other . . . is a face that is weak and certainly not a common English face." He followed these with composite portraits of sailors, military officers, consumptives, and other human kinds. "These ideal faces have a surprising air of reality," he wrote. "Nobody who glanced at one of them for the first time would doubt its being the likeness of a living person, yet, as I have said, it is no such thing; it is the portrait of a type and not an individual."

With lectures, demonstrations, and articles, Galton was a brilliant popularizer of his ideas. He made composite photographs of ancient coins, to reveal the consensus profiles of Cleopatra and Alexander the Great. (He thought Cleopatra's looks "simply hideous.") Thanks in part to his showmanship, a fad for composites arose among enthusiasts for the new hobby of photography. In the 1880s, gentlemen all over the Western world turned cameras on family members, prostitutes, picturesque peasants, and members of different classes, tribes, and races.

One Frenchman who lived near the Pyrenees noted the considerable difference his plates showed between the "race of the country" and another human kind, those, he said, who were the descendants of charcoal sellers who had been brought to the region to chop down trees during the Middle Ages. (The association with wood makes one wonder if these people were cagots.) As for the considerable difference that interested the photographer, I looked at his plates with my eye, formed by a different nation, in a different century, and saw none.

The new enthusiasts were fascinated and excited at the prospect of seeing a human kind, a category made flesh. "At the beginning of our experiments," wrote the French pamphleteer, "we experienced a singular emotion to see, slowly emerging in the pale light of the laboratory, this impersonal face that exists nowhere on earth, that one could call the portrait of the invisible."

In Vienna, the young Ludwig Wittgenstein, not yet a philosopher, was intrigued by this "portrait of a probability" that Galton had devised. He had a composite photo made of himself and his sisters, yielding a compound Wittgenstein of their shared features. In this he was following Galton, who had written that the composite photograph "portrays an imaginary figure possessing the average features of any given group of men."

Yet Galton didn't apply his method to "*any* given group." He did not combine ten or twenty images at random to yield a composite picture, though of course any set of images would work. (Realizing this, one hobbyist had written to Galton to say a blending of "the

ape tribe and some low-caste human face would make a very curious mixture.") A hundred years after Galton's invention, for instance,
the American artist Nancy Burson used a computer to blend the faces
of Stalin, Mao, Hitler, and Pol Pot into the composite face of dictatorship. Sort photos of people according to any rule you please — by
birthdate, number of letters in their names, favorite color — and
you can blend them into one face. The crucial act isn't creating an
image; it's deciding on the rule.

Galton believed this decision was no problem at all. He imagined
that his groupings were based on objective measurements and mathematical laws, applied through techniques recently imported from
astronomy and physics.

Earlier in the nineteenth century, the mathematician Karl Friedrich Gauss had solved a vexing problem for observatories all over Europe: when different people take many measurements of the same
thing, like the position of a star, they don't report the exact same
result. So which report was right? Gauss saw how the discrepancies
could be corrected. They followed a pattern. For any particular measurement, most people's versions fell a little below or a little above an
average; the further a number was from that average, the fewer people
would report it. For each planet and star, then, it was possible to find
both the answer that was most common and the one that was most
typical.

This general principle underlay Galton's claim that his composite
profile of Cleopatra was more accurate than any single image: it
smoothed away any unusual this-coin-only details and left features
that many different coins had gotten pretty much the same. Gauss's
point was that an astronomical observation that was very close to
many others was much more likely to be correct than one that was
far from that average.

A graph of this relationship between each measurement and the
number of people who produced it will come out looking like a bell.
Most people's results, close to the average, are in the center; a few
people are far out, falling where the curve slopes away. That's the bell
curve, or "normal distribution" — a bedrock of modern statistics.

Inevitably, someone would apply Gauss's technique to measurements *of* people, rather than by them. The modernizing, centralizing

governments of post-Napoleonic Europe were gathering such numbers — population sizes, births, marriages, deaths, tax payments, suicide rates, crime rates — in unprecedented quantities. The continent
was producing, as the philosopher Ian Hacking has pointed out, "an
avalanche of printed numbers" about human beings.

In 1835, the Belgian astronomer Adolphe Quetelet made the leap,
in his best-known book, *On Man*. Quetelet observed that multiply-
ing a person's height in meters by itself would give you a number
quite close to his weight in kilograms — unless he was one of the
unusual people whose measurements fell at one extreme or the other
of the curve. This observation created a new human kind: the
height-weight proportional person, beloved of gym trainers and
personals advertisements. (Today's Body Mass Index is still called the
Quetelet Index.)

Quetelet's goal was an objective science of society, but his response to the graphs was certainly hot cognition. He saw them
as moral and aesthetic guides — as if, as the critic Allan Sekula has
pointed out, this measure of people's differences was a measure of
their worth. For Quetelet, that thick part of the bell, where most
people clustered, was a place of virtue and beauty. That "center of
gravity," he wrote, where the "average man" would be found, was
"the type of all which is beautiful — of all which is good." And so
another new human kind was forged: the "normal" person, a being
who isn't just mathematically typical but morally, psychologically,
and politically desirable.

This was a big jump, from the realm of numbers to the emotional
world of truth, beauty, and goodness. Imagine, for example, that your
Body Mass Index is not normal. This means, mathematically, that
most other human beings' scores are closer to the average of all
scores than yours is. By itself, that says nothing else about you —
how you might do on a different test or how you vote, or whether
you're a good person.

The results don't even prove that the test is worthwhile. Perhaps,
as some argue, the Body Mass Index is a poor indicator of physical
condition. The bell curve has no opinion. It simply graphs the scores.
Do those scores make any sense, or have any use? Not the curve's

department. No one disputes that IQ test results fall on a normal distribution, as Richard Herrnstein and Charles Murray noted in their book *The Bell Curve*. Instead, arguments over that book turn on whether there is such a thing as innate intelligence, and whether IQ scores really measure it.

In other words, "normality," in statistics, is intellectually and morally neutral. It's just a description of how measurements will arrange themselves. At this scientific level of analysis, the human kind called "normal people" is meaningless. After all, it has no particular measurement associated with it, so it can't be graphed.

Nonetheless, most people want to be members of this human kind. We insult our enemies by implying that they aren't in this category with us, in words like these (from former Czech prime minister Vaclav Klaus, about his enemy Vaclav Havel): "He is the most élitist person I have ever seen in my life. I am a normal person. He is not."

How could Quetelet and Galton get away with associating averageness with goodness and beauty? Such an unscientific link should have struck their readers as unsound. That it did not suggests the human mind has a blind spot about the strangeness of this idea — a blind spot that derives from mental structure.

A good analogy for this is the blind spot in your field of vision, which is a consequence of the eye's architecture. At the back of an eye is a spot where optic nerve fibers enter. There are no photosensitive cells in that spot, and so you never register the light that lands on it. That's just how your eye is organized.

Something in the mind's workings made many nineteenth-century readers willing to believe that people who share a height-weight measurement must also share virtue and beauty. If that inclination doesn't come from facts, it must come instead from the only other possible source: the way the mind is organized. Readers attached assumptions and feelings to neutral categories like average man and normal person. That's what persuaded them that "normal" describes a real and desirable tribe of human beings. That's another indicator that mental rules for human kinds exist in their own realm, separate from that of logic.

Not all psychologists agree on this. Some argue that human-kind categories are pretty accurate representations of reality. Steven Pinker of Harvard, the linguist and cognitive scientist, says stereotypes — the psychologist's word for the human-kind beliefs that we use to make predictions — are largely "good statistics about real people." Agreeing with him, Jonathan Haidt, a psychologist at the University of Virginia, told me, "Most stereotypes are true."

Theirs is not an argument for forgetting Hume's observations. No one believes that *everyone* in a stereotype fits the profile. It is, as Hume noticed, a matter of probabilities. But if a trait is more likely to be found within some human kind than in others, then a stereotype might be better than nothing for making predictions, no matter how often it yields false positives.

That's the argument of Lee Jussim, a social psychologist at Rutgers University. For example, he says, predicting heads every time you toss a penny will pay off in the long run because the odds of a penny coming up heads are indeed just slightly larger than the odds for tails. Jussim suggests an analogy: Suppose 6 percent of the imaginary group Kampalese Americans are counterfeiters, while only 1 percent of other Americans counterfeit. "If you are in the FBI going after counterfeiters," he asks, "where should you look? You probably would spend a disproportionate amount of time among Kampalese" — even though 94 percent of them are *not* counterfeiters.

Still, Jussim adds: "Because you will be spending so much time investigating innocent Kampalese, Kampalese leaders can, with more than a little justification, protest that the FBI is harassing Kampalese-Americans."

The claim that stereotypes are good statistics, then, is a claim that people's usual judgments about probabilities are sound. This depicts stereotyping as a sort of rule-of-thumb version of a Galtonian process statisticians call the *analysis of covariance* — measuring how closely two different measurements are linked. In human beings, height and weight tend to covary, in that big people are likely to weigh more than small people. In that way, perhaps, being Kampalese covaries with being a counterfeiter more than being Italian does, and so the stereotype does useful work.

Is this, though, really what people do? Many social psychologists say no. They don't believe people's perceptions of human kinds are stable enough for statistical thinking. After all, if I'm not even aware that I am perceiving you as Kampalese, and if in a few minutes I might stop and perceive you instead as female or as a professor, then how can I run statistics about you?

This controversy might make you wish we could compare human-made stereotypes with statistical inferences made some other way — say, by some nonhuman artificial intelligence. A purely rational device, one that only did computations based on good information, would be a fine tool to test the statistical validity of stereotypes.

Of course, such machinery is available. It's in use every day, wherever and whenever computers are applied to questions like, "Whom should we be stopping to search at the airport?" Thanks to these machines, we can get an idea of what "good statistics about real people" look like when they are created without the involvement of human minds. And by that measure, stereotypes do not yield good statistics at all.

In fact, in 1998 a U.S. aviation official, Cathal Flynn, told a congressional hearing that computers can do this kind of figuring *better* than human beings. American airports were then installing the first computer-based system for finding dangerous passengers. (More recent experiments to find connections among categories — like that done by NASA's Ames Research Center on passenger information supplied by Northwest Airlines, or the experiment devised by Torch Concepts, a Pentagon contractor, to work with passenger records from JetBlue Airlines — work on the same principle.)

Into this first computer-assisted passenger screening (or CAPS) system went some two dozen different pieces of information about each passenger, taken from the airline computers. Out came a score, which, if it was above a certain number, caused the passenger's luggage to be "targeted" for a search. In other words, CAPS was machinery for making inductions about human kinds. Its score was a measure of the probability that a passenger was dangerous (low, but worth searching), based on the relationship among various other categories of which that person was a member.

People speculated about what these categories might be — one-way ticket buyers, people who pay in cash, last-minute trip-takers — but the authorities wanted to keep the details secret. What is striking, though, was that the machines' categories for people weren't coming up with the same results as the human kinds that people use themselves.

No CAPS criteria, testified Flynn, "none of them, have to do with ethnicity of people; none have to do with association with names, with ethnic groups; none have to do with race or religion." The Justice Department had checked to see if the program unintentionally had the effect of singling out any particular race or religion or ethnic group for hard scrutiny and found that it did not.

Why didn't the computers act like people? Beliefs about human kinds arise from hidden, unconscious activities of the mind. But computers must operate with categories created by explicitly stated rules. That's the crucial difference. In fact, you don't need a computer to see this contrast. Any set of definitions for human kinds, combined with clear procedures, will yield a different account of human kinds than does the largely hidden machinery of the mind.

Another government agency's history has shown how "good statistics about real people" can be generated without computers, to correct the *lack* of good statistics in human hunches. In the late 1990s the U.S. Customs Service was searching a higher percentage of travelers classified in the American system of human kinds as nonwhite — even though the nonwhites didn't have a much higher rate of smuggling than the whites. After controversies and lawsuits, the Service decided to ban, completely, the use of traditional human kinds as a basis for a body search.

Its handbook for officers was changed to include a new prohibition: "*Never* use a person's gender, race, color, religion or ethnic background as a factor in determining any level of suspicion." A variety of new procedures were put in place to track searches and make sure this rule is obeyed. For example, the Commissioner of Customs receives a daily report on searches at all the country's ports of entries, with a breakdown by race, nationality, ethnicity, and gender. The entire service went through retraining, which stressed how to think in a more consistent, systematic, and delimited way — transparent in reasoning and confined to the here and now. "When you're questioning someone, don't look at their color, listen to the answers," as a department spokesman described it.

Customs inspectors were told instead to look for signs of nervousness — shaking hands, rapid breathing, cold sweats, averted eyes, and so on, as well as oddities that are relevant to their search for contraband: Does the person have strangely thick-soled shoes, for instance, or an unusual gait? They were also trained to look for atypical behavior: actions that stand out against the pattern created by what other travelers are doing. That's *normal* in its strict statistical meaning — what most travelers are doing here and now. Nothing could be more different from the untrained mind's irrational, ill-defined, emotionally charged sense of *normal,* which means, basically, people who look and sound and act in ways that you have learned are acceptable for your kind of people.

One practical consequence of this new approach was an important arrest. Shortly before the turn of the millennium, a traveler arrived at a border post near Seattle off a car ferry from Vancouver. The inspector asked him some innocuous questions. And he found that the man's trip wasn't like that of most other people in line. His route from Vancouver to the ferry had taken him three hours out of his way. Moreover, he seemed nervous. The inspectors decided to search his car.

They found explosives in the trunk. The traveler was Ahmed Rassam, who was part of a conspiracy to bomb the Los Angeles airport over the New Year's holiday. As the Customs Service trainers like to emphasize, he was not caught because he looked Arab or spoke with an accent. He was caught because of categories that narrowly confined themselves to the question at hand — because his itinerary was odd, and his hands were shaky.

Data soon confirmed that well-targeted methods for creating truly good statistics about real people could spot more criminals than do human-kind predictions based on race, ethnicity, or gender. In 1999, the last year before these procedures were completely in place, the Customs Service searched 23,108 people and found smuggled cocaine, heroin, or Ecstasy in 533 instances. In the first eight months of 2001, the service had logged 734 seizures — but it only searched 6,111 people. And minorities were no longer disproportionately targeted.

Human-kind beliefs, then, are not just composite portraits of the people we've encountered or heard about. If they were, stereotypes would not be contradicted by the logical categories we've created for computers and institutions like the Customs Service. And if rules for classifying people don't come from information about those people or from logical thought, then they must have another source. And there is only one candidate left to be that source: our brains.

In other words, human kinds are what happens when the real world meets the human mind. They aren't just perceptions. They're *beliefs*.

So, does that make human kinds all fiction? Is the category "normal people" a fraud, a bit of bogusness, that we can forget about? You could believe that, but if you did, you would be crazy. You would be trying to live in the world with only one mode of knowing anything — the way of just-the-facts data collecting and scientific theorizing. No "normal" person lives like that.

Instead, people cycle through different means of understanding the world — subatomic knowledge for physics class, emotional and intimate knowledge for a family dinner, cultural and political mode for deciding about a vote in an important election. Each of these modes of understanding requires that you accept its categories. For example, you can pay for your groceries with bits of colored paper, which the cashier accepts, because both of you agree that those pieces of paper represent value. Take a plane to another country where people don't share the faith, and your bills are just paper. Money is real because we all believe it is.

This is why there is one foolproof way to bring a new human kind into being: convince people it already exists. Draw their attention away from the workings of their minds and persuade them instead that the human kind in question is a Galton-style entity: a result of measurements and analysis. We now have standardized tests in schools; tests of intelligence and personality; tests for dyslexia and autism and attention deficit; genetic tests for susceptibility to illnesses and differences in responses to medications and other treatments — the list is long and ever-growing. Once experts define a kind of person and offer a procedure to reveal who belongs, then that kind is well on its way to practical reality.

The philosopher Ian Hacking of the University of Toronto, who has thought keenly about the human kinds created by experts, has pointed out that the process doesn't end with the first act of persuasion. Once a human kind has attracted belief, its members take part in defining it.

A good example is the human kind Americans now call "gay person." In 1975 the American scholar Clarence Arthur Tripp published *The Homosexual Matrix,* which, in essence, offered a redefinition of a human kind. He discussed homosexuals without the widespread assumption that there was something wrong with this kind of person. The message of his book was that a person could be a member of both the gay kind of human being and — here comes that powerful word again — the *normal* kind.

Many people read the book and treasured its message. One of them was Larry Kramer, a movie producer and writer, who warmed to the point that gay person and healthy person were not mutually exclusive categories. "I remember reading it and saying, 'Wow, that's me,'" Kramer has said, "and I'd never had that reaction before in reading a book about homosexuality."

Kramer himself went on, in the 1980s, to help change what "gay" means to most of his fellow citizens. He took up furious activism in response to inaction on the AIDS epidemic. (Among other things, Kramer founded the groups ACT-UP and the Gay Men's Health Crisis.) As a consequence, Americans' concept of gay person today is likely to include images of pride parades, of political engagement and solidarity. You can call it community if you approve or the homosexual agenda if you do not; either way, this notion is a far cry from the image of gay people I was taught as a child in the 1960s: isolated, apolitical, and not normal.

Hacking has called this sort of change a *looping effect:* A category of person starts out as an idea in someone's mind. That person convinces other people that he or she is onto something, and the idea spreads. Then people who belong to the newly minted human kind start using the concept to guide their behavior and understand themselves. That creates evidence this kind of person is "really" out there.

Six years ago in the United States, for example, red and blue states signified nothing more than results on postelection maps. After the

2000 presidential election, though, people began to use the concepts of red state and blue state to define fundamentally different kinds of voter. By the 2004 election, several loops later, *red* and *blue* had come to mean fundamentally different kinds of *person*. The terms now stand for an array of beliefs and practices — about religion, family life, and culture. The terms have come unmoored from their original, election-related meaning, and Americans speak of red or blue people, places, and symbols, rather than red or blue voting.

This is just what you should expect of a looping effect. People, as Hacking notes, "are aware of what they are called, adapt accordingly, and so change, leading to revisions in facts and then knowledge about them." Looping effects go on in perpetuity. Once a human kind is defined, the people in it even change how they think and act, to better fit the definition. But their very act of pondering and debating the definition causes it to change as well.

Again, this observation does not mean looping human kinds are pure fiction. Were gay people invented by Kramer, or C. A. Tripp, or Karl Maria Benkert, who coined the term *homosexual* in 1868? Certainly not. Same-gender sex and affection were recorded millennia before Benkert came long. To describe a looping effect is not to claim that it is baseless.

Yet there is a knee-jerk, debunking rhetoric that claims all human kinds are socially constructed and so must be all fakery and fiction, with no necessary connection to actual people and their actions. That stance isn't worth a lot of attention.

To see why, imagine applying the debunker's approach to money. It would be easy. You'd point out that the bills in someone's pocket are really just bits of colored paper, with no value outside the zones where people believe in them. You'd have made an obvious point that reveals nothing about how money works and that won't have any effect on people who tomorrow will still need to earn money and spend it, whatever their beliefs. The important aspects of money follow from the laws of economics that govern it and the ways people are affected by their belief in money, and the needs and desires that grow from that belief. If you're satisfied by the notion that money's a mirage, you'll never come to grips with those laws, needs, and beliefs.

As I've mentioned, human kinds are real in just the way that money is real. If enough people believe in a kind of person, that kind will take its place among the realities of life. Yes, it's a mental process, not ultimate reality, that makes us believe nowadays that gay people are a human kind with a common outlook and culture, while left-handers are not. Nonetheless, because of that mental process, millions of people live their lives in a way not possible before the belief existed. It's silly to be content with pointing out that beliefs about human kinds are inventions, not discoveries about an objectively real world. So what? Those inventions, once made real, have more impact on people than all the plagues and earthquakes ever recorded.

In their political and cultural forms, the widely credited human kinds — races, nations, cultures, religions, political movements — have shaped lives, changed lives, and as the morning news always reminds you, ended lives too. So they aren't illusions: they don't go away when you think about them. They aren't pure fantasies, either: we don't hallucinate skin color or mannerisms or test scores. We see them.

But this shouldn't lead you to the opposite idea — one that, as it happens, Larry Kramer has been promoting.

"I want our people taught about in schools," Kramer once wrote. "*Our people.* Doesn't that sound wonderful? *Our people.* Yes, we are a people. And we are exceptional. And we have been exceptional since the beginning of time, as sure as any other Adams and Eves." This is a view that some scholars apparently share, at least in part. The historian Jonathan Ned Katz affirms the value of finding historical figures who were gay, because, as he said at Yale — at a talk sponsored by the Larry Kramer Initiative for Gay and Lesbian Studies — "evidence of our past existence worked against the feelings of inferiority of a people told directly or indirectly that they had no history."

Think about this notion of a people existing "since the beginning of time." In Kramer's rhetoric, it suggests there is some property of gayness, shared by people today, and the ancient poet Sappho of Lesbos, and men arrested in fourteenth-century London for same-gender sex acts, and Abraham Lincoln (according to Kramer; Tripp, whose last work, published posthumously, was an argument that Lincoln's supposed homosexual side is key to understanding him, was more cautious). Such an essence stays the same, even as generations pass and languages, laws, customs, and politics all change.

Essentialism, the belief in such properties, is the upside-down mirror image of anything-goes-ism. Instead of claiming that our concepts have no connection to reality, essentialism says they have a permanent, unbreakable link. Essentialism is the comforting belief that the human kinds we talk about today are never-changing, hidden truths about people.

You might think that all those wonderful bell-curve measurements of human traits would have put an end to essentialism in the nineteenth century. After all, the bell curve shows that measurements of human beings fall along a wide range, with most people in the broad middle. This was what David Hume had intuited a hundred years before modern statistics: differences among groups are differences in averages, not absolute essences.

So, for example, the average man has more muscle mass than the average woman, but this does not mean that I could outrun a female Olympian. If I say "men are stronger than women," I have said something true about probability, but not that all men share an essence that makes them stronger than all women. Since all human beings are very similar, it follows that almost all differences among human kinds are going to be of this probabilistic sort. Essentialism should be a dead letter in a world run on mountains of statistics. And it would be, if human kinds weren't made according to their own laws.

But human kind-mindedness does follow its own laws, one of which is that people feel strong emotions when human kinds are in question. And so, when statistical reasoning meets essentialism, it's essentialism that wins, almost always. If you believe that men are from Mars and women from Venus, you're ignoring probability and proceeding as if all men have one essence and all women have another. That kind of thinking is pervasive in the way people talk about human kinds.

That mental habit certainly helped Francis Galton succeed with his composite photographs. When he displayed the face of "the officer in the Royal Engineers," he was actually *hiding* a bell curve's worth of variation — the range of differences among all the individual faces that went into the image. Then when he contrasted the officer photo with "the" face of the enlisted man, the people in Galton's audience could only think about how different those two types were. Had they been able to see the full range of variation in the faces, they might have noticed that there were soldiers whose appearance edged into the officer range and officers who looked soldierish. People would have noticed that the bell curves overlapped. Galton forestalled that, and it was the mind's love of essentialism that let him get away with it.

Much the same rhetorical strategy lives on today, visible wherever people try to create a new human kind or make a trait-based category into more of a tribe, a coherent thing made of people. Feminists who say that all women innately have a different morality than men do, or dwarves who ask if you know Attila the Hun was a Little Person, are saying about their people what Kramer says about his: something exists that makes us what we are, and it has always existed, and we all share it. So believe!

Essentialism, though, makes no more sense as an explanation for human kinds than arbitrary "social constructionism." Today's gay essentialism, for example, is hard to square with the historical record. The problem isn't, of course, that the terms *homosexual* and *gay* are recent coinages, because homosexual acts predate both our words and our species. But what people in Western countries mean by gay nowadays is a person who is like a heterosexual, emotionally, sexually, and culturally, except that his or her intimate feelings center on same-gender people. This category — gay person as straight person with one little difference — is new in history. Different times and places have divided up the range of sexual behaviors in many other ways, and as historians and anthropologists often point out, there is no particularly good reason to claim that today's must be the right one.

There are and have been societies in which adolescent boys become the sexual partners of adult men, then grow up and take wives. The ancient Athens of Plato and Pericles was one such place, and parts of Papua New Guinea another. Were these men gay or straight? Some societies had no sanctioned human kind for same-sex lovers but did have one for people of one gender who take up the clothes, jobs, and privileges of the other. Are such people gay or straight?

Suppose Lincoln did have sex with his friend Joshua Speed, as Tripp has suggested was likely. Both Speed and Lincoln nonetheless became fathers and husbands in conventional nineteenth-century families. This doesn't mean Tripp must be wrong to assert that Lincoln's primary affective life was focused on other men. But it does mean that having a "homosexual side," as Tripp puts it, did not mean for Lincoln in the nineteenth century what it means for Larry Kramer in the twenty-first.

Essentialists can't be satisfied to note that people have noticed same-gender sexual behavior in many times and places. Essentialism requires that people be, in some deep sense, "the same" in all times and places. But people in those other times and places haven't talked about the subject with our human-kind categories. Ancient Western classifications for sex seem to have included three different concepts that we would lump together as "gay": sex between older men and younger ones, in a mentor-pupil relationship; sex between men; and sex between women. Ancient law codes made distinctions about human kinds based on what kinds of acts they perform: the receptive partner in male–male sex acts was seen as a different kind of person from the active one. Many cultures that have categories for gay sex have none for gay families. Those cultures included, until very recently, many in Western Europe and North America. Never mind Lincoln; Oscar Wilde, lover of young men, loyal husband and father, would not have called himself gay either. From the viewpoint of centuries, both gay and straight are the oddball categories — attempts to divide a wide range of sexual behavior into two (and only two!) essentialist pigeonholes.

Any historian will tell you that today's human kinds do not map well onto other times and places. This does not mean we can't understand those other people, but it does mean we need to translate from their thinking to our own.

To this, essentialists say, in effect, Who needs a translator? Everything is the way it seems to us. Essentialists want to go through life as if categories didn't depend on the mind that creates them. That's just as distorted as "social constructionism" debunking, with its suggestion that categories for people have no connection to how those people look or act. The philosopher Catherine Z. Elgin coined a useful phrase for these viewpoints: one holds that concepts are absolute; the other claims they're arbitrary.

In the last few decades, insight into the workings of the brain has shown why both these views are poor accounts of the mind. It's now well established that thoughts, feelings, and perceptions depend on *both* the mind and the world outside it. There is no discovering any fact without the mind doing some inventing; there is no inventing an idea without some reality check.

Human kinds are concepts — mental images of the categories we use to get through life. If they did not work at all, people would not use them. So they cannot be fantasies, to be cast off at will. Yet human-kind concepts change all the time, as I've mentioned. So they aren't eternal essential facts about people. Like any other thought, categories for people are a hybrid, made partly out of reality and partly by the mind itself.

To figure out how human kinds are made, then, the right place to look is *between* the absolute and the arbitrary, as Elgin puts it. That's where the mind comes to believe in a human kind like "normal people," "gay people," "Czech people," and so on. To look at that, though, it's better to start with a more general question: How do we come to believe in categories for *anything?*

Four

Birds of a Feather

Peddler: Wallets, wallets, I got nice wallets, genuine leather.
Teenager: I don't carry no fucking wallet! 'Cause I'm gangsta!

— OVERHEARD ON STREET CORNER, SIXTH AVENUE
AND 8TH STREET, MANHATTAN, SPRING 2004

When you use a category, you treat different individuals as if they
were all the same — interchangeable instances of at least one trait
they all share. This is a great skill, and probably why brains have been
such a success in evolution.

Being able to categorize means you don't have to reexamine every
rock on the road, because you can apply experience from the last
rock to this new one. If the rock you are noticing was thrown at you
by, say, a protester in a mass demonstration, you don't need to learn
his name and question him about his beliefs to learn why he is in the
street throwing rocks. One demonstrator, like one rock, is the same
as another.

For centuries, this sort of pigeonholing was thought to be simply
a matter of matching a thing to a list of features: you look at something or someone, and you decide what traits apply to them, and
then you know whether they are or are not members of your category. That was the classical definition left by Aristotle, who derived
the term *category* from a verb that meant "to accuse."

He had declared that some defining features were *necessary:* being a person, for instance, is required to be an Olympic champion. No ape could be an Olympian, then, by definition. Other features were *sufficient:* if a person wins a gold medal in the Olympic Marathon, he or she belongs, by dint of that fact alone. So all categories had crisp boundaries — a person either has necessary and sufficient traits for the category Olympian, or doesn't.

It was Ludwig Wittgenstein who pointed out that this is not how people actually think. His example was the category "game." Some games are mere amusements, like ring-around-the-rosy; others involve team competition, like soccer; some involve luck, like board games with dice; others involve skill, like chess; others involve both, like gin rummy. In our time, we could add, some involve computers and hand-eye coordination, like *Tomb Raider,* and others involve computers and luck, personality and thought, like *Sid Meier's Civilization.* Some are played with acquaintances whose names you know, and others are played with people you never meet, except by modem. Some are Olympic meets.

Our conviction that all these are games does not arise from a set of features that they all share, because no such set exists. Instead, Wittgenstein said, we sense all these different things are games because of their "family resemblance." In his maturity, Galtonian portraits apparently were still on Wittgenstein's mind.

The classical idea of a category has lost ground ever since Wittgenstein's critique was published in his *Philosophical Investigations* in 1953. By the 1960s and 1970s, many psychologists and philosophers had become convinced that a "probabilistic" theory of categories was better than the classical theory for describing the real thoughts of real people. Rather than tick through a classically crisp yes-or-no checklist, people looked at an object and toted up how many traits it had. Belonging in the category was a matter of having *enough* traits, not any particular one.

One strength of this idea is that it explained why all members of a category are not equal. The psychologist Eleanor Rosch of the University of California, for example, found that people in her studies repeatedly rated *robin* to be a better example of a bird than *penguin,* and *desk chair* to be a better example of a chair than *electric chair.*

In classical theory, that's impossible; an object either has chairness or it doesn't.

One place to see the difference — and to understand how widespread the probabilistic theory has become — is the *Diagnostic and Statistical Manual of Mental Disorders,* published by the American Psychiatric Association (APA) and used by psychiatrists to treat disease (and get paid by insurance companies). The second edition, or *DSM-II,* published in 1968, had a classical-category definition of "depressive neurosis" — a list of defining features. After a long effort to make the manual more systematic, the APA published its next edition, the *DSM-III,* in 1987. There, the psychoanalytic term *neurosis* had been purged, and the illness was now called "dysthymic disorder." But there was another change: it had also become probabilistic. The book said a diagnosis requires a persistent depressed mood plus any two out of six possible symptoms.

The late Ziva Kunda, a social psychologist, pointed out this shift. As she observed, following the *DSM-III,* three people showing a persistent depressed mood could all be diagnosed with the disorder without sharing any other single symptom. (The fourth edition, or *DSM-IV,* published in 1994, contains many changes, but it still offers a two-of-six list.)

Nonetheless, many psychologists and anthropologists weren't satisfied with the "probabilistic" view. It doesn't answer the root question: Where does the list of features come from in the first place? (Obviously, the ones in the *DSM* come from committee meetings, but the "official" written concepts we use in specialized jobs are not a model for what takes place in the mind.) After all, as one cognitive scientist puts it, a category is not just a grouping of objects but "a grouping of objects that makes sense to the perceiver." What causes a grouping to make sense?

The critics had another objection. The list-of-features idea also seems to miss one of the most important aspects of categories: we often rely on them to tell us about *hidden* connections — the link between things that *don't* share obvious traits. A good example is that point the psychologist Kurt Lewin made about a traditional nuclear family: A child is much more like other children than it is like its mother and father, and the mother resembles other women more than she does her husband. Yet everyone would agree that mother, father, and child fit together in a human kind of their own.

Categorization isn't the only aspect of human kinds. Most of the ones that matter most involve more than shared traits. They draw on that second aspect of human kinds, which I've already mentioned: their aura of being a "thing made of people," a single entity whose members have obligations that stem from their membership. Lewin suggests that only this second aspect matters. A number of psychologists have agreed with him that categorization by itself is not worth much attention. Men are similar to other men, which makes "men" a mere category, but husbands, wives, and children depend on each other to act in particular ways, which makes families meaningful groupings.

Yet many meaningful groups don't involve any personal dependence at all — I feel for my 290 million fellow Americans, but most of them aren't cooking me dinner or asking me to water their plants. Lewin's point is actually better understood as an observation about categories in general: we want a category to tell us something important about its members. A lot of important things, like who your parents are, or what diseases you might be prone to by heredity, are not evident by looking at obvious similarities.

In the 1980s, scientists proposed a new theory that appears to take care of these objections: both the problem of how the mind knows to look for "invisible" traits (like the connection between dissimilar-looking family members) and the problem of how it finds them. (If a basis for a category isn't apparent to the eye, after all, then how is it perceived?) The new approach was based on experiments on how little children learn.

When toddlers picked up categories like "living thing" and "dog," it turned out, they weren't referring to lists of traits at all. Rather, the categories that made sense to the children were those that helped them explain to themselves how the world worked. In other words, categories were neither lists of necessary and sufficient features, nor lists of traits that could be counted up. Categories aren't lists at all. They're explanations.

Some researchers, in fact, now think the best model for a developing child's mind is the scientist's. They believe that children, like scientists, learn their categories and concepts by making theories and testing them — that a child sorts out the differences between the cat and a robot toy in much the same way that a biologist would work out important distinctions among species. Others reject this "theory theory" and assume that the child need not work so hard. Their argument is that concepts are constructed by following a few basic principles.

Underlying differences among the ideas, though, is a common, pragmatic way of thinking: categories (and concepts, which are representations of categories) arise out of the needs and purposes of categorizers.

That's a departure from the classical idea that categories reflect objective reality. It's also a contrast to the Enlightenment notion that categories reflect the shape of our minds. The pragmatic idea is that categories are made of world, mind, *and* practical circumstances. In this outlook, it's virtually meaningless to talk about a category without talking about who is using it and for what purpose. To a pragmatist, the origin and meaning of a concept consist of what happens in the world when the concept is used — how it is, in the jargon of some philosophers and scientists, "operationalized."

If this view of categories is correct, then each category you can think of — types of sedan, bones of the hand, prime numbers, you name it — is a solution to some particular person's particular problem. You could think of any category, in fact, as the answer to a person's question.

Some categories are widely shared, because the world makes the same sorts of impressions on us all. Yet each person also has categories made for his or her life, which are different than those of anyone else. The psychologist Lawrence Barsalou of Emory University has one that includes "children, jewelry, portable TVs, paintings, manuscripts and photograph albums." The category? "Things to take out of a burning home."

If categories are the product of problem solving, then they aren't facts. They're thoughts; mental actions that you take to cope with your current circumstances. But they're *tethered* thoughts, with responsibilities to reality. They can't be just whatever you say.

For instance, nothing about plants in a nearby park compels you to categorize them the way other people do. You're free to group them by color or smell or distance from your house, if you like. There are experts who might divide them, for instance, into the poisonous and the nonpoisonous, but that's no concern of yours.

However, if you plucked a couple of berries off a branch, ate them, and then felt sick, that poison/not poison distinction suddenly would be a lot more interesting. You'd probably want to make use of it, in fact, and once you do that, you've limited your freedom to categorize any which way you please.

This is because the concepts "poisonous" and "nonpoisonous" depend on rules for deciding which is which. Accept the categories, and you agree to play by those rules. If you don't — if you say, for instance, that you'll decide anything with yellow flowers is poisonous — then the categories won't do the job you need them for.

To be good for anything, then, categories have to address the problem they're supposed to solve. They are not mystical glimpses of objective truth. Those plants in the park can be grouped in many different ways. But categories are not arbitrary, whimsical thoughts, either. Once you've decided you want to distinguish daisies from deadly nightshade, you have to follow the rules that produce that distinction.

If categories are called up as needed, it follows that, as your needs change, you'll use different categories — often, different categories for the same thing. I am writing this on a Friday, which is also October 1, which is also the day my monthly mortgage payment is due. Same day, three different slots for it.

This kind of variation also applies to human kinds, the categories we use for people. We may not see it because our lives are organized to support our beliefs. But any traveler knows that as circumstances change, so do perceptions of what kinds of people there are and what kinds you belong with. A disruption of the usual, confirming routine reveals human-kind flexibility.

The experience of Charles Johnston is a good example. He grew up in North Carolina as a white man with ordinary eighteenth-century American attitudes toward nonwhites. Then, in 1790, he was seized by a band of Shawnee Indians. Their only other captive was a black slave. In his memoirs the white man recalled: "The poor Negro, whom I should have kept at a distance under other circumstances, now became my companion and friend, and I felt quite at home." Those circumstances had placed Johnston in a situation where the human kinds "white" and "black" were not useful; where, in fact, another way of dividing human beings (Shawnee versus English speaker) was a better fit. And so circumstance was enough to make Johnston set his lifelong race divide aside.

Almost two centuries later, the U.S. racial divide remains foremost among its human-kind divisions. Yet people still ignore it when another map of human kinds becomes more useful. In 1968, Peter Binzen, a writer on education, was spending his days in the public schools of northern Philadelphia. It was an era of high racial tension, riots, and a national presidential campaign by a white supremacist, George Wallace. Still, Binzen writes, "It was clear to me that among teachers the racial gap was not as wide as the age gap. The older teachers stuck together; often I would find half a dozen of the old-timers sitting in a classroom at lunchtime, munching sandwiches and watching soap operas on the class TV. These groups would be mixed racially, but rarely would I see a young teacher lunching with the veterans, or vice versa."

More recently, an Arab American medic, Ramzy Azar, had a similar experience, with national categories, rather than racial ones. He was translating for wounded Iraqi prisoners of war during the 2003 U.S.-Iraq war. Though he wore a U.S. Navy uniform, as soon as the enemy soldiers heard him speak Arabic, Azar said, "I saw a change in their demeanor, and saw them relax." There was "an immediate cultural bond. To them, I've become like a brother, and I'm their advocate."

Ziva Kunda, the psychologist, found that the circumstances that change the mental map need not be as drastic as a kidnapping or a war. In her experiment, she had volunteers meet with an African American doctor to discuss their health. Half the group enjoyed the meeting, because the doctor told them they were in good health and doing everything right. The other half were told they had poor habits that needed to change. People who got good news were far more likely to talk about the man as a doctor; those who didn't like what they heard were more likely to refer to him as a black guy, rather than to his occupation.

For Daniel Saab, of the Dearborn, Michigan, police force, this experience is so familiar he has a plan for managing it. "Sometimes if I go into a household and they're all Americans," he told a reporter, "I'll cover my name. I don't want them to think of me as Arab. I want them to think of me as police."

These are stories from day-to-day life. You might object that written, formal definitions of human kinds, drafted by governments, look more permanent than an individual's feelings about his surroundings. But these categories, too, depend on the goals of the categorizers. For example, "Hispanics" are a race to the United States Department of Justice when it enforces provisions of the civil rights laws. But Hispanics are not a race to the Bureau of the Census. As George Lakoff of the University of California at Berkeley has said, "When you ask different questions, you get different answers."

If that applies to all concepts, then, it applies to that special set of concepts that are human kinds. Each is the solution to a problem, the answer to someone's question. Race was part of Johnston's question when he lived in a world of white masters. However, when he became a captive of the Shawnee, his needs were different. In the new context, with the new question in his mind, race mattered far less than the ability to speak English.

So human kinds are *creations*. They don't just happen when the mind meets the world. That mind has to need a category for some purpose, or it won't bother to make one. How, though, do you make a category for yourself to use?

Apparently, you do it by ignoring some of what you know, while paying heightened attention to the rest. Imagine, for instance, that you're walking along the seashore with a friend. Poking around at the surf's edge are some seagulls. (An ornithologist would call them herring gulls and laughing gulls, because to an expert, looking around with a different purpose than a layperson, "seagull" is not a true category. Assume you're not a bird maven.)

Now, the gulls don't act and look exactly alike. Some are bold, others shy; some are bigger than most, some smaller. Some are dingy, some fresh-feathered. One might be limping.

When you call them "those gulls over there," you tune out those variations and focus on the aspects they share. It's a little like using the speedometer while driving a car. From moment to moment, you might be going 62 miles per hour, then 63, then down a hill, 68,

then up the next hill, 59. You ignore these moment-to-moment variations and tell yourself, "I'm driving at 65."

The mind works, from top to bottom, by this kind of averaging,
or selection. Each of its many subdivisions takes in a chaotic, messy
signal from other parts and then sends out a sort of summary — a
useful representation of what the incoming noise is "really" about.
That, as the neuroscientist Alfonso Renart of Boston University says,
is what the brain does with its 100 billion neurons and their trillion
connections. Computation, he says, "is just losing information in a
smart way."

Imagine turning from that gull at the beach, to look at a friend
walking along beside you. She's moving. The light is changing. You
blink constantly. Your eyes are making constant tiny jittery motions
within their sockets. None of that affects your perception of your
companion. You don't imagine that she turns into a different person
if a cloud passes over, or that she disappears when you blink, or that
she is shaking in an earthquake because your eyes are moving all the
time. All those were eliminated when your brain's visual processing
centers, in the back of your head, summed up the rush of signals that
came in from your eyes. That "executive summary" cut large parts of
the signal that came in, sending something clearer to other regions of
the brain.

Those other regions, though, don't treat the summary like a final
product; they take it in as just one more ping in the noisy signal that
they, in their turn, will sum up. And their summary goes to still other
regions, which will average that with the others that they receive. So
output from one part of the brain becomes input for others; one section's "final product" becomes "raw material" elsewhere. Light hit-
ting your eyes is translated into signals which tell that you are seeing
a face; that representation then gets sorted by face-recognizing brain
cells, which report that this one belongs to a friend; their report in
turn goes elsewhere, where your experience of your friend today
can be sorted with memories of other times you have seen him. And,
by the way, though I have made this sound like a sequence, it's not.
All these things are happening more or less simultaneously.

Sometimes the "corrections" that the brain imposes on perception aren't right, and you experience an illusion. For example, if you

saw a gull fly from the right of your visual field, approach a cliff, then disappear behind it, you would strongly expect anything that flew out from behind the cliff on the other side to be that gull. Thanks to this phenomenon, called the "tunnel effect," experimenters have found that people cling to their perceptual map, even when it is wrong. If researchers roll a green ball behind an obstacle, then push a yellow one out the other side, most people feel they saw a single ball — it just changed color as it traveled!

So our thoughts, feelings, and perceptions are the products of a vast process of averaging, summarizing, and then passing the summaries along for more processing. It is happening at many different time scales, from the microseconds it takes for your brain to correct for the jittery movements of your eyeballs and create a steady image of these words, to the years of living that create a "feel" for a nation and its people.

This doesn't sound too different from Francis Galton's idea that concepts were "blended impressions" — averaging out all the slight changes and differences around you into a single picture, as his composite portraits made a single face stand for all the officers in the Royal Engineers whose photographs he'd obtained.

But Galton ignored context and scale. You only average out what you need to think about at the moment, and on the scale that's relevant to your situation. Your slight alterations in speed over ten minutes average out to 50 miles per hour; your best friend's many different expressions, stories, hairstyles, and so on average out over years to your sense of her; decades spent in the landscape of your homeland averages out to a sense of "my country."

Change your circumstances, and your goals change. That alters both the direction of your attention and the scale. You might attend a demonstration with your attention on politics, using human-kind categories like "moderates" and "extremists," formed over years. If violence should break out and you find yourself dodging rocks or running from the riot police, your time scale will be a lot smaller. (Fear elongates the perception of time.) And your human-kind categories of the moment will be much simpler. They might be, for instance, "people who are trying to hurt me" and "everyone else."

Yet, as I've mentioned, some human kinds transcend their context, and come to feel eternally true and always relevant. Anyone can recognize that a human kind like "people on the 8:15 ferry" tells you only which boat those people ride on (until the people on the boat decide it means more). Yet we assume that categories like "German" and "Hindu" and "old person" tell us much more about people.

Why? Given that we are capable of changing classification systems all the time, why bless certain categories — like race or nation or religion — with permanent relevance? As we've seen, it's not "good statistics" that make us do this. Quite the opposite. We don't gather statistics and then make human kinds; we begin with human kinds and then go out and measure. What makes us decide some valid categories are real and important, while others are just accidents?

One answer is "other people." Human kinds are convincing when others are already convinced, not only because we want to conform but also because, as a practical matter, people's beliefs organize their lives and thoughts. This is the looping effect that Ian Hacking has described. The more aspects of life that Americans can describe in terms of blue states and red states, the more those categories will be meaningful human kinds.

Another aspect of convincingness is what could be called a "founder effect" — an accidental pairing of a set of people with some easily spotted feature. In genetics, a founder effect arises when an unusual mutation appears among a small band of relatives or in a single individual. Suppose this "founder" has many descendants who all identify themselves as members of the same human kind. If that human kind can't or won't marry often with "outsiders," then the usual effect of sex — bringing the distribution of human genes in any human kind back to the species average — won't occur. The unusual gene will persist among members of that group, at rates higher than in most collections of people. For example, Tay-Sachs disease is caused by a mutation on the *HEXA* gene, which can occur in any human being. But the Tay-Sachs mutation turns up with higher-than-average frequencies in a number of human kinds — Louisiana Cajuns and Ashkenazi Jews, to name two.

Perhaps there is a purely mental equivalent of the founder effect, which speaks to the needs of the human-kind part of the mind. Such an effect involves an arbitrary, accidental linking of people with some feature or activity that's easy to perceive and talk about. The more this happens, the more a human kind convinces us of its validity.

When I was a child in New York City, one of the distinguishing traits I learned to associate with Ashkenazic Jews was a fondness for Chinese food.

The sociologists Gaye Tuchman and Harry Levine, who grew up with this tradition, trace it to the history of immigration in New York City. Jewish immigrants from Eastern Europe arrived in great numbers around the turn of the last century. They brought dietary laws from their former life. Chinese restaurants did not observe these laws, but they also didn't conspicuously violate them, because Chinese cooks didn't mix milk and meat. (They used no milk or cheese at all.) Chinese restaurants were affordable, and unlike those of other ethnic groups, they weren't perceived as hostile to Jews. In fact, eating Chinese food came to be seen among upwardly mobile immigrants as a sign of sophistication and urbanity.

That's a *cognitive* founder effect — an accident of circumstances that connects a kind of people with some activity or trait and makes it theirs. After which, of course, looping effects can take place: in the second and third generation of Jewish families in the New York City region, Chinese food was, as a friend of mine once said, "what your mother brought home on Sunday night."

Another kind of imagery that seems to capture the attention of our human-kind faculty is a type of rhetoric that the historian Eric Hobsbawm has called "the invention of tradition." It's a way of slapping a coat of essentialism on those looping effects and founding accidents.

In a collection of essays on the subject, Hobsbawm's colleague Hugh Trevor-Roper notes that the supposedly ancient traditions of Scotland — kilts, clan tartans, playing bagpipes — are all recent. In fact, none is much older than Hume's essay on national characters, published in 1777. The kilt, invented by an Englishman, was a creation of the early industrial revolution. It replaced a one-piece shift because it let a workman move more easily while felling trees or

working in a crowded factory. Clan tartans were standardized in the
1740s by the British Army, when it created its Highland regiments.
The association of particular patterns with particular clans derives
from a fake manuscript created by a pair of wily forgers. From the
mid-eighteenth century forward, cloth manufacturers encouraged the
idea. They had plaid to sell.

In the next century, Europeans elsewhere took interest in "national dress," which was one expression of a shift in fashionable taste
against Enlightenment values. In the wake of the Napoleonic Wars,
which had been fought in the name of the "universal rights of man,"
thinkers turned against rationalism. Where Hume had noted that
people everywhere are similar, that nations change, and that many
different traits can be the basis for a human kind, new taste preferred
a contrary idea: that humanity divided into eternal "peoples," each
with its own essence, which is expressed in language, folktales, traditional costumes, and the like.

The invention of tradition remains an important part of political
rhetoric today. It helps persuade people that some human kinds are
the basic units of politics — the real divisions that matter — while
others are "just theories."

Among the world's other invented traditions is the strict divide
between Hutu and Tutsi, which was the basis for genocidal killings
in Rwanda in the 1990s. As Mahmood Mamdani, a political scientist
at Columbia University, has explained, these seemingly ancient tribal
boundaries are only about a hundred years old. They were accentu-
ated in the last years of the African-ruled state, for reasons particular
to its place and time. And those same human kinds were then emphasized even more in the 1920s and 1930s under Belgian colonial
rule, when a theory about racial origins was used to divide schools,
governments, and churches into Hutu and Tutsi spheres. The resulting human kinds were certainly real. (They organized the 1994 slaughter of hundreds of thousands of people.) What they were not,
though, was ancient.

Another politically potent invention has been noted by the social
anthropologist Thomas Hylland Eriksen of the University of Oslo.
A central tenet of India's Bharatiya Janata Party, which ruled the coun-

try until 2004, is that India should be true to its ancient religious essence, its *hindutva,* or Hinduness. Eriksen points out that hindutva is itself alien to Hinduism. Unlike Islam, Christianity or Judaism, Hinduism was never a religion with authorities who decided what was in and what was out. The sense of a well-defined character for the religion, then, was borrowed from non-Hindu enemies. Specifically, it was borrowed from European colonialists' ideas about national souls (that romantic essentialism that sold kilts). The idea also had affinities with Muslim notions of a pure community of believers, distinct from the infidels. In other words, Eriksen notes, "Hindutva has double origins in Western Romanticism and Middle Eastern political Islam."

As is often the case when the subject is human kinds, the strangest aspect of "the invention of tradition" is the one that almost never gets talked about, because it's too obvious and uncontroversial. Why should people care about the *age* of their loyalties and practices? The Hutu-Tutsi divide and the ideology of hindutva are potent political forces right here, right now. What difference does it make that they're recent inventions?

The answer is probably rooted in the bad habits of essentialism, toward which we are strongly biased by the rules of human-kind thinking. People really dislike evidence that essentialism is wrong. And this makes some sense: if a concept you depend on for your politics and way of life was hatched a few generations ago, then it follows that the concept might not endure too far into the future. If that's so, then it cannot represent an unchanging, eternal essence of Hinduism, or Tutsiness, or American spirit. If you want to believe you're connected with all your fellow Hindus, or Tutsis, or Americans, dead and alive, because of a shared essence in all of you, then you might find the thought that everything was different fifty years ago to be a problem.

Let's recap. Thanks to looping effects, people who believe in a human kind will act as if it is real, which is all that's required to make a human kind have practical effects in the world. Founder effects help people tell one human kind from another, helping to make those human kinds feel real (and helping them forget other equally logical ways to divide up the human race). And invented tradition gives to the resulting belief a reassuring flavor of timeless essences — the gut feeling that "things were always this way."

The convincers that I've just described — looping effects, founder effects, inventions of tradition — are mental amplifiers, making some human kinds seem important. Other categories, like "people on the same bus" and "left-handed people" and "soccer fans," don't get the treatment. They aren't imbued with traditions and loopings and founder effects. So scientists don't go looking for the common gene shared by all the people on the bus, though such a gene could be found.

Francis Galton, measurer and classifier of physical features, was looking in the wrong place. He thought he could calculate his way to an objective map of the human kinds, in which his own beliefs did not figure. But there is no such map, and there can never be one.

Galton refused to believe that his human-kind categories arose from any mechanism other than pure counting and analysis. "No statistician dreams of combining objects into the same generic group that do not cluster toward a common center," he wrote. "No more should we attempt to compose generic portraits out of heterogeneous elements, for if we do so the result is monstrous and meaningless."

It was because height measurements for men in the British Isles obeyed the bell curve, he said, that they could be taken as a single people, even though they were "much mingled" in their ethnic origins "and although Ireland is mainly peopled with Celts." And if by contrast a grouping flunked the bell curve test, it wasn't a proper category. "It clearly would not be proper to combine the heights of men belonging to two dissimilar races," he wrote. "A union of two dissimilar systems of dots would produce the same kind of confusion as if half of the bullets fired at a target have been directed to one mark, and the other half to another mark."

Galton argued here that the British made sense as a people because their measurements fell on the bell curve. He was wrong. *Any* large collection of height measurements would fall on the curve, even if they were drawn from every continent on earth. His sense of Britishness as a real human kind came from the operations of his own mind — from a bias for essentialism, amplified by looping effects, founder effects, and invented traditions.

Still, the argument drags on, in our own century, about which human kinds — races, religious castes, sexual orientations — are "real." Most biologists believe today's common rules of thumb for race — white, black, and yellow — are meaningless as science, for the same reason that ornithologists hate the term *seagull*. Notions of race hide, rather than reveal, real facts about the species. However, race still has its apologists. Their claim is that today's human-kind *beliefs* line up with objective, valid *measurements.*

A decade ago, the author and physiologist Jared Diamond of the University of California at Los Angeles demonstrated why this makes little sense. Yes, he wrote, differences in skin color correlate with some measurable differences among people. But that concordance isn't special. Many *other* biologically real distinctions lump people into human kinds that have nothing to do with our ideas of race.

For example, people whose ancestors lived in the tropical regions where malaria is common often inherit genes that help protect against that disease. At the same time, human populations move around; people today don't live where their ancestors did. If a biologist were to group people according to the presence or absence of these "anti-malaria" genes, then North European Swedes and South African Xhosa would belong to the same human kind — the one that lacks the genes. Meanwhile, Nigerians and Italians, populations in which a higher-than-average number of people possess those genes, would be together. Similarly, there are people whose bodies keep making the enzyme lactase, which lets them easily digest milk. Many other human beings, though, lose the ability to make this enzyme after the milk-suckling years of infancy. If you divide the human species into adults-tolerant-of-milk and adults-who-can't-digest-milk, you place the Swedes with the Fulani, a West African people, while most other Africans go into the same box as the Japanese and the Native Americans.

A few years ago I recalled Diamond's observation in a room full of young neuroscientists learning about the physiology of taste. They (and I) had all sampled scraps of paper imbued with 6-n-propylthiouracil, a ghastly tasting chemical known as PROP.

It tasted ghastly to me, anyway — bitterer than anything I could remember. Others in the room found it merely unpleasant. And a few people could not taste it at all. Tom Finger, the University of Colorado neuroscientist who conducted the demonstration, explained why: Only those with particular versions, or alleles, of the genes for taste would sense PROP. Anyone without the alleles would taste nothing. Moreover, some of the "tasters" had more taste-receptor cells on their tongues than others did (another genetic difference). We were the "supertasters," revolted by PROP because we had more cells firing in response to it.

As I looked around the room, now divided into the three human kinds of supertaster, taster, and nontaster, I noticed the dividing lines. Among the ten supertasters were six men and four women; six North Americans and four Europeans; nine people who would fit the vague American category "white" and one person whose ancestors were Japanese. Among the ordinary tasters were two people of what Americans vaguely call Asian ancestry, four North American whites, and two Europeans. The three nontasters were two men and one woman, also describable as two North Americans and one European.

Using PROP, Finger had shown us biologically real human kinds: our three groups were meaningful consequences of genetic differences. But they had no connection to race — or to gender or nationality. For example, of the three German citizens in the room, one was a supertaster, one a regular, and one a nontaster. One of the Spaniards was a super, the other a regular. Taster, nontaster, and supertaster are just one of the infinite number of potential schemes for dividing humanity that we do not use. It's a gene-based framework that's certainly as "real" as most ethnic groups. (In fact, given that taste buds are tied to genetic differences, the taster-supertaster line is probably more biologically based than ethnic boundaries.)

One more example: to find a biologically real, oppressed minority in any country, look for the left-handed people. They're disparaged in proverbial phrases like "left-handed compliment" and "sinister atmosphere" (*sinister* derives from the Latin for "left"); a few die every year from using tools made for righties. Yet there are no social movements or political parties or literature courses devoted to them.

Left-handers aren't asking for lefty-only dorms on college campuses because no one believes in that category as a meaningful human kind. Just as no one believes in human kinds like "people who live at odd-numbered addresses" or "people who can't carry a tune." Give me any hundred people selected at random, and I can divide them every which way, into groupings that will fit some real measurement system.

The important thing to understand about human kinds like race, ethnic group, nationality, and sexual orientation is not that they're baseless. It's that they make no more sense than alternative categories, which we do not use. That's how we know that the source of our beliefs is not physical evidence about people.

One "race realist" has derided this sort of argument as merely hypothetical game playing, saying, in essence, who cares about these alternate universes? In the real world, people go by race. But there is nothing theoretical about the gap between belief and measurement in human kinds. As I've mentioned, it's a practical problem for law enforcement, where reliance on racial and ethnic categories proved less effective at catching the bad actors than reliance on precisely defined categories.

It's also a problem in medicine. The medical historian Richie Witzig has shown how doctors who ignore Diamond's point have made mistakes. Witzig's research turned up a child with sickle-cell anemia who almost perished because no one thought to check for the disease. After all, the boy was white (descended from Sicilians), and "everyone knows" sickle-cell anemia is a disease of black people. Conversely, Witzig notes the example of an African American man who nearly died because his doctors thought he must have that African American illness, sickle-cell anemia. He did not. He had a bleeding stomach ulcer.

Essentialists about race or ethnicity often accuse skeptics of claiming that there are no differences among human beings. This argument misses the point. The question is not whether people differ but why we hang our essentialist beliefs on one type of difference — skin color or language, say — while ignoring others.

Galton illustrated the point when he lumped the Anglo-Saxons of England and the Celts of Wales — two human kinds that can easily

be treated as separate on the basis of language, culture, and genetics —
into one category. Meanwhile, he excluded Hindus and Zulus. His
calculations cannot tell why that makes sense.

Of course, the Anglo-Saxons and the Celts of the British Isles are
linked by more common history than are further-off lands of the
once-global British Empire. But Galton was not making a claim about
history. He said the human kind called British people made sense as
science. He was treating information about *history* and information
about *biology* as if they were of the same nature.

Doing this comes so naturally to most people that it's worth spending a little time on the human kinds that many of us, today, believe
to be eternal, unchanging aspects of the human condition. They
aren't. They're concepts — mental images of categories that people
use to get through their lives. As such, these ideas are like any other
thought: they have a birthdate in human history, in a time when they
arose for particular reasons, belonging to the people who devised
them. Let's look at some of them.

Race

Henry Louis Gates Jr., the chairman of Harvard's Department of
African and African American Studies, remembers learning as a small
child in West Virginia about white people. There are two kinds, his
father explained — Italians and Irish. How to tell them apart? Italian
names, his father explained, ended with an "o." Irish names began
with one.

As Gates's story illustrates, each person makes human kinds out of
the differences he can learn about and see in everyday experience. A
lot of those differences can't be perceived until we have acquired a
fair amount of knowledge — like language and the alphabet, which
let young Gates use the position of an "o" to make an important distinction. Many modern human kinds require a lot of training to perceive. It takes education and experience, for example, to know the
difference between a Shia and a Sunni Muslim.

For some differences, however, less training is necessary. When people speak a different language, wear different clothes, move and act in ways you don't recognize, or have a different color skin than you are used to seeing, your perception that they're different from Us feels immediate. Young Gates had to learn about the difference between Italians and Irish people, but he could see a difference in skin color around town.

This sense — that the human species divides into kinds of people whose differences are obvious and cannot be hidden — is part of the rhetoric of race. The other part, usually, is an assumption that the easily perceived difference stems from ancestry and can't be changed.

In one sense, this notion of an easily spotted human kind whose members are in it by birth is ancient. To tell Us from Them, people have always seized on the differences they could perceive most easily and, to make their lives easier, just assumed that the categories had no element of choice. The ancient Greeks saw a line between themselves and peoples who neglected to speak Greek, those makers of outlandish speech sounds — *bar-bar-bar-bar* — that marked them as barbarians. Their Persian enemy Xerxes declared himself, in inscriptions, the king of many different kinds of people. *Race* is as good a word as any for the sort of overarching differences among people that depicted Persians as one human kind and Greeks another.

There's a big gap, though, between a general notion that people use easily noticed physical differences to sort human kinds and a claim that *today's* particular version is true and eternal. Most people in North America use *race* nowadays to mean a particular set of human kinds — the black, the white, and the yellow kinds — defined first and foremost by the amount of melanin in people's skin. This set of categories for people, like any other, has a history, dating back to the nineteenth century, or perhaps the eighteenth, or perhaps the sixteenth — historians don't agree.

A few academics who call themselves race realists have claimed that today's North American race map describes real, enduring divisions in the human species. That essentialist belief has required them to insist that race has *always* meant more or less the same thing, which is an idea most anthropologists and biologists reject out of hand. Race doesn't even mean the same thing today, from country to country. Census figures are hard to compare among nations because their racial categories don't line up.

In fact, racial boundaries have never been clear, and they still aren't. For example, the epidemiologist Robert Hahn and his colleagues examined the birth and death certificates of infants who, sadly, died within a year of their birth in the United States between 1983 and 1985. More than 40 percent of the babies classified as neither black nor white — as Asian, for example — were placed in a different category on their death certificates than on their birth records. It's not surprising that Americans are much better at deciding who is black and who is white than they are at using other categories, since Americans for centuries have been taught about the black and white races. Still, more than 4 percent of the infants who began their short lives as "black" ended in a different human kind — most likely the white one, as that was where almost all of the reclassified infants ended up. The likely explanation: mothers supplied the race information for the birth certificates; funeral directors filled out the documents after death.

Does this mean that there is no such thing as race? Such a claim might come as a surprise to, say, Gates, whose childhood town was organized along a racial divide; for that matter, it surprises any African American in a big city who can't get a taxi to stop on a Friday night. Human-kind categories don't need a logical or factual basis to be used in day-to-day life. They just need to be convincing to the mind, and nothing is more convincing than practical, lived experience. Categories, remember, are problem-solving thoughts, and a mind presented with racial problems is only doing its job when it creates racial concepts to understand the world. Organize life along racial lines, then, and people will believe in races. And because human kinds are probability judgments, not absolutes, those believers won't be swayed by contrary evidence — like black people whom doctors can't identify as black.

Asking if race is real, then, is like asking if money is real. Both questions are meaningless without a framework. At the political and cultural level of analysis, races are real enough, because people believe them to be. So is the value of the bills in your wallet, for the same reason. Genetics, though, is a different framework of knowledge. At the genetic level, most African Americans have European ancestors as well as African ones; genetically, almost all variations in human DNA are found in all races. As the chemistry of ink on your money gives no clue to its economic value, so human genetics doesn't support today's notion of race. Is *race* a valid idea? That question doesn't make sense without a second one: *Valid for what?*

Nation

The word *nation* evolved from the Latin *nasci,* "to be born." In the ancient Roman world, then, *nationem* had the connotation we would now use for race or ethnic group: people born of a common stock. For centuries, though, the term also has designated the inhabitants of a particular region, and this ambiguity — is the nation a thing created by birth or by territory? — haunts the word.

In the Middle Ages in Europe, religion, social class, and feudal obligations outweighed the call of one's nation. As I've mentioned, most Europeans then were considered part of a single Christendom, and their ruler governed from rights over particular peoples — whether or not he lived in their territory or spoke their language. Since the French Revolution, however, European political ideas have stressed cultural and territorial concepts over these older ties. Exported to the rest of the world, these ideas now organize the way most people pay taxes, do business, vote, and travel.

One reason for the quick rise of this novel human kind is its association with political power. Nations are also states, with governments that have the means to control their citizens. Hence, the second ambiguity about the concept: Does a nation *have* to be a state?

Nations trigger human-kind thinking just as intensely as an older idea like race or tribe. Nationalism remains one of the most potent political forces in the world, and millions have died "for the nation" as ancestors died for gods or families. It's likely that the vagueness of the idea — which can mean an ethnic group, like "the Germans," or

a shared ideology, like "the Americans," or a territory and government, like "Nigeria" — is part of its success. "Nation" excludes no
human-kind belief. You can think of yourself as a nationalist by blood,
by location, by conviction, by mystic ties, or by any combination of
those criteria.

Ethnic Group

Ethnos is ancient Greek for a people or nation. The word was used in
the Christian Bible to signify peoples that are not Us — in other
words, heathens: non-Christians and non-Jews. This meaning passed
through Latin into English: ethnics were the pagans. That usage died
out in the eighteenth century, but the root word was taken up in the
nineteenth, to apply to a new kind of "not Us" — the tribes and nations that Europeans were discovering and conquering. The terms
ethnography and *ethnology* were coined to refer to these new fields,
from which emerged concepts like ethnocentrism. *Ethnic,* as a word
more or less meaning "tribal," emerged in this epoch.

Ethnic group is a very recent term. It arose in the 1940s, when
American scholars began to use it as a way of talking about non-
WASP white people, including Americans who saw themselves as
Jewish, Italian, or Irish. *Ethnicity,* then, is a back-formation from more
precise ideas, and so today, the concept is something of a mess. No
standard definition exists.

Most scholars use *ethnic group* to describe people who are thought
to belong together because of shared traits that are inherited, not
chosen. That inheritance may be genetic, but most concepts of ethnicity allow the shared traits to include language, culture, religion,
or social class. Many recognized ethnic groups combine several elements from that list.

Many of these definitions stress that people in an ethnic group
will see themselves as descendants of the same forebears — a kind of
giant family. This notion need not be true. What counts, as the German sociologist Max Weber pointed out in the 1920s, is that it be
believed. In fact, recent work in population genetics suggests that

Weber's instincts were correct. A team led by Raphaëlle Chaix of the Centre National de la Recherche Scientifique in Paris analyzed genetic markers in the male lines of men from five different ethnic groups living in Uzbekistan: Kazakhs, Turkmen, Uzbeks, Qongirat, and On Tort Uruw. All had traditions that told of their group's descent from a common ancestor. But the analysis showed that members of each ethnic group were no more closely related to fellow ethnics than they were to men in the other tribes.

Aside from sharing stories of common ancestors, people in an ethnic group also often are supposed to look and behave, on some measures, more like each other than like outsiders. Most definitions of ethnicity also include marriage restrictions — part of what defines an ethnic group is that its members marry one another and don't mate outside their human kind.

So does ethnicity include race, religion, and nationality? Yes, says Donald L. Horowitz of Duke University, a leading expert on ethnic conflict. No, says the University of Washington's Pierre L. van den Berghe, a sociologist and Darwinian, a true ethnic group must invoke a common ancestor. Ethnicity, he likes to say, "is kinship writ large." And does the word *group* after *ethnic* make any sense, given that members of an "ethnic group" may be scattered over several continents and speak many different languages? Some scholars say no, preferring van den Berghe's term, *ethny.*

Despite the unsettled state of the experts' debate, most ordinary people nowadays place a lot of faith in the importance of ethnic groups. The belief that ethnicity is inescapable — that we're all "born that way" into our ethnic kinds — supports the muddled notion that everyone in an ethnic group has the same experience of life. From this derive the often illogical lumpings of contemporary American politics — policies in education and corporate life, for example, that treat all African Americans as the same, even though some African Americans are children of privilege while others are impoverished new immigrants.

Ethnicity is often said to be pervasive in people's lives, in a way that other human kinds are not. You need to do bosslike things to be seen as a boss, for example, and act fatherly to register as a father. But many people act as if ethnicity is *always* relevant in all situations, no matter what you do or say. As with race, this feeling can become a self-fulfilling prophecy, because it causes most aspects of life to be organized on ethnic lines.

For people whose access to markets, politics, education, religion, and culture do not depend on ethnic human kinds, ethnicity can feel like nothing special — just one of many categories for people. A native-born American may feel Chinese in one conversation, female in another, and Bostonian in a third. Meanwhile, a newly arrived immigrant, without English and without American connections, may find his whole life organized by his Chineseness, and so feel differently. Ask a different question, get a different answer: the meaning of ethnicity, like that of any human kind, depends on who is using it and what he needs to accomplish with the concept.

Class

Francis Galton set great store by social class — a human kind defined by the way its members make their living. When he created composites of men in the Royal Engineers, he separated officers and enlisted men, and remarked on the refinement of the upper-crust men. Similarly, Karl Marx saw classes defined by their relationship to the means of production: those who labor and get their income from their efforts, the workers; and those who don't work, getting their income from returns on money, the capitalists. In much of the industrialized world, *working class* implies physical labor, *white collar* means technical or managerial, and *upper class* means highly paid workers or those who get their income from investments. (The American term *middle class* designates all the others and so does not describe a class at all. It's a synonym for "normal people.")

Ordinary talk gives social class all the traits of traditional human kinds. We speak of working-class speech, white-collar child rearing, working-class neighborhoods, upper-class tastes in food, clothes, and movies. Marriages across class lines look and feel "mixed" like marriages across religious or ethnic divides. Sir Michael Marmot of University College, London, has pointed out that in Britain even differences in average height correlate with class lines.

So why is it easier, politically, to make people unite as citizens of the same nation or believers in the same religion than as members of the same class? One reason, as the psychological-anthropologist Lawrence A. Hirschfeld suggests, may be that it's harder to be essentialist about class. The category is based on work and income, so by definition, you can change your class. And yet its tribal aura makes that change much more difficult than people think.

Ideology

An ideology is a set of beliefs, thought to be coherent and consistent by the believers — and by their enemies — which are used to define a human kind. As a general rule, you scorn others' ideologies as unrealistic and strange, and seldom examine your own. Communists, fundamentalists, and proglobalization technocrats, for example, are all human kinds defined by ideology.

In modern times, ideologies have rivaled older human kinds in their numbers of adherents and in their fatal consequences. The creation and maintenance of human kinds held together by fascism and communism, for example, probably killed at least as many people in the twentieth century as did racism or nationalism.

Nonetheless, ideological human kinds aren't given the legal and cultural status of supposedly more fundamental tribes arranged by nation, ethnic group, or religion. The murders of alleged Communists and their supposed sympathizers in Indonesia in 1965–66 are not legally a genocide, because that crime requires the victims to belong to a religion, ethnicity, culture, or nation.

Perhaps ideology hasn't yet acquired the trappings of those other human kinds. But it may be that ideological categories lack some of the features that convince the mind's human-kind faculty. Communists do not, for example, claim that all members share descent from a single ancestor. Nor are they expected to marry only among themselves. Nor do they share languages, customs, foods, and folk-ways. Contrast that with the worldwide religions: they also lack the ancestor claim, but they do require that believers share at least a few physical actions (for example, baptism in Christianity), and they stress marriage within the faith.

Originally, as the writer and critic Terry Eagleton points out, *ideology* meant the opposite of what we intend today. Coined by Antoine Destutt de Tracy, a French revolutionary and intellectual, ideology was to be the study of how ideas arose from the interaction of human nature and the physical world. Tracy conceived of it as a branch of zoology.

It was Napoleon who reversed the word's meaning, complaining of "ideologues" who clung to their liberal dreams against the facts of nature and tradition. The sense of ideology as a belief that disregards reality and material life was perpetuated by Karl Marx and is now part of what most people mean by the word.

All these human kinds certainly don't *feel* like inventions. But if the mind makes categories to answer its needs of the moment, then we should not be surprised that those categories can be canceled, as were the cagots of France or the paekchong of Korea; that categories can be redefined, as "white person" has been in the United States to include the once-rejected children of Irish and Italian immigrants; or that categories can be separated from their markers, as tattoos have parted from sailors and convicts. It also should not be surprising that human kinds are *local:* created to suit the needs of particular people at particular times and places, they are not easy to translate across continents and centuries.

This is why, as the sociologist Clara E. Rodriguez has pointed out, census figures around the world are difficult to compare. Different nations use different definitions of race and ethnicity.

Even within a nation, census figures are not consistent over time. As Rodriguez recounts, in the first half of the twentieth century, a person with seven white great-grandparents and one black great-grandparent was white in Oregon, but not in Florida — or Indiana, Missouri, Nebraska, North and South Carolina, and North Dakota, all of which considered a person black who had one black great-grandparent. The U.S. Census Bureau classed Mexicans as a race in the 1930 census, never before or after; Armenians were not white until a court decided they were in 1909.

Judges have had to define and redefine human kinds for centuries. In the United States courts, an 1854 decision held that Chinese people were Indians under American law. An 1893 case classed Japanese as Mongolian. The category Hindu, used in the 1930 and 1940 censuses, included Muslims and Christians — it was intended for all people from the subcontinent. Courts and politicians were also vexed for decades by the question of whether these Hindus were white. The 1910 census said they were (though it noted that they were not seen that way by most Americans). The 1920 census bureau, leaning on that popular sentiment, decided that Hindus weren't white after all.

When some Hindu citizens challenged this decision, the Supreme Court upheld it, on the grounds that the people of the United States believed that a Caucasian was a European sort of a person, whatever the science of it all. As a result of this decision, at least sixty-five naturalized Indians lost their citizenship. Even for black and white, those American lodestars, definitions have moved over time. In nineteenth-century Virginia, *white* meant anyone less than one-quarter Negro. It was not until 1924 that the state legislature barred anyone with the infamous "single drop" of Negro blood from marrying a white person.

Francis Galton measured and calculated without ceasing in his effort to find the true divisions among human kinds — whites and Negroes, officers and commoners, Jews and Gentiles, criminal types and decent people, the talented and the mediocre. But the source of these categories could never be revealed by any physical measurement of people's bodies or their actions. The source was in his head.

The root mystery of human kinds lies in the problem Galton ignored: why the mind picks some traits to mark human kinds and ignores others. You don't believe in today's races, ethnic groups, national characters, and other human kinds because you went out and measured people. It's the other way around. First, you learned the categories, as Gates, for example, learned that there are black people and white people, and that the white ones divided into Irish and Italians.

Then, with those kinds of categories to organize your thoughts, you learned how blacks and whites differ, and how to tell the Irish from the Italians (and men are from Mars, and women from Venus, and southerners are charming, and northerners efficient, and so on and on).

So if you are convinced that your society is truly divided into black versus white, or Muslim versus Hindu, or Blue versus Red — and not into left-handed versus right-handed, or parents versus the childless, or clear-eyed versus nearsighted — there must be a basis for your feeling that the first list of examples makes sense while the second one does not. That basis isn't in the facts, because the facts will support many alternative categories. The obvious answer — "because those are what everyone else believes" — is true enough, but it doesn't explain much. If we believe in race and ethnicity because our parents did, and because that's the way the world is organized, the question remains: Why did *they* believe it? How did society get organized this way and not according to some other set of categories?

Looping effects, founder effects, invented traditions, and other rhetoric do indeed work on the human-kind faculty of the mind. But why do they work? What rules govern that faculty, making it believe in some human kinds and reject others?

Five

Mind Sight and Kind Sight

There are things which are only things; and there are things which are also signs of other things.

— ST. AUGUSTINE

April 2001. I'm in line to check in at a Los Angeles hotel, for a conference on social-cognitive neuroscience. Ahead of me at the desk is a wiry man, speaking in what, to my ear, is an English accent. He's sporting a black leather jacket and a head of hair dyed three different colors. So he stands out in a crowd of academics in T-shirts, uncomplicated haircuts, and sensible shoes. I notice him and classify him quickly.

This is L.A. He's probably with a band. I go back to looking around for people I know, or expect to meet, or want to meet.

Nothing could feel simpler than this moment that some social psychologists call "person construal": (a) see someone; (b) classify him; (c) decide, on the basis of that human kind, what to do about him.

Everybody does this, automatically, constantly, to very high levels of detail and precision. It's not just for strangers. Because all of us belong to more than one human kind, we also classify and reclassify people we know, and ourselves, as situations change. (Sometimes it takes a second or two to switch from one context to another, and you have to explain to, say, your office colleague that you didn't recognize him on the treadmill in his sweats.)

As I would soon see at this scientific conference on person construal and other forms of social cognition, this job of pigeonholing people requires no conscious thought. That's significant. A few people, by great effort, have made themselves experts in difficult mental activities, like calculus, jazz piano, or piloting helicopters. Person construal is more complicated, mentally and emotionally, than any of those. Yet human-kind classification doesn't need to be taught. Without work, without awareness, we human beings are experts at sorting people into kinds. And we're experts at talking about it.

Up in my room, for instance, I came upon this sentence in the hotel's guide to the neighborhood: "In a strip of Sunset that goes from trashy to chic without changing area codes, Bar Marmont resides on the higher end of elegant cool."

Not many words, but look how much they told you about the kinds of people you can meet at Bar Marmont (and about the kind of person who wrote that description). Where did that knowledge come from? Did you have to think about it, draw up lists, or make calculations? My guess: no. You read the words and formed, immediately, a picture of the relevant human kinds. And you got some sense of how you would feel among such types of people, and what you could and could not comfortably do around them.

It doesn't matter that your picture of the Marmont may not agree with mine. No doubt an Angeleno would learn more from this sentence than I did, visiting from New York (I don't get that bit about area codes), and maybe I got more out of it than would a first-time visitor from Khartoum (who might not know that U.S. area codes refer to telephone numbers). In that way, this description is like a map: easier to read if you're familiar with the local area but informative enough for anyone who knows how to unfold it.

And anyone *can* unfold it; whether you're familiar with its imagery or alienated by it, every person who can read this sentence will know that it is about human kinds. There is no information here about the physical space, nor anything about the individual Joes and Janes who hang out there. Everything that sentence has to tell you, about the sights, sounds, and rules of conduct that you'll find at the bar, follows from the *types* of people there. That, and nothing else, is the subject. And anyone who reads it knows this and gets that kind of clue from it — immediately, effortlessly, and in detail.

In a real sense, then, that sentence is in code. It connects one mental realm (perceptions, like sights and sounds) to another (knowledge about kinds of people). It was that code that I used when I decided, without thinking about it, that the man in line was probably in a band. Morse code can be sent by telegraph clicks or signal flags or a hammer banging on a drainpipe, and this code also reached my awareness by different means at different times — *looking* at a person's appearance at noon, *reading* about a bar forty-five minutes later. The code isn't confined to one medium. Looking around in line, or reading in my room, I was translating perceptions into information about the human kinds that were relevant to me at the moment: hotel employees, other journalists, scientists of various disciplines, grad students, and on the periphery, that guy ahead in line.

An object or action that transmits code is leading a double life. It is both a physical object or event (air vibrating, causing my ear to signal my brain) *and* a pointer to other, nonphysical facts. This sentence, right here, has just such a multiple existence. You see black shapes on a white background, but you also see what they represent — letters, words, sentences, and ideas. The book is an object made of chemicals and wood pulp, and you can perceive its weight, shape, and color. But you also perceive what those stand for: the thoughts that are encoded here.

Codes are rules that establish a correspondence between one world and another, which lets you perceive the not-obvious and not-physical realms. They give you a way to see objects or events as signs of other, less-obvious knowledge. And these codes are, quite literally, in your brain, where 100 billion cells create them and maintain them. Code after code after code has transformed the light that reached your eyes from this page into your awareness of the book — as an object, as a collection of inky shapes on paper, as words, and as ideas.

It all begins at the back of your eye, where light-sensitive cells "fire" in response to light energy. That signal then travels down 1.5 million neurons that stretch from each eye back into the brain. (If you're listening to this book instead of reading it, a similar process is starting at your ears.) The vision researcher William K. Newsome of Stanford likes to point out that those 3 million little electrical signals are all your brain has to work with to represent everything you see.

Within the brain, the signal from your eyes triggers responses in a large swatch of territory toward the back of your head — the visual centers, where the signal from the optic nerve is decoded and turned into a new message, which is sent on for another act of decoding at the next station. Without this work, that initial signal from the eyes is useless. If you could somehow see "directly," everything would be upside down, since that is the way images arrive at the retina (it is the brain which corrects for this); the world would be jiggling and wiggling like the inside of a washing machine, because your eyes make tiny jumping motions constantly as they scan the world (the brain filters out these jitters). A dog seen through a picket fence would look like pieces of dog, hideously chopped up and left on the lawn. Watching the dog chase a ball behind a shed, you might be astonished to see another dog and another ball emerge on the other side.

All these moments of not being astonished — of seeing more than what is in the signal — are the contribution of coding. "Vision," as Newsome says, "does not happen in the eye. It happens in the brain." And what is true of vision is true of much of the rest of reality. From a few cues, codes supply a lot of correction and detail.

A good example of this is the results from a set of experiments in which volunteers were shown movies of little lights moving about. When those lights are arranged into a pattern that suggests arms, legs, and a human body, people instantly "read" the bulbs as a person in motion.

Codes are everywhere in life, at all different scales and levels of description, as the theoretical biologist Marcello Barbieri has pointed out. At the base of the whole enterprise, deoxyribonucleic acid, that famous DNA at the center of each cell in your body, is a good example. It's a molecule but not *just* a molecule; in the right context, it's also a code, carrying instructions for making proteins, the building blocks of life. Sure, in some situations DNA is just a blob of nothing special. It isn't doing much inside a stray hair that's caught on a brush, for example. But when DNA code comes in contact with the right receiver, the molecule can be turned into information that has nothing to do with the molecule itself — recipes for making a person and a record of the evolutionary history that links us to the first living things.

To "get the message" in a code, then, you have to be prepared. First, you need a set of rules for making the translation (a codebook, if you like, setting out how X in the message means Y after decoding). And second, you need a translator to use the codebook, an agent that can apply the rules.

The cells that make up your body have that codebook and translator in their globby innards: cell parts shaped to use the laws of chemistry and physics to interpret DNA. Their constant decoding keeps you alive. Geneticists, having more or less cracked the code, do the translating differently; they use lab equipment. Their procedures let them state, with a very high degree of confidence, that DNA in that hair on the brush is very, very probably yours.

Like geneticists, neuroscientists talk a lot about codes, because the brain is run on them. (Think of all the codes involved in reading these words.) For all but the simplest and most-studied processes, this trail of encoding, and reencoding, and reencoding again is very hard to follow step by step. Instead, scientists can judge that codes are being received and understood by observing what people do — or just by asking them. When they do that, of course, researchers are no longer at the neuroscientific level of analysis. They're working at the psychological level: the realm of Mind rather than Brain.

At that level, too, Barbieri points out, codes are at work. It may not be possible to point to a particular path in the brain for them, but the codebooks are clearly in there. Experiments over the past few decades have found more than a few.

In 1957, the developmental psychologist Roger Brown showed that asking English-speaking children to look for a "sib" caused them to search for a thing, while asking about a "sibbing" caused the kids to look for an action. The kids didn't know what sib and sibbing meant, so meaning couldn't be their guide. Brown had found evidence of a mental faculty for grammar — for telling nouns from verbs. It wasn't conscious thought. No toddler could say, "I know that nouns and verbs are distinct," but young minds followed that rule anyway. More recently, the psychologist Gary Marcus of New York University played strings of nonsense syllables at three- and four-month-old babies, and he found that even these infants showed more interest in the combinations of sound that fit the rules for assembling words than in the combinations that were completely random.

Of course, nothing about the sounds *themselves* told the babies where the words were. A code doesn't reside *in* the material that conveys it. Without the right codebooks and decoders, DNA is just a molecule; brain-cell firing is just electrochemical noise; and people with tricolor hair are large mammals with access to peroxide and dye. A string of DNA reads as a gene, and neural firings are experienced as religious ecstasy, and multicolored hair tells me what sort of person I am looking at, only when the codes get *processed* — when their message reaches a place where it can be decoded. The message needs to arrive at the right place, where the codebook and translator await it. There, the translator consults the codebook for rules like "this pattern of electrochemical signals means the edge of an object" or "sounds with this pattern are important and sounds in other patterns don't matter." And that raises an important question: How does the interpreter know what to do? Where, in cells, brains, and minds, do the codebooks come from?

For the cells that decode DNA into recipes for proteins, the knowledge is built in. Evolution has honed the cell into a fine interpreter. The uncoiling and copying of DNA proceed inexorably. Rules for interpreting genes are part of the cell's chemical and biological form.

In the brain, though, codes can't be constrained this way. If they were, then all your responses to the world would be inflexible and rote. Nothing you experienced could change your responses. People do have codes of this sort: uncontrollable reflexes, like blinking when startled.

But humans and most other animals have brains that can handle a wider range of experience. We have to adapt to changing conditions. So our codes can't be preset at birth. They must be able to respond to the world as we find it. They must be learned.

You weren't born knowing how to read, for example, or even how to understand all that babbling and yapping that adults did around you when you were an infant. You were not born, for that matter, knowing how to see or where your hand was. The codes that tell you what brain signals correspond to what objects and events were not built in. You had to *create* them. You experienced the world and, in doing so, made the codes you needed. Naturally, in the last century the mind sciences were preoccupied with the question of how exactly you do it.

Fifty years ago, many scientists thought the mind had a single, all-purpose codebook creator: a mighty intelligence that took in experience and figured out the rules for everything, from how to throw a ball to grammar to etiquette at dinner. In other words, people were thought to be very smart, in a general sort of way. The mind began as that blank slate proposed by the seventeenth-century philosopher John Locke, and worked with any and all impressions it received.

Locke's heirs in the twentieth century were the adherents of behaviorism, which held that the mind's innards must be forever inaccessible to science. Instead, proper psychologists would study the process indirectly, by observing what went into the black box of the mind (the stimulus) and then what came out (the response). According to stimulus-response thinking, for instance, a child learned to understand and then to speak by hearing talk and then deducing the rules for making proper words ("flew" not "fbew") and putting them together ("he flew," not "he flied"). Psychologists could study that all-purpose single-code learning because it obeyed a simple general principle.

Today, mind science has largely abandoned the general problem-solver model. Its fundamental flaw was that people can't possibly be as smart as it claims. Language learning is the first and greatest example of this criticism. There are rules for the combination of sounds, so that, as the linguist Noam Chomsky says, an English speaker knows that *strid,* though a word he has never heard before, could in fact be an English utterance, while *bnid* could not. (An Arabic speaker, operating under different rules, would say just the opposite.) Similarly, there are rules for the combination of words and word fragments to make new words. English speakers know, for example, that the "k" sound at the end of *electric* turns to an "s" when "-ity" is added to create *electricity.* They know when to put "en-" in front of a word to make a verb like *enfold* or *enrage* and when to put it at the end to create verbs like *fasten* and *loosen.* Such rules allow an English speaker who has never heard the word *mockingbird* to know that it's legitimate and to venture a guess as to its meaning. If *birdingmock* and *ingbirdmock* were equally acceptable, that would be much harder.

To learn a set of complex rules like this should be difficult. It is difficult, in fact, for adults; no adult learns a language with thoughtless ease. But toddlers do, every day, everywhere. And they do it, Chomsky pointed out, without enough evidence.

"It's called the 'poverty of stimulus' argument. We all got what we know about language on the basis of essentially no evidence," Chomsky has said. Research on child learning has detailed the many ways in which kids learn without the information that a general-purpose deduction machine would need. Paul Bloom, a psychologist at Yale who has studied how children master words, notes that much of what parents say to children *should* leave the kids utterly befuddled. Parents say "sleep" when everyone is awake, for example, and "now we brush our teeth!" when nobody is doing it.

Among the accomplishments for which Chomsky is famous is defining this problem and offering a solution: children learn what they need to, without good evidence, because they are born ready to decode it. "If you assume that knowledge either comes from inside you or outside, you're left with the basic assumption that everything you know about language is innate, except for some trivialities."

Obviously, this is not a claim that you were born knowing your native language. Infants can't speak Chinese or Hindi or German. But most linguists now think you *were* born with the ability to make the right codebook for whatever languages you heard people speaking in your toddler years. That "codebook writer," if you want to call it that, was in place and ready to go to work — to listen for, examine, and decipher human sounds and to figure out the rules for translating sounds into words, sentences, and thoughts.

So the precise codebook is not built in, but the ability to *make* the code is. You weren't born a blank slate. Instead, you were born ready to make the connections between the firing of cells in your brain and the rest of the universe — including, for instance, how to make light into sight and how to tell where your body is in space. You were born with a whole staff of codebook writers, each specialized to pluck the right information from the world and assemble rules for dealing with it.

Chomsky's revolution has left scientists arguing about exactly how many specialists the mind is divided into, how they should be defined, and how they work together. From neuroscience to philosophy, many, if not most, scholars hold that the mind is a collection of specialists, each doing its job and only its job. Some of these specialized codemakers, decoders, and code-creators work outside of your awareness. Some contradict one another. Some can be affected by conscious thought. And some cannot.

Some researchers believe most of these codes are "built in," needing only a little bit of nudging from the world outside our heads. Others lean the opposite way, holding that a few principles are all we start with, and the rest is shaped by experience. As Marcus has pointed out, the usual approach to those arguments, until recently, was to pick your side and ignore evidence from the other.

Yet, as he says, experiments supply evidence for both sides. Sight, as I've mentioned, requires specialized light-sensitive cells. They root themselves at the back of each developing eye in the womb. After birth, they must link to regions in the back of the brain that will translate their signals into information about shape, position, color, and distance, among other properties. This array of codes and translators gets "wired up" very quickly in a newborn brain, which is certainly evidence that the capacity to make a visual code is built in.

Yet it's also true that these codes can't be generated in the dark. They need the guidance of experience; the brain areas dedicated to vision won't work if your eyes send no signal. The same principle seems to apply to the multiple codes involved in language. For both seeing and speaking, there seems to be a "critical period" early in life, when the codebooks can be written. Kittens whose eyes were covered during their critical period grew up blind, though their eyes and brains were healthy. Children not exposed to language during *their* critical period never learn to speak a human language.

In any event, arguments between the nativist and experientialist theories don't affect the essential point here: the mind is a collection of specialists. Very little of its work involves general-purpose problem solving. Instead, it relies on specialized codes, each dedicated to its particular job.

One example of this principle is morbid fact, recounted by a former emergency services police officer in New York City, whose job it was to rescue suicidal people from the Brooklyn Bridge. "The amazing thing is someone will pull over on a bridge, lock their car and then jump — like they were planning on coming back," he told a reporter.

That would be hard to explain if the human mind were a single, coherent, unified entity. Such a mind would think, well, I'm not coming back, no point in locking this thing. But the mind is multiple, and the street-smart part that learned always to lock the car is not affected by news from elsewhere in the brain — not even news that the whole multicode enterprise is about to be canceled.

It is conventional wisdom that tut-tuts about how a man brave enough to fight in a war can be a moral coward, or how a terrible father can be a great musician. For neuroscientists and psychologists, there is no conundrum there. The mind is made up of many separate operators, working with separate codes. In fact, one of the mysteries of contemporary mind science is not the psyche's fractured nature, which is well established, but the opposite: somehow, each of us believes, against the evidence, that we are all coherent, consistent, unified minds.

Where is the border between a physical description of neural signals, the realm of Brain, and an abstract description of rules for the code, the realm of Mind? The answer depends on whom you ask, and when. If, like most neuroscientists, you agree with Steven Pinker that "the mind is what the brain does," then you expect the boundary to disappear eventually. Descriptions of Mind (for example, grammars for language) will match descriptions of brains — like scans of people's brain activity as they read. And a scientist will use whichever one best fits the question she wants to explore this morning.

Scientists don't have such a complete picture yet. They're not close, and there is even a respectable body of opinion that claims this goal is unattainable. The issue is whether concepts formed in one sort of inquiry, psychology, can be perfectly matched to those created by another, neuroscience. Here, too, neither extreme position makes much sense. It's ridiculous to claim that the physical activity of the brain has no effect on people's souls, because brain damage changes people's character and behavior. At the same time, attempts to pinpoint exactly how psychic experience is incarnated in the brain have so far failed. All those pretty images of depressed brains and mathematical brains and loving brains are partial guesses. No one has managed a complete neural map of a memory or feeling.

For most of the people attending the Los Angeles conference on social-cognitive neuroscience, those interesting debates were beside the point. Maybe Mind reduces to Brain and maybe it doesn't. In the meantime, though, there are many more manageable questions that can elucidate the codes on which minds, brains, and bodies depend. Understanding how those codes are made and "read" is the first step. It makes possible a second: figuring out how each code — from DNA, to electrochemistry, to the accent that tells you where the speaker grew up — depends on and relates to all the others. That second objective is still a long way off. But, most scientists at the Los Angeles conference said, the only way to get there is to try.

For many, the starting point is the neural code. The cells that make up your nervous system and much of your brain — the neurons — each hold a mild electric charge. When something nearby changes the electrical balance that holds this charge in check, the neuron "fires" — an electrical blip travels away from its center, down its long trunk, the axon. At the far end, the electrical blip prompts reservoirs of specialized chemicals to release their molecules. These are the neurotransmitters, made famous by the drug industry in the 1990s: serotonin, dopamine, and scores of others.

These molecules carry the signal from cell to cell. They cross the synapse, the tiny gap between an axon and neighboring neurons. When the next neuron picks up the signal, its own chemistry changes: it may be made more likely to fire in its turn, or conversely, it may be tamped down by the signal and made less likely to release its electrical charge.

This system of signals — across a trillion synapses among the 100 billion neurons — is fast and vast enough to process many codes at the same time. For example, the codes that let you read these words, and breathe, and sense how you feel, physically and emotionally, are all ticking along simultaneously. It's easier to imagine a chain of neurons leading back from your eyes into the brain (and this is what nerves are — axons). But most neurons in the brain itself are surrounded by thousands of neighbors, so the number of possible signals each can get, and the number of patterns it can join, is immense.

That's how electrochemical blips can become everything you experience — every thought, emotion, and perception — but only after each blip has been decoded and reencoded many times over.

Over the past fifty years neuroscientists have developed techniques for tracing codes, sometimes neuron by neuron, by placing electrodes on or near the cells and recording when and how they fire. It's difficult, dexterous work, lowering a thin piece of glass or metal around the cell's delicate membrane, then properly calibrating a rack of electronic instruments to pick up the signal and amplify it. The cells aren't easy to pinpoint, and they are delicate, all too easy to puncture. The electric current to be measured is minuscule, about 70 millivolts (an ordinary D cell battery, by comparison, puts out about 1,500 millivolts). So electrophysiologists often have to check for interference from current in overhead lights, or a nearby piece of office equipment, or the metal rack that holds their instruments.

Such techniques helped establish that some brain codes can be read by solitary neurons. In the 1950s, the neurophysiologists David Hubel and Torsten Wiesel followed the pathways of vision backward from the eyes of cats, into a region of the brain called the striate nucleus. (Their work is the source of the critical period concept.) There, by recording from individual cells, they found that some neurons would fire in response to straight lines in the visual field but not to the sight of a border between a light and dark area. Other cells did just the opposite. In other words, in this part of the brain, individual cells were tuned to fire only when they received a particular kind of information.

A possible inference from this work was that a complete picture of an object is made by many different specialist cells, each firing for its particular part of the whole code. Somewhere further up the hierarchy, then, there should be neurons that receive signals from these separate actors and put them together into a complete picture. Perhaps you would perceive your grandmother because you had a "grandmother neuron": a single cell where signals encoding light and shadow, texture and edges, faces and names, and childhood memories would all converge. When that cell would fire in its turn, you'd become aware that you were looking at your grandma.

That hope helped draw scientists to the difficult and productive techniques of recording from neurons. They learned a great deal in the following decades by recording from single cells and tracing circuits cell by cell.

However, the epoch of the grandmother neuron ended, as neuroscientists became convinced that most codes live *among* neurons, not *in* them. In other words, your perception of your grandmother probably isn't a blip from one cell that received a lot of inputs. Rather, it's likely a pattern of coordinated firing by millions of neurons, all over your brain. That would make it a bit like the Times Square "zipper," which gives news headlines in moving letters spelled out in lightbulbs. No single bulb encodes the letter "P" or the word *President* on the zipper. Instead, all the bulbs flash on and off in a patterned way, which reads, to the pedestrians in Times Square, as the word *President* gliding along the side of the building.

What single-neuron work suggests, though, is that the "bulbs" aren't completely interchangeable. In order to perceive your grandmother or anything else, you need neurons dedicated to information like edge, shape, distance, and color; neurons that encode emotions like love (or fear — let's make no presumptions about your grandmother); and neurons that encode the memories that tell you who this old lady is. Most neuroscientists now believe many such matters are taken care of by groups of cells that are specialized for a particular task. In other words, neurons that read the code for the edge of a surface won't work with a different code, like the one for distance. You don't have a grandmother *neuron,* then, but your ability to perceive your grandmother nonetheless depends on specialized *regions* of the brain.

Evidence for this idea came first from the practical experience of neurosurgeons. For example, curving over the sides and top of your brain, a little behind the crown of your head, is a layer of brain cells that receive signals from different parts of your body. (They were discovered by a Canadian surgeon, Wilder Penfield, who electrically stimulated the area in his awake patients and asked them what they were feeling.) Right next to the temple in front of each ear, there are cells that get signals from your tongue; a half-inch or so up the slope of your brain, there is the area that senses the teeth for that side of your body. Further up are the brain cells that get signals from the face. Keep following this narrow track of cells up the slope, and you'll pass over a map of your hand and trunk. The map then continues down the other side, into the narrow canyon between your two brain hemispheres, where the map ends with an area that responds to half your genitalia. Across the chasm, on the other lobe of the brain, is the map of your other side.

This map is not to scale: it doesn't reflect the proportions of your body but rather the relative importance of the parts. A human figure proportioned just like the map (the *sensory homunculus*) is a staple of medical textbooks. It has big genitalia, a tiny trunk, and a huge face, with colossal lips and tongue.

Just behind this map of self-sensation is another, the *motor homunculus,* which follows the areas you can control with your conscious mind. Genitalia and teeth don't show up on it, but face and tongue are, again, immense relative to the rest. And bigger still is the region devoted to the hand.

These maps aren't fixed at birth. Instead, they are the result of a preset program of development interacting with the environment. The infant flails around, and the signals his brain gets from his actions go to a region dedicated to sensing the body. Repetition is important: neurons that fire together become more likely to fire together in the future, so a synaptic pattern that is reinforced every day becomes well established. Soon enough, stable patterns of firing emerge, and the map is set.

It turns out that the brain is covered with such easily created, reliable maps. Taste buds link to a little map of your lips, mouth, and throat, for instance, and among the thirty or so regions that play a role in vision is one that responds point for point to each light-sensitive cell at the back of each eye. There are regions whose shape and size mirror the things they map. Professional string-instrument players, whose left hands have to move quickly and precisely, have a larger field devoted to that hand than do ordinary people. Conversely, brain maps of body parts that have been lost, such as a finger cut off in an accident, actually shrink.

Maps persist longer than their parts. Amputees often feel lost limbs, for example. The neuroscientist V. S. Ramachandran, who has studied these phantoms, had a patient who, when brushed on the cheek with a Q-tip, felt the touch in his missing hand. When touched on the upper lip, the man felt it there and at his long-lost index finger. Ramachandran found a second map of the missing hand on the man's upper arm. None of this surprised him. On the body map Penfield discovered, "face cells" are on one side of the "hand cells," and "arm cells" are on the other. (After he published his findings, Ramachandran heard from an amputee who now understood why she had sensations in her phantom foot whenever she had sex. Feet are next to genitalia on the sensory map.)

These many maps stretch all over the cortex, which forms a coat of thickly interconnected neurons that covers the brain's other structures as bark covers a tree. (Cortex is Latin for "bark.")

To get through the day, though, the mind needs many codes that aren't literally maps. You need to understand not only where your body is at the moment, for instance, but where it will be if you take the Number 7 bus. You need to be able to recall that you've been on the Number 7 bus before. And if you should see people running like hell away from the bus stop one morning, you need to understand what their actions tell you about this particular morning's commute.

The codes that tell you about such matters are not literal point-for-point body maps like the sensory homunculus. But they probably work by the same principle. Experience of the world guides specialized parts of the brain to write "codebooks," synaptic patterns in your brain, and you learn to trust those codes. They fill in your picture of reality from a few signals. With a map of your morning commute, you can tell that people running from the bus stop is out of the ordinary and that something unusual is happening.

An image of your commute coordinates memories and knowledge about yourself and society. That involves many more kinds of information than a map of your hand. Such a "higher-order" representation is probably encoded in what Antonio Damasio of the University of Iowa has called *convergence zones* in the cortex — regions where information from different codes converges on groups of cells that combine it all into a new signal. In one such region behind your forehead, for example, codes about taste and codes about smell are likely blended into a new kind of information: flavor.

On a mental map like "a typical Monday at the bus stop," there is no physical object to represent. Nonetheless, there is still a representation — one that includes time, relationships, and activities as well as a physical space. Such a higher-order code is like the literal map of the body in another way too: people assemble these maps easily in early childhood. And from then on, we don't notice that we're using them to perceive reality.

The first hints that this is so emerged some seventy-five years ago, in work by the English psychologist Sir Frederic Charles Bartlett. He studied memory with a simple experimental procedure. He would ask his students to read a folktale, wait a few hours or a few days, and then retell it.

He was careful to select a story that they had never heard before. (It came from anthropological accounts of the Kathlamet people of Oregon.) As you might expect, the student versions left out many details. When they did recall something, they often changed it to make it more familiar. (For instance, they made "peanut" into the more British "acorn" and described paddle-wielding warriors as "rowing" their canoe, the way proper English undergraduates would handle a scull.) The students also *added* details that weren't in the original. Where the story read "That Indian has been hit," some recalled an Indian being killed, others an Indian being hit by an arrow. Recalling a warrior in the tale who says he will not go into combat because his relatives don't know where he is, "but you may go," many of Bartlett's volunteers added an explanation, like "you have no one to expect you," or "you have no parents."

The students were unaware that some of their "memories" were actually alterations or additions. They imagined they were simply recalling what they had read. It felt so right that they did not see where the story stopped and their own contribution began.

Bartlett decided the students were confident about their memories because they came to the story with a ready-made mental map. When they read about Indian warriors, they thought of arrows. No matter that the story did not mention arrows; no matter, either, whether the Kathlamet people really used arrows. Arrows came to mind because when English undergraduates in the 1920s read a story about American Indians, they "knew" that arrows would fit in the picture.

Just as the students were using codes within codes to transform the shapes on paper into letters and words and read the story, then, they were using more abstract codes to interpret it. As their vision centers "told" them what they were seeing, so these more abstract processes "told" them what and who the story was about.

In other words, the visual centers of the brain can be tricked, seeing a succession of still images as a movie, so higher-order maps of the world can be fooled. Bartlett's students trusted their sense of human kinds, which caused them to "remember" facts that they had not learned from the story. Once the students had seen enough detail to call up the relevant map, a pattern seemed to complete itself in their minds, and they felt no difference between what they had learned from the outside world and what they had supplied. To describe this kind of structured knowledge, Bartlett reached for a Greek term for a framework: *schema*.

The idea had almost no impact at the time. Bartlett was publishing in the 1930s, when behaviorism and its "black box" notion of the mind held sway. Proper scientists weren't supposed to wonder what went on inside the box. Compared to the precise measurement of stimulus and response, Bartlett's concept looked vague. Scientists like ideas they can use, which pose questions they can answer with experiments. The schema concept was considered too imprecise for practical work.

It took a person who wanted to *build* a thinking box to appreciate that Bartlett's idea was practical. Forty years later, Marvin Minsky of MIT's Artificial Intelligence Laboratory was searching for ways to make computers act less stupidly. The problem was that, for computers, all possible inferences were alike. A machine has no "common sense" to tell it, for instance, that a paddle is more likely to be in an Indian canoe than in a ceiling fan. So if you tell a computer that people who buy plane tickets at the last minute in cash likely are terrorists and then tell it that many terrorists have been killed, it can infer that buying a plane ticket in cash can lead to death, until a programmer straightens it out. Yet in order to work in the real world, computers needed to be able to tell the difference between flooding coach class with light and flooding it with water.

Minsky saw that Bartlett's schema — or, rather, its equivalent in computer code, which he called a frame — could supply that missing sense of the world. Minsky conceived of a schema as an application form with blanks ready to be filled in. Computers programmed to fill in such forms could avoid logic traps. So, if a robot must go in and out of rooms, it would be programmed with a form for "room." The form would have slots for descriptions of four walls — not eight, not one — and some furniture of the sort people sit on. No Humvees or diving bells.

That frame would give the machine a stable map of the world, but it would also be flexible, because the same details would serve many schemas. As you can be asked to give your address on a tax form, a college application, or a mortgage, so the slot for "wall" could be used by the robot in many different ways. That was how the machine could move around a building and know, for instance, that the ceiling of a room on the first story was the floor of a room on the second.

As Minsky and his colleagues were developing the frames theory in artificial intelligence, many psychologists were abandoning behaviorism and looking for a new model of the mind.

Meanwhile, as the historian Derek de Solla Price has pointed out, intellectual metaphors tend to be drawn from the latest, snazziest technology. Nowadays, we like networks as explanations for human behavior, because we're impressed with the Internet. Plato had compared the mind to a chariot; Sigmund Freud's images of high-pressure emotions being blocked and redirected come from an era of locomotives and other industrial machinery.

In the 1970s, the most exciting new machine was the computer. When psychologists turned to what was then called cybernetics, they found the frames idea and rediscovered Bartlett.

Nowadays, his insight — described as schemas, frames, scripts, mental maps, platforms for understanding and other names — is almost a truism. It's now accepted that we don't just have codes for "low-level" processes like perceiving objects and finding our own hands. We also have codes guiding our thoughts and feelings about much more abstract matters, like who and what people are, and how they live.

I just described these codes as "higher order" because they combine more different kinds of information than the ones "below." The coding that tells you about the edge of a table is less complex than the ones that tell you that someone you just met is a trustworthy, decent sort of person. That contrast between elaborate and simple might tempt you to think that one sort of code is more *convincing* than the other. That, for instance, basic information — salty or sweet, bright or dark — takes priority over nuanced maps. Other people, I learned, lean the opposite way: they think we're more inclined to trust the codes that need more connections.

This may be a temperamental difference among people who think about such subjects. Some of us trust our guts, and others prefer our heads. Neither bias may help with neuroscience, though, because the brain does not seem to have a preference.

Consider the simple act of taking medication for, say, an upset stomach. You take the pill. It works. The nerves that monitor your body for you report that your pains have decreased. That's a bottom-up process — from humble stomach up to magnificent conscious mind. However, people who *believe* they've taken medicine often feel better, too. That's a top-down effect: conscious mind signaling to humble stomach that the pain is gone. In that case, your relief isn't coming from your body at all. Instead, it derives from your knowledge of doctors, pharmacies, and prescriptions — very complicated, specialized, multiple-code information that quells the simple message of pain in the gut.

Top-down effects must be part of the reason human kinds are so important to us. Such processes connect our map of human kinds to our sense of our personal health and well-being. Human-kind news can make us feel joyful for no physical reason ("our country won the World Cup!") or depressed about the death of a martyr two thousand years ago. If we depended only on our nerves' reports about our immediate situation, we could not be affected by such stories.

But we are. In fact, the sense of human kinds has been shown to change even basic perceptions of reality. In the 1930s, for example, psychologists at Columbia had volunteers look at a pinpoint of light shining on the wall of a darkened room and estimate how many inches, or fractions of an inch, the light had moved. In fact, it didn't move at all. Such a light seems to jump because of the eye's constant motions. The brain's correction process needs clues from the whole visual field. A pinpoint of light in the dark provides none. (This is why a star in the night sky will seem to dance if you stare at it.)

The volunteers, who individually had to guess about the light's movement 100 times in a row, soon settled on a narrow range of estimates. But when they were put in a room with two other volunteers, the students abandoned their own range and converged on the little group's.

In the 1950s, another set of experiments asked volunteers to look at a vertical line and then pick which of three other lines was closest in length to the first. Each volunteer thought he was part of a team assembled in the room. Actually, though, everyone else there was acting. Their job was to insist on an obviously wrong estimate, so that the lone volunteer would find himself odd man out. His estimate was right, but it wasn't the team's.

Faced with the choice between measurable reality or the opinions of the team, most people went for the team. They changed their estimates. They didn't say that they'd seen correctly but chose to get along with the others. Instead, they decided that the group must be right. (If these results sound like an abstruse bit of lab manipulation with no practical meaning, consider this: on three-judge U.S. Courts of Appeals that consist of two Republican appointees and a Democratic appointee, the Democratic appointee is more likely to vote on the conservative side of cases than he does on panels where he's not alone.)

It would be wrong, then, to think some of the brain's codes are about "real things" while others are "all in your mind." Mental codes influence each other. People who have just seen a photograph of maggots and rotting food will judge someone's ethical lapse more harshly than do others — one kind of disgust apparently communicating with the other. So, too, eating with someone will likely make you more receptive to what she has to say. One experimenter found that volunteers who heard the name Michael Schumacher in the lab wrote faster — the speediness of a famous race-car driver leaking over into their scribbling. Almost everything going on in your brain right now is exerting its subtle electrochemical pull on everything else.

This is part of the reason even a simple human-kind perception — light waves strike my retina, getting encoded as neural signals, which are then turned into shape and color and distance, and then into hair and a jacket and a face, and then into an instance of a category like "rock musician" — is a challenge to explain. All those codes are being sent to their proper interpreters, to be transformed into information by neurons, and then routed to other neurons that treat the finished work as raw material for a new code, again and again, in microseconds, and practically simultaneously. It's a lot to describe. By comparison, even the vast global economy in all its details is simpler.

In some ways, that global economy might be a model for the way the brain makes, moves, combines, and consumes its different codes. Perhaps my conscious thought "that guy must be in a band" is a bit like a finished pair of jeans in a store. The jeans emerge from a score of different workplaces around the world — cotton growers in Egypt, copper miners in Chile, dyers and fabric cutters in Italy, seamstresses in China, designers in New York, marketers in Los Angeles. So these words, too, emerge from the distinct activities of many different parts of the brain, each receiving material, processing it, and passing the finished work on to another workshop, where it's treated as raw material for a fresh operation. In other words, the process is "recursive": products are plugged back into the processes that created them.

A lot of global manufacturing happens in parallel, and this too is true of the brain's work. The neurons that "told" me I was looking at a person did not wait until I had scanned every object in the room for edges and shapes, just as fashion designers don't wait until they're told the cotton for their clothes has been grown and harvested.

The ships that carry jeans can also carry CD players, and cotton grown for jeans can also be used for sheets or bandages. In the same way, a neural pathway is used for different codes at the same time. There is no logical connection between the experience of taking in a nice meal and the experience of taking in a new business proposition, but in some parts of the brain, aspects of the two different thoughts share a berth.

Brain and economy share one other key trait: no central authority runs either, so no single place in either system is the key to the rest. People who don't believe this about the economy are crackpots, with their theories about secret societies that rule the world. When it comes to the brain, though, gnomes-of-Zurich explanations are still popular. The general rule might be that we all prefer to say that whatever part of the mind we understand best is the part we will believe is in charge.

So, the mind as described by theologians is a top-down sort of a place, in which our most complex beliefs and feelings — careful thoughts about ethics, soulful meditations on faith — should rule over cruder impulses to eat, have sex, hurt enemies, and so on. Conversely, the mind described by specialists in animal behavior is a bottom-up kind of system, in which those urges we share with other creatures are really running the show, and big thoughts are a by-product.

But the brain, like the global economy, is both a bottom-up *and* a top-down system, and a side-by-side system, too. A lot of economic activity happens because of bottom-up demand, like the desire of each and every one of us to eat pretty often. However, there is also a great deal of trade that takes place for top-down reasons: to fulfill wants that people never felt until they saw a movie or heard a song on the radio. After the movie *Finding Nemo* became a worldwide hit in 2003, for example, millions of children wanted a pet clown fish like the title character. The world economy responded, and more clown fish were taken from tropical reefs. By year's end, divers in the Pacific nation of Vanuatu were complaining that the species was no longer seen there at all.

In the brain, bottom-up processes for self-preservation can certainly tell you that you're in danger, make your heart beat fast and your gut churn, and get you to run away. But that can't explain why people overcome such fears, to do their duty as soldiers, or to rush headlong into death as religious martyrs. "Duty" and "martyrdom" are top-down thoughts — arrived at by thinking and talking — yet they can overcome that bottom-up system for saving one's hide.

The mind of a person who pits faith against danger, as does a martyr, is certainly not a bottom-up system, in which animal responses like pain and fear "tell" the conscious mind what is real and what it is to do. Such a person would never hold to her belief in the face of a threat. Nor is the mind just a top-down realm, where belief tells the eyes and ears what to see. (If that were so, martyrdom would be easy for anyone.) Instead, both processes are happening at once — bottom-up perception guides belief, but top-down belief also guides perception.

Once I had decided that the man at the conference was a musician, I made everything I perceived about him into a sign of his musicianness: the way he stood, for instance, and his luggage. (Was that an amp?) I did not, first, notice those details and then, second, decide he was in a band. It was the other way around: I decided he was in a band and then noticed the details that fit the schema.

A well-known demonstration of how complex thoughts work top down to shape human-kind perceptions was orchestrated nearly thirty years ago by David Rosenhan, a professor of law and psychology. He and six volunteers — three other psychologists, a psychiatrist, a painter, and a homemaker — checked themselves into mental hospitals, each claiming to hear a voice that kept saying three words: "empty," "hollow," and "thud." That was all they did to be psychiatrically interesting; they did not alter their behavior in any other way. In each of the twelve hospitals they tested, they were admitted without question as mental patients.

Once inside, the pseudopatients immediately stopped talking about their voices, and, if they were asked, claimed that they no longer heard them. Nonetheless, all were confidently labeled schizophrenics and kept confined for weeks. (The average stay was nineteen days; one person was kept for nearly two months.) In the context of the psychiatric ward, their ordinary actions were taken as symptoms. For example, when they paced (remember, they were stuck in the ward, which is kind of boring), they were described as nervous and on edge. One of the fakers told a psychiatrist that he'd been closer to his mother as a child but then had become closer to his father as a teenager. "Ambivalence in close relationships," wrote the psychiatrist. The only people who suspected the experimenters of faking were other patients.

A second experiment reversed the situation. Rosenhan warned the staff of a teaching hospital that he would try to sneak in some pseudopatients, but he never managed to recruit any. Nonetheless, psychiatrists at the hospital labeled scores of people as fakes.

To explain this 100-billion-celled, trillion-synapsed system of codes, scientists break it down into smaller segments, offering questions experiments can address. Before you can diagram the whole global economy, you track how that pair of jeans gets made, or a teapot, or an ad campaign. This approach has had some spectacular successes in the mind sciences, and it will, I think, explain human-kind-mindedness eventually. I want to look, now, at some of these separate pieces.

First, though, one last point about my true tale of human-kind thinking — that man in line who, I thought, after all my mental codes had done their work, was a rock musician.

He wasn't. The man with the three-tone hair was David Perret, a neuroscientist at Scotland's University of St. Andrews and one of the star speakers at the conference. Just a reminder, then: nothing about mental codes guarantees that they're correctly representing reality. In fact, the more scientists learn about our beliefs, the less reliable those beliefs look. If the theme of science for the last five hundred years could be boiled down into a sentence, it would be this: the world is not what you believe it is.

Six

Looking for the Codes

The eye sends, as we saw, into the cell-and-fibre forest of the brain, throughout the waking day, continual rhythmic streams of tiny, individually evanescent, electrical potentials. . . . A shower of little electrical leaks conjures up for me, when I look, the landscape; the castle on the height, or when I look at him, my friend's face and how distant he is from me they tell me. Taking their word for it, I go forward and my other senses confirm that he is there.

— SIR CHARLES SHERRINGTON

We have no need to go picking out miracles and remote difficulties; it seems to me that among the things we see ordinarily there are wonders so incomprehensible that they surpass even miracles in obscurity.

— MICHEL DE MONTAIGNE

People are born to be attuned to other human beings. All of us are naturally inclined to become experts on each other.

Several decades ago researchers established that infants keep their eyes on things that surprised or interested them, while turning away from other sights. That's how experimenters know that just-born babies, hours out of the womb, react to human faces. Adult faces, and pictures of faces, and even crude cartoon renderings of faces hold newborns' attention where other sights don't.

Human beings appear to be ready to pay attention to faces from the beginning of their lives. And like the brains of monkeys, people's minds "fill in" missing perceptual details from a few clues. Shown a few lines on a piece of paper, we see a face. Watch a few lights moving in the dark, and we see the arms, legs, and torso of a body in motion. That monkeys also do this, of course, is evidence that these codes evolved long ago, to help our ancestors live in troops. That's one reason such experiments are done with animals. Another is that important coding regions in an animal can lead researchers to the corresponding part in the human brain. The basic structure of a mammal brain has not changed that much over evolutionary time, and primate brains are very similar.

We perceive people as people, then, quickly and easily — whether we want to or not. That makes people-perception different from, say, birdwatching, which requires conscious effort. Birders have to learn to see and hear their quarries, in places where untrained people see nothing. But no one has to be trained to connect the sights and sounds that add up to a person. Everything needed to write the codebook for people came free at birth.

Even more important than the codes for hands and faces is the one that lets us see minds. Those develop a bit later in life. Newborns, already drawn to faces, need a couple of years before they realize that people are more than just bodies — that there are *minds* moving the bodies. At some point in toddlerhood, children begin to "get it." In one experiment that helped to show this, a researcher playing with a child would pretend to hit his own thumb with a toy hammer, yelp, and then make reassuring gestures to show he wasn't really hurt. In that situation, ordinary kids, and the developmentally disabled ones as well, looked up at their playmate's *face.*

Understanding that other beings have minds is a very big deal and the codes we have for the job, unlike the ones for faces and bodies, apparently are not shared with other animals. Yet these codes for "mind reading" work like any other: they assemble themselves early in life, without conscious learning, with very few cues. Just as your brain supplies the missing body when eyes see only a constellation of lights in the dark, so the brain also fills in when it sees actions that "should" have a mind behind them. One of the first and most striking illustrations of this inclination emerged from an experiment conducted in 1944, with a short film.

The movie is simple, barely a minute long. On the screen you see geometric shapes: a little circle within the corral of a large rectangle, which is open on part of one side. Outside is a big triangle. The little circle moves outside the box, the big triangle descends, and the two shapes bump. Now here comes another triangle, which is smaller — about the same size as the circle. It bumps up against the big triangle several times until the bigger shape drifts away. Then the little triangle and the circle float into the box. The big triangle follows, but it won't fit in the opening. It stays outside, bumping against the "gate."

In their experiment, the psychologists Fritz Heider and Mary-Ann Simmel showed that these simple shapes and movements were all people needed to trigger the code for other minds. When asked to write down what they saw on film, people told how the circle had left the box, gotten pushed around by the big triangle, then saved by the small one. Many saw a love story — the little circle pursued by the big, bullying triangle, rescued by the plucky little triangle, and living happily ever after. Later researchers, using the methods I've described to peek into infant minds, have shown that babies, even before they can talk, will "get" this kind of movie. Then, too, babies between nine and twelve months were found to look longer at these kinds of films if the abstract shapes had cartoon faces on them.

Codes that tell about minds are important for getting along with other people, so it isn't surprising that these codes are activated constantly as we get through a day. In fact, such codes are so important for our sense of reality that they're activated even in situations where they're not appropriate to reality. The computer crashes, and you yell at it. The remote control doesn't work, you fling it across the room. Bad remote! The sun is shining on the day of your wedding, and you thank God.

Other parts of the mind know the computer didn't decide to crash, because it has no mind; you know, too, that today's sunniness probably doesn't mean God is smiling on your wedding, since this same golden light is also falling on funerals. Yet this knowledge doesn't matter to the mental code for other minds. With few hints, those codes "fill in" the picture, telling you things happen because of the actions of thinking, feeling beings. Heider and Simmel's experiment showed how little of a hint the code needs.

People in the experiment saw the code stuff—those lines and motions on a screen—but they also saw *past* those lines and motions to perceive what the code represented: invisible entities we call minds. Instead of talking about triangles and directions and speeds, the codes told of journeys, loves, and hopes. Thanks to those codes, viewers assumed that visible activity had invisible causes. Most important, they knew that these invisible causes were the ones that mattered—"the triangle wants to go inside" felt like a better explanation than "the triangle is bumping up against the aperture." That's encoding: treating what is literally there as a representation of something else, which can't be perceived directly.

Most of the time, this code is interpreting the minds of other people, not computers and weather deities. It tells you how to understand what they're doing. Your code for other minds is what tells you that the actions of other people are *about* something. The code tells you, without your having to think about it, that thoughts and feelings are better explanations than the actions you can literally see. That's so clearly important to being human that Hollywood screenwriters have made a truism of it. In the movies, any character who lacks these mental codes for mind reading will turn out to be a space alien or a robot.

In the second of the *Terminator* movies, for example, the teenage hero is fighting back tears, but Arnold Schwarzenegger's character doesn't get it. In his flat machine voice, he asks, "What is wrong with your eyes?" We, the audience, see tears; the machine sees only water. That's one way we know he's not a human being.

Yet there *are* people who apparently lack this code—who see water pooling in your eyes and don't "get" that these are tears. They don't decode noise and movement as the work of underlying minds, any more than a blind person watches a sunrise. The codebook isn't there between their ears to put sights, sounds, smells, and touches together in that way.

As you might expect, this is a big problem. It has been well described by the English writer Mark Haddon, in the voice of Christopher Boone, the hero of his novel, *The Curious Incident of the Dog in the Night:*

And one day Julie sat down at a desk next to me and put a tube of Smarties on the desk, and she said, "Christopher, what do you think is in here?" And I said, "Smarties."

Then she took the top off the Smarties tube and turned it upside down and a little red pencil came out and she laughed and I said, "It's not Smarties, it's a pencil."

Then she put the little red pencil back inside the Smarties tube and put the top back on. Then she said, "If your mummy came in now and we asked her what was inside the Smarties tube, what do you think she would say?" because I used to call Mother Mummy then, not Mother.

And I said, "A pencil." That was because when I was little I didn't understand about other people having minds.

From that difficulty flow many other problems getting along in the world as the rest of us have made it. Not being able to read the codes for other minds means not being able to read the signals that pass effortlessly among other people: it means not knowing what they're understanding about each other while you're left in the dark and not knowing what they mean when they try to communicate with you in their shared code. Haddon says it's like going through life behind the one-way mirror of a police interrogation room. Everyone can see your mind, and they can all see each other's. But you can't see theirs.

After all, a lot of ordinary conversation isn't about the meaning of words — talk about the weather or how the soccer team played last night is just code stuff, a surface that represents something else, and that something else is the state of the speakers' minds.

Imagine having no choice but to take words literally — to think that someone who says "I could eat a horse" actually wants to eat a horse, or that a question like "How's it hanging?" requires an answer about how it, in fact, hangs. You'd be missing all those aspects of life that you learn not from words but from tone, intonation, knowledge of social rules and of individuals. Not being able to put all this together, these people are often baffled by their inability to read the message hidden in the code, which is not about eating horses and what hangs but about the thoughts, feelings, and plans of other minds.

Lacking a code for perceiving minds, the world of other people will scare and perplex you; it is full of meaningless, random, unrelated noises and sights that other people read as related signs of a coherent something. "When adults spoke directly to me, I could understand everything they said," writes the engineer Temple Grandin, who is one of the people who lacks this code. "When adults talked among themselves, it sounded like gibberish."

If you don't receive the signal, you don't send it back out, either. Other people will find you strange and impossible to reach. The writer and neurologist Oliver Sacks, when he met Grandin, noticed that one of the ways she felt different was that she seemed to expect everything in her conversation to be explicit — to be *in* the words, not under them. "She spoke well and clearly, but with a certain unstoppable impetus and fixity. A sentence, a paragraph, once started, had to be completed, nothing was left implicit, hanging in the air."

People with this difficulty were defined as a human kind in the mid-1940s and given a label. They're called autistic. And their inability to share the codes that we use to make sense of other people makes them, as the autistic writer Jim Sinclair puts it, "'foreigners' in any society."

In the same essay, Sinclair asks the parents of autistic children to remember this and to try to imagine what the absence of this code must be like:

> You're going to have to give up your assumptions about shared meanings. You're going to have to learn to back up to levels more basic than you've probably thought about before, to translate, and to check to make sure your translations are understood. You're going to have to give up the certainty that comes of being on your own familiar territory, of knowing you're in charge, and let your child teach you a little of her language, guide you a little way into his world.

The "mindblindness" of autism has been mapped in the 1990s by the British psychologist Simon Baron-Cohen, who coined the term (and devised the Smarties test). Most people have codes for a "theory of mind," which makes it easy to see personalities and goals in the movements of triangles and circles. That lets a child be in sync with mother, siblings, and others.

Some autistic people have multiple problems understanding the world, but not all do. If they're smart and determined, those whose other codes have developed as usual can substitute conscious thought for unconscious codes. "High-functioning" autistics can learn, for instance, that water coming out of someone's eyes means that the person is distressed, even if they cannot have the instant, costless certainty that the rest of us experience when we notice someone crying. So, for instance, the autistic British writer Donna Williams tells herself not to walk away from people as they talk to her: "It is a mechanical effort to remind myself that such actions may dent their feelings." (In fact, Baron-Cohen's Autism Research Center has devised software that teaches autistics the language of expressions.)

The faculty that lets most little children quickly write themselves a code for "theory of mind" is an ability that resembles that other capacity I mentioned earlier — the one that tells people (and apes and monkeys) to read certain sights as information about the bodies and movements of other creatures. In fact, the two codes — for other bodies and other minds — share some pathways in the brain. As the body code "fills in" missing information and tells you that moving lights are a person, so the mind code "fills in" the connection between words and face and movements to tell you that the source of all that fuss at the other end of the room is a mind, like yours, with its own experiences and its own knowledge of the world.

So, ordinary people with no mystic powers engage in spectacular feats of mind reading when they do ordinary things, like eating dinner together or talking on the phone. At such times, they sense one another's moods, feelings, and plans from few clues: a shrug, a sigh, a trace of a smile. Mind reading is part of how we decide whom we're talking with and how they stand with us. With a few important exceptions, which I'll get to below, most every human being is this sort of mind reader.

But we are all, also, I think, *kind* readers. To make sense of another person, we don't just ask the mind question — "Who is this person?" We also ask the kind question — "*What* is this person?" What type does she belong to? What knowledge about human kinds can I bring to this encounter to help me understand it?

Mind reading is for individuals. It works best, as you might expect, with someone you know well. You "read" a parent, sibling, or child-hood friend because long years have made you an expert in that in-dividual. Mind reading also works with people with whom we share many codes, as any traveler discovers when she meets someone from her country in a foreign setting. A person who eats what you eat, worships what you worship, and holds to the same notions of rude and polite as you do, who saw the same movies as a kid and watched the same sports too, is a lot easier to talk to than someone else who doesn't "get it."

Mind reading requires a lot of attention and a fair amount of pre-liminaries to establish that, as people say, "We're in sync" and "We understand each other." (That was the point of that conversation I mentioned between the liberal white commentator Paul Begala and the conservative African American ex-congressman, C. J. Watts. Sports talk created common ground, where each could be sure the other would read him right.)

A lot of life, though, doesn't require that degree of attentiveness to another individual. Much of what we do follows a limited script. Lawrence Hirschfeld of New School University uses the example of the collector in a tollbooth on the highway. "If someone is a toll-booth attendant, when I drive up to the booth with my money in my hand, all I need to think is 'tollbooth attendant,'" he said. "A lot of our encounters follow scripts like that."

Suppose, though, you want to get to know the toll-taker and to see him as an individual. You'll need to get in sync, find ways to communicate, so you can figure out how to interpret him. You'll put out a conversational feeler. Sports is good. Or maybe cars. Something to give you a sense of him. Obviously, that first sense doesn't come from knowledge of him as an individual. You don't know him. In-stead, you get that first rough guideline by figuring out what *kind* of person he is.

But this "person construal" is not the only use you make of cate-gories for people. In the course of a day a typical person asks herself questions like "What would a good mother do in this situation?" or, "Is my work up to the standards of my profession?" or, "Have I be-haved as a good Christian should?" We also use human kinds, in other words, to place ourselves — to orient our actions with ideas about what we are or should be.

This mental faculty engages when we first encounter an unknown person or find ourselves in an unknown situation — the process that answers, as Neil Macrae says, that first important question — not "Who is that?" but "*What* is that?"; not "Who am I in this encounter?" but "*What* am I?" In most face-to-face meetings, kind reading always precedes mind reading. We know each other first as types.

Now, this doesn't prove that human beings have a predisposition to see kinds. Coding for human kinds could be learned, as is driving a car or playing soccer — very common skills but not part of the brain's built-in tools.

Driving skills, though, aren't found everywhere, in every person, nor are soccer skills. But kind-mindedness is. In that, it's more like puberty or the ability to learn a language: part of every person's human nature.

The evidence? There is apparently no people known to history or anthropology that lacks a distinction between "us" and "others." Famously, the name many societies use for their own people is also their word for "human being." Then, too, there is no collection of people anywhere that lacks divisions into smaller subcategories — distinctions between those brown-shoe Navy vets and black-shoe veterans, or Generations X and Y, or my family and yours. Some of these categories are local, like East Side versus West Side in Manhattan; but others appear everywhere.

For example, definitions of a "good man" and a "good woman" vary from culture to culture. (Female chastity is more highly prized in Saudi Arabia than in Sweden.) But there is no people who lack a distinction between good people and those who are not up to the standard. Dividing people into overlapping categories is something all human beings do (with exceptions for which there are ready explanations, usually involving brain damage).

Universality, though, isn't a sure sign that some ability or trait is "built in" to the mind. Again, driving is very common all over the world, but the ability to learn to drive is unlikely to have evolved its own special faculty in the last hundred years. A better clue to a code's being part of human nature is the way that people with difficulties about that code have come by their troubles. If you can't drive a car, it could be because no one ever taught you. But if you can't see colors like red and yellow, this can't be because you missed a few days of art class. Absence of such a code can only be the result of some physical fact — a genetic oddity or an injury.

As I've mentioned, amputees often have to cope with codes that insist their missing extremities are still attached; then, too, people with medial temporal lobe damage can no longer make new memories out of their experience. If a particular gap in someone's abilities correlates with damage in a particular brain region, it could well be that the neurons in that region are necessary for the circuit that supports the necessary codes together.

This criterion certainly applies to the codes we use to understand other individuals. A person with Capgras syndrome, for example, tells his psychiatrist that the people he knows aren't real: he is convinced they're exact duplicates of the actual people. Other patients fail to recognize their reflections, wondering who that is in the mirror. The psychiatrist Leslie Brothers has called such cases "misidentification syndromes": they are instances in which some part of the chain that links perceptions, thoughts, and feelings has broken. In Capgras syndrome, people see spouse, relatives, friends, and neighbors perfectly well, understand what they say, and know their names. But a part of the brain that relates those codes to "mind reading" is cut. These strangers don't feel "right." They must be fakes.

Misidentification syndromes arise from injuries to the brain — lesions or tumors. The problem is physical. Now, if you were to lose your favored hand, you could learn to write with the other. But, evidently, if you lose certain vital components of the circuit that tells you about other individuals, you cannot learn to feel that these strange robots around you are people. That suggests another useful standard for distinguishing the built-in specialists of the mind from the results of general-purpose learning: mental codes, in addition to being universal, depend on particular brain circuits.

It is also a good bet that those circuits are essential because they're specialized — dedicated to the tasks in which they participate and not to any other. That would help explain why a person can lack a particular kind of perception, as Capgras sufferers and autistics do, yet have other mental abilities in good working order. The converse must also be true: there should be people with problems in other areas who, because they have a code intact, turn up with surprising abilities. In Williams syndrome, for example, retarded people with major cognitive problems can nonetheless chatter brightly, in complex, grammatical sentences. That suggests that syntax is one of those codes that the philosopher Jerry Fodor has called a "module": a self-sufficient system, needing so little contact with other parts of the mind to work that it will operate even when other parts are missing.

A couple of other indicators to consider: A specialist code will work fast. Focused on those parts of experience that it can interpret, undistracted by everything else, it can work more quickly than processes that require more input from different parts of the mind. Then too a system dedicated to one job, primed to work as soon as it "sees" the right code, will engage whether you want it to or not and whether you know it is engaged or not. Its operations won't just be quick; they'll be involuntary.

Let's tote up these criteria. If a particular way of perceiving, thinking, or feeling has its own mental apparatus, it should be found in everyone, localized in the brain, fast, and not under conscious control. All of this implies another characteristic: it'll be hard to turn off, ignore, or think around.

For example, the language codes insist on working, whether you will or no, and those codes say this particular stream of sounds is made of words and meaning. A basic code persists in telling us its messages, even when other parts of the mind "know" these messages can't be right. These codes map the world for the mind, and the mind has a hard time setting those maps aside. This is why you are able to read the following sentences: *In raedinng a wrod, the olny neceassry tihng is taht the frist and lsat ltteer be at the rghit pclae. Yuor mnid supppleis the wrods form tohse cuues alnoe. It tnues out all tohse woorngly palced lteters.*

Another good example is sight. We notice the codes for vision only when one interpreter is made to contradict another, as they do in an optical illusion. In an "Ames room," for instance, the wall opposite the viewer is slanted so that one of the opposite corners of the room is several feet closer than the other. If one six-foot-tall person stands in the far corner and another six-footer stands in the near one, the person looking in gets the impression that a dwarf is in one spot and a giant in the other. The code for rooms includes the expectation that walls will be parallel, and when they are not, we literally don't believe our eyes. Instead, we're left with the puzzling sensation that comes of using maps that contradict one another, as one part of the mind tells us we're looking at freaks while another notices that both people in the room look normally proportioned.

One of the most familiar of such illusions is the movie — an optical illusion whose sensation we have learned to love. One part of the mind "knows" that we're watching people running from meat-eating dinosaurs; another knows we're just watching light on a screen. It's often entertaining to play with the contradictory messages of different mental codes. They're an endless source of puzzles and jokes. For example: time flies like an arrow, but fruit flies like a banana.

Be they as familiar as *Jurassic Park* or as odd to look at as an Ames room, though, illusions work for a single underlying reason: the brain trusts its codes. When it perceives a small piece of a pattern, it "knows" the rest is out there. The amputated hand is actually missing, Clint Eastwood's moving image is actually a quick succession of stills, that weird room violates the mental map for rooms. None of that matters. Parts of the mind that know these things cannot dismiss the dedicated code, which "knows" to fill in the rest of the form in the usual way.

If I'm right about kind sight, then, it should show the traits of other codes that seem to grow naturally in the seedbed of the mind, without conscious learning. As I've mentioned, thinking in human kinds certainly appears to be universal, so that's one I can check off. There is also evidence that kind sight has its own codes.

A few years ago, the psychologists Paul Bloom and Csaba Veres, then of the University of Arizona, created a new version of the Heider-Simmel film, in which each of the three moving shapes was replaced by a group of five tiny objects that moved together. The pair then showed this film to some student volunteers. Would they see three actors (the three collective groups) or fifteen (each member of each group)?

It turned out that most people saw three. Like people who had seen the Heider–Simmel film, these students interpreted the abstract shapes as having desires and experiences. But they attributed those mental states not to each individual object but to each group. People certainly understood that they were looking at collections of separate individual objects. They described the characters as "a group of blue things," for example, and called each group "they," not "it." But they somehow knew not to bother thinking about each individual thing on the screen; something in their perception told them that the place to look for meaning here was at the collective level.

That is evidence of a mental code for groups — a specialized bit of mind that tells you when people should be seen as a single thing, rather than as separate individuals. As I've mentioned, I think this perception of belonging together in a "thing made of people" is one of the defining traits of a human kind. (The other is categorization: belief that your membership in a human kind explains your past and predicts your future.) It's much easier to see this aspect of group belonging when it's attached to institutions with names and boundaries, like "the air force" or "the Social Democrats" (more about why in a minute). But the aura of a thing-made-of-people attaches to *all* categories with human beings in them. The air force is more of a group than a category, while mothers are more of a category than a group. So we're more likely to hear that the air force "decided" to take action. Yet it's not impossible to say (and believe) that "mothers vote for good schools."

A mental code for human groups, then, is important to understand, and the Bloom-Veres film suggests a way to do so. It's true, of course, that the little doohickeys on the screen were not people, but that's not relevant. Computers are not people, but we yell at them when they crash, and the weather is not a person, but we curse it when it rains out our Sunday. The code for understanding minds responds to cues, even if those cues don't *come* from minds. So, too, I think, the code for human kinds responds to cues that say, "This is a sign of people acting like a single person."

What might those cues be, though? What are the sights and sounds that the mind reads as code stuff — as signs of invisible information about an entity made of people? One of the first attempts at an answer was published some fifty years ago, but it remains a basis for current research. It was worked out by the late Donald T. Campbell, a philosopher and social scientist who taught at Lehigh University in Pennsylvania.

I've already mentioned how people can be organized in ways that make them seem to belong together — that make it easy to perceive them as one thing and difficult to think of them as separate individuals or as members of many different human kinds. Solomon Asch's flying wedge of police, marching down the street, is difficult to perceive as a collection of separate Janes and Joes, or as blacks and whites who happen to be walking together. You think of them as the police because they have been arrayed in a way that makes you perceive that human kind.

Campbell wanted to explain why that works. He saw that group-sight must work according to its own rules, outside of consciousness — just as language has rules that tell you that *mockingbird* is a proper word, but *ingbirdmock* is not; just as your theory of mind tells you that water trickling from the eye is a tear. A theory of kind must have a grammar.

The phalanx of marching cops wasn't Campbell's example, but it illustrates his theory well. Notice, first, how every officer in the group is dressed alike, in a uniform. Though people are attuned to differences in facial features, gait, and body type, we won't pay attention to those variations when other sights are telling us, "They're all the same!" Those distinct faces are partly obscured under looka-like headgear; the variously shaped bodies are all in uniforms of the same color and cut. And the difference between this one's mince-step and that one's slouchy lope is suppressed by their march rhythm. Obvious, visible similarity definitely speaks to the human-kind code. When it sees birds of a feather, it assumes they flock together.

Also notice the simple physical nearness of each cop to the others. As Campbell put it, "Elements close together are more likely to be perceived as parts of the same organization." In our everyday talk about groups and our place in them, we invoke this feature when we say, for instance, "Going through training together, we've become really close."

Another fact about the group is one that Campbell (following the Gestalt psychologists of his day) called "common fate." The unit's march takes its members in a single direction and puts them all in one place at the same time. The mind picks up the contrast with the milling, wandering, hazy cloud of onlookers. People sharing an event will apparently activate your human-kind code. This too is reflected in everyday speech, in clichés like "We're all in the same boat," "Are you on board?" and "If we don't hang together we'll all hang separately."

Then, too, as the police march together, they appear part of a larger pattern. Campbell called this "good figure." Armies call it close-order drill. Being in sync with others, which the historian William H. McNeill has called "muscular bonding," is part of what convinces people who march together, or dance together, or sing the same song, that they are all One. In ordinary talk, we might say, "We're in the groove."

Now imagine someone from the crowd — a little kid, say, who has spotted his older sister — jumping in among the uniforms. He'd stand out, and he'd probably be removed. That sight suggests that this group resists intrusions, that it will enforce an invisible boundary. What is enclosed within a border tends to be seen as a distinct whole. See a sign that says "Members Only" or "Authorized Personnel," for instance, and you sense that everyone on the other side is part of a single entity.

Finally, Campbell noted that we're also impressed when we see people who share information more quickly than we can. If the order comes to run ten blocks east, the police unit quickly goes. Random people plucked from the sidewalk would need to exchange a lot of information ("We're heading east," "Which way is that?" "Does anyone have a map?" "I want to rest here for a second," and so on and on). The police don't.

So, Campbell realized, efficient information-sharing tells the mind that people belong to a single thing. This too is part of our everyday rhetoric of solidarity. We say, "We understand each other so well" or "We really speak the same language." When the Rev. Jesse Jackson gathered together a group of African American officials and reporters and said, "Let's talk black talk," he was invoking this aspect of human-kind codes.

Campbell's 1958 paper was an effort to get precise about that part of the human-kind code that produces "things made of people." When people are arranged to seem similar, physically close, headed for the same fate, prone to coordinate their acts, resistant to intrusions, and able to communicate easily with one another, he suggested, then they satisfy your mind's syntax for a thing made of people. That prompts you, looking on, to feel those people are acting as a single being.

Campbell believed that each kind of perception helped make the group seem more like a real object — made the thing seem more "thingy," like an object that takes up space in the world, and less like the product of human thoughts. The more a group is like an entity, he wrote, the more it will be believed in. *Entitativity* remains a subject for psychological research today.

Campbell did not say, though, that these cues were specialized for *human* kinds. Maybe we think of a flying wedge of cops as a single thing because we've seen flocks of birds and cases of beer, and this general things-together syntax is applied to people by analogy. If there's a special mode of thought for kinds of *person,* there should be instances in which we group people together that can't be explained by the way we class other stuff.

Good evidence that human kinds are indeed special is the way they "scale up." You can only watch so many uniformed people march by before you lose count. Yet there is no upper limit on the number of people you can call members of one human entity. You needn't see 290 million Americans to accept that they form a nation. So our ability to imagine populous human kinds mustn't depend on the mental mechanism that tells us a couple dozen pigeons all belong to one flock. We need to see the animals doing Campbellian things to decide they form a single entity made of birds. We don't need to see any members to believe in gigantic things-made-of-people like nations and world religions.

One possible explanation for those huge human kinds is that they really belong in the other half of the human-kind problem. Perhaps giant groups are not really entities at all, but simply categories of person. You could argue, for instance, that the concept "Americans" is like the concept "pigeons": a definition that doesn't require you to observe anything about members of the category. But, as I've said, human kinds don't feel like this. They create expectations that neutral categories don't. For example, most Americans expect other Americans to care more about jobs lost in North Carolina or Michigan than they do about the people whose lives get better by taking those jobs after they've moved to Manila or Bangalore. People debate that ethical stance, but pro or con, the argument is made in the language of obligations and expectations: it's either "Americans should stick up for Americans" or "All people have a claim to my compassion." In other words, we argue about *which* human kind applies — should I act on my membership in the American category or in the human-race category? — but not about what membership means. It means expecting that other people will behave toward you in a particular way, only because you're a member, not for anything you've done or failed to do.

This aspect of human kinds — the way they create claims on people and limit what they can do — is not what you'd expect of a mere category. It is what you'd expect of a coherent, bounded entity, whose members have obligations to one another. So the hugeness of human kinds, those things-made-of-people that can number 290 million or one billion or more, really does indicate that we think of them as entities. As I've mentioned, human kinds combine the nature of a category and of a team. They feel to us as if they were both a simple category (mothers are people who have children) and a big team — a thing-made-of-people that has thoughts of its own (mothers want good schools).

So the hugeness of human kinds does matter: How can we believe in a meaningful connection to people we have never met and never will, to people who are too numerous to count? I can be convinced by the organization of a platoon of cops that they're a group, but something else must convince me that millions of people can be too. The existence of that something else is good evidence for a human-kind faculty. If people perceive human kinds without any physical evidence, then their knowledge must come from inside their minds. Another line of evidence for a specialized human-kind detector comes from experimental work that scientists have done to see how kind sight develops.

Taking their cue from previous work on specialized faculties, like language and theory of mind, some researchers have looked to small children. The idea is to study the capacity when it first blooms in the mind, to see how it arises and develops. So when Lawrence Hirschfeld and his colleagues (he was then at the University of Michigan) went to look for the mental roots of human kinds, it was to toddlers they turned, in experiments with children in Michigan, Korea, and France.

In a typical experiment in this series, the researchers showed three sets of color-wash line drawings to 109 toddlers from around the university campus in Ann Arbor, where Hirschfeld was then a professor of psychology. Each set included drawings of an adult and three children of the same gender. The adults in the pictures varied according to three kinds of obvious, outward cues: body build (thin versus stocky), occupation (wearing tools, a stethoscope, or a police uniform), and color (dark versus light).

Asked which kid depicted the adult as a child, the children generally matched the racial types instead of body build or occupational types. The children showed that same tendency when asked to choose which pictured kid was the adult's child. Yet when Hirschfeld's team asked which pictured kids and adults were most *similar,* the children were as likely to match images by occupation and body build as they were to use race.

With that contrast, Hirschfeld's experiment neatly distinguished between surface appearances and invisible facts — the kind of knowledge that requires a code to interpret. The visible facts told the kids that there were many kinds of similarities in the pictures in people's clothes, body build, and skin color.

When they matched kids and adults only by color, these children were treating the visible facts as code stuff. Their minds saw the visible cues as representations of a fact they could not see. It told them to ignore similarities in build and clothing and treat color as the deciding trait for grouping people together. Hirschfeld, I think, had turned up evidence for kind sight.

This does not mean that certain human kinds are real while others are not. But it does mean that human kinds with attributes that satisfy the kind code will be easier to think about and easier to feel right about than others. Race is easier to learn and be convinced by than, say, economic class, Hirschfeld believes, because the cues that translate into race are more easily encoded than the cues that represent class.

The ease with which we see "things made of people," and the evidence that even small children class people on the basis of "hidden" traits, are both evidence for a human-kind code that is both universal and distinct from other forms of thought. What about another important criterion for a mental code — automaticity? Theory of mind, like understanding language, works whether or not we want it to and even works in situations where other parts of the mind know it can't be right. (That's what yelling at the computer for being contrary is about.) Many mental modules work outside conscious awareness. They decode and encode without our knowing that we're thinking.

Does our sense of human kinds operate this way, quickly and in the dark, without our knowing it? Work in social psychology suggests the answer is yes.

Some eighty years ago, the American journalist Walter Lippmann borrowed a term art historians had taken from the printing trades, where it signified the inky metal plate that was used to make repeated copies of the same text — the "stereotype." In his 1922 book *Public Opinion,* Lippmann wrote, "We notice a trait that marks a well known type, and fill in the rest of the picture by means of the stereotypes we carry about in our heads." His examples, from 1920s America: Agitator. Intellectual. Plutocrat. Foreigner. South European. From the Back Bay. Harvard man. ("How different from the statement, 'He is a Yale man.'")

Lippmann defined a stereotype much as David Hume defined "undistinguishing judgments" about national traits. Lippmann's stereotype was a generalization that you imagined would apply to every single member of a given group. It was oversimplified and often secondhand (learned from other people, movies, the radio, not personal experience). It was by definition not totally reliable, since no member of a group of people is exactly the same as any other, and it was resistant to change. People held their belief in a stereotype, even after contrary evidence. Their reasons, Lippmann wrote, were simple: "The stereotype not only saves time in a busy life and is a defense of our position in society, but tends to preserve us from all the bewildering effects of trying to see the world steadily and see it whole."

Psychologists took up the concept shortly after Lippmann's book appeared, though their emphasis was a little different. They focused on what people said they believed, and on the contrast between those beliefs and the supposedly more accurate measurements made by smart people, such as psychologists. This was in line with the spirit of Lippmann's book, which had suggested that modern life was so frenzied and complicated (in 1922!) that voters ought to trust boards of experts to tell them what was what.

As Lippmann had told them, psychologists assumed that any stereotype is a mistake in thinking — "an exaggerated belief associated with a category," as the esteemed American social psychologist Gordon Allport declared at mid-century. Prejudice, then, could be defined as the thoughts and feelings you expressed as a consequence of your mistake. And discrimination was the action you took, personal and political, because you were prejudiced. (These supposed mistakes of fact, attitude, and behavior were usually studied separately, but the theories are more or less compatible.)

Some stereotypes, Allport said, were complete falsehoods; others were based on a "kernel of truth," but all were errors. His interpretation became a part of his nation's secular theology. Many Americans now believe that stereotypes are doubly wrong: both the opposite of "truth" (as defined by experts) and the opposite of "right." As late as the 1990s, some social psychologists were still assuming that stereotypes were the consequence of people's innate desire to do as little thinking as possible. "A stereotype," wrote one pair, "is a sluggard's best friend."

In the past fifteen years, though, many researchers have decided that what Lippmann called stereotypes were not based on faulty reasoning. This is because they aren't reasoning at all. Instead stereotypes work outside of consciousness, according to their own rules.

A good example of the way psychologists' views have changed is the work of Anthony G. Greenwald of the University of Washington and Mahzarin R. Banaji of Harvard, who found that people associate good and bad traits with human kinds, without knowing what they're doing.

You take their Implicit Association Test (IAT) at a computer keyboard, while the screen flashes a series of words. Some of these are proper names, like Brad or Latisha, and others are positive or negative adjectives, like "paradise" or "hatred." Almost all test-takers show a marked difference in how quickly they associate good traits with one set of names instead of the other. The same goes for the negative attributions. Some of the name lists, like the one that includes Latisha and Brad, contrast names that strike Americans as "white" with those that sound "black." Another version used lists of male and female names; a third offers "old" names, like Wilbur, and "young" names, like Tiffany. If it takes you longer to associate positive traits with a name like Wilbur than with a name like Tiffany, that suggests that you have a harder time seeing old people in a positive light.

Many people who take the test find that their results aren't just surprising but actually contradict their stated beliefs. "Ivy League students who consider themselves enlightened or even radical in their egalitarianism are the most perturbed," Banaji says.

Almost invariably, the American students find they have an unconscious favoritism for white over black and often for male over female. Banaji herself ruefully admits that she tests out with a pro-male bias. (My test results said I slightly favor white over black, while not showing much gender bias. And that I have quite a chip on my unconscious shoulder against old people.)

Human-kind categories are not just terms that we apply to other people. We also apply them to ourselves. That process, too, appears to stand apart from conscious thought. In a 1999 experiment by Margaret Shih, a social psychologist at Harvard, Asian American women took a math test. One group was asked first about their living arrangements, with a number of questions about coed dorms and houses. The other was asked questions about what languages they, their parents, and their grandparents spoke, and about how many generations their families had lived in America. Shih reasoned that the coed questions would remind her volunteers of their gender and call up stereotypes of women; the questions about ancestry and language would call up their sense of themselves as Asian.

Many Americans believe that women aren't too good at math. Many Americans believe that Asians are. Shih thought these assumptions would have an effect on the people who applied the stereotype to themselves.

She was right. Volunteers who had been reminded of their Asian identity got an average of 54 percent on the math test. Those who had been reminded of their female identity scored 43 percent. The women in Shih's study were not just alert to which of many possible groupings was relevant; the choice of grouping affected how they thought. Similar results have been found with other human-kind concepts. Old people reminded of the geezer stereotype perform less well on memory tests than other elderly people. And African American college students reminded of the gap between black and white college achievement score less well on a subsequent test.

Apparently, mental codes for human kinds, applied without awareness to ourselves and other people, have effects that we don't reckon or intend — effects that are sometimes at odds with our conscious thoughts. Social psychologists established decades ago that the familiar, no-thought-required human-kind categories are much faster in operation than the concepts we have to learn and argue about. Experiments have shown that people are quicker to find words about, say, a soccer hooligan if the words are consistent with their stereotype of the hooligan. Moreover, if they're put on a treadmill or distracted by a video playing in the background, their reliance on the stereotype is even greater.

Perhaps it's not surprising that a mental code that works quickly and automatically, and resists distraction, is mostly outside the conscious mind. That's what researchers have found, in any event. Even young American radicals committed to racial justice react differently to black names than to white when they take Banaji and Greenwald's test. Coding is triggered by messages that go right past the rational parts of the mind. And if they're evoked that way, they're probably created that way too. As you'd expect for an important, universal, independent mental code, the process is fast and automatic.

This gap between conscious thoughts and the automatic workings of a code causes one of the frustrations of parenthood. You want your child to speak as you do, but instead he talks like the other kids in the neighborhood. (For immigrant parents, of course, this is literally a difference in language. When the young mind's language-maker looks around for its clues about what "we" speak around here, it listens to the whole world, not the parents.) Similarly, parents want their children to believe "as we do" about politics and morals. But the human-kind map sorts people according to the child's actual experience. It learns what the kinds are and what their traits are, without regard to parental hopes or hypocrisies. (This doesn't mean its experience is good or natural. Learning "how we do things around here" has nothing to do with whether "how we do things" is right.)

The late Paul Moore, former Episcopal bishop of New York City, described the contrast between abstract, hopeful, consciously chosen beliefs and the ones children pick up from the interaction of human-kind codes and the way their environment is organized. It's in a part of his memoir that recalls his early years as a white minister in a poor and racially divided neighborhood:

> One day, we were in the kitchen entertaining a black woman, the first who had come into our house. We were thrilled that at long last a person of color had come to visit and we were on our best behavior, as was she. After a few stilted, nervous attempts at conversation, we began to feel at ease. Just then, the door flew open and Pip, as we called our three-year-old son, Paul, rushed in, sobbing hysterically.
>
> "What on earth's the matter, Pippy," I asked, as I held his shaking little body.
>
> "Some fucking nigger stole my truck!" he cried.

Let's sum up: More recent work confirms that stereotypes work outside awareness, responding to experience in their own ways, whatever we may wish in our conscious minds. Add that to the other characteristics of kind sight: it's present in all minds. It works on its own, without needing other parts of the mind to create its message.

It operates quickly, without our willing it. Those are all characteristics of a specialized mental code — a means of understanding reality that we do not learn but simply experience, because the mind sets it up for us automatically. Language is like that; theory of mind is too.

There are a couple of other criteria for a specialized mental code, though, that I haven't gotten back to. One is a clear connection to the known biology of the brain.

In the past few decades, neuroscientists have had great success in linking specialized processes of the mind to particular regions of the brain. Some of their evidence has come from new techniques for analyzing brains, including those beautiful images made in functional MRI scanners. Another line of evidence has come from unusual neurological patients: when a mental code is distinct and specialized, there turn out to be people who seem normal in most ways but lack only this particular code. And, conversely, doctors come across people who have lots of mental difficulties but no trouble with this one code.

It's worth asking, then, if kind sight is one of these faculties — a mental operation that can be related to maps of the brain and is missing in patients with damage to those parts. The answer is probably yes.

Seven

How Mind Makes World

We think that the grass is green, that stones are hard, that the snow is cold. But physics assures us that the greenness of grass, the hardness of stones, and the coldness of snow, are not the greenness, hardness, and coldness that we know in our own experience, but something very different. The observer, when he seems to himself to be observing a stone, is really, if physics is to be believed, observing the effects of a stone upon himself.

— BERTRAND RUSSELL

I can't recommend being fourteen years old. It was exciting, but also confusing and kind of alarming. I remember an exhilarating feeling that I had no idea what lay ahead and probably wouldn't be up to meeting the challenge. This feeling combined with the smell of eucalyptus and the sound of Rod Stewart singing "Maggie May."

The song was playing every day on the driver's radio as the bus carried us to high school through the humid air of a northern California September. The song brings it all back — a scent, a pleasant mugginess, and the golden sunlight of that place, in that season.

Such are the mental experiences we call memories. They glue together different codes, the results of fusing signals for sights, sounds, body states, and emotions. Memories emerge from regions of the brain where disparate types of information converge.

Among those convergence zones are the temporal lobes, which, roughly speaking, stretch inside the left and right sides of your skull, from your eyes to your ears. The central part of each temporal lobe is rich in cells organized to make connections — to relate different bits of information to one another.

I don't recall every bus ride that year, because not every one felt important. But the first one did: it was novel to be making this trip, and I knew I was starting a new phase of my life, in a new town. Temporal-lobe regions connect pieces of information all the time, but few of those links are consolidated into memories. It's as if each connection is a *candidate* for a memory — one that will not register unless it's marked as worth the trouble.

To know what's worth marking, Antonio Damasio of the University of Iowa has proposed, involves other codes — ones that tell the brain about your physical and emotional state. That information appears to act as a sort of guide, marking the coincidences and connections that are worth keeping. I remember the song, and the eucalyptus-scented breeze, and feeling fourteen, because they accompanied a major change in my routines and surroundings. The conditions of my daily life were changing, and I could not possibly get through a day unless I paid attention to my new insides, my new surroundings, and the links between those two realms.

I recall the period, but no particular day. Yet if the bus had crashed on one of those trips, I would probably remember the details of those few seconds very clearly — as I remember learning on a June morning in 1968 that Senator Robert Kennedy had been shot; as I remember the morning of September 11, 2001, in New York City. Fear and grief are emotions that create "flashbulb memories": intense recollections of the sights and sounds that happened to converge on us at the same time as the awful emotions. Those impressions may not be accurate — people often revise their memories after they hear what others say about the same experience — but they'll be strong.

What we call memory is no doubt a fundamental brain function. It would be difficult for animals to get anywhere if they couldn't connect sights and sounds and smells into a mental map of their surroundings. A lot of temporal-lobe research, in fact, has focused on how this region is involved in mice and rats learning to get through a maze or find food.

Without such connections among codes, no creature could tell cause from effect; no one would know, for instance, that the sight of a flame and the sensation of heat were linked to the pain of getting burned. Without such connections, we'd have no way to say things like "The last time I saw clouds like that, it rained." If we couldn't link sights and sounds and feelings, we wouldn't even know that the face in front of our eyes and the voice in our ears belonged to a single being.

The temporal lobe's crucial role in memory became apparent in the 1950s, when surgeons removed large parts of the lobes in the brains of patients suffering from epilepsy. The last-ditch measure worked, but it had an odd effect on patients. They seemed as intelligent as before and weren't acting differently, but they had strange new flaws in their abilities to remember.

One such patient, known by his initials in the medical literature as H. M., found himself unable to make new memories. Like anyone else, he could recall a word or a phone number for a few minutes. (In fact, H. M.'s case allowed neuroscientists to distinguish short-term memory and long-term memory.) And actions H. M. had learned before the surgery, like riding a bicycle or tying his shoes, were still with him. What he could no longer do was recall anything he'd experienced more than a few minutes earlier.

H. M., who now lives with his wife in Canada, has been studied by the psychologist Brenda Milner for decades. She knows him well. But he doesn't know her; each time she visits, he makes her acquaintance from scratch. H. M.'s old memories, though, seem to be intact. For instance, he knows that he's acquainted with another of his psychologists, because they were children together in the same school before he had his surgery.

Reports about patients like H. M. spurred speculation and research on how particular parts of the brain might be linked to particular experiences of the mind. According to the "triune" model, the human brain had a "reptilian" section, not much changed in form from when it first evolved, before mammals existed. On top of that were supposed to be regions, highly developed in mammals, where strong emotions and drives were forged. Layered above that, in turn, was the supposedly uniquely human part — the "new cortex," so called because it had recently evolved in our species, unlike the old cortex structures that we share with cats, rats, bats, and other mammals.

Perhaps this model caught on because it mirrors familiar religious traditions. The model implies a rational mind, the better angels of our nature, sitting on top of animal passions that it must control, though it doesn't always succeed.

Then, too, the model seemed confirmed in the 1990s by new techniques for imaging the brain.

These techniques — functional magnetic resonance imaging (fMRI) and positron-emission tomography (PET) — shoot radiation at the brain and then use a computer to analyze differences in the signals that bounce back. In fMRI, for example, the computer maps whatever "region of interest" the researchers have picked, showing where oxygen-rich blood is flowing. Since firing neurons take up oxygen, this reveals where neurons are firing more strongly than elsewhere in the brain. The computer's end-product is often a striking multicolored picture, to which the experimenter can point and say, "When we startled people, THIS is what lit up."

Taken to extremes, this sort of talk makes brain science sound like phrenology, the nineteenth-century pseudoscience that classified people according to the bumps and curves of their skulls. Just as phrenologists talked about the "math bump," reporting about neuroscience can slip into the claim that this or that spot in the brain is where, say, depression makes its home.

Recently, though, many researchers have decided that neuroscience needs to shed its phrenological aura. There is no "language bump" or "sadness bump," just as there is no sharp division between brain regions of feeling and thought, virtue and vice, soul and animal. Instead, the work of the last decade portrays a brain in which all these aspects of the self are commingled.

So nowadays you're a little less likely to read that emotions live in the limbic system — a set of structures involving parts of the neocortex and the adjoining inner sides of the two cerebral hemispheres, which the psychiatrist Paul MacLean, who proposed the triune brain theory, had defined in the 1950s as the seat of emotions.

Joseph LeDoux of New York University took a hard look at this concept of a distinct home for emotions in the brain and pointed out its flaws. The first is that the definition of the limbic system has been fuzzy. One of the important temporal-lobe structures for memory is the hippocampus, a curved body inside each lobe, under the cortex. The hippocampus is old cortex, yet the work on H. M. and other patients showed that it was essential for memory, which is a higher-order human faculty, not an emotion.

The second problem with the triune brain concept is that the structures usually identified as part of the limbic system could not be linked to any specific emotion. For example, LeDoux has become well known for his work on the role of the amygdala in fear, but he notes that the frontal cortex is also involved in that emotion. Meanwhile, the amygdala (which is divided into at least twelve regions that don't all do the same thing) is also involved in sexual arousal and other exciting, nonfearful experiences.

The amygdala "is a learning area," Paul Whalen, a neuroscientist at the University of Wisconsin told me. "And what interests it most are the things it has had less experience with — situations where it doesn't know what the relationship is between the first thing it noticed and the second."

In other words, people do have an emotional brain, but it does not consist of a neatly separate emotion sector distinct from regions dedicated to perceiving, acting, or thinking. Neuroscientists will never declare that love or fear or language has a single address in the brain, because those experiences draw on neural activity from all over — not just between the ears either but all over the body. We feel our hearts go pitter-patter with love, we talk with our hands, we experience fear as "butterflies in the stomach" because the nerves that control those organs and report back to the brain about them are also involved in the codes.

In fact, many scientists, including Damasio and George Lakoff of the University of California at Berkeley, argue that the brain's relationship to the rest of the body is no different from that of hearts and hands. The brain is, in their term, "embodied," so that it makes little sense to speak of the brain as if it existed independently. That's the mistake that Damasio called, in the title of his first book, "Descartes'

Error." (In the seventeenth century, René Descartes had held that the human soul must be separate in nature from the body.)

It shouldn't be surprising, then, that current descriptions of the physical brain are hard to line up with labels for mental experience, like emotion, action, or perception. Those concepts describe how people act, not how their brains are physically organized. Why should the anatomy of the brain, as described in 2004, line up with notions about the mind that were formed thousands of years earlier?

Think, for example, about the nearest computer. You can start it up and use a Web browser, an e-mail program, perhaps a word processor or a spreadsheet. The architecture of the machine makes all these applications possible. But if you take the PC apart, you will not find a word-processor region amid the circuit boards and transistors; no part of the hard drive will turn out to be the e-mail center. The principles that apply to your experience of the computer — the software — are different from the ones that govern its physical organization.

Many scientists now believe the same is true of the brain. Analyzing it as an organ of the body requires them to see it in a different light and perhaps with different categories than those of the mind. The idea of memory itself, for instance, might not be so useful. It's an image of people retrieving indelible records from some library in the brain and then relating those records to the present. Yet such records do not exist.

As the British science writer John McCrone has pointed out, your brain is tuned for signals that are relevant to your situation at the moment — "not for retrospection and contemplation but for intention and anticipation, for looking forwards rather than backwards, outwards rather than inwards, for being selective rather than merely retentive." Trying to predict what will happen, getting you ready to take action, guided by your needs and emotions of the present, your brain doesn't always distinguish between accurate and inaccurate memories or between memory and imagination.

So it may be that traditional, folk-psychological notions of memory, perception, thought, emotion, and free will do not join neatly to concepts like neuron, amygdala, and neural code. Some researchers think the concepts won't fit together at all.

One reason they believe this is that brain anatomy, unlike computer architecture, is not a settled subject. For one thing, anatomy derives from the purposes of those who use it. So the brain according to a doctor treating Alzheimer's disease is not the same as the brain according to a neuroscientist trying to understand memory. And neither of those is exactly the same as the brain according to an evolutionist, whose main interest is how the human organ evolved from those of ancestral animals.

Even within a single field, though, where some brain structures like the hippocampus and amygdala have been well defined, many others still aren't. Scientists debate about the shape and location of brain parts and about what they should be called; for instance, what's sometimes called the orbitofrontal cortex might be better combined with parts of the anterior cingulate cortex and given a different name.

Meanwhile, the placid voice of journalism tells you that this part of the brain under your temples "is called" the temporal lobe, which is certainly nice and clear. But that description hides a lively science, where the best researchers disagree on such topics as "What, if anything, is the medial temporal lobe?" (That was the title of a major presentation at the Society for Neuroscience's annual meeting in 2003.) There is a nascent Human Brain Project working to make it easier for scientists to deal with one another's concepts. Its leaders have agreed already on this principle: "To develop a standardized nomenclature for the brain now," says one, "is a big mistake. Because nobody knows what it should be." Many researchers expect the neuroscience of 2050 will not use today's map for the brain regions nor our terms for mental life, either.

"We might need to invent a new set of terms that can translate between the different ways of describing social behavior," writes Antonio Damasio's Iowa colleague Ralph Adolphs. Such new terms, he suggests, might "correspond more closely to the neural processes that underlie them."

When brain scientists relate language, or fear, or moral judgment to neurons firing in a particular area, then, they aren't looking for the one spot where that mental experience happens. Rather, they are seeking the different stations of a network. For example, memories enlist many different parts of the brain, not just the hippocampus. Yet people whose hippocampi are damaged have trouble with memory. So that part of the brain is *not* a phrenological memory box. But it could be an essential part of a larger circuit.

The sense of human kinds is at least as widely networked as the ability to remember, so mapping a human-kind circuit isn't going to lead to modern phrenology; scientists aren't going to find a prejudice bump or a patriotism region. They need to understand the circuit for a different reason: the brain links concepts of human kinds to bodily states.

In the brain's convergence zones, codes that represent human kinds like Buddhists or normal people or Red Sox fans trade signals with cells that track your heart rate, your hormones, and your immune responses.

That's the reason you can be enraged at the sight of strangers halfway around the world burning your nation's flag. It's the reason you can be physically sick after eating safe food, if it violates the taboos of your religion. It's the reason levels of the hormone testosterone decline in the bodies of fans who have seen their team lose an important game (as documented in a remarkable paper by the University of Georgia psychologist James M. Dabbs and his colleagues). This is why human kinds are so different from categories for things like sailboat-kinds or deciduous-plant kinds. Categories for people have effects on our bodies. The brain, where mind meets matter, makes that possible.

One of Antonio Damasio's demonstrations of this principle came from work he and his colleagues did with patients who have damage to their amygdalas. The experimenters gave each patient a wager game to play in which the strategy for winning was clear after a few rounds. People with undamaged brains caught on and switched to the best approach. People with amygdala damage stuck to what they had started with. They did this even though they had no trouble describing how and why the other strategy was better.

Different codes for different purposes: The people in this experiment could perceive a better method but without an amygdala on the circuit, they had no motive to switch strategies. Their strategic insight wasn't enough; to act, a person needs other brain codes to mark insight as important and relevant — to his or her particular body, right here, right now, in this particular situation.

That dependence also works in the other direction. If your amygdala is sending signals to a part of the brain that perceives rules for games, it is a safe bet that this part is sending signals back to the amygdala. The late Francisco Varela, a neuroscientist at the Centre National de la Recherche Scientifique in Paris, called this the brain's "law of reciprocity": if region A has nerve fibers connecting it to region B, then B will have its own, separate pathway back to A.

So, for example, the amygdala fires above its usual rate whenever it gets the signal that you have noticed something new. Usually, it rapidly calms down. But it will keep firing if what you're perceiving is startling, terrifying, or sexually arousing. Some other part of the circuit is deciding which of those states you're in. Considering the significant difference between an angry snake and a willing sex partner, these other parts of the circuit must be pretty important. If it's true that you can't have useful thoughts without emotions, it's equally true that you can't have emotions without thoughts to tell you what they mean.

Human kinds, then, are not just categories. They're also guides. They tell you what a perception means. They encode the sight of bleached hair as information about the person sporting it, telling you what he probably is (someone into punk-rock style) and probably is not (an investment banker), and so what to expect of him. Those same thoughts also tell you what you are in relation to this stranger, by calling up your knowledge of what human kinds *you're* a part of.

Human kinds are also guides to *action*. Once I've classed myself and the stranger as, say, employee and boss, I know which game to play and which rules apply — how to speak, how to dress, and how to behave toward this other person. Then, too, human kinds are guides for self-monitoring. Suppose that I'm at lunch with another person from the office and I say, "Whoa, go easy on the french fries, guy, you know you're on a diet!" If the human kinds that apply are those of close friendship, then I'm playing the game well. But if my tablemate is my new boss, I've just insulted him. My sense of human kinds tells me if what I am doing is appropriate.

In the past couple of decades researchers have found a number of regions in the brain that do indeed seem to be required for the three mental processes I just listed: classifying things, learning rules, and evaluating oneself. It would make sense that those regions are involved in human-kind thoughts and feelings.

The amygdala and the hippocampus would likely be involved in such a circuit, because they seem to be required for a mind to learn rules and distinguish one context from another — for learning, for example, that a bikini is appropriate for the beach but not for a funeral. As for the rest of the system, experiments in the growing field of social neuroscience have found a number of other regions that would almost certainly have to participate in kind sight.

Consider what scientists can say with confidence about the moment when I noticed David Perret in the hotel and (erroneously) classified him. I was able to see him because of activity in my visual-processing regions. I noticed that he stood out in part because my amygdala helped mark this unusual sight for attention, and thanks to my temporal lobes, I could then apply all the invisible background knowledge I need for life with other human beings — how people behave in hotels, how to tell leather jackets from tweed, and so on. I was also getting signals from my somatosensory centers about my physical condition right then, telling me that I wasn't particularly troubled by the scene in front of me. (If I had been in a heart-pounding, sweaty panic, my mind would have been at pains to explain it as somehow caused by what I was seeing.)

But where were all these codes and codes of codes being put together into a sense of human kinds? A likely site is the prefrontal cortex, which wraps around the frontmost section of your brain, that part of it that juts out over your eyes like the marquee of a theater. You can get near this area by putting your thumbs just under your eyebrows and pushing up a little. Right above your thumbs when you do this, nearest the orbits of your eyes, is the underside of your brain: the orbitofrontal cortex. It's also called the ventromedial cortex, as it lines the ventral (underside) medial (central) region here. In contrast, another stretch of cortex, the dorsolateral, runs along the sides and top of the front of the brain.

The orbitofrontal cortex has direct links to the amygdala, the hippocampus, and the brain regions that process sights, sounds, and smells. And the two cortices also have such connections to each other. That anatomy prompts Damasio and other neuroscientists to suggest that the orbitofrontal cortex is a convergence zone where perceptions, memories, emotions, and information about your body are all received and combined. (The likely convergence of codes for taste and smell, to create flavor perception, is also part of the orbitofrontal cortex.)

An interesting experiment recently took such ideas down to the scale of the single neuron. Hiroto Kawasaki, Ralph Adolphs, and their colleagues at the University of Iowa were working with an epileptic patient who had come in for brain surgery. Unusually, the search for the cause of his seizures required an electrode to be inserted into his brain. (The usual methods, involving an electroencephalogram, had not worked.) So the researchers were able to monitor solitary neurons in the man's right orbitofrontal cortex. The scientists showed the patient pictures of faces (some nice, some nasty) and of events (some neutral and again, some nice or nasty, like warfare and mutilating accidents). Each neuron fired in response to the unpleasant pictures, while staying silent for the nice and neutral ones.

This response was extremely fast (probably firing before the patient knew what he was seeing). The researchers believe the cells could be part of a loop from the cortex into regions of the brain involved in emotion. That could be a circuit linking different mental codes — the ones that tell the patient what he's looking at, and the ones that give a sense of how it feels to look at it, and what he can do about the sight.

Among the abilities that the orbitofrontal cortex appears to make possible is the learning of rules and conventions. People who suffer injuries to this region, Damasio says, often go from being upright, reliable citizens to shiftless, rude, unsociable misfits.

His most famous example is a nineteenth-century American railroad worker named Phineas Gage, who survived a bizarre construction accident that sent an iron rod through part of his orbitofrontal cortex. Gage supposedly went from being a good employee and all-round solid citizen to being a careless, irresponsible character who troubled his friends and couldn't hold a job. (I say supposedly because one scholar has carefully documented a case that the Gage story is, basically, a myth.) But Gage is not the only evidence neuroscientists have. Many patients with orbitofrontal damage have social-rule troubles.

As a region that combines codes about memories, emotions, perceptions, and the body's sense of its own well-being, the orbitofrontal cortex seems a likely place to look for codes about human kinds, which, after all, involve memories, emotions, perceptions of people, and a sense of the body's safety or lack of it.

It's already known that the orbitofrontal cortex is involved in detecting the rules and customs that people use to get along with others of the same tribe. And one study does suggest that damage to the orbitofrontal cortex alters human-kind thinking. Elizabeth Milne and Jordan Grafman, of the American National Institute of Neurological Disorders and Stroke, found that people with orbitofrontal injuries could not use stereotypes. Unlike a comparison group of normal people, these patients, when they took an Implicit Association Test for gender, showed no preference.

Of course, if there is a human-kind faculty in the brain, it will likely draw on many different regions. The orbitofrontal's neighboring dorsolateral cortex is another possible part of such a circuit. It's a region where codes for rules are translated into action. It has direct links to its orbitofrontal neighbor for both sending and receiving neural messages. And the dorsolateral sends out direct connections via nerve fibers to parts of the brain that code emotions.

Another region with a link to the dorsolateral cortex is a small stretch along the inside walls of each brain hemisphere, called the cingulate cortex. It's an area that seems to help code for judgments about your actions. A circumstance in which the frontal part of this region — the anterior cingulate cortex — gets more active is when you notice you're making a mistake or failing to adhere to some rule or strategy. This code appears to be part of any kind of self-evaluation, from how accurate your pitch was to how good a person you are.

So, for instance, the anterior cingulate cortex is involved in evaluating physical pain, helping to judge the extent of the damage. The same pattern of activity has been found in people who feel the *social* pain of rejection by a group of other people. One team of researchers at Stanford also found that people's scores on a test for self-esteem predicted the amount of activity in similar areas of their cingulate cortices. The higher a person's self-esteem measure, the less active the anterior cingulate cortex region appeared to be in an MRI scan. Research on nine people deemed to be suffering from post-traumatic stress disorder after the 1995 sarin-gas terrorist attacks in the Tokyo subway turned up distinct shrinkage in their left anterior cingulate cortices — a hint that being terrorized might cause this region to "burn out."

If a brain code is distinct and specialized, it's possible to knock out parts of the brain that support it without injuring the rest. In other words, a genetic oddity, illness, or injury like Phineas Gage's might result in someone who lacks *only* that one code. Conversely, there could be people who have serious brain impairments elsewhere but whose ability to produce that one code is unaffected. If a certain kind of brain injury, then, prevents a person from stereotyping, it may be that stereotypes come from a specialized mental code of their own.

There is other evidence along these lines. People whose amygdalas have been completely destroyed appear to feel that *everyone* is "my kind." They are too trusting, taking everyone at face value, and are easily gulled because they have no suspicions. Patients with such damage have a difficult time recognizing negative emotions in other people's faces. In one experiment, in fact, they had an easier job of perceiving an angry fight from a photo *after* the faces in it had been blanked out.

At the opposite extreme are the kind of people currently labeled psychopaths (or sociopaths; their official diagnosis currently is "anti-social personality disorder," whose signs include a callous disregard for others, irresponsibility, and lack of guilt about misdeeds). For them, *no one* is "my kind": everyone, from parents to friends to strangers, feels like a nonperson, a means to an end. If the amygdala-less patient's world is one where everybody is Mom, the psychopath's appears to be a world where everybody is just a toll-taker on the highway — a living thing who is to be used to reach a goal.

Sociopaths often are successful because the rest of their mind is unimpaired: they're smart enough to be able to counterfeit the vibes of friends, sons, lovers, and comrades even though they don't feel the bonds of human solidarity. They have a particular psychic deficit, one of human-kind thinking. If physical damage is involved in their condition — to amygdala or orbitofrontal cortex, or both, among other regions — what it has removed, it seems, is the code for literal and metaphorical kindness.

This is not how sociopaths are usually described. Instead, they're considered to be people who lack a moral sense, or empathy, or both — which implies that the rest of us have those capacities and apply them to everyone.

Obviously, we don't. In fact, normal people treat others as objects, as things to be used, all the time, with no offense taken. To return to Lawrence Hirschfeld's example, the toll-taker in the booth doesn't expect you to ask how he's feeling and say you empathize with his troubles. To him, you're a car; to you, he's an instrument on your commute.

What sociopaths do differently from normals is refrain from distinguishing one kind of person from another. They feel toward *everybody* as the toll-taker feels toward you, and as you do the toll-taker. Autistic people are sometimes complained of because, lacking a theory of mind, they also don't feel the need to act differently toward one kind of person over another. "He treats me like a stranger," say their parents. (The rest of us know better; we only treat *strangers* as strangers.)

What kind sight lets us do, as I mentioned, is learn and follow intricate rules for treating people just as, and only as, they should be treated — *given the kind of person they are, and the kind we are, in the situation we meet them.*

These rules have to be complicated because there are many different human kinds, and what is appropriate for one is not for another. Men in most parts of the world talk differently to women than to each other, and people treat children differently than they treat the old. The system is finely calibrated, even in societies where people are theoretically equal.

Then, too, it's a system that we have to tune constantly because our situations change all the time. The same person may be in one human kind — the boss — at lunch and another (Mom) at dinner. The orbitofrontal cortex and the amygdala, among other regions, appear to be required for adjusting to these changing contexts, because people who cannot make these distinctions have damage there. So we need these parts, apparently, for mapping human kinds — for knowing to treat your mother differently from a stranger on the bus.

Is it simply that sociopaths can't *tell* the difference between Mom and a stranger? This seems unlikely. They could not counterfeit so well if they didn't understand how other people's emotions and actions are guided. What seems to differ in sociopaths is how they act, not what they see. What they lack, in other words, is not the map of human kinds but the rules that attach to it.

These rules are important to us. We care that other people follow them, if they are also in our kind. We want our soldiers to behave with honor and our leaders not to be disgraced, even though we'll never meet the soldiers or the leaders. Also, we want our kind, whatever it is, to be in the category covered by the rules. For instance, we want to be considered normal even though being labeled "not normal" by someone we don't know has no effect on our lives. We want the applicable rules to be followed, too. We're outraged by small slights that have no practical effect — "I was here first, but you took their order before me!" — because those slights connote that we aren't getting what we are due.

It's probably significant, then, that the brain circuits identified as important for learning and following rules — including the amygdala, temporal lobe, and the orbitofrontal and dorsolateral parts of the cortex — are also those that look important for human-kind thinking. Maybe it isn't surprising that these regions also appear important in thinking and feeling about moral questions. Morality, after all, consists of ultimate rules that define who we are and what we must do to stay in that most desirable of human kinds, the good people.

A bit more eerily, the orbitofrontal cortex also is engaged when people perceive something as beautiful. One study found it active in people listening to music. Another found the orbitofrontal cortex active when people were deciding that paintings were lovely. And the same stretch of cortex has been found to "fire" more during a number of the activities that make up a religious practice: meditation and the ritualistic repetition of important or comforting activities.

As I've mentioned, neuroscience isn't phrenology. Many different parts of the brain are involved in these distinct mental experiences, and the involvement of the same region in more than one does not mean the experiences are equivalent or even that they depend on the same neurons. That said, the overlap may be suggestive of ways that the mental experiences might be associated with one another and perhaps how they might have some shared processes. It's at least worth thinking about how a region important for human-kind thoughts and feelings is also one that helps you sense the beautiful, the good, and the Godly.

Like any other code, the one that places people into kinds feels natural and obvious; we don't recognize that it is shaping our perceptions, making us see "the police" where, with a different code, we would see Harry, Jane, and Joe. As with all codes, small children learn to use it, and all small children appear to pick it up in the same way. (This is why researchers go to the trouble of working with three-year-olds.) Like all codes, the one for human kinds makes us think our perceptions are straightforward and natural and true. And it makes us think we know where those perceptions come from. But the actual sources of those perceptions are signs that are recognized outside our conscious minds, according to rules of which we are not aware.

If that's so, it follows that human-kind code can be manipulated in experiments. It should be possible to make typical, conscious, aware people see human kinds where they had not, and reckon with those new kinds, and feel for them. It should be possible, too, to make those people *stop* believing in human kinds by changing the conditions of the experiment.

That does sound weird — but it has been done.

Eight

Inventing Tradition in Oklahoma,

or

What I Did on My Summer Vacation

I was now . . . an immigrant in an altogether different physical reality. Here everything demanded revision, and I was aware that my senses were being adapted to the chemical and tactile demands of the new place — its atmospheres, its hidden variations had to be absorbed.

— SAUL BELLOW

For twenty-two Oklahoma City fifth graders in the summer of 1954, the offer must have sounded like a dream: Come spend three weeks in the Sans Bois mountains, at a 200-acre campground with swimming holes, streams, canoes, baseball diamonds, campfires, caves, and snakes. Explore the woods where Jesse James's gang hid out! Have cookouts! Play tug of war! Advance social psychology!

This last, not mentioned in the brochure, was why the University of Oklahoma picked up almost all the costs. The camp was actually an elaborate experiment. As the boys, all strangers, assembled their campfire universe, their counselors observed the birth, life, and death of human-kind feelings, like geologists measuring a steaming fresh volcanic island, just emerged from the sea.

This exercise in what Donald T. Campbell called "experimental anthropology" was designed by Muzafer Sherif, a brilliant and eccentric psychologist who himself was a refugee from human-kind violence. Born just before the collapse of the Ottoman Empire, in what is now southeastern Turkey, he had found himself in the crowd on May 15, 1919, when a Greek army took the city of Smyrna and set about killing every Turk it could find. The man next to Sherif dropped, bleeding, and he saw the soldier pull out his bayonet. He was paralyzed with terror and the knowledge that he was next. But just then something else got the soldier's attention, and he turned away. (Three years later, the Turks would return the injury, burning much of Greek-held Smyrna to the ground.)

Threatened for being part of a human kind, a lot of people would become more loyal to their endangered identity. Many German Jews persecuted by the Nazis, for example, felt themselves to be more Jewish and less German than they had before. Muslims in post–September 11 New York City are more likely to use religion to identify themselves than nationality, which was not the case in the 1990s. But some people become detached not only from their kind but also from the passions of kind sight. Sherif was one of these.

In later life he was proud that the Christian missionaries who taught him as a boy had failed to convert him from Islam, but he was no chauvinist. What had brought him to live in the United States, in fact, was a prison term in Turkey for his opposition to its fascist-leaning government in the 1940s. (Colleagues from his grad-school days had to organize a campaign to spring him.)

Sherif let his Turkish passport expire, but he never applied for U.S. citizenship, remaining literally and psychically a stateless person until his death in 1975. Ostentatiously unmoved by the boundaries that mattered to other people, he liked to tell stories of puzzled Americans trying to fit him into a human-kind system that saw all people as white, black, yellow, or red. Was he a mulatto? Or a Cherokee? After he'd taught at the University of Oklahoma for a number of years, he liked to refer to himself, in his thick Turkish accent, as an Okie.

Like many scholars, Sherif studied just those parts of life for which he had no intuitive feel. He'd been in danger just because he was a member of the "wrong" kind. To many people, such a story seemed a self-evident part of life. To him, it was a profound mystery, and he got no answers from the standard explanations of his time.

By the middle of the twentieth century, conventional wisdom had settled on a tragic model for mob violence, war, persecution, prejudice, and genocide: the cause must be some barely controlled impulses toward death and destruction, which escaped whenever they could, like steam from a cracked boiler.

This idea was not new. What the moderns added was the claim that it was science.

One of the first ventures of this sort was *The Crowd,* published in 1895 by the French journalist Gustave Le Bon. Members of a mob, he wrote, have no defense against their "ancestral savagery," which is always at the ready. Crowds resemble simple, emotion-driven individuals, Le Bon said, like women, and primitives, and children. Le Bon based this on histories and novels about the Paris mob during France's revolution of 1848 and the three-month period in 1871 after the country's defeat in the Franco-Prussian War. When his book appeared, it well suited the conservative politicians who routinely came to Le Bon's regular Wednesday luncheons. His theory seemed to lend the support of science to their low opinions of lower-class people and of political protests and upheavals.

A generation later, in anti-Semitic Vienna, stunned by the disasters of World War I, Sigmund Freud had his own reasons for detesting mass movements. His 1921 essay on group psychology begins with long quotations and paraphrases of Le Bon's work. In a group, Freud wrote elsewhere, "The individual is brought under conditions which allow him to throw off the repressions of his unconscious instincts. The apparently new characteristics which he then displays are in fact the manifestation of his unconscious, in which all that is evil in the human mind is contained as a pre-disposition." Being a powerful, degenerate, overgrown version of the individual self, the crowd was dangerous because it lacked the more sophisticated psychic defenses available to the individual to protect himself from the innate appeal of aggression and death. "In consequence of this primary mutual hostility of human beings," Freud wrote, "civilized society is perpetually threatened with disintegration."

The notion of universal human depravity leads most thinkers quickly to the notion that some people — not the thinker, of course — are more depraved than others. In 1950, a group led by the German refugee philosopher Theodor Adorno published an immense book describing an "authoritarian personality," which, the group said, was marked by a tendency to be overly fearful and respectful of authority, while being hostile and domineering to "inferiors." Conventional values, a sense of a sharp division between right and wrong, and disdain for nonconformists and minorities were also supposed to be authoritarian traits.

The book made no allowance for the way a person's behavior depends on his surroundings and his goals. People can act authoritarian about their nation but not their ethnic group, or vice versa. But to Adorno and his colleagues, an authoritarian was that way at all times and in all situations. The explanation was that aggression, blocked from being released at harsh parents, would pop out of the safer vent aimed at minorities and nonconformists. Meanwhile, figures of authority would take on the attributes of the parents and be feared and obeyed at all costs. A nation of authoritarians would tend toward dictators and paranoid politics: hence Nazism.

The authoritarian-personality school had a family resemblance to Le Bon's ideas, not only in the assumption that savagery is lurking in the mind, waiting to be let out, but also in its dressing up of humankind feeling as objective research. As Le Bon described his class enemies as savages, so Adorno implicitly condemns as dangerous and narrow those who aren't like Adorno. (He often wrote in this vein, whatever his subject.) The book suggests that good, smart people like the reader are naturally interested in how to fix bad, stupid people, those authoritarians.

Such views — that human beings are born bad, or in the modified form, that people you happen to dislike are bad — have comprised the dominant strain in Western thinking for centuries. In the Christian world, it was expressed in the doctrine of original sin, which holds that even a newborn infant is evil, bearing as it does the taint of the universal parents, Adam and Eve. As Frederick Crews has pointed out, Freud himself explained that his theories were a restatement of what the church fathers had said. Europeans had had long training in this tradition. Recast as science, then, it felt right.

Nowadays, historians and psychologists think Le Bon was wrong. Street mobs actually appear to behave much like any other collection of people who come to see themselves as one, like a corporation or a Boy Scout troop. Their members seek to fit in, to be in sync with one another and to meet one another's expectations. Crowds that turn violent have been prepared for it by leaders who persuaded their members they were entitled to act. And evading responsibility isn't a universal trait of crowds at all. At American lynchings in the 1920s, some of those present had their pictures taken for posterity.

Some of the clearest modern evidence against Le Bon comes from Otto M. J. Adang of the Police Institute for Public Order and Safety in the Netherlands. He was a firsthand observer of 225 violent street clashes at soccer matches, political events, and other hot spots for three and a half years in the 1990s. Using a system of codes for classifying aggression, which he'd originally developed watching chimpanzees, he assembled his observations into a compare-and-contrast database. When a crowd became violent, Adang found, the number of people in it actually trying to hurt anyone was always low, never more than 10 percent of the rioters. The rest yelled, threatened, waved their weapons, and posed no danger to anyone. The more risky an act was — hurling oneself at a shielded line of riot police, for example — the fewer people did it. Most of the real violence he saw took place when the police were around to break it up. Like a man in a street brawl who hurls himself at another, counting on his friends to pull him back, the rioters acted craziest when someone was around to keep a lid on things.

For Le Bon, the mob was made of people who destroyed private property and fought the troops of the government he supported. He saw only how members of that mob treated their enemies (who included him). Le Bon's theory was propaganda for his kind — prosperous conservative Frenchmen of the time. It offered stereotypes always invoked to describe any enemy — "savage," "cruel," "bloodthirsty." Because people like him were the targets of the mob's fury, he thought fury was all that a mob was capable of. He wouldn't imagine, then, that men in lynch mobs could still tip their hats to the ladies who watched the body burn.

Fifty years ago, however, most authorities followed Freud, who had followed Le Bon. The urge to pillage and massacre was supposed to be boiling away in the human soul, ready to emerge at the slightest chance. The notion that rioters could be making fine judgments about what they owed to their fellow rioters didn't fit. Psychologists preferred a metaphor of effortfully controlled power.

Freud proffers the imagery of pipes and tanks storing a pent-up desire for pleasure, which he called libido, and a pent-up desire for death, among other high-pressure substances. In a similar vein, an American school of psychology held that aggression was a consequence of frustration, with more of the latter producing more of the former. In the 1950s the German ethologist Konrad Lorenz devised a similar model of mental plumbing in which fear and aggression were either vented in frequent short bursts or built up with no outlet, then exploded.

Freud and Lorenz's imageries of blocked pipes are now described as hydraulic models of the mind. The models live on in phrases like "He's under a lot of pressure" or "She needs to vent a little." When you use such a phrase, you make it difficult to imagine such emotions under fine control. After all, boilers don't explode carefully.

Easy to say at the dawn of the twenty-first century, but very few people thought this way when Sherif was working at Columbia in the 1930s or even when he worked in Oklahoma in the 1950s. He seems to have realized that the enemy of insight into human kinds is "what everyone knows" — the accepted wisdom of the professionals. In the 1940s, he pointed out that the sources of frustration for most people were the privileges of others — yet the privileged were seldom the targets of violence. Why, he asked, were less-frustrated people — for instance, white southerners in the segregated United States — more aggressive than African Americans, who were far more frustrated?

Then too, if parenting styles determined a nation's politics, the authoritarian theory is a claim that most German parents were harsh in the 1910s while most British parents were more touchy-feely. Not very plausible. Anyway, the notion that a country's political character is inevitably set by the preceding generation fails to explain how a supposedly authoritarian country can vote in a nonauthoritarian regime, as has happened in Spain, Portugal, South Africa, Taiwan, South Korea, and other countries in the twentieth century.

These explanations left no room for change in human-kind feelings or perceptions, and Sherif saw that as another fatal flaw: clearly, people's definitions of human kinds *did* change. One 1943 study of American students, for example, found that their descriptions of other nations' traits had been much affected by World War II. In fact, descriptions of the Japanese and the Chinese had switched places after the war began. The Japanese, who had been portrayed as progressive and artistic, were now called sly, treacherous, and deceitful, while the Chinese, depicted in 1930s surveys as sly and treacherous, were now held to be reserved and courteous. Another study, published in 1951, found that American descriptions of the Russians had changed from brave and hardworking in 1942 to cruel and conceited in 1948. Some scholars have tried to save the notion of accurate stereotypes by claiming that these surveys measured *attitudes* toward Chinese, Japanese, and Russians, not people's definitions of these human kinds. This is ingenious but not convincing. It requires you to believe that people talking about human kinds are just mouthing off, and don't mean what they say.

Lest you imagine that Americans are particularly flighty, two Indian psychologists found similar changes in their country. India and China spent most of 1959 tensely disputing a border. In that period, traits that Indians had ascribed to the Chinese went from artistic, religious, industrious, friendly, progressive, and honest to "aggressive," "cheat," "selfish," "war-monger," and "cruel."

Political conflict alters people's perceptions, and that's no surprise. It turns out, though, that people's list of essential traits for groups can be changed by less dramatic circumstances.

For example, in 1960 Lutfy N. Diab, a psychologist at the American University of Beirut, asked Muslim students there to choose words from a list and apply them to various national and ethnic groups. Americans were likely to be described in fairly negative terms — *if* the category Americans came after Germans on the list. If instead Americans followed Russians, then the students were more likely to describe Americans with positive words. In a second study Diab found that the students, in comparing thirteen national and ethnic groups, rated the French as base, selfish, materialistic, and mean. He then asked a second group to rate the French vis-à-vis only the four most unpopular groups on his list. In this new context, the French were seen as sociable, artistic, cultured, and democratic. In other words, when you ask people to define a human kind like "the Americans" or "the French," their responses depend on what happened just before you asked.

Sherif saw exactly what was wrong with the midcentury's conventional wisdom about human kinds. A person's representations of human kinds must not depend on some unalterable core in his soul. If that were so, ideas and feelings about human kinds would never change. Stereotypes do change though, so people's beliefs must be affected by their experience. On the other hand, Sherif knew that human-kind perceptions, especially in their emotional aspects, did not emerge out of "good statistics about real people." The Japanese did not abruptly stop working hard and become sneaky after Pearl Harbor, however Americans felt. How could these concepts have a basis in reality, and yet be so changeable, so dependent on accidents like the order in which nations appear on a list?

Sherif solved this problem with a brilliant insight. The source of stereotypes is not the person being stereotyped, he said, nor is it in the mind of the person doing the stereotyping. What stereotypes really describe is the *relationship* between those two parties.

I remember the moment when I read this in the faded pages of a book in the New York Public Library. It's a flashbulb memory — when all my amygdala and other temporal-lobe circuitry put me on high alert. Mark this! So I recall cool autumn light fading in the high windows and the smell of old tobacco that they could never get out of the carpet in the room where writers and researchers were given their work spaces. I had been reading in the literature on war, violence, aggression — man's inhumanity to man — for months and finding a bottomless sea of platitudes. Here instead was an idea. And unlike the original sin view of humanity or the hydraulic model of the psyche, Sherif's idea could be related to today's science of mind.

Sherif does not anoint a winner in the old debate about stereotypes and prejudice. Instead, like many great insights, his observation redefines the argument. Are stereotypes "good statistics about real people"? Obviously not. Are they, then, fantastic, arbitrary notions? Obviously not. Human kinds emerge from relations *between* people (or, to be more strictly accurate, from perceptions about those relations).

If I fear Japanese soldiers, my extremely negative stereotype of Japan will always be accurate enough — as a measure of my fear, even though it may strike others as ludicrously wrong information about Japanese life. And if I, like the cops in Lee Jussim's example, am anxiously looking for people who might have committed a crime, my inclination to suspect Kampalese Americans because of their slightly higher crime rate is a reflection of my particular job concerns.

Hence, Sherif realized that it makes no sense to talk about stereotypes without stereotypers. Concepts don't exist in some world of bodiless ideas. They're in the minds of particular people, coping with particular problems in their particular time and place. This was why Americans' descriptions of the Japanese could be admiring in 1938 and contemptuous in 1943. And this is why the ancient Greeks, whom we see today as proud and brilliant, were considered by the Romans to be glib, deceitful, childlike, and untrustworthy. As the historian Orlando Patterson has pointed out, the Romans knew the Greeks as slaves. And masters have been consistent in the way they have described slaves throughout the world, from ancient Rome to medieval England to antebellum North America to dynastic China.

The consistency is not in the slaves, who came from every sort of religion, culture, and race. Nor was it in the masters, who ranged from Caligula to Thomas Jefferson. The common thread was the *relationship* of master to slave.

It's hard to think consciously about things you have learned to do without thinking. However, in a series of experiments in the 1990s, the psychologist Alan P. Fiske of the University of California at Los Angeles and his colleagues asked people to take note of the difference between perceiving a person and perceiving a *relationship* to a person. They asked people to keep track of mistakes in which they confused one acquaintance with another — like calling someone by the wrong name or telephoning the wrong person without thinking. Their volunteers recorded both the kind of person involved and their relationship to that person. (In other words, if you called Dave when you meant to call Sam, you might note that Dave is Asian, tall, and outgoing and that he's a client and occasional handball partner.)

It turned out that *relationships* predicted people's mistakes, not the physical and psychological characteristics that we think we use to distinguish human kinds. If you confuse Dave with Sam, it is much more likely to be because both are clients, or employees, or occasional handball partners, than because both are Asian, or outgoing types, or Republicans.

Once you see that stereotypes depend on perceived relationships among different human kinds, the question of how objectively accurate they are disappears. We think the human-kind code is based on facts about people. Instead, it's based on facts about how we relate to those people at the moment we categorize them — what we want, or expect, or fear from them. Mental codes interpret human kinds as if they were things that have dimensions and persist through time. But the information that makes the codes work is not about things. It's about actions — what we're doing and planning to do as they relate to what other people are doing. That was what Sherif saw.

Unfortunately, Sherif was swimming against a Freudian tide. When that tide receded in his field, he was dead, and the new ideas were not framed in his terms. To this day, most public thinking about human kinds and human-kind emotions focuses on the stereotyper and the stereotypee, ignoring the third, defining variable: the relation that makes them see one another in the first place.

A good example of the consequences was a disagreement in 2003 between an anthropologist and a psychiatrist. The psychiatrist Willard Gaylin had written in his book *Hatred* that no one could

"pretend to distinguish the Irish Protestant from his Catholic equivalent in physical appearance, speech patterns, Irish traits, Celtic
humor or even cultural values." Reviewing the book, the anthropologist Mel Konner of Emory University replied: "But in fact, as
psychologists in Northern Ireland have shown, any child can tell
them apart, not from physical but from numerous cultural traits
beyond religion and politics."

Any child in Northern Ireland, certainly. But not any child on
earth: a Nigerian or a Tibetan kid plunked down in Northern Ireland would not be able to do it. In order to see and feel a difference
among human beings, you need to see and feel the relationships that
define that difference. Gaylin, knowing that most people on earth are
not versed in Ireland's relationships between Catholic and Protestant,
implies those tribes are not "really there." Konner, looking at the capacity of all children to learn code for human kinds, says no, the difference is not illusory — people learn it and live by it. So who is
right? Are human tribes imaginary and kind of absurd? Or are they
facts of life that have to be accepted?

Certainly, human-kind beliefs can change, as Gaylin implies: there
is no material or logical reason why the bloodshed in Northern Ireland could not end tomorrow. But Konner too is partly right. No
one can just *decide* to stop seeing people as Protestant and Catholic,
in a city organized on those lines. What connects the factual, inescapable tribal world to which Konner alludes with the mental realm
Gaylin describes, where minds *invent* differences and minds can be
changed? Something must, because both those realms exist.

Sherif's great idea points to the link. It's because relations endure
between one category of person and another, he suggests, that
human-kind beliefs can last for centuries. But those relations can
change, so human kinds are also capable of vanishing or being altered beyond recognition. Look at how people perceive the interactions between two groups, and you'll find the source of their
human-kind beliefs.

The Robbers Cave camp was the greatest test of this idea. The
twenty-two boys from Oklahoma City schools were bused to the
camp in the Sans Bois mountains, in two groups of eleven each. All

were white, Protestant, middle-class kids with no obvious problems, as similar to one another as could be.

The bus was late on June 19, when the first group gathered, and kind-consciousness being ever active in the human mind, the waiting boys had already begun sorting themselves, asking, for instance, if "us southsiders" could stay together. When the boys got off their bus, though, they discovered that they were all going to live in one bunkhouse. As they showed the boys the ballfields and the camp's one mess hall and canteen, the "counselors" (Sherif and his collaborators) made sure that the children knew they had the run of the place. When the boys in the other group arrived the next day, they found a different bunkhouse, and the experimenters saw to it that they didn't cross paths with the first contingent.

The boys spent their first week exploring, choosing places to swim and things to do. They also — automatically, and without anyone's finding it odd — created "our" ways of doing things. Each group settled on a favorite swimming spot, its preferred route to it, its style of dealing with scrapes and sprains. By the end of the week the boys agreed that they should have a name for their band so they could stencil it on their T-shirts and hats. The first group picked the name "Rattlers" and spent long hours working out what its symbol would be and how to imprint it on the shirts. Though the boys already looked alike, it was important to them to look even more so.

After supper on the sixth day of camp, after they'd stenciled their emblem, the Rattlers learned they were not alone. They could hear other boys in the distance, playing on the ballfield — boys who, also on their own, had invented folkways and given themselves a name: the Eagles. When the Rattlers heard unknown voices, "The immediate reaction was to 'run them off' and 'challenge' them," Sherif reported. Over on the other side of the woods, where the Eagles were also learning that there were other boys around, one of the Eagles gave the adults a nice demonstration of how the human kind code works.

To place an unfamiliar person, that code has to begin with what it already knows: the human kinds that are already on its map. When a feeling of fear or anger about that stranger needs explaining, then, it's no surprise that the code suggests human kinds that prompt such feelings — even if they don't make sense in the new context. In 1950s Oklahoma, for instance, a white boy's code for "not our kind" included politics; bad people were Communists. The code also included men who didn't fit the standards for how men should act; bad people were sissies and cheats. And in that segregated society, the map included race.

That's the code the Eagle boy used. Just who, he wanted to know, were "those nigger campers" he could hear but not see? He would soon learn that the enemy campers were white kids, just like him. This did not change his attitude toward the other group, because he was not using human kinds to guide his feelings. He was using feelings to guide his choice of human kinds. Each boyish tribe's enemies had to stay enemies, despite new facts. So when it turned out that everyone involved was white, this boy would abandon racial categories and use others to explain their feelings.

There's nothing here peculiar to kids or summer camps. Sometimes people perceive that they're different from some other kind of person and feel threatened. But brain circuits work in both directions: often, people feel threatened first and then perceive a difference. For example, hundreds of thousands of people, perhaps as many as 2 million, were killed, supposedly for being Communists or Communist sympathizers, during Indonesia's 1965 coup d'état and its aftermath. Many of these people, perhaps even the majority, weren't leftists. But they were dead. An explanation was needed. They were not killed because they were deemed Communists; they were deemed Communists because they had been killed.

The slurs the boys of Robbers Cave would soon hurl at their "enemies" were like that — in fact, "Communist" was one, along with "sissy," "cheat," "baby," and "dirty shirt." To explain the feelings of threat and competition that Sherif's manipulations had created, the boys summoned every undesirable human kind a ten-year-old white boy could think of in their time and place and tried to fit it onto their rivals.

Freud arrogantly called this kind of line drawing "the narcissism of minor differences": the boys stretched to set each tribe apart precisely because they were so alike. The arrogance lies in the assumption that someone else — Gaylin, maybe, or Freud — can decide *which* differences are minor and which are not. Today Freud's spat with his rival Carl Jung, and the contrast between his Viennese milieu and that of provincial Austrians, would strike most people as trivial. I doubt he saw them so. His catchy phrase invites you to condescend to people whose differences don't matter to you, letting you imagine that this gives you insight into their problems. But it doesn't. When it comes to human kinds, all differences are *equal:* equally minor, because we can find differences so easily between any two people; and equally grave, because once a difference is taken seriously, it has power to alter thoughts and feelings.

As they tried to make familiar human kinds work in this new environment, the boys were also elaborating the new categories. That involved pressing even chance events into service.

One boy's impulse to jump in the creek with no suit made nude swimming the Eagle way. Another boy hurt his toe swimming and didn't mention it; that was enough to make toughing it out a Rattler custom. An hour or two with no swear words in the air was turned into the solemn belief that clean language was part of the essence of Eaglehood. Meanwhile, the Rattlers cursed a blue streak. That was the Rattler ethos, handed down, like Rattler emblems and Rattler songs, from the dawn of their seven-day history.

The newborn categories quickly suppressed alternatives — other ways of sorting people that, true as they might have been elsewhere, were not relevant in camp. Among the Rattlers, the southsider clique dissolved. Among both bands, talk of "our" swimming spot and "our" field sprung up only after the boys knew there was another gang nearby. This feeling extended to everyone; fishermen and hikers passing through the state park would also cause the boys to fret about interference with "our" territory. Their passionate sense of Eagleness and Rattlerdom was marking the entire human world. Innocent adults with fishing rods were not welcome in the Rattler or Eagle empire.

Sherif had been one of the first psychologists to document the power of these conventions, which he called social norms. Twenty years before Robbers Cave, he had established how easy it was to get students to change their perceptions of facts, like the length of a printed line or the amount of wavering they saw in a projected pin-point of light. All they had to learn was that their answer was not near that of other people in the experiment, and most people's per-ception changed to line up with the group average.

At Robbers Cave, he saw social norms being born. "Our" swim-ming hole; "our" attitude to swearing. The boys soon proved willing to force these new folkways on any nonconformists. For example, one of the Rattlers didn't want to wear the newly minted Rattler symbols on his shirt. Another boy told him he could not play in any games without a proper Rattler emblem.

The most important part of this human-kind story is the part you don't remark on. No one wonders why the kid did not stick to his taste in shirts. Our brain codes fill in the missing facts. We all know how it feels to need to fit in with the family, the kids at school, the people at work. Sherif doesn't even need to spell out that the boy gave in. He just turns up in the game, and we know what happened. Of course he put on the shirt. Who wouldn't?

I am not arguing that pressure to belong is always bad.

One of the Rattler boys jumped into the creek after several days of not swimming, to cheers from the others. They yelled that he should *dive*. For two minutes, he hesitated on the diving board while a circle of Rattlers in the water called out encouragement. He plunged in. That made another boy take a swim for the first time. Then he too dived. Then one of the boys who swam but had been afraid to dive also climbed to the board and took his turn. Being Rattlers had forced these boys to change, but it did not diminish them. For these three, at least, the pressure of being Rattlers propelled them into a summer flight, through warm air, into cool water. Alone, without the de-mands of their new tribe, they could not have done it.

Throughout that first week, then, the emotional force that crack-led around the campers was desire — to be part of a "good" kind and to avoid belonging to the bad ones. This desire was strong enough to make the boys want to have instant traditions and symbols and, more important, to make each one willing to curb his behavior to fit these new social norms. It was an emotion about the self. Each boy felt this about his person and his body. The boys were desperate, now, to be worthy Rattlers (or Eagles) and to see the Eagles (or Rattlers) triumph.

Once the boys had formed the tribes Sherif expected, he devoted the camp's second week to their bilateral relations. He wanted them to go sour. The counselors set up a tournament of combined games — baseball, tug of war, and tent pitching, plus events whose scores the experimenters could manipulate to keep the suspense up, like cabin inspections, skit acting and song singing, and a treasure hunt. Each boy on the team that won would get the sort of swag boys of the time enjoyed: penknives, medals, and trophies.

Baseball came first. The Rattlers arrived for the game on what they considered "their" ballfield. The Eagles approached, waving their sacred flag and singing. It only took a moment for one of the Eagles to call a Rattler a "dirty shirt," and then all was razz. The Rattlers, for instance, called one chubby Eagle "Tubby," "Fatty," and (here comes race thinking again) "Little Black Sambo."

The Rattlers won the game. By dinnertime, the Eagles were saying they preferred not to eat with those Rattlers. The next day, after the Rattlers again won the main event, a tug of war, more than one weepy Eagle talked about leaving camp. What was the use? The Rattlers were bigger. And because a couple of Eagles had left with homesickness in week 1, there were only nine Eagles to the eleven enemies. The camp was rigged. It was hopeless. Unfair!

By this time, both groups had clear leaders. The Eagle chiefs pulled their band back together by starting a war. They stole the Rattlers' flag from the ballfield, set fire to it, and put the charred remains back up. Eagle morale improved. Rattler vexation rose.

After that, Sherif writes drily, it was unnecessary for the counselors to introduce any more incentives. The next evening, after the Eagles enjoyed their first victory in the games, they came back from dinner to find their cabin had been Rattler raided, its screens torn and its beds turned over. They wanted to retaliate. When the talk turned to gathering rocks to stone the Rattlers, the adults shut down the cabin for the night.

And so it went, eye for eye and tooth for tooth between the two little cultures, until the week's end. After the Eagles won the tournament and got the prizes, the Rattlers struck hard. They raided their enemies' cabin, messing up beds, piling up gear, setting boats loose from the dock — and stealing the most prized of the trophies for the winning team, their knives. The Eagles came back from dinner, found the theft, and rushed to war.

Ten feet in front of the Eagles cabin, both groups made their stand. You want your precious knives, said the Rattlers, then get down on your bellies and crawl, and we'll give them back. Kids from both sides began punching one another, and the adults again moved in before any boy got hurt.

The week had been rich in human-kind thoughts and feelings. Boys held their noses when they were near their enemies. They asked for separate but equal fireworks for the Fourth of July. On a written test to measure how their new human-kind feelings affected their perceptions, all the boys said their team tossed beanbags farther than they really had, while the other team covered less distance than it really had. One Rattler abruptly dropped his pencil in midtest; he'd noticed it was Eagle brand.

Fourteen days after they had arrived as strangers, then, these look-alike boys, all born around the same time, from look-alike households, had turned into two exclusive, disdainful tribes, yelling "dirty bums" and "sissies" at their neighbors whenever their paths crossed. It had all been "experimentally produced from scratch," as Sherif put it.

So far, so bad. At the end of week 2, though, Sherif and his crew were only two-thirds done with their experimental anthropology. It would be a mistake to jump to conclusions about the work at this point. And who would want to?

Here's who: thinkers who believe in the "original sin" view of human nature. The cognitive scientist and best-selling evolutionary psychologist Steven Pinker, for example, was apparently determined to shoehorn Sherif into a Freudian view that, as he puts it, people are innately "a nasty business." In *How the Mind Works,* Pinker depicts Sherif's project as a sort of Oklahoma *Lord of the Flies.* The psychologist Judith Rich Harris, who has many interesting things to say about groupishness, is fairer to Sherif, but also stresses tribal violence.

Actually, the only original sin in Pinker's account is the omission of Robbers Cave's third and final week. Those who spin the case for pessimism think they are part of the solution to the world's problems (hard-nosed realism and all that) but the only way to shoehorn Sherif into their belief system was to ignore the point of his work.

After millennia of Judeo-Christian and Islamic tradition, it is all too easy for people to think that "good" emotions are fragile and "bad" ones are strong. So decades of peace in Yugoslavia from 1945 to 1990 and Rwanda until 1957 are treated as a fluke, while later persecution and genocide supposedly boiled up or broke out or came to the surface.

In this, Le Bon in his time, Freud in his, and Darwinian pessimists in ours all get a free ride from religious tradition: their views feel right because they fit what these institutions have taught for centuries. Conservative Christian Darwinians recognize this affinity.

Pinker has said we must not reject the notion of human nastiness just because the thought is unpleasant. But it is equally important not to accept it just because it is familiar. It feels like something we have heard all our lives. But is it true?

Muzafer Sherif did not think so. The central insight of his work is that kind sight is a servant, not a master. We think in human kinds because of what we see around us and what we feel, inside us, that we want to do. In contrast, if you assume the default setting on a person is "evil," you can expect, eight times out of ten, to see an obedient slave of this drive to do bad. (The other two times you'll explain as the product of a fragile civilization.) Whatever you want to call the source of badness — original sin, or the id, or selfish genes — it should prevail, most of the time, in most places. But if human-kind emotions track relationships between different human kinds, then those emotions will change with the relationships. Sherif reasoned that his food fighting, kicking, shoving, jeering campers felt as they did because they saw the relationship between their groups as competitive.

If he were wrong, and theories of original sin were right, then the boys' raiding and sneering would continue until someone stomped on their feelings in the name of civilization. The last phase of Robbers Cave, the one Pinker doesn't mention (and the one Sherif called the main objective), was a plot to disprove the original-sin model, getting the boys to *abandon* their tribal divisions and perceive themselves as one big happy twenty-kid entity.

That plot was a total success.

Its first step, at the beginning of week 3, was blocking the faucet leading from the camp's one water tank with a sack. Both sides pitched in with tools and suggestions to unblock the spigot. Some boys drifted away from the ongoing work to catch lizards or carve wooden whistles, and the adults noticed that they didn't avoid members of the "enemy" group. Still, at dinner that night, a threatened Rattler-Eagle food fight took place as promised. The next morning, when the Rattlers learned they might go on an overnight campout at a lake, their top dog asked, "Are those damn Eagles going?" On the other side of the divide, another boy was asking, "Do we have to do it with the Rattlers?"

Sherif and his team then introduced another goal that all the boys would have to work on in common: a movie. The adults explained that renting *Treasure Island* would require them to come up with some money; the camp couldn't cover the expense without their help. What should they do? Make the other gang pay, said the boys. After some to-ing and fro-ing, though, one of the Eagles suggested that each group pay an equal share and the adults the balance. The boys voted as a single group to accept this idea. Yet they were still thinking tribally, putting their kind-perceptions above emotions about individuals or "all of us kids." As the boys did the math, they realized that each of the nine Eagles would have to contribute 39 cents while each of the eleven Rattlers could get by giving 31. As usual, it's important to think about the dog that didn't bark: no boy wanted to change the plan. What struck them as fair was that each *band* was equal, not each camper.

The boys enjoyed the movie, seated by groups but as a single audience. From then on, the food fights gave way to a treaty. They would take turns going in to eat first — Rattlers for breakfast, Eagles for lunch, and so on.

Later that day, Sherif's team took the boys on the overnight camping trip, at a lake some sixty miles away, and staged some more predicaments. First was a "breakdown" of the truck that was sup-

posed to go pick up food for their lunch. All twenty boys pitched in
to get the truck rolling, until the adult at the wheel announced that
they'd gotten it started. Then it turned out that the food, when fetched,
needed to be unpacked and set up. Cans needed to be opened, meat
cut, melons sliced. After discussing which group would be in charge
the boys got the work done together. As they ate, one Eagle said to
a Rattler: "You never thought we'd be eating together?" The other
boy just laughed.

Sherif had given each group their tents and poles in a mix, so that
each band had to ask the other for missing pieces. This went
smoothly. After their meal, they went swimming in the lake and had
a cheerful splash-fight. Then they made dinner, ate, and cleaned up,
with no regard to group lines. Neither the splashing nor the eating
was divided into Rattler and Eagle.

The next day Sherif's team staged another mechanical breakdown, so that only one truck was available to take the boys to the
Arkansas state line, which they all wanted to see. This was a moment
of truth. They could stay true to their Rattler and Eagle loyalties and
make two separate sixty-mile round-trips. Or they could decide to
go as one. Sherif was not letting them slip their boundaries by accident. They had to choose.

It was quite a debate, because their feelings were now mixed, but in
the end the boys who wanted to make separate trips or skip the whole
thing gave way to the ones who wanted to share the truck. On the way
to Arkansas, the boys traded stories about the raids and fights, like veterans of a long-ago war. Slights and attacks that had made them furious before made them laugh and brag now. Then one boy started
whistling. He chose a song bound to appeal past their Rattler and Eagle loyalties: "The Star Spangled Banner." The boys sang for about half
an hour, politely alternating Eagle songs and Rattler songs.

At supper the boys once again entered as groups and sat according
to their lines, but conversations were friendly. That last night, the
boys decided they wanted to go to the camp's corral, where they
roasted marshmallows. Then each group performed skits for the
other. The next day was the last of the camp. At breakfast and lunch,
the boys sat higgledy-piggledy, with no regard for Rattlerdom and

Eagleness. The frequent opinion polls he was taking also told Sherif that attitudes were changing: overwhelmingly hostile sentiments about "the others" had been replaced by overwhelmingly positive feelings. Meanwhile, the bands' ratings of their members had gotten somewhat less enthusiastic. It was as if the need to puff up their members had quieted, along with the urge to disparage the enemy. When they took seats on the bus for the trip home that afternoon, the boys ignored Rattler-Eagle lines completely.

They stopped for snacks on the way, and the Rattlers spent five dollars of their prize money on malteds — for all Eagles as well as all Rattlers. Once again, the math of the situation tells the story: if they had been feeling as they had on the night of the movie, yearning to do right by their tribe, they could have had more food for all the Rattlers and nothing for the Eagles. As they headed back to their homes, those lines had ceased to matter.

It is a strange experience to read about these passions, welling up from the shallows of little boys' tiffs. How familiar it all feels; even as their days proved how quickly human-kind feeling could change, the boys thought and felt as if those kinds were spiritually deep and practically immovable. Who would have thought an Eagle would ever eat with a Rattler?

Still, this is not why I've gone into such detail here about the neglected conclusion of Sherif's experimental anthropology. The important point is that Sherif's last phase yielded results that were just as dramatic as the earlier ones, which are overemphasized by Pinker and other pessimists. Muzafer Sherif was able to create a reconciliation with no more difficulty than he had created the two tribes and their hostility.

Do circumstances cause people's perceptions about human kinds to change? The answer at Robbers Cave was yes. Do human-kind feelings have a particular direction, then — do they tend to the bad (as Pinker tells us) or, for that matter, to the good? The answer at Robbers Cave was no.

Of course, most people don't create tribal bonds from scratch. Sherif's kids were very much alike, so he didn't learn anything about what would have happened if the boys' new tribes had conflicted with the ones they used at home. What might have happened if these white boys with their racial slurs at the ready had found that half their new cabinmates were black? The Robbers Cave results suggest that what shaped each boy's tribal sense there was not what he *was,* but what he was *doing.* Perhaps what we learn from parents and institutions about "our kind" can't compete with the lessons of our own experience. But Sherif had no evidence one way or the other for that.

Someone else did, though. In 1963, Lutfy N. Diab tried to repeat the Robbers Cave procedure with eleven-year-old boys in Beirut. Eight were Christians, and ten Muslims. Not surprisingly, given the historic tensions between religious communities in Lebanon, fighting broke out between the two teams of campers, the Blue Ghosts and the Red Genies. After three Genies threatened a Ghost with knives stolen from the camp kitchen, Diab decided he had to break the camp up without reaching the reconciliation stage.

The striking fact about his camp, though, is that the fighting was not along religious lines. The Blue Ghosts consisted of five Muslims and four Christians; so did the Red Genies. The three Genies with the knives were all Christians, but so was their Blue Ghost victim. Fourteen of the eighteen campers had come from fiercely religious schools, yet in the camp, separated from the outside world, when they could easily have chosen to see themselves as Christian versus Muslim, they chose instead Ghost versus Genie.

A few years later, a Dutch experiment found a milder, but similar effect. There, researchers created two teams, one of which consisted of members who said they supported legalizing euthanasia, while the other was split into people on both sides of that issue. When they were forced to choose whether to help a fellow team member who disagreed violently with them or instead to help a nonteam member who was on their side politically, people chose the teammate over the political ally.

In the fifty years since Sherif worked at Robbers Cave, scholars in many fields have caught up with him. Historians, anthropologists, and political scientists no longer flinch at the thought that human kinds depend on people's goals and circumstances. They have recog-

nized, too, that there is nothing modern or novel about this phenomenon. In 1481, for example, a Jewish rabbi recorded in his diary
that he had befriended his Christian fellow passengers on a ship from
Palestine to Italy. He and his friends were taken for Christian merchants, he wrote. But "after they heard that I was a Jew, they were
much astounded, but still, *because of their former love for me* they could
not change their attitude."

The recurrent principle here is that there are circumstances in
which face-to-face experience with people overcomes doctrines
about our bonds to people we never met. One historian, David
Nirenberg, found this phenomenon in records from the medieval
kingdoms that would later unite into Spain. There, he writes, "despite
repeated ecclesiastical condemnation, Christians, Muslims and Jews
drank together, gambled together, went to war together, lived in the
same neighborhoods (sometimes in the same house), established business partnerships, engaged in all forms of commercial exchange, even
watched each other's religious ceremonies and processions."

Nirenberg also cites the report of a bailiff in the town of Daroca,
who complained that a Muslim bandit in his prison had been sprung
by a band of Christians. When the bailiff told the gang's leader that
he shouldn't include Muslims in his crew, the man replied that "he
would form factions with Muslims as well as Jews, to the displeasure
of anyone who said otherwise." Fourteenth-century Spain was a land
where Jews brought their complaints against fellow Jews to Christian
law courts. It was a land where the Confraternity of St. Eloy, a union
of Muslim and Christian blacksmiths, donated a candle to the Virgin
Mary every week, and where Christian and Jewish butchers formed
associations to buy and pasture animals together.

Similar in its themes is Peter Sahlins's history of the Cerdagne region in the Pyrenees, through which the boundary between modern
France and Spain has run. Sahlins describes how the newer categories, "French" and "Spanish," overlapped with older loyalties to
village, quarter, province, region, and Catalan ethnicity. Historians
and sociologists used to follow a model which predicts that identities
should be stronger the closer they are to home — that village trumps
valley, which trumps region, which trumps nation, and so on up.

Instead, Sahlins writes, loyalties in the Cerdagne shift among these levels, depending on circumstances and the goals of the people involved, and this has been the case for at least three hundred years.

The work of these contemporary historians feels different from what most nonprofessionals think of as history, in which big, collective entities like France and Spain interact, carrying all their people with them. That's a picture of tribes and nations and religions shaping individuals; the theme of the newer work is that people use identity, not the other way around.

That approach is even more widespread among political scientists, whose interest is in the way concepts of human groups are used for political ends. David D. Laitin of Stanford proposes that ethnic behavior in politics ought to be understood as a form of rational choice: individuals, trying to advance their interests as best as they can, choose among possible ethnic stances according to how well the choice serves those interests. We all say what we need to say (that we're permitted to say) to get ahead. After all, Laitin says, the rigid ethnic boundaries in which we moderns live are "fairly recent inventions."

Evidence from all over the world suggests that people make creative use of whatever human-kind concepts they can. An anthropologist found this was the case in parts of Nepal, where individuals and even entire villages readily change their ethnic affiliation and their position in the caste system. It was the case in East Africa, where Donald Campbell, whose ideas about entatitivity I've mentioned, went with another social psychologist, Marilynn Brewer, to do research on ethnicity in the 1960s.

Campbell and Brewer were surprised to find that "which differences are emphasized under what circumstances appears to be flexible and context dependent; this flexibility permits individuals to mobilize different group identities for different purposes."

Meanwhile, anthropologists were reporting that the entities didn't have the kind of neat edges implied by phrases like "Pathan culture" or "Ibo folkways." In the villages and countrysides where they made their observations, they found that, to name a few examples, there were circumstances under which people in the Kachin Hills of Burma changed their ethnic identity, and members of Pakistan's Pathan eth-

nic group would become Baluchi if they found they could not succeed in a life lived by Pathan rules. Today's anthropological texts are
filled with accounts of how people change their group identities — in
order to make a living; in order to get power and status, or simply to
live another day. The title of a review in the journal *Current Anthropology* sums it up: "Creating Culture through Choosing Heritage."

Sherif's contemporaries in the academy were also, for the most
part, unaware of the way mental codes work, with perceptions,
thoughts, and emotions all interacting, shaping one another. They
thought the human race consists of a few obvious kinds whose traits
we perceive directly, no matter where we stand and what we're feeling. Sherif was far ahead of his time in thinking his way free of that
assumption. His campers perceived the Rattler and Eagle traits they
needed to perceive, changing them as the Rattler-Eagle relationship
changed.

Demonstrating that, Sherif and his colleagues anticipated a key
tenet of current cognitive science: that our sense of reality is created
by the mind. And they showed how our sense of human kinds con-
tributes to that creation, marking some people as teammates and
others as enemies, making those labels feel as real as sunshine and
as accurate as two plus two equals four. Most amazingly of all, they
showed that this human-kind filter on reality works according to its
own rules. That's why the experimenters could manipulate the boys.
It's also why others, throughout history, have succeeded in manipulating millions, to much more sinister ends.

Nine

Them, We Burn

From what sort of education will this first form of the moral life
spring?

   We acquire habits of conduct, not by constructing a way of living
upon rules or precepts learned by heart and subsequently practiced,
but by living with people who habitually behave in a certain manner: we acquire habits of conduct in the same way as we acquire our
native language.

— MICHAEL OAKESHOTT

How do Americans get around all their constitutional safeguards and
repress rivals, strangers and scary others? Morality. We are bound to
honor our fellow citizens and their rights, unless the neighbors turn
out to be bad.

Then they can be — and often are — stripped of their lives, their
liberty and their legally acquired property.

— JAMES MORONE

In early 2003, *Paddler,* a magazine for kayakers and canoeists, published a small photo of smiling young people standing on a beach.

Scattered around were equipment, wet suits, and tents. It was a typical picture of a wilderness trip, except for one detail: they were naked.

This wasn't obvious, though, because everyone was artfully arranged behind bags, equipment, and one another. They weren't showing as much flesh as the typical billboard or magazine advertisement for a line of lingerie.

Nonetheless, some readers were furious. In its March-April issue, the magazine published a letter from one. He was trying to raise his children right and encourage their interest in sports, and he didn't want his kids to see such things. He was canceling his subscription.

I don't think he meant photos of sexual behavior, because none was visible in the picture. Nor could he have meant displays of body parts usually kept private, because none of those could be seen either. What he did not want his children to see, I suspect, was something more abstract: people breaking a rule.

Adults everywhere reserve certain kinds of talk and activity for themselves. Some of it would be harmful to children, like drinking whiskey or smoking tobacco or having sex. Much of "grown-up" behavior, though, isn't like that. The urge to protect children from bad language and disturbing thoughts, the reason we have family hours for television shows and ratings for movies, is rooted in the desire to teach: we want them to learn the rules and respect them. We don't want them to see that the rules don't always apply, or don't apply to some people, or that there are people living nearby who don't bother with them.

This desire to transmit regulations appears to be a universal human trait, found in all societies. Some anthropologists believe it is a sign of an important link: between, on the one hand, that part of the cortex that notices and obeys rules and, on the other hand, the cultural authorities who devise laws for "our people" to follow. It's the connection, in other words, between mental codes that support vision, language, and music, and societal codes — of conduct, of law, of honor.

I have mentioned that every mind creates categories out of its experience. Since a lot of experience is the same for everyone, though, there's a great deal of agreement between us: my experience of fire is not exactly the same as yours, but it's not that different. Our bodies and our brains, tuned to learn things that keep us alive, have absorbed the lesson that fire is hot and that it burns, so when you tell me about a fire, I can be pretty sure we're talking about the same concept.

Societal codes must work the same way: what assures us that your idea of honor or fair dealing is the same as mine is shared experience, which taught us both the same lessons as we figured out the world. It makes sense then that brain regions engaged when we figure out natural laws — like fire is hot — are also engaged when people deal with social laws, like "Say thank you when someone gives you something."

The catch, though, is that human laws don't get assistance from our experience of the natural world. Everyone's experience of life is guaranteed to cause him or her to create concepts of fire and heat and burning that will match other people's. This is not true of concepts like *clean, respectable,* and *honorable.* To make people get the same lessons out of their experience of life — to make each individual's brain write the same code — that experience must be engineered. Just as a child learns a language because he hears it and doesn't hear others, so that child learns particular rules for being a person because they're what he sees people do. Life could teach him other lessons; instead of learning that men and women are equal, for instance, he might learn that they aren't. But alternative rules have been excluded from his day-to-day life.

This engineering of experience is what we call culture. Ethnic, religious, national, or corporate, it's what allows a human kind to teach newcomers how "our people" solve the problems of life. It represents a tradeoff: your culture excludes experiences that don't fit, that might teach useful lessons. The compensating gain is that, thanks to your culture, you did not have to figure out the world from scratch.

After all, learning what foods were safe to eat, and how to keep warm in cold weather, and how to get along with others around you would have taken a lot of time and effort and might well have killed you. Culture restricts your perceptions, but in exchange it gives you the benefit of others' knowledge. As the anthropologist Naomi Quinn of Duke University has put it, these codes are answers to repeated problems of life: "Cultural models of this kind evolve because culture and brain together can achieve shared solutions to human tasks that the individual brain alone is ill-suited to perform."

Among those jobs is managing one's self. That's evident from the difference between adult emotions and those of very small children. Adults weep for serious, tragic experiences; toddlers cry if they have to leave the playground. Adults laugh at funny things; kids will giggle over dumb, embarrassing stuff. Though kids can feel grief and joy almost from day one, growing up means learning what to feel grief and joy *about*. Children don't know that falling-down wails are appropriate for national catastrophe, but not for failing to score a Mars bar. They must be taught. As they grow, they learn how to attach their emotions to other people's sense of what is fitting, which means they learn "what we do" — the rules followed by the human kinds among which they live. A child who fails to pick up these rules will spend life trapped in the little prison of the self, pushed here and there by strong emotions, without a guide to say which ones make sense to other people.

This isn't to say that everyone everywhere learns the same specific rules. The wake appropriate to an Irish funeral would be anathema in Syria; healthy sexual experience in the eyes of most Swedes is bad conduct to most mainland Chinese. What's common to everyone is the ability to seek "our" rules and learn them.

A child in any society is a tiny foreigner. Adults laugh at her cute mistakes of behavior, sigh with impatience when she tries to do the impossible, explain patiently how to get along in "our" world. Like a grown foreigner, the child is intelligent, eager, willing to learn our ways but not yet fully educated in the sounds and motions that signal "I am one of you." The child cries tragically because it's time to leave the park and go home; she hasn't learned how we match emotions to occasions. Or a foreigner says "Wassup?" to his new boss, because he doesn't yet know that "we" talk that way to friends, but not to higher-status people. Stranger and child are both probational people, learning how to be part of Us.

Compared to chimpanzee troops and wolf packs, human societies accept new immigrants easily. Part of the reason could be this universal experience of learning culture in childhood. We have all been instructed in "how we do things," because we have all been children.

And almost everyone has taught one of these little strangers something about "our ways."

Quinn has pointed out how much culture depends on this innate knack for learning "our" rules. Though child-rearing methods differ from place to place, she says, they all serve one purpose: shaping the child's life so rules are easy to spot and master. Parenting strategies all "engineer the child's experience," Quinn argues, so that the local culture feels right and obvious.

That engineering makes constancy for the child. The codes he is learning — say please, say thanks, don't hit — are convincing because parents create a world in which the rules always work. It's much easier to figure out a game if everyone plays the same way.

Parents the world over also link their lessons to strong emotions, Quinn says. As I've mentioned, emotions tell what about daily life is worth noticing and remembering. This was the point of Antonio Damasio's results in the card-game experiment: people notice patterns in their experience and work out the underlying rule, as his patients did in the card game. But without strong feelings to say "Mark this!" those people had no motivation to act on the rules they'd perceived.

The emotional manipulations of child raising, like the rules, are not all the same in all places and times (many Americans praise, many Chinese shame) but, Quinn argues, their effect is uniform: they establish the connection between "our" way of doing things and intense feelings.

Strong emotions mark the rules as important. Boys don't cry. No one works on the Sabbath. Women cover their hair in the street. The young child soon learns that such patterns are not just regularities in life, like dark following sunset. Instead, these have a personal bite; when a child disrupts them, adults (and other kids) make sure that he or she feels shame, guilt, fear, and pain. It's consistency in child-rearing that makes "our way" feel natural — as if the rules for "please" and "thank you" were built into the fabric of reality, like the rules that tell you fire is hot. But it's shame and pain, or joy and love, that mark these childhood rules as "urgent."

So child-rearing practices teach that there are learnable rules for "our way of doing things" and also ensure kids know that breaking the rules is painful. There is another aspect, though, also found, Quinn says, in all child-rearing cultures: a child who is learning cultural codes is told constantly that he is being good or bad. In other words, a kid's experiences, as engineered by his caretakers, doesn't just tell him the rules are natural and that he'll suffer for going astray. They also tell him that the rules define who is good.

In this way, practical guidelines for life — this is how to speak to your elders, don't forget to brush your teeth — take on the emotional aura of morality. The conscious mind knows there is a difference between a rule like "we drink tea with breakfast" and one that states "thou shalt not kill." Yet any traveler knows that the feel of moral rules rubs off on the merely practical. For example, if you're used to coffee, that breakfast tea feels *wrong*. What is different, what violates your expectations for how people act, strikes you, however mildly, as just "not right."

If a child's brain needs a clear, constant environment in order to learn the mental code that is "the way of our people," then it's a problem when the child sees someone not obeying the rule. And if a child must learn that it is bad not to follow our rules and good to obey them, there's potential for confusion if the people across the street are ignoring them.

No wonder we care about other people's morals — even those of people we will never meet. For the brain to learn the codes of conduct that "our kind" use to get through life, it wants to live in an environment that confirms that lesson.

A German colleague of Quinn's told her a story. He was riding his bicycle across the street against a red light (rarely done in Germany, but there were no cars on the road). He heard a shout, doubled back, and came upon a dog and its very angry owner. "Can't you see," the man said, "that I'm trying to teach my dog to wait for the light?"

Later in 2003, in its July-August issue, *Paddler* published another letter, from a reader offended that others were offended by the photograph. What harm did the photo do? "Just go on to the next page," this letter writer suggested. For people who say their moral values include individual freedom and diversity, this is a common reaction. They're the sort of people who would say, "Why do I have to be involved in teaching your dog to mind the stoplights? Mind your own business!"

But those of us who think we are immune to the mix of moral and human-kind feeling are deluding ourselves. If you aren't offended by photos of naked people or by bikers who run red lights, it doesn't mean you lack moral outrage. Are you fine with eating dogs? Aborting a female fetus because sons are more desirable? How about incest between consenting adults, vasectomized and ligated to make sure there are no offspring? If you have no problem with the incestuous couple (a rare response), would you shrug off the news that they had been sentenced to death by stoning?

Even self-consciously unjudgmental people must judge. (Most tolerant people cannot stand intolerance, for example.) Whatever your moral beliefs, they will bring you to the point where you must say of someone, "No, that is not acceptable." So any ethical code automatically leads you to think about an especially important human kind: moral people.

Now, you have learned the rules of the game for your kind — the way "we" do things. (Whether "we" is defined as a religion, a nation, an ethnic group, or an ideology is not relevant to the point.) As Quinn notes, the people who raised you made those rules convincing by linking them to words about right and wrong. That special human kind, the good people, overlaps with another: *our* people.

Morality is for us "good people," however we define "good," and anyone who seems good must be at least a possible member of our kind. Which has been lucky for the human race; we can accept strangers with strange ways if they seem morally sound. Yet the logic also works in the other direction: out there, we feel, are people we cannot ever welcome. It's not their accents or their taste in music; it's our sense that their morals aren't acceptable.

Obviously, there are human kinds without this aura of ethics about them, like shy people or women on the 8:15 ferry. In fact, it's likely that *most* human kinds feel morally weightless when we think about them — including human kinds like African Americans, liberals, and Muslims. As general terms, these concepts have no connection to our bodies and our feelings. However, once a human kind actually affects the experiences that most interest your brain — your individual life, in your own particular body — then moral emotions are engaged. The person who says "Buddhists" and means a word he read in a book is not using the same concept as a person who uses that same word to mean people he actually met every day in a nation filled with Buddhists.

The difference between a concept and a human kind in actual experience has come to interest social psychologists. In one recent study, the University of Virginia psychologist Jonathan Haidt and students Evan Rosenberg and Holly Hom surveyed thirty-two members of an all-male "mostly white, not very liberal" campus fraternity about how various traits would affect their desire to admit a new member.

The members actually liked the prospect of admitting men from different ethnic, religious, and social classes into their club. But the men were much less willing to admit hypothetical candidates who differed on what Haidt calls the "politico-moral" categories — students with different attitudes toward sexual ethics or drug use, for example. Not surprisingly, the fraternity brothers said they'd have less trouble accepting people with different moral attitudes in a seminar than in a frat house where they lived. Shared rules for life matter more among roommates than they do among people meeting in a neutral setting twice a week.

These results hint at how human-kind psychology will turn out to be different from today's commonsense picture. We want to talk about how each Joe or Jane has feelings toward each human kind — how Joe is prejudiced against, say, Lerians. But as Sherif showed, human-kind feelings and even human-kind perceptions depend on the situations in which people find themselves. If Joe should have to cope in a situation where nationality is irrelevant, he might not even notice who is Lerian and who is not. Or he might exempt a friend from his general notion, as this short verse describes:

> Phokylides says this: "Lerians are rotten." Not
> "This one's rotten, not that one" — no, the lot.
> "Except Prokles." And Prokles? He's Lerian.

There is nothing modern about this sort of thinking: this poem is well over two thousand years old.

These attitudes can only be compatible in the same head if this single word "Lerian" actually stands for two different concepts: (1) the general abstract notion of Lerian is not the same as (2) the concept of Lerians derived from their contact with an actual person's life.

This difference — between human kinds we experience ourselves and human kinds we only hear about — may account for the difficulties of a beautiful theory in twentieth-century efforts to reduce prejudice. Fifty years ago, social psychologists had high expectations for a proposition by Gordon Allport, a Harvard psychologist and the author of a highly influential book, *The Nature of Prejudice.* Allport proposed that prejudices could be reduced if people from different human kinds met as equals, had some shared goal to work for, and had support — or at least no opposition — from the law.

This "contact hypothesis" contributed to the U.S. Supreme Court's 1954 decision in *Brown v. Board of Education,* which declared racial segregation to be unconstitutional. It's also the root of the argument in the more recent decision by which the court upheld a system of affirmative action to promote admission of nonwhites into the University of Michigan Law School. Allport never said mere "goodwill contact" could overcome prejudice; in fact, he said exactly the opposite, warning that successful contact required the conditions he specified. Nonetheless, his idea led to today's conventional wisdom that contact among different human kinds — diversity — is in itself good for mind and soul.

Yet scholars now agree the contact hypothesis is a muddle. Some studies suggest that prejudice goes down with contact, but others find the opposite. Actual contact sometimes makes people *more* prejudiced. On many American college campuses, for example, the emphasis on diversity has led students to join one of these diverse human kinds and shun much contact with the others.

The problem, I think, is that Allport's hypothesis assumes stable, unchanging human kinds: it expects that people have a fixed idea of race and that they apply that idea in the same way, at all times, in all places. But human-kind perceptions emerge from the ever-changing circumstances of life. Walking down the street, I might be a man on one corner, a white guy two blocks later, and a middle-aged person a few streets farther down.

The contact hypothesis ignores each person's mental churning through different possible human kinds. The theory can only be proved or disproved by measuring the prejudice that Group X feels toward Group Y before and after contact. It's not too surprising, then, that the theory is mired in arguments over what terms like *prejudice* and *contact* mean.

More successful than telling children not to be prejudiced against, say, the Christian kids, is persuading them not to *see* Christian kids, because another set of human kinds — say, Blue Ghosts and Red Genies — is more relevant. In the 1970s, the American social psychologist Elliot Aronson devised the "jigsaw classroom." His approach places students in small groups and forces them to work together on tasks, for example, learning about twentieth-century history. Racial, ethnic, gender, and school-clique boundaries don't count for the task: The kids must work together to master their subject. The idea is that these preclass human kinds fade in importance and the kids' shared work comes to the fore. As Aronson told a reporter, "Someone can tell you over and over that the short fat kid with pimples is really sweet. But there's no substitute for being in a small group with that kid and seeing that he's warm, funny and clever."

In long-standing political conflicts, exactly the opposite happens. Life is organized in a number of ways to *prevent* alternative human kinds from forming in anyone's mind. Child rearing in such places is a kind of antijigsaw classroom, where there are only the political human kinds, and the freedom to create alternatives — Rattlers and Eagles, Blue Ghosts and Red Genies — is sharply controlled by the authorities.

Which brings us back to morality. Remember, we are all of us members of many overlapping human kinds; I am an American, a man, a white person, a Democrat, a New Yorker, and so on. I am also, I hope, a good person or at least a not-bad person. *That* human kind, the moral one, created by our upbringing, is on almost everyone's map. Now, suppose I want you to dislike Lerians and never get close enough to a Lerian to see him as part of any of your human kinds. One of my best strategies would be to convince you that Lerians are *morally* wrong.

This turns out not to be difficult. We're prepared to connect moral values with our way of eating or talking or worshipping already, because that is how in the first place we learned morality — the rules our parents gave us for what we do. And no moral system makes sense without judgments that some people, by their actions, aren't acceptable.

This boundary between us good people and the rest need not be narrowly drawn; "good people" can enfold many different human kinds. But the boundary has to exist, as the Milton scholar Stanley Fish has pointed out. In John Milton's England, the moral boundary took in many forms of Protestantism. But it excluded Catholics. There is always, for any moral kind, a refusal point when people say, as Fish puts it: "not X; them, we burn."

Decades ago, students were taught that people find these limits by reasoning from abstract principles, like "killing is wrong" and "honesty is the best policy." But reason may not have that big a role. Moral sense may well be like the products of other mental codes: automatic, unconscious, and shaped by innate biases, which make humans behave differently than reason would dictate.

For example, the philosopher Peter Unger of New York University came up with a thought experiment that shows how moral perceptions part ways with neutral computation.

Unger's example is Bob, who has retired as the proud owner of a fabulous car, a Bugatti. He loves driving it and caring for it, and he likes the security of knowing that he can sell it for a lot of money if he needs more funds to keep himself comfortable. One day, though, Bob sees a runaway train heading straight for a child playing on some distant tracks. The only way he can save the child is by pulling a switch that will send the train onto another track — and right into his beloved Bugatti.

What to do? Suppose Bob said to hell with the child, whom he didn't know, and so saved his car, and his retirement, and his nice life. Many people would think ill of Bob.

But many of those people, if they were asked for, say, $200 right now to help a charity keep a hungry child fed and healthy from age two until age six, might well say no. Most wouldn't condemn some-one else for refusing.

Yet, Unger pointed out, the two situations — Bob saving his Bugatti and you keeping $200 to spend on your life — are logically the same. You have more than you need to keep yourself alive, while other people are in danger of disease and starvation. Something makes the two situations feel different to most people, but whatever it is, it's in their heads, not in the facts of the case.

Philosophers and psychologists who have tried to explain the dif-ference have implied that selflessness is kind of like a lightbulb, shin-ing brightly on those close to us and ever more dimly with each added increment of distance. Lack of generosity, they imply, is a conse-quence of our theory of mind: we care about minds that are close to us (even if it's the family dog's mind, or the car's "mind") and not about minds that we never see or hear, because they live in Novaya Zemlya.

Yet this explanation doesn't square with people's actual behavior. Al-most no one uses mere distance to calibrate charity. Odds are, you have at some point in your life sent a donation to help far-off strangers — flood victims, a child in a newspaper story who needed an operation, victims of crimes or political oppression. Odds are, too, that you've avoided helping someone you see often, like the homeless man near the office or the elderly shut-in a few doors away. If distance were the only predictor of altruism, Americans would be cooking and clean-ing and doing errands for one another, and sending no money to re-build countries hit by the Indian Ocean tsunami of 2004.

Another flaw in the distance idea is that it is static. For the sake of a clear argument, it portrays a world in which people don't change — in which they either give money to flood relief or save it for a nicer vacation. But people can and do change. (If they never could, after all, there'd be no earthly reason to argue about Bob's Bugatti.)

The real difference between your middle-class life and the Bugatti story is that the runaway train is a freak crisis, but appeals for help ar-rive in the mail every few days. Bob has to make a single irrevocable decision, but real people make moral choices constantly. And those choices wander. People in offices with an "honor system" coin box for bagels and coffee, for instance, cheat more when it's raining heavily. They also cheat more near Valentine's Day and during the Christmas season. It's easy to speculate about what might cause these variations or why cheating in these Washington-area offices declined after the September 11 attacks, but my point here is simpler: whatever makes people choose to cheat or be honest is not constant. It varies.

Part of that variation — that aspect of human nature that makes it impossible to be sure how altruistic a particular person will be toward another — is in the mental code for human kinds. We make our moral choices about others based on the human kinds in which we place them and the relationship of that kind to our own.

That's one reason moral choices can change. When the supposedly worthless bum is reclassified as a fellow citizen, your calculations about helping him change too. Or conversely, if you convert to a charitable religion after a Scroogey period, you'll probably become more generous, or try to. Those who receive your new largesse aren't reclassed into a new human kind necessarily, but *you* are. Again, a new relationship, new human-kind mapping.

It is not hard to see, either, how moral feeling sparks up when we hear about actions by people we feel are our kind, even if those actions have no effect on us personally. If someone is a member of the same human kind as you are, then his behavior is in a sense yours as well. If he gets away with X, then suddenly you belong to the kind of people who do X. If X is wrong, this is intolerable. So citizens do not wish their soldiers to commit atrocities, even if they never learn of them. Thinking about morals is thinking about human kinds.

Without human kinds, in fact, we can't make moral judgments at all. Here's another hypothetical story: Claire walks down a busy shopping street with her father. It's a beautiful day, so when he heads into a store, she keeps strolling along. A few minutes later, you run into her. Do you have any feelings about this?

I bet you don't. Your mental codes have probably supplied implied facts that weren't in the story and left you with a fairly neutral impression. In this case, for instance, you might assume Claire and her father are both competent adults. Suppose, though, that Claire is five years old. Now how do you feel about her father? Try another variation. Suppose Claire is an adult and her father suffers from dementia, so that he can't figure out what sort of store he is in. How do you feel about her breezily waving him off?

A careless caretaker is ugly in most people's sight, but that's not the point here. You can easily imagine other variations that change how you feel. Suppose the father is a genocidal war criminal; by treating him normally, as if he were an ordinary man, Claire is implicitly excusing his crimes. Or suppose you know the father knows Claire is an addict, eager to sneak off to buy drugs. Each of those possibilities changes the emotional picture.

Until lately, moral psychology did not pay much attention to those emotions. As I've mentioned, *reason* was supposed to be the key to moral thought and action. Yet, as Jonathan Haidt of the University of Virginia points out, moral emotion is certainly consequential. Before you start thinking about the rights and obligations of the two people in this story, you experience a clear, strong, instantaneous feeling about it. Such moral emotion is just as clear to mind and body as the ones psychology is used to exploring — feelings about yourself or those close to you. What makes a moral emotion different, Haidt says, is that it wells up in response to acts that don't touch you directly.

So you don't need to know Claire to feel something when you learn that she is five and her father left her to wander the street alone. Her situation has no possible impact on your well-being or that of anyone you love. (After all, she doesn't exist; I made her up.) Nonetheless, you have feelings — anger? disgust? — toward Claire's father, that fictional person, because of his actions.

Many religious and philosophical traditions are suspicious of those feelings. If human nature is nasty, then its emotions are likely nasty too. Certainly they must not be trusted as a guide. Instead, people become morally sound by conquering feeling with the rational mind. Reason is the way up, emotion the hindrance.

Informed by this intellectual tradition, the Swiss psychologist Jean Piaget described the development of morality in children as a progression. In early stages, the child claims, for instance, that lies are "naughty"; at the end of the process she can think critically about a

moral rule like "no lying." A similar progress from feeling to reasoning is implied in the work of the late Harvard psychologist Lawrence
Kohlberg, who proposed that children's moral development began
with a stage in which they would try to get rewards and avoid
punishment. The end of the process was supposed to be a person
whose morality was centered on "ethical principles appealing to logical comprehensiveness, universality, and consistency."

In the 1980s, Kohlberg was criticized for using interviews with
American boys to make a claim about human nature. Other cultures
sort things differently, said the anthropologists. And women, said the
Harvard psychologist Carol Gilligan, go through different stages than
do men. But today's psychologists see a different problem: schemes
like Piaget's and Kohlberg's tacitly assume that moral reasoning can
be separated from the emotions.

These days, research on ethical behavior is thriving, but it is not
research on moral *reasoning*. After all, feeling and reasoning are inter-
tangled. So the emphasis now is on moral emotions and the possibility that, as Jonathan Haidt puts it, "the emotions are in fact in charge
of the temple of morality, and that moral reasoning is really just a
servant masquerading as the high priest." Other researchers aren't so
convinced, thinking these processes, like so many others, are likely
to be both top-down and bottom-up, with emotions sometimes
guiding conscious moral thought and moral thought sometimes
guiding the emotions.

A third position in the debate is that *neither* emotions nor reason is
in charge. It's possible that the mind has a dedicated code for moral
judgments, separate from both conscious thoughts and feelings —
like the code it has for grammar in language. That's the position of
Marc D. Hauser, a psychologist at Harvard.

It could be, too, that what we traditionally call morality is not one
activity in the mind. The philosopher Joshua D. Greene of Princeton
University, for example, argues that an impersonal moral question
("Should a person let another human being die to save five others?")
involves different mental codes than a question that touches you directly ("Do you kill the person next to you to save five other
people?"). When he and his colleagues performed MRI scans on

people wrestling with these dilemmas, they found the two types of questions prompted two different patterns of brain activation.

The study of moral psychology is busy and thriving because it has been liberated from the notion that moral conduct is equal to cool, emotionless rationality. Yet the ancient tradition that reason must be master lives on in a different way. Research on ethics still ignores the importance of human kinds.

Take a look at any text on ethics you like: it will assume that once you're capable of a moral thought or feeling, you will aim it at all comers. It might even hold, as does the Princeton University philosopher Peter Singer, that morality requires "equal consideration" for the interests of all sentient creatures, no matter the unpleasant consequences for you, your loved ones, people like you, your country, or any particular human kind. But even thinkers who acknowledge the validity of preferring one's species, or nation, or family still use generic terms like "the" child or "society."

Yet moral thoughts and feelings make no sense when seen from the point of view of "society," which is no point of view at all. Toward a person of no kind — a generic human who may or may not need special help, may or may not have done evil, may or may not be the same skin color you are, may or may not have earned the respect of your society, and may or may not share your religion — you have no moral feelings. Why should you? Real-life ethical action is a set of fine discriminations among the human kinds we see in the world. Even Peter Singer, a utilitarian so rigorous he extends the principle of greatest-good-for-the-most to animals as well as people, spent extra time and effort on the care of one individual of a special kind — his aged mother.

More practical than philosophers, the professional manipulators of the human mind — clergy, politicians, raisers of money and of consciousness — learned long ago *not* to make their pitches in the language of abstraction. To take action on behalf of faceless, distant strangers, the mind must clothe them in human-kind terms. And people do this easily.

To be included in the moral emotions of human kinds, in fact, you needn't even be human. Singer once recalled for a reporter how his father, an asthmatic, would walk along a waterfront and empathize with fish gasping desperately next to the fishermen who had caught them. "He used to say how cruel that was," Singer said. "He didn't understand how people could think it was fun."

Getting you to feel that my cause is morally right, then, is a matter of getting you to feel that you belong to the same kind as the people (or animals, or grasslands, or sculptures) that I want to help. Not because you're similar on the surface (though similarity helps) but because, underneath appearances, you and those others are all a part of the community of the ethical.

We are all children of one God, I might say. We are all parents, I might say, from Beijing to Boston, wanting the best for our children. We are all united in our great cause, I could say. All these forms of rhetoric invite you to imagine strangers as if they were the same moral kind of person you are. These are words that tell you those other people are held, as you are, within an entity: a thing with those Campbellian traits that tickle the groupish half of the human-kind faculty. If we are all children of God, then we share proximity to one another and a common fate. If we are all parents, we share both common fate and similarity. And if we are united in a cause, we have a common fate, internal communication, and a boundary defining who we are against those who are not with us. Never mind that you've never met your fellow members in Cambodia. They're with you.

A remarkable example of this mix of moral and human-kind rhetoric is an open letter against lobster fishing written by the actress Mary Tyler Moore in 1995. Lobsters, she wrote, "are fascinating beings with complex social interactions, long childhoods and awkward adolescences. Like humans, they flirt with one another and have even been seen walking claw-in-claw! And like humans, lobsters feel pain." Lobsters are like you! (Similarity gets your kind-code working.) And they flirt and hold hands! (You can understand them, see?) That suggests that you and those hand-holding crustaceans can communicate more efficiently than some other kinds you can imagine, like "people and sea slugs."

That's the perceptual cue Campbell called "internal communication." It's a message in human-kind code for that department of your mind. It says that information is passing more easily inside the lobsters-and-people community than outside it and invites you to perceive that lobsters are "part of us." That another part of your mind might be thinking "what a crock" is, of course, not relevant here. As I've mentioned, it's the nature of these separate codes to work in their own way, whatever your conscious mind may think.

People who write effective fund-raising letters are not setting out to speak the hidden code of human kinds. Like the many medicines we use without knowing how they work, rhetoric has been honed into an effective form, and that's all that people using it need to know. But we can say now *why* this imagery works: it speaks to parts of the mind outside your conscious awareness. Speaking in the specialized code of that part, it links human kinds that don't relate to your experience with a human kind that always does — the one called "good people."

Of course, the existence of good people assumes that others are bad. I may want you to eat lobsters, not help them. In that case, I apply the same rhetoric in reverse: I invite you to believe that the boundaries of one human kind — race, nation, class, sexual orientation — coincide with this other boundary, between the good and the bad. Moral pride and moral anger, those feelings that tell us some action or person is not merely odd but not "right," are powerful reinforcers of boundaries.

This simple and important division, good people versus bad people, is different from the human kinds that guide you in dealings with others, like "boss" versus "drinking buddy." And those categories don't line up with the human kinds defined by politics and culture talk, like "fundamentalist Christian" versus "secular humanist." But if the moral boundaries can be made to *look* like a perfect fit with the other ones, then — click! — the world is simple. Instead of undercutting and overlapping one another to make a varied, changing map of humanity, the human kinds all seem to line up. Drinking is *evil*. Secular humanists have *no morals*.

In such a light, acts you would accept in "good people" take on a different hue. Such a view told whites in America's Jim Crow South to feel nothing strongly when white men whistled at white women; it told them to feel a murderous rage about the same whistle if it came from a black man. It tells a Hindu in Mumbai that a naked sadhu in the street is a holy man, while a naked hippie from Copenhagen is offensive. This code tells most of us that murder is awful but that killing enemy soldiers is not.

One of the shocking aspects of Muzafer Sherif's summer-camp experiment is that he was able to create this kind of moral feeling in his two instant tribes. Even though they had never heard of Rattlers and Eagles until they invented the names, the boys attached a full array of moral feelings to the human kinds they'd made. At the height of their war, campers in each group saw their enemies as cheaters and cowards — not as kids from another team but as kids from a different morality. That's a hint that moral feeling can be triggered by the human-kind faculty, for its own reasons. As those reasons have nothing to do with morality, the boys' situation should seem paradoxical: they felt sure the opposition was immoral, not because of any ethical test but because it was the opposition.

This feeling — what is not "us" is not moral — should strike people as deeply weird, but it doesn't. We are so used to it in our own lives that it doesn't seem odd. Thanks to the human-kind faculty, we grow up applying moral emotions to people and actions in which there is no moral issue. Many of our feelings about right and wrong are actually feelings about Us and Them.

Muzafer Sherif's camp was a simplified world, without the overlapping and crosscutting human kinds that guide real life. His boys organized themselves into competing groups because they arrived in separate buses, lived in separate housing, and were told early on that they would be playing against their opposite numbers. As critics pointed out, his work impelled the boys to form teams and had nothing to say about how, in daily life situations, people choose among many available human kinds. It's the kind of choice you might make on meeting a Christian and Arab American male police officer, for instance: Is this a Christian, a man, an Arab, or a cop? When you don't have a camp counselor telling you which team you are on, how do you choose? When that conundrum is mixed with powerful emotions about right and wrong, the problem becomes as mysterious as it is important.

Ten

"Our Common Humanity Makes Us Weep"

I am a human being. Nothing human is alien to me.

— TERENCE

The last day of April 1944: On Nazi-occupied Crete, a band of British commandos and Greek guerrillas has managed to kidnap the commander of the German forces, General Heinrich Krcipc. For three days they have been force marching him from cave to cave. Everyone is desperate. If they're found by Kreipe's troops, his kidnappers know, their fight will be hopeless, and they'll die; if that happens, Kreipe knows, they will kill him in their last stand.

Yet this morning the sight of dawn breaking on Mount Ida reminds the general of a poem. It is the beginning of an ode by Horace: "You see how Mount Soracte stands out white, covered deep in snow." Keeping watch on the prisoner is one of the British commandos, Patrick Leigh Fermor. He surprises Kreipe by taking up the Latin, reciting the rest of the poem. It happens to be one of the few he knows by heart.

"Ach, so, Herr Major," Kreipe says, and for some time the two men look silently at the peak.

"It was very strange," Fermor wrote years later. "As though, for a long moment, the war had ceased to exist. We had both drunk at the same fountains long before; and things were different between us for the rest of our time together."

In that moment, one set of human kinds receded in those two minds and another came to the fore. The two men felt themselves to be one kind, sharing for a moment not just the Latin language and a classicist's sensibility but the exact same words. Of course, they knew the war had not really ceased to exist. It hadn't vanished from other minds. Of course, they knew that it could not vanish from theirs, nor did they wish it to. Fermor was a dedicated soldier; he had spent two years hiding in caves and dodging enemy patrols before the "snatch." General Kreipe, a loyal officer, wanted to escape.

Nonetheless, their shared feeling wasn't a whim; as Fermor writes, it changed the way they acted with each other. Kreipe, who was duly delivered to a British boat and ended up at a POW camp in Canada, later described his treatment as "chivalrous," and he was among the guests when the kidnap team reunited in 1972 for a commemorative banquet in Crete. At that time, Fermor said that he hoped there were no hard feelings. None, said the retired general.

A conscious mind makes decisions and swears oaths to treat the enemy as an enemy, always. But consciousness is a tight, bright spotlight roaming over a restless ocean of mind. Elsewhere in that ever-changing sea of perception and feeling, things change without conscious intent. All that's required is a message, set in human-kind code, touching the human-kind decoder. You — the you who thinks you know yourself — need not be involved. And so one dawn sixty years ago a soldier found that the code dividing the world into Horatians and non-Horatians mattered more, for that moment, than the one dividing armies.

This shifting of the map is not an exotic experience of guerrilla warriors. Kind switching comes a lot in the ordinary ups and downs of life. One woman, for example, has described "a painful and disturbing sense of separation" from her sisters because of her good fortune: she doesn't share the family gene that makes its carriers likely to have cancer. No one would want such a gene, and the medical news hardly outweighed years of family history. Nonetheless, she said, "now they belonged to a club that I didn't necessarily want to join, but still hated being shut out of."

It's at moments of mixed feelings and uncertainty that we can see ourselves switching from one set of human kinds into another. These are moments like the one experienced by an affluent white mother in a wealthy New York neighborhood, when she felt more connected to other mothers, though they were poor and nonwhite, than to her childless neighbors. They are moments described by one returning American veteran of World War II, who would leave his friends to talk to a total stranger who happened to be a fellow Marine.

Such changes in perception are easy to explain if there's a distinct human-kind faculty of the mind. In fact, they're to be expected. If your sense of human kinds is constantly responding, outside your awareness, to signals in its own code, then it is not referring to your consciously chosen commitments. The hunch will come to you that, whatever you may wish to believe, a different set of human kinds applies.

This is the human-kind equivalent of an Ames room or other optical illusions, where the mind knows one thing but the eyes see another. A soldier in France's brutal war against its Haitian rebels described the contrast in a letter home: "One cannot stay in a rage indefinitely, and our common humanity makes us weep sometimes."

This natural suppleness of the mind frustrates those in charge of human-kind boundaries. Rulers try to orchestrate daily experience so that the human kinds most relevant for daily life are what those rulers prefer. Yet the minds of their subjects remain open to other ways of seeing. When the Catholic Church's Lateran Council of 1215 required mandatory badges for Jews and Muslims, one of its stated reasons was that the people of Europe could not tell which group was which and so failed to keep to their own kind.

Centuries later, the Nazi regime reintroduced the church's old idea, requiring that Jews wear a yellow Star of David at all times. Joseph Goebbels, the Nazi propaganda chief, found himself exasperated by the population's response. The new rule, he wrote in his diary, "has had the opposite effect from what we intended. . . . People everywhere are showing sympathy for them [the Jews]. This nation is simply not yet mature; it's full of all kinds of idiotic sentimentality."

It's easy to dismiss that "sentimentality" as mere mood, which altered no laws and saved no Jews. Yet changes in human-kind perception do sometimes have practical effects. For example, a Nazi administrator in charge of occupied territories around the city of Minsk actually did act on the conflict between his political map of human kinds and his contrary perceptions.

The official, Wilhelm Kube, was troubled by transports of German Jews into his fiefdom. In these arrivals from his own country, he saw signs of their membership in the ranks of proper human beings: "Among these Jews are front veterans with the Iron Cross first and second class, war wounded, half-Aryans, and even a three-quarter Aryan," he wrote. A few lines later, he added: "I am certainly tough and ready to help solve the Jewish question, but human beings who come from our cultural sphere are something other than the native bestial hordes."

Kube's devotion to his "toughness," his genocidal duty, was grotesque, but the sort of conflict he recorded has been experienced by many soldiers, even when they fought in noble causes. It is easier to fight effectively if the enemy does not feel like a part of the human community. The problem is that the mind-set is hard to maintain. We do not like to use only one human-kind map all the time. It takes work.

Curtis Le May, who served as an American bomber pilot during World War II, described this mental effort with unusual clarity:

> You drop a load of bombs and, if you're cursed with any imagination at all you have at least one quick horrid glimpse of a child lying in bed with a whole ton of masonry tumbling down on top of him; or a three-year-old girl wailing for "Mutter . . . Mutter . . ." because she has been burned. Then you have to turn away from the picture if you intend to retain your sanity. And also if you intend to keep on doing the work your Nation expects of you.

Your human-kind code sees what it sees, not what your leaders wish it to see nor even what you wish it to see.

In creating and uncreating the Rattler and Eagle war, Sherif had instigated human-kind perceptions and feelings that arose straight from the immediate needs of the boys who experienced them. In contemporary terms, Sherif reads like those practical people who insist that ethnic terror and religious violence are "really" about practical matters like jobs and contracts. His experiment was a model of what he called "realistic conflict."

That idea is a good antidote to the purported explanation of violence as an inevitable clash of cultures, ethnic groups, or other human kinds. For instance, when religious riots broke out in late 2002 after the Miss World beauty pageant in Nigeria, news reports touted the outrage of Muslims confronted with this secular show of female flesh. Yet many rioters had never heard of Miss World, and the violence began four full days after the insult that supposedly prompted it. The first people attacked were all supporters of one candidate for governor in an upcoming election. The Nigerian politicians who pointed out all this were acting in a thoroughly Sherifian way. They were saying this supposed clash of cultures was actually driven by a struggle for political power in the region.

Yet there is a problem with realistic conflict theory. It suggests that human-kind codes follow rational perceptions about the real world, that my kind's hatred of your kind must derive from some dispute over tangibles, like oil revenue or political patronage. But if human-kind codes have their own rules, there is no guarantee that they will agree with reason. The key to my human-kind thinking about you is my *perception* of how my kind relates to your kind (once I have decided which kinds we belong to for this particular place and time). But that perception of mine might be shaped by human-kind rules, without reference to politics or economics.

A decade or so after Sherif's Robbers Cave experiment, another refugee scholar came up with a method for examining *non*realistic perceptions of human kinds. His name was Henri Tajfel.

He was born in Poland in 1919, within a few months of the day that Muzafer Sherif was nearly bayoneted for being a Turk. Tajfel's family was Jewish. In a different venue, then, with different codes of the human kinds, he found himself in the same species of danger.

Since Jews were barred from taking advanced degrees in Polish universities, Tajfel went to France to study history, and he was there when Germany invaded Poland in 1939. He joined the French army and soon found himself a prisoner of war. For the next five years he lived on identity's razor edge, knowing that his life depended on how his captors classified him. As a "French POW," he was kept with other captured soldiers in German and Austrian camps. Had he been classed as a Polish Jew, he would have been sent into the Holocaust.

Trying to find his home at war's end, Tajfel soon learned, as he wrote years later, that "hardly anyone I knew in 1939 — including my family — was left alive." So he took up work in rehabilitation centers for war orphans and turned from history to the study of psychology. In 1954, he had won a scholarship to an English university with an essay on prejudice. "The interviewers must have decided that I was exceptionally well-qualified to know what I was talking about."

Working in the 1960s and 1970s, Tajfel concurred with Sherif's antiessentialist understanding of human-kind perception. He too saw that human kinds must emerge out of the mind's interaction with its surroundings — that they were dynamic thoughts. "Groups," he liked to say, "are processes, not things."

But he was not satisfied with Sherif's method of making groups for study. In a little world of two lodges, two swimming holes, and two competing sports teams, the boys were impelled to perceive a world with two kinds of person in it. Tajfel wanted to create circumstances without clues. He wanted to see just how little it would take to trigger human-kind coding in people's minds. He ended up concluding that the bare minimum is very little indeed.

Tajfel's laboratory-made human kinds were painstakingly contrived to be without meaningful relationship to the real world. For instance, he might show his experiment volunteers a slide show of paintings, asking which ones they liked. Then he would divide the volunteers into two groups. One bunch would be told they had all preferred the paintings of, say, Vassily Kandinsky and the other that they all preferred works of Paul Klee. (In fact, the participants hadn't heard of the painters, didn't know which paintings were which, and had been assigned at random.)

After they learned that they were, say, Kandinsky people, volunteers were asked to help divide a payment the entire group was getting for being in the experiment. Each volunteer did this by filling out a form with multiple blanks: one for each person in the experiment — fellow Kandinskyans and all the Klee folk too.

The point was to focus people's awareness on a human kind that they *knew* was of no real importance. Most of the first experiments were done on British teenage boys (though later work with women and girls found no gender difference). These kids were schoolmates who had known one another for years, but the painter-preference groups deliberately mixed up the familiar categories of their lives, like age, grade in school, accent, clique, and religion.

What the kids should have done, according to Sherif's theory, is award money just about equally to members of both groups. After all, the Klee and Kandinsky preference caused no realistic conflict.

Nonetheless, in these minimal-group experiments, "Kandinsky" people gave more money to other Kandinskyans and "Klees" to Klees. A statistical analysis of their choices turned up another striking fact: the choices they were making didn't lead to the maximum possible payoff for their side. Instead, they created the maximum possible *difference* between their side and the other. In other words, Kandinskyans were making sure they were as far ahead of Klee folk as possible, even when it meant they personally made less money. Later experiments tried to make the nonsense groups even more arbitrary — letting both groups know, for example, that they had been divided by a coin toss into "heads" and "tails." Participants still favored their nonsense groups over the other team's.

Later studies have found a similar bias in favor of "our gang" even in nonsensical circumstances. One experiment literally involved nonsense. It found that English speakers rated the syllables "xeh" and "yof" (meaningless in English) to be much more pleasant when they had been paired with the words *we, us,* and *ours* than with the words *they, them,* and *theirs.* The same researchers later found their volunteers quicker to associate positive adjectives like *skillful, competent, careful,* and *courteous* with "us" words and quicker to associate unpleasant adjectives like *sloppy, irritable, wasteful,* and *gullible* with "they" words.

One of Sherif's students, now a political psychologist, has found that the best predictor of a candidate's winning a vote was the voter saying the politico was "our kind of person." You could interpret this to mean that people start with a clear idea of what "our kind of person" is and then look for people to match. But Tajfel's minimal-group work hints at the opposite. Sometimes we begin knowing who we're with, favor those people, and then find similarity to justify what we've done.

In my high school, our student body was organized by astrological sign. Yes, we were in California, in the 1970s, but actually there were good reasons for using this set of human kinds. Our school was 50 percent African American and almost 50 percent white, with heavy concentrations of both poor people and the well-off. Needing a way to administer the place, one that would not divide students into racial or class groupings, our teachers used birthdays. It's easier to remember that you're a Capricorn than that your birthday places you in Section 5.

As you might expect from Tajfel's experiments, we Tauruses soon came to feel that we belonged together. But the daily sorting of kids by zodiac also had an effect on our teachers. More than one came to think maybe there was something to astrology after all. "I've never seen so many kids who liked being alone," one said to me. "It makes you think."

Yet an astrologer would have said our categories were not meaningful, because we were lumped together with no attention to the planetary details that practitioners use to draw up their charts. And no one on the staff tried to tell us that astrology is a worthwhile system of human kinds. It was just a way of marking birthdays. But once these categories became "real" in our little world — once they determined which kids would go to which homerooms and class picnics — even sensible teachers were tempted by them. Automatic mental codes told them that the groupings they saw were real human kinds.

Sherif had missed this unrealistic aspect of human kinds. Yet it's important, because a map of human kinds doesn't always emerge from conflict between political or cultural groups. Some kind of map has to come *before* conflict. Before Muslims and Christians can fight in the streets, as they did in Nigeria in 2002, the people involved must believe themselves to be Muslims and Christians and not divide themselves into some other set of human kinds. Of course, in such a conflict, people have no choice about the lines that determine whether they live or die. You couldn't end a religious riot by saying, We're all children of the same God, and now let's imagine ourselves as parents or soccer fans. But battle lines have an origin before the fighting began, in a time when people *did* have a choice. The alternative to this idea is a tautological circle: the reason we fight as my tribe against your tribe is because . . . we fight.

To show how human kinds arise out of political and cultural circumstances, Sherif had re-created those circumstances in miniature. Robbers Cave was a microcosmic version of twentieth-century political life, its two cabins arranged like the two races of America's color line or the two sides of the Cold War. Tajfel showed that the mind didn't need those circumstances to see human kinds. *Any* circumstances would do.

Sherif had demonstrated how politics and culture don't create our maps of human kinds directly. He suggests that we don't believe in racial and religious and national divisions because we're told to but rather because our daily experiences are organized to make those categories relevant and useful — and to make other ways of sorting people useless. For example, in Lebanon in the 1960s, so much of the human world was organized along religious lines that boys who thought in other terms would have been at a disadvantage. But all it took was a few days in a different environment (the experimental summer camp that Lutfy Diab set up) and the boys quickly switched to another set of human kinds. They went from seeing themselves as Muslims and Christians to Blue Ghosts and Red Genies as soon as that second set of categories became better for getting through the day.

Tajfel suggested that your categories for people may be quite separate from such realities. That doesn't mean you're free from society's politics or its traditions. But it probably means that those politics and traditions work on your mind in subtler ways than Sherif imagined. It doesn't take wars or riots or unfair laws to make you believe in particular human kinds and then act on those beliefs. Your mind responds to much slighter cues.

Those cues, Tajfel argued, came from the mere act of sorting people. His emphasis was on classification — the way human kinds are seen so easily as important categories that tell a lot about the people in them. His intellectual heirs in psychology have followed that line. It's "self-categorization," argue Tajfel's former students and collaborators, that powers human-kind perceptions.

That's one side in a long-running debate: Are human kinds basically a type of *category,* created to explain people (as in "they're Chinese, so they work really hard in school")? Or are human kinds mostly a type of *entity,* which we imagine as a living being (as in "the Chinese have decided to pursue economic growth")? As I've mentioned, it's pretty clear that human kinds are *both,* so the argument is about which aspect is a fundamental mechanism, and which is an aftereffect.

Thinkers who focus on the "thingy" aspect of human kinds point out that those are the ones that have real impact on people's lives. To these scholars, it's obvious that the human kinds that deal in life and death aren't *categories* like Kandinsky fans and Klee fans in the lab, but *entities:* nations, ethnicities, religions, and other organized collections of people whose memberships oblige them to one another in various ways. Donald L. Horowitz of Duke University, a leading contemporary scholar of ethnicity, put it this way: "Since ethnic groups do not compete in merely one task or one game but in lifelong games, the competition has an urgency, a centrality, that the experiments do not capture."

According to Tajfel's critics, he created idle games — Klee or Kandinsky, who cares? — that obscure the real work of the human-kind faculty, which is teaming up with others. Tajfel thought the Kandinsky fans were favoring each other just for being Kandinskyans. Skeptics say something in the situation must have told the human-kind part of the mind that the Kandinsky fans did or at least could make up an entity, a thing made of people, not just a pigeonhole.

What's interesting about today's debate on entities versus categories, though, is what *isn't* in question: whether your mental codes are triggered by classification alone or by an inbuilt scanner for possible allies, both sides agree that what happens inside your head is important. Individual experience matters for the study of human kinds, as both Sherif and Tajfel realized early on.

That may seem obvious enough, but Sherif and Tajfel were pioneers. Not long ago, the study of such human kinds as race, nation, ethnicity, and tribe presumed that individual experience made little difference. Those human kinds were envisioned as monolithic entities with compulsory memberships. People were born into their tribes and creeds, and nothing about their individual, subjective experiences — the thoughts and feelings that made Jane's life different from Joe's — was supposed to be relevant. Human beings were either In or Out.

That was, for example, the doctrine of William Graham Sumner, who coined the terms *in group* and *out group* in his 1906 book, *Folkways.* Sumner, one of the first American sociologists, was a Yale professor and one of the nastiest of his country's social Darwinists. In his sermonlike essays and books (he was a former Episcopal minister), he declared that nothing should be done to interfere with those at the top of society (the "captains of industry"), nor should anyone waste time on its losers. "A drunkard in the gutter," he wrote, "is just where he ought to be, according to the fitness and tendency of things. Nature has set up on him the process of decline and dissolution by which she removes things which have survived their usefulness."

Sumner's rabid laissez-faire writings aren't much read these days, but his thoughts about human kinds live on. He coined the terms *mores* and *folkways* to describe shared practices of a human kind. He also invented the term *ethnocentrism,* which he defined as "this view of things in which one's own group is the center of everything, and all others are scaled with reference to it." In the course of explaining his idea, Sumner differentiated between "the we-group, or in-group, and everybody else, of the others-group, out-groups." The in-group is the sovereign human kind, he explained: "Loyalty to the ingroup, sacrifice for it, hatred and contempt for outsiders, brotherhood within, warlikeness without — all group together, common products of the same situation."

Much of this is dead wrong. "Brotherhood within," for one thing, does not mean "warlikeness without." The anthropologist Elizabeth Cashdan of the University of Utah combed a database of field reports on 186 traditional societies all over the world, looking for the sources of loyalty to one's ethnic group and of hatred of outsiders and found no connection between the two. The one type of information that could predict hostility to outsiders, she reported, was this: how much violence and hostility people felt *within* a society, toward each other.

Similarly, Otto Adang, who tracked European soccer hooligans, found that the most violent among them weren't the ones with the most team spirit. Instead, they were the wife beaters and child abusers — men who turned to violence in *all* their relationships. Using different theories and methods, Marilynn Brewer and Donald Campbell's East African research also found that people's high ratings for their tribes did not cause them to feel hostile or contemptuous of other human kinds.

Sumner was wrong, then, to assume that love for one's kind required hatred of others. But that was not his most important mistake. A more fundamental flaw in his theory is its assumption that each of us belongs, at all times, to a single in-group.

Each of us is simultaneously a member of many different human kinds, and each of us is capable of inventing new ones. You can be, for example, male, Japanese American, a parent, a Republican, and a Methodist; you can, with no trouble at all, decide tomorrow to join up with other people who happen to live in your neighborhood, or who happen to share your interest in antique cars or butterfly collecting. As Lawrence Hirschfeld puts it: "Anyone in any human society, no matter how small, has a very large number of affiliations, allegiances and coalitions that can be invoked at any time."

Each of us places himself in whatever human kind feels relevant to the needs of the moment. Understanding human kinds, then, is a matter of seeing how this ever-changing mental dance produces the permanent-feeling human kinds we call tribes, races, religions, and nations. To solve the problem, though, you have to see it, and Sumner didn't.

Nonetheless, psychologists and anthropologists today, with their interest in subjective experience, may have a new use for Sumner's idea. The crucial distinction he made — between Us and Them — is not a measurable fact about people, but perhaps it *is* a fact about how the mind works. Perhaps this sense of Us and Them is embedded in the human-kind codes, as part of the grammar it uses to divide the world. That would mean that invisible mental calculations about who is Us and who is Them would be part of our perceptions. If that's so, then Sumner's crude notions of in-group and out-group, though not a reflection of reality, may help describe how the mind thinks about reality.

For instance, the sense of who is Us and who is Them may be part of the process we all use, as we move through the day, for deciding which human kinds are relevant at the moment. When you walk into a room filled with people, you might not think about race or religion or gender and then decide who in the room is part of Us or Them. Instead, you might begin with feelings and perceptions about Us and then settle on a human kind — race, religion, gender, politics, soccer, what have you — to explain the feeling.

That is what Charles Johnston, the white captive of the Shawnee, did when he befriended a black slave. He switched his human-kind boundary from color to language in the new situation, but in doing so he preserved something: a feeling of shared troubles, companionship, and solidarity. A feeling of being among Us.

Among those who have invoked Sumner's old idea in this new way is E. O. Wilson, the Harvard evolutionist whose *Sociobiology* is the foundation of modern Darwinian approaches to psychology. Noting the connection between moral judgments and human kinds, Wilson writes: "Altruism is characterized by strong emotion and protean allegiance. Human beings are consistent in their codes of honor but endlessly fickle with reference to whom the codes apply. . . . The important distinction is . . . between the ingroup and the outgroup, but the precise location of the dividing line is shifted back and forth with ease."

Suppose, then, that part of what your mind takes in about your surroundings is whether you're among Us — without regard to what particular label "Us" attaches to. That observation would not come to you as a calculation. It would be a feeling. Perhaps your human-kind faculty takes note of those traits of a true group that Donald Campbell identified — similarity, coordination, ease of information flow — and sees, in addition, that you're a part of it.

This process is not at all like the rational mind's ability to check a piece of paper to see if we belong — to look at your boarding pass, for instance, and get on the right airplane. The signs to which your emotions respond are outside your awareness, and as they shift all around you, they give you different messages. You're either on the plane or not; but feeling that you belong is something that comes and goes.

Nor is it exactly like an animal's ability to tell if an unknown arrival looks or smells or sounds "right." Your emotional responses are not so stable, because they are not geared simply to a physical indicator, like smell or sound. They're geared instead to the *meaning* of those indicators. The mental codes that tell who you belong to converge with codes that interpret signs and symbols. That's likely how a simple and primitive calculation — who is with me and who is against me? — can lead to the infinite variety of overlapping human kinds in which we live.

I literally felt this importance the day I met the primatologist Frans de Waal. The chimpanzees he studies — a group of twenty or so in a basketball-court-sized enclosure surrounded by a high chain-link fence — had never seen me before. When I walked up, they shrieked and hooted; the males' hairs stiffened, making their shoulders look bigger. A well-aimed piece of rock-hard "monkey chow" conked me on the temple, announcing, Hello! Chimpanzees don't like strangers!

The great difference between the Us-Them emotions of chimps and those of human beings is that human beings have a different method of determining who is friend and who is foe. Apes use sight and smell and memories of what has taken place between the stranger and their troop. Human beings, however, have an immense mental apparatus for mapping the world of human kinds. They can refer not only to their own face-to-face experience (do I know you?) but also to a set of *symbols* that indicate who is part of "our kind."

The chimpanzee looks for smells and sounds and sights that tell it who is part of its troop. The human being looks for *signs*. This is a huge difference. A chimp, meeting a stranger, can only feel that the newcomer is not right. A person meeting a stranger can feel, because of the signs the stranger displays, that this unknown person is one of "us." His skin is the same color as ours, even if he doesn't speak our language. He speaks our language, even though his skin is a different color. He is not of our color or language, but look, he's carrying a soccer ball. He's playing our game.

Rather than deciding how to treat one another by sight, smell, and memory, de Waal and I used a different mental code. We tested each other for *signs* that we belonged to the same human kinds. Things warmed up when we spoke in French; they cooled when I quoted a skeptical colleague of his, whose point I obviously thought made sense; they warmed when we hit on a book we had both read and cooled when he mentioned primate work about which I knew nothing and warmed when we talked about pets. (We both owned cats.)

As we spoke, it was as if we were drawing imaginary circles, some of which took us both in, some of which did not. Every word we exchanged carried, in addition to its agreed-upon meaning for speakers of English, another meaning that was particular to the space between us. We were sorting out what we could expect of each other, with clues about what we were and who our friends were; and we were establishing how intelligible we were to one another, which would define how much each of us felt completely human to the other. We were figuring out how we could "play the same game."

One obvious point about this contentless "we-feeling" is that it's a desirable state. You want to be in it. The Sudanese novelist Tayeb Salih describes the emotion as it floods the mind of a man who has returned to his village after seven years away: "I felt as though a piece of ice were melting inside of me, as though I were some frozen substance on which the sun had shone." What he has gotten back, he says, "is that life-warmth of the tribe."

Life-warmth, we-feeling, is easy to associate with the familiarity of foods, street sounds, and light through a childhood window. But smells and sights only *represent* the feeling; they don't create it. We-feeling is about people, not things. It is a sense that your knowledge of other minds is correct, so you can tell for sure what people mean, and what you should do, and how your acts are being understood by others. That is the sense of being among our kind. It's "that absence of self-consciousness, that ease and fellowship and sense of common values which make for intimacy, and sanity, and the quick give and take of familiar intercourse," as Virginia Woolf once described it.

"We" are the people you laugh with, not at. Among "Us," we feel at ease and normal; we're all using the same map of the human world, and, as the anthropologist Fredrik Barth put it, "playing the same game." (That's not always a metaphor, either: the most prestigious universities in the United States are often referred to as a set of schools who play the same game against one another. They call themselves the Ivy League.) "We" might not love one another as individuals (we may even hate one another), but there is a sense that "we" are "good"; that moral law applies to all our dealings. The Golden Rule — do unto others as you would have them do unto you — was made for Us. For good or ill, we're supposed to treat one another as people.

Usness can be exciting or moving or routine or unnoticed. But all human beings, everywhere, will go to a great deal of trouble to get and keep this feeling. With it, you cross streets, confident that drivers will not run you over; quarrel with friends or spouses, sure that they won't kill you for it; get in elevators, buses, and trains with total strangers, knowing that however you annoy them they won't haul off and punch you. We all trust that strangers will deliver our mail and keep our electricity running and cure our illnesses because they say they will, and people keep their word to others who are part of Us, even if they never met them. We trust this feeling of "Usness" with our lives. We all do, from the subway rider jammed with hundreds of others in a metal box to the lonely trekker in an Arctic wilderness whose life depends on the care taken by the unseen people who made his tent and his dried-food packages.

Our capacity to draw such circles of trust is not confined to our species. In fact, you can see the distinction between feelings of Us and Them quite clearly in attitudes toward animals. Imagine that you're walking down the street and you spot a cat. Unless you hate cats, what you feel is probably rather neutral — maybe awareness that a living creature is nearby, awareness that it is a cat, but no particular interest in its fate. If it looks thin and sick, well, too bad. If you see someone feed it, that's nice of the person, you might think, with no special emphasis. The cat is not a thing; it is alive, and you are attuned to living things. But the experience of that life — whether it feels good or bad to be the cat, whether it is flourishing or dying, its life history until now — is not of any particular concern to you. It is alive, but it is an object. It is one of Them.

Suppose, though, that this is not any cat but *your* cat, the family pet. Now your feelings are different. What is it doing there in the street? Is it safe? What should you do? All of these questions puncture your indifference to living-things-in-general. Everything you would have ignored in the other case, all those questions of what it is like to be the cat, now matters a great deal. To some extent, of course, this is because you have a one-on-one connection with the animal. It sat in your lap, purred in your ear, followed you from room to room when it was small, and all these things awoke your code for your relationships with individuals. But that is not all that is involved in your response; if it were, parents would not care for their children's pets, and spouses would not tolerate animals that preferred their mates. No one would help look for other people's lost animals, either. People feel for pets they don't like or even know because of a different code   the one for "my kind." When you know the cat is your pet or the pet of someone in your family, neighborhood, or clan, you feel emotions appropriate to one of "us." Appropriately, the English language labels those emotions "kindness." The stray is Them; the pet is Us.

Even in death, it's better to be one of Us than one of Them. In 1795, for example, one Lewis Avershaw was hanged on Kensington Common in London. As people then would say, he "died game," with a flower in his mouth, chatting with people who rode alongside as he went to the scaffold. For months afterward, people visited the spot where his body had swung in chains, as if it were a hero's grave. An Englishman among Englishmen, he was killed with respect, as one of Us. English people, accustomed to public hangings, knew that this mattered. In 1759, Adam Smith had reminded readers in his *Theory of Moral Sentiments:* that a man on his way to the scaffold has "the sympathy of the spectators [which] supports him . . . and saves him from that shame, that consciousness that his misery is felt by himself only, which is of all sentiments the most unsupportable."

Frank Embree was hanged from a tree near Fayette, Missouri, 1899, in just such a misery, to judge by the photos of his death that someone made and carefully preserved. The crowd stripped him naked and horsewhipped him, then posed him, front and back, on a buggy for the photographer. He stared straight into the camera. Around him in the photo, clothed men smirk and grin. Many such murders in the Jim Crow South were photographed, in fact, and some were made into postcards. On such a card, a photo of a charred corpse, someone had scrawled, "This is the barbecue we had last night" before mailing the card to his parents. Unlike Avershaw, Embree, a black man in a white-dominated state, died as one of Them, as a living object. That's the difference between a hanging and a lynching, between punishing one of Us and disposing of one of Them.

Smith understood it. "Human virtue," he wrote, "is superior to pain, to poverty, to danger, and to death. . . . But to have its misery exposed to insult and derision, to be led in triumph, to be set up for the hand of scorn to point at, is a situation in which its constancy is much more apt to fail."

Desire for emotional cues that you're among Us is very old in the history of life. It can be found in all animals that live in groups to get their living. Schools of porpoises, flocks of parrots, cagefuls of rats, and troops of monkeys are all keen to sense who belongs and who does not. In many species, young members of one sex or the other must leave the safety of the troop when they're grown, and it's always a big crisis. Many die. Staying in the troop, for an animal that doesn't have huge claws and teeth, is the best way to survive.

In a society where you meet and work with strangers all the time, getting acquainted is a play of symbols about the human kinds you might share. Any common ground — shared college, shared taste in movies, I-used-to-live-where-you-live — can help. Any drawing of a line that excludes you ("You like Westerns? I can't stand them") is a little dark cloud that asks to be watched for trouble. It's one less brick in the imaginary wall of shared humanity that's building around you.

Once, sitting down to interview a brilliant scientist who was famously hostile to journalists, I pointed out that we had graduated from the same college. He lit up like a bulb. Conversely, another scholar reminded me as we shook hands that I was the second writer to interview him on the same topic for the same publication. He'd liked the first one. "We understood one another, we got along," he said, smiling sadly. "Perhaps because she's European, and I'm European." Perhaps. Though a mere American, I got the message.

In face-to-face meetings with strangers, the British evolutionist Robin Dunbar once said to me, "It's all about establishing trust." Face-to-face, as strangers standing in a lunch line at a conference, we were engaged in the process we were discussing.

Dunbar is known for his proposal that the human brain evolved to reckon with about 150 individuals.

But human beings don't have relations only with other human beings. We also have relationships to human kinds. We have concepts that tell us that we can trust a total stranger because he's a fellow Hindu; trust him more, in fact, than we trust people we have known all our lives who are Muslims. When Dunbar and I spoke, we were surrounded by such signs that we could trust the strangers around us — the conference organizers who had said they would give us lunch, the cooks who threw away the spoiled vegetables instead of shrugging and throwing them into the pot. Dunbar and I could read each other in the way that de Waal and I had, but the background of our personal encounter was this more general sense of being among Us. We had only to see and hear the codes that told us these strangers were our kind.

This is likely one reason people care so much about symbols like headscarves and choices on the menu. If there had been nothing halal at lunch that, say, an observant Muslim could eat, *her* sense of being among Us would be undermined. The conference paperwork would tell her she was welcome, but her emotions might lead her to feel that she was not.

This fine-tuned awareness doesn't depend on likes and dislikes for individual people. Nor is it exactly a perception of human kinds, either. The mental faculty that tells me I am among southerners or Puerto Ricans or Hindus does not tell me if I am welcome or rejected. What tells me if I'm in the game is rather my perception of signals that are specifically about how my human kind relates to the ones I see about me.

To go back to my example, a Muslim scientist at the meeting could look about and see indicators that Muslims were not the majority in the room. But what emotional significance would that fact have? Would it tell her she would be uncomfortable or that it was not a problem? That she would learn by noticing if the lunch menu made accommodation for people who keep halal; if people seemed to stare or remark on her headscarf; if, in short, she was going to be reminded of difference or encouraged to forget it. Symbols can tell us about human kinds. But the way we use those symbols, communicate without words about them, tells us what the human kinds *mean* in any given situation.

What does a U.S. Army uniform "mean," then? To a certain extent, it stands for a specific human kind. But the other part of its meaning is determined by how people respond to it. That's only somewhat a matter of how they think and feel about this particular tribe, the U.S. Army. The other part of their response is about Us and Them.

Feeling securely a part of Us, then, can happen anywhere. "We" may be Her Majesty's forces, or "we" may be the two men on the mountain who know Horace. Peter J. Richerson, a biologist at the University of California at Davis, points to the difference between what happens when his lecture class sits down in front of him for the first time — quiet talk, borrowing of pens, flirtations — and what would happen in a hall full of young macaques or chimpanzees (screams, blood, injuries, and perhaps deaths). The human ability to imagine that a stranger is not an enemy, that a stranger can feel like Us, is an essential part of our humanity.

"Getting acquainted is a series of negotiations, of decisions that the other is OK. You need the face-to-face contact to judge the other's honesty," Dunbar told me, in the lunch line. But before you can get to that stage, you have to be sure the other person knows the rules — that an outstretched hand or a wink means the same to you as it does to him, for example. As the anthropologist Francisco Gil-White points out, the details of those rules don't matter. Is it safer to drive on the left or on the right? The answer depends on where everyone else drives. What keeps you from head-on crashes is being able to learn what rule they're following and then follow it yourself. This is part of the essential work human kinds do, by answering the question C. Neil Macrae, the social psychologist, defined: Not *who* is this, but *what* is this? What kind of person you see tells you what rules to apply. Knowing that we can figure out human kinds tells us that we can learn the rules — how they do things around here — no matter where we are.

If Dunbar is right, and our capacity to track individuals tops out at 150, then this code of human kinds must have been a powerful amplifier. Instead of knowing 150 people, our ancestors could know thousands, by knowing their *kinds.* Getting acquainted with Dunbar took a few minutes; getting to know large numbers of people in any of his human kinds — citizens of the United Kingdom, bearded men, scientists — would take many more lifetimes than I have. But I long ago included, on my code of human kinds, a category for scientists, and I tend to trust its members.

Instead of having to establish a one-on-one connection with each, then, I can substitute the category "scientist" whenever I perceive signs that fit. When I trust a whole kind of person, it isn't Dunbar's watchful, bearded face that I envision but a huge hall of mirrors, with hundreds, or thousands, or hundreds of thousands of Dunbars in it, all of whom I can count on to follow certain conventions. That, I think, is how the human-kind calculator works. And that suggests a reason human kinds are linked with emotions about morality. "We-feeling" seems to be the guide that tells us who is appropriate for the kind of relations that morality governs.

Such relations, of course, are not always smooth. As Jonathan Haidt likes to point out, "There is more to morality than altruism and niceness." "We" don't necessarily get along. We may quarrel or even fight. In fact, many regions have a history of cycling through intermarriage, trade, and warfare — a pattern that the royal houses of Europe followed for centuries. A saying in one African tribe supposedly held, "They are our enemies. We marry them." Similarly, members of the Mae Enga tribe in New Guinea told anthropologists, "We marry the people we fight." The connections between intermarriage, trade, and war led the anthropologist Lawrence H. Keeley of the University of Chicago to speculate that they are all aspects of a single process.

So the feeling that someone is part of Us does not require that you find him or her pleasant to be around. Rather, Usness is a sense that someone is fit for the respectful exchanges of goods, services, information, and emotions that constitute life in a human community.

When the feeling of Usness clings to our opponents, we fight with a rule book and with respect. "Those guys," said an American soldier in Afghanistan in 2002, "got their pride like we got pride, fighting for what they believe in, that Taliban stuff, whatever it is." When instead we feel that opponents are Them, not part of the community of people fit to play the game, then there's no need for rules. A person who feels like one of Them isn't fought; he's dealt with, like an infestation of ants. Just as we would not trade benefits with him, so we would not trade punches. Killing someone who doesn't feel to us like a part of the human community does not, in fact, seem like killing a person. Perceptions of Themness are an emotional license for cruelty and murder. That seems straightforward enough: Us good, Them bad, even if no one human kind is Us 100 percent of the time.

The complicating element is that human kinds aren't literally things. Even well-bounded nations are mostly ideas, beliefs, and feelings, inside our heads. Which means our sense of human kinds, and their emotional impact, is always changing. We shift from feeling as if we belong to feeling that we do not; we see people as fellow members of Us one minute, then just breathing things — Them — in the next. And our human-kind categories ramp up our feelings, so that we can have shifting feelings not just about Robin Dunbar but also about scientists-in-general or Britons-in-general.

A harmless pageant of moods, maybe. But what if those thoughts can be *prevented* from shifting? Then Themness, this sense that some people are not fully human and not to be trusted is no longer a passing thought. It leaves the realm of psychology and becomes a political fact. Some of the myriad human kinds you see, then, feel as if they are not, never were, never could be, part of the human community. Their misery, then, does not feel like human misery. Their blood flowing in the gutter is not human blood.

So the human ability to sense Usness comes at a cost. Because you can get the emotional security of feeling we are part of Us easily, you can lose it just as easily. As travelers know, it can vanish in an instant. When it does, your emotions send up an alarm. Because if you aren't part of Us, you're one of Them.

These are not our respected opponents, whom we may fight to-day and trade with next month and marry next year. They are simply not present in our thoughts or feelings. Such people are "completely off the record," as a white driver told a black hitchhiker in the American South in 1959. (The black hitchhiker was actually a white writer in disguise.) Among Us, we keep an eye on the consequences. Will this give offense? Will this cause hurt feelings? To Them, we can say whatever pops into our heads. The same hitchhiker encountered another white man, who questioned him about black people and sex and asked to see his penis. That capacity for "theory of mind," which lets us understand other people so well, is switched off when it comes to Them.

Not surprisingly, these mental states — We-feeling and They-feeling — are intense physical experiences. When the American law professor Gregory Howard Williams, as a twelve-year-old on a bus in the segregated United States of the 1950s, learned that his Italian father was actually African American, the feelings he experienced sound like panic:

> All of us are white, I said to myself. But for the first time, I had to admit Dad didn't exactly look white. His deeply tanned skin puzzled me as I sat there trying to classify my own father. Goose bumps covered my arms as I realized that whatever he was, I was. . . . Fear over came me as I faced the Ohio countryside and pondered the discovery of my life. . . . I'm not colored! I look white! I've always been white! I go to "whites only" schools, "whites only" movie theaters and "whites only" swimming pools! I never heard anything crazier in my life!

Williams's intuition was correct. We-feeling is good for your health. It lowers your heart rate, reduces stress hormones, makes you sleep better and think more clearly. Conversely, a sense of being Them is bad for you. A sense of being Them, a nonrecognized nonpart of human community, pushes your mind and body toward jumbled thinking, anger and sadness, and a shorter life span. So an innate preference for good human-kind feelings over bad ones, for feeling like Us and not like Them, is no sideshow. It's one of life's main events.

Eleven

No Humans Involved

"NHI — No Humans Involved"

He was a Peuhl herdsman — a different tribe from ours — and didn't speak our language well. Although he might have been about our father's age, we didn't call him by the respectable title of Ata, or papa, as we did other adults, for he was a "foreigner."

— TÉTÉ-MICHEL KPOMASSIE

A tribe that we want to enslave. The government and the scientists give out that the people of this tribe have no souls; so they can be used without any scruple for any purpose whatsoever. Naturally we are interested in their language all the same; for of course we need to give them orders and get reports from them.

— LUDWIG WITTGENSTEIN

Music wafts up the stairs of a subway station in Manhattan. A violin. Plaintive and dignified, the tune echoes and reechoes off concrete and steel. I don't recognize it. Nonetheless, I can place the human kinds to which it seems to belong. My mental codes tell me this is

Eastern European music, possibly a folk tune or a composer's imitation of a folk tune. It sounds like it was written in the nineteenth century.

When I get to the bottom of the stair, I see the violinist — pale, blond, bearded. Eye agrees with ear; he fits the music. Listening to him intently is a black man in his fifties or sixties, who codes the music as I did. He, though, isn't pleased.

"Come on, man," he says. "Whyn't you play something *American?*"

The violinist looks at him, still playing, without rancor. The audience is asserting its taste. He responds, with a graceful phrase that turns the Old World melody into a blues number.

"That's better," says the other man. "That's it. You ain't in Russia now. Play some soul!"

We human beings have a great deal in common with other animals. Yet we do things no other creature can, and this musical encounter exemplifies a number of them. Only a human mind could, as I did, associate a sequence of sounds with a people and a place, without meeting the people or visiting the place. Only a human mind could care enough about the sound to want it changed, yet not so much as to want to kill the source of the sound. And only a human being, told that he should switch kinds, could shrug and literally change his tune.

This ability is probably one of the reasons we human beings dominate the planet. It is what permits us to live and work in giant human kinds — those things made of thousands, millions, even billions of people that we call corporations, cities, armies, nations, and religions. Without a way to feel that a stranger is part of Us, we would all be stuck living in troops of one hundred and fifty relatives and allies, trusting only those whose every expression, scar, and wrinkle we had known all our lives. Ants, bees, and termites cooperate on this massive urban scale, but they do it because they share genes. The human way is different.

The human way is to share *symbols,* which are flexible and various, to manipulate our Us-Them emotions, which are inflexible and simple. That's how the musician could change his human-kind status in the eyes and ears of his audience — how he could make himself a nonstranger, using the human-kind code that both men shared.

It is the reason, too, why I feel Us–Them emotion for total strangers who are fellow Americans. Symbolic indicators tell me their kind: accents, words, information only Americans care about (like National League playoffs instead of rugby tournaments), certain tastes in food and movies, certain forms of clothing and decoration. In an encounter with someone new, we just look for the right *signs* that he's trustworthy, one of the right people — in other words, one of Us. It's a neat trick. Thanks to it, we run the planet.

How, though, do we learn these symbols? What makes them work when they're run through the human-kind code of the mind? No doubt, much is simple this–means–that association. Mental codes overlap, and different brain circuits communicate constantly.

Some of these (or at least the capacity to learn them) are built in. It is much easier to get children to fear snakes, for instance, than to get them to fear electrical sockets. However, it's clear that a lot of our associational talent is free-floating. We can connect almost *anything* we have experienced to anything else. In other words, when the child is gathering material to feed his or her code for human kinds, anything can serve the purpose. The material does not have to be moral, or accurate, or desirable. It just has to feel relevant and be easy to perceive.

Physical appearance fits the bill. The Christian rulers of medieval Spain required their Muslim subjects to wear a particular hairstyle, as did the Taliban in Afghanistan. In most Western societies, this sort of inflexible requirement that people dress to represent their kind has been replaced by a requirement that each of us make such choices. We call it fashion. It is supposed to be a pleasure now instead of a burden, but in any event it is the same business of choosing markers — hairstyle, jewelry, clothing, tattoos — to represent the kind we belong to.

Many other indicators of human kind come to us via eye (flags, statues) and ear (music that we can place on the code of territories and ethnicities, or languages that, before modern standardization, would let hearers distinguish two speakers who lived only fifty miles apart). These are the sorts of indicators ("if Y is present, then this is Group X") that the political scientist Harold Isaacs, following the English philosopher Francis Bacon, dubbed "the idols of the tribe."

These are not the only senses that present us with simple human-kind indicators. The perceptions also arrive through the nose. Even with its comparatively limited capacity for distinguishing smells, the human nose can tell us where we are on the code of human kinds. Not for nothing do many religions use incense in their ceremonies; not for nothing do people who dislike a particular country or region speak of its nasty odor. "When I was fighting in Korea they were a poor country; they used human waste as fertilizer," an American veteran once said to me. Fifty years after he left, his face still contorted into the familiar about-to-spit look, a universal indicator of disgust. "The whole country smelled of it," the man said. "And when I got back, everything in my duffel smelled of the place. It was months before I got that smell off me."

Touch, too, tells where we are among the human kinds. So does the sense known as "proprioception" — the brain codes that tell us where the body is in space and where its limbs are. Both senses feed your sense of human kinds by relating your experience to your habits. Clothes you aren't used to wearing, for instance, pinch in the wrong place, they're the wrong texture, they're too hot and confining (or too skimpy and exposing). Or consider situations in which you're dressed in your usual fashion but no one around you is. Something is amiss, you sense. The people around you are wearing costumes instead of proper clothes. Or the people around you are dressed for the place and occasion, but you're like the guy who came to the wedding in cutoffs.

In the same sense (pun intended), unfamiliar movements make you uncomfortable. I grew up in a Western country; bowing to others, which feels natural to people raised in Japan, strikes me as strange and awkward. I have no religious attachment. So when once I found myself in a Jewish prayer service, I had no idea that the man in front of me would step backward, expecting me to do the same. I got a heel on my toe; he landed on the strange, gristly softness of a foot instead of the floor he was expecting. But I think the real reason we were flummoxed in that moment was that our body-in-space codes were telling us that the other man wasn't playing by the same rules.

The most visceral human-kind messages, though, don't come from eye, ear, skin, nose, or the body's gyroscopes. Instead, they come on the tongue. Food and all its related customs place us among the human kinds with amazing precision. Consider the Kansas worker for the 1990 United States Census whose job was to interview people who had not mailed in the required form. She was assigned to an apartment complex that housed many immigrants from India. As she approached the door of her first prospects, she said, she could smell dinner cooking. And the odors made her sick. "I never smelled anything so terrible in my life," she said the next day, as she quit the job.

Cultural training makes much use of this kind of food sensitivity. Nothing could be clearer and easier to learn than the rules that make sure a child eats what "we" eat and avoids perfectly good food that isn't "for us." In the 1950s the anthropologist Herbert Passin heard this from a Korean informant, describing his memories of a man who belonged to the paekchong: "I would often see him in his shop cutting off chunks of raw beef with his knife and eating it right then and there."

Wow. Yuck. Except that ordinary Koreans also ate raw beef, as Passin's informant knew. "Of course," he added, "we eat raw beef too, but we treat it with spices."

People often justify their dietary restrictions as healthy. (Vegetarianism is better for you, say observant Hindus; pork carries diseases, say observant Muslims.) Millions of healthy pork eaters around the world give the lie to those claims. But these sentiments aren't really about medical matters: they're an appeal to human-kind emotions, a way of saying, "Our way is natural and right for the human body." They strum a web of associations that people learned as children: whatever is part of our way feels good, true, and beautiful. Not because it is, but because it's ours.

It seems odd at first glance that a wide-ranging, omnivorous animal like Homo sapiens would have the capacity to learn such a lesson, with the kind of intensity that foiled the poor census taker. But the psychologist Paul Rozin of the University of Pennsylvania has offered a theory to explain it. He reasons that human ancestors ranged all over the world; they could not have done this with a hardwired program that required only foods from one region. At the same time, many plants and animals are poisonous. A band whose children could not be convinced to avoid "bad" food would not see many grow into adulthood. Better to have infants prepared to eat anything after weaning (so they can live anywhere) but then put them through a period of intense, emotional learning to prune the list of possible foods down to what's safe in a particular locale.

There's a hint here of the reason food learning gets incorporated into the code for human kinds. Both mental processes represent local knowledge — what's right for us. And while people think of food cultures as national, ethnic, or religious — remember how loving Chinese food became a Jewish trait in New York City — most people have little trouble associating foods with *any* human kind. Food can stand for social class, like Joe Sixpack's beers; or personality types, like the dinners preferred by a real meat-and-potatoes kind of guy; or genders (if a married couple in a restaurant orders a big salad and a hearty stew, which is likely the woman's?). Food habits can be emblems of regional human kinds, as in southern cooking, and generational ones. Take a look at who is eating in any American restaurant you pass at 5:30 P.M. — not too many people under sixty.

Food preferences probably originated as mental codes that serve the body: to keep an animal from being poisoned or made ill. But when our circuits for eating right are summoned to work with the human-kind code, their meaning changes. Those feelings about the body are in essence transferred to a new object: instead of being disgusted by bad food, we can be disgusted by bad *actions,* deeds unworthy of our kind. Rozin has delineated this process of "moralization" in the realm of disgust, but he and his colleagues note that such connections also involve other basic emotions. That is, no doubt, one of the ways in which the realm of nations, religions, tribes, and political parties connects to the realm of fears, hopes, loves, and pains of the individual mind.

If we come to feel intense love, intense hatred, or intense disgust for a human kind — an ethnic group, a social class, a political movement — it is not likely to be for the reasons our conscious mind supplies. Just as you learn to drive a car without being able to say exactly how you coordinate your mind and muscles with the machine, so you learn to feel good toward some human kinds and badly toward others. In both cases, your brain is perfecting a code that works without your knowledge.

My guess is that early in the history of every society, people discover these powerful codes — the hidden language of Us and Them, which speaks directly to the unconscious mind. Perhaps it was the same sort of process that discovered strong drugs and poisons hidden among the many plants and animals used for food. Like beer or wine, these discoveries had mind-altering effects: getting people to feel strong emotions about human kinds changed how they acted.

That's a powerful drug in the hands of people with the authority over others. As historians have noted, rulers have used such power to promote their interests: they have worked, as the historian James Given puts it, "to penetrate the souls of ordinary men and women and reshape them according to elite conceptions of proper behavior and right order."

That task is not difficult. All a ruler need do is arrange the lives of his subjects so that their human-kind codes are shaped to the ruler's liking. With such codes in place, the masters of society could lord it over subjects who were bad people, not really Us. Ordinary subjects would not ask why those people, so much like themselves, were not considered human. Moreover, ordinary people would work hard to avoid becoming like those bad kinds. Rulers could punish those who resisted their domination by consigning them to the ranks of the despised.

Even more to their advantage, fear of being cast out dams up the normal ebb and flow of human-kind feelings I discussed before. Left to your own devices, you may cycle through feelings of Usness and Themness with anyone. For example, someone may find that a total stranger reminds her of her father and, at other times, her father feels like a total stranger. This is because the human kinds that become relevant at any given moment depend on a given situation. Once your senses tell you that a stranger is bad, however, you'll want to avoid classing yourself with him or her. The fear of being one of Them pushes against your frequent perception of sameness. Difference is all you may permit yourself to see.

Still, the mental codes for empathy are also strong and ancient. When the code for human kinds conflicts with the codes that impel people to cooperate with *any* other human being, sometimes the human-kind code loses. To the endless frustration of those in charge, their subjects sympathize, like, admire, and even love the "wrong" people.

A friend of mine grew up in the South before segregation ended. As a little girl, she remembers asking her mother why elderly African Americans would step out of the way when she walked down the street. Weren't they old people? Shouldn't she be the one making way for them? Her story reminded me of the Christian bandit in medieval Spain who told the Christian authorities he'd gang up with Muslims or Jews, no matter what anyone thought of it. He, too, had decided to value his experience above the lessons of those in charge.

All societies have means, though, of *enforcing* the official rules: laws and customs that work hard to sustain particular human-kind beliefs against the mind's natural fluidity.

Given how easily people team up with other human beings and how many different categories we all use for people, powerful persuasion is required to blind us to other people's potential as teammates.

Stigma fits the bill. The word is Greek for "mark"; it was originally a term used in classical Europe for the brand or cut made on the body of a slave or criminal — a permanent, inescapable sign of not-belonging, which could always be seen no matter what human kind its bearer felt a part of and no matter what he did.

You could argue that stigma imposed on one person can be justified; it might be (and often was) punishment for a crime. But stigma imposed on an entire population can't be just, because it falls on babies and other innocents. At the population level, stigma isn't about justice or about people and their actions at all. It is a kind of mental curare for the human-kind faculty. Stigma paralyzes the normal shifting process by which people might see another person as a fellow citizen in one context, a typical man in another, and a Christian in a third. Stigma tries to lock its victim into one human kind, all the time, in all contexts.

You and your friends and even your enemies can be many kinds of person in the course of a day. In contrast, stigmatized people, when the rhetoric works, are always and only one kind of person — the bad kind. The trick doesn't always work; stigma, like any other human-kind concept, depends on the goals and environment of the people involved in it. As the sociologist Erving Goffman pointed out, what is a stigma in one context may be fine in another. But when it does work, stigmatizing imagery blocks the usual flow of a person from one human kind to another. For example, other people may be parents and Methodists and Welshmen, but the man who has been to prison is always, first and foremost, an ex-con. Stigma, when it succeeds, creates what Goffman called a "spoiled identity."

Authority need not confine itself to words and images about bad people; it can actually *create* them. This is done by *forcing* the traits that signal "not one of Us" onto the bodies of despised people. Rulers crippled and marked criminals, so they would not look "right" as they hobbled past. They refused education to certain kinds of persons who would then be seen as stupid. They placed slaves under constant stress and then derided them as emotional and flighty.

People who live in societies without branding, public flogging, or scarlet letters can well imagine that humanity has outgrown the tricks of physical and rhetorical stigma. But those strategies are still with us, and they still work. The human-kind code has not changed in the past few centuries. The same buttons are there, still being pushed.

Consider one common sign of stigma: the association of a human kind with death. Such a link, the psychologist Jamie Arndt of the University of Arizona has found, makes people in his experiments angry. He sat volunteers at computers, where some saw a word associated with death flash by on the monitor, long enough to register but too quickly to be noticed by the conscious mind. They went on to read essays about foreigners, moral renegades, or critics of American culture. Another group of people just read the essays. Those who had been reminded of death were far more hostile to the foreigners. (Arndt and his colleagues have performed more than forty studies like this, in five nations, with similar results.)

Suppose the suggestion this work points to is correct — that reminders of death spark an Us–Them surge of anger at outsiders? What if the outsiders' very presence was a reminder of death? Other people might then feel the anger, the uneasiness of that association, without realizing its exact cause. They'd just feel that Those People really were not right.

Far-fetched? Maybe, but in many societies, the handling of corpses and slaughtering of animals were assigned to "low" classes of people, whose work linked their kind to feelings of disgust. The paekchong of Korea, besides being killers (they were butchers), also had the task of carrying coffins and leading the horses at state funerals.

Today the world's democracies do not force particular classes or ethnic groups to tan hides and haul corpses (though we do make uneasy jokes about undertakers). Nonetheless, that death association remains effective. Here, for example, is the late feminist writer Andrea Dworkin on the male gender: "Men love death. In everything they make, they hollow out a central place for death, let its rancid smell contaminate every dimension of whatever still survives. Men especially love murder." And then there is the gay activist and writer Michelangelo Signorile, writing about how the socially conservative senator Rick Santorum and his wife lost a baby, Gabriel Michael, shortly after delivery in 2003. Signorile notes that the Santorums took Gabriel Michael home after his death, so their other three children could hold him and say goodbye. Then the journalist lowers the death boom: "I mean, how much more perverted can you get," he writes, "than walking around with a dead, five-month-old fetus and having your kids caress it?"

At the other end of the American political spectrum, the right-wing commentator William Bennett, in 1998, was quick to draw the public's attention to a study that claimed the average life span of a homosexual man in North America was forty-three. Other conservatives repeated this number with delight.

As it happened, that study was erroneous. The sample it used was drawn from the ranks of men who placed ads looking for casual sex partners — people far more likely than the average gay man to contract HIV infection. The journalist and author Andrew Sullivan rebutted the claim in print, and Bennett recanted. But the myth, with its suggestion that a political enemy is the friend of death, continues to circulate. (In 2004 the antiabortion activist Randall Terry repeated the claim in an interview about his gay son.) The lure of this image — They Are Close to Death — is strong.

The association with death is far from the only rhetorical trick that appeals directly to our unconscious mind, to make us fear or hate a particular human kind. Another common one works on our ceaseless desire to exchange stuff with other people. What is exchanged might be goods or favors or information; it might be dinners or child care or gifts. Whatever the specific items, the common ground of communal life is this endless trade: If I invite you to lunch, I can expect that you'll invite me someday; if I help rebuild your damaged fence, I know you'll do me a good turn later. Some psychologists now speculate that the mind has a separate, fast-acting, specialized code for maintaining this way of life: a built-in "cheat detector" that makes us all keen to spot people who aren't playing by the rules. (More about this later.)

An array of human-kind tricks has evolved that seems to work on this cheat detector. By stigmatizing certain people as unworthy of taking part in exchanges, these techniques make us feel that those people are not, somehow, fully human. They aren't playing the same game, we feel; we don't want to loan them money, invite them for dinner, or let any of them marry our sister. The stigma puts the cheat detector on high alert.

One of the crudest ways to prompt this perception is to suggest that some other kind of person is not really human at all. At its most extreme, this involves classifying people as not alive — as things. Consider the words of Toshimi Mizobuchi, a veteran of the Japanese Army's Unit 731, which performed biological warfare experiments, including vivisections, on prisoners during World War II: "They were logs to me. Logs were not considered to be human. They were either spies or conspirators. They were already dead. So now they die a second time. We just executed a death sentence." The organization of complex bureaucratic societies has made this image easier to embrace. It's easy to see people as numbers in computers or pieces of paper in a file cabinet.

However, the distinction between alive and not alive appears to be rooted deep in our brain codes. We find it hard to convince ourselves that living things are not alive. (We're much more likely to go the opposite way and ascribe life to things.) Accordingly, a more common way to gin up negative emotions about a human kind is to concede that, yes, Those People are alive — just not human. They may, for instance, be animals. The ancient Greeks called slaves *andrapoda,* the "human-footed stock." *Yotsu* was a pejorative term for Japan's class of outcaste people in the sixteenth-century Tokugawa period (whose descendants, the *burakumin,* still face discrimination in the twenty-first century). The word means "four," as in four-legged. Among nineteenth-century white settlers in Oregon, one wrote, "It was customary to speak of the Indian man as a Buck; of the woman as a Squaw; until at length, in the general acceptance of these terms they ceased to recognize the rights of Humanity in those to whom they were so applied. By a very natural and easy transition, from being spoken of as brutes, they came to be thought of as game to be shot, or as vermin to be destroyed."

It's an effective piece of imagery: It has been rediscovered in so many times and places. In mid-2004, Brigadier General Janis Karpinski, whose troops had abused prisoners at the Abu Ghraib prison in Iraq, told the BBC about advice she'd received from another U.S. Army officer, Major General Geoffrey Miller. Karpinski said Miller, who was then running the military detention facility at Guantanamo Bay in Cuba, had told her to train the prisoners like animals. "He said they are like dogs and if you allow them to believe at any point that they are more than a dog then you've lost control of them." Calling a person an animal, or like an animal, also triggers other associations, about which more in a minute. Here let's focus on one aspect of the comparison: most animals are not a part of our moral and psychological economy. In the joking prejudiced phrase that Americans used in my childhood, you wouldn't want your sister to marry one. Animals don't engage our moral emotions. (If one does, we explain that the creature is an honorary person, "part of the family," "my child.")

Reciprocity is the mental code that's fired up by this rhetoric. It isn't just about unpleasant associations with animals. If that were so, then despised people around the world would always be depicted as subhuman. But these human kinds are imaged as both less *and* more than human, sometimes in the same sentence. Here is this, by Horatio Bottomley, an English writer who was complaining, at the start of World War I, about British subjects who were trying to change their German-sounding names: "You cannot naturalize an unnatural beast — a human abortion — a hellish fiend. But you can exterminate it." A beast can do much less than a human; a fiend can do much more. But both stand outside the human community. You wouldn't want either to marry your sister. Either one is unfit to be part of Us, as Aristotle long ago observed: "He who is unable to live in society, or who has no need because he is sufficient for himself, must be either a beast or a god."

Still, it's not easy to imagine that a human being is not human. With a brain tuned to pay close attention to other minds, you are constantly taking in evidence that others act and feel as you do. Your codes for interpersonal relationships impel you to treat them normally. You can learn to use a top-down code about human kinds, which tells you not to pay attention to signs of others' humanity. But it is not easy to maintain. A lot of the rest of the mind pulls against it.

Words alone are often inadequate to sustain the fiction. Accordingly, for thousands of years, those who held power over others have had methods for making the metaphor real. In order to make "wrong people" seem like animals, make them act like animals. When the Rattlers told the Eagles that they would have to crawl on their bellies, the boys were reinventing an ancient technique, the one used by ancient armies when they made the losers march under a yoke. In the twentieth century, it was much invoked during China's Cultural Revolution, when supposed counterrevolutionaries attacked by the Red Guards were made to walk on all fours and eat grass. This effort to make real what words depict can and has been taken to a ghastly conclusion. In northern Europe from the fifteenth century onward, people would engage in "gypsy hunts," with a bounty for each gypsy taken, dead or alive. In Denmark, one such hunt on November 11, 1835, killed 260 men, women, and children.

We twenty-first-century people imagine that we are free of such crude concoctions. Yet the imagery of They Are Animals is still around. Like the imagery of They Are Close to Death, this one persists in modern politics. A reader wrote Britain's *Daily Telegraph* in November 1998 to compare the "nauseating life style" of gay people to "that portrayed in the recent BBC 1 program 'Wildlife on One,' showing the activities of the pygmy chimps." She wrote it; the paper printed it. There are no more hunts for humans in Western Europe, but the mind has not changed.

There are still other ways to suggest lesser-human status. Despised kinds can be depicted as childish and flighty, be they Greek slaves of Roman masters, black slaves of American masters, homosexuals in mid-twentieth-century America, or women in many male-dominated societies. Or a group can be described as descended from some morally defective ancestor. Europeans once told each other that gypsies made the nails for Christ's crucifixion. Similarly, the paekchong of Korea were supposedly descendants of people who had helped the Mongol Kitan tribes in attacks on Korea in the thirteenth century. Among those classed as "mean people" (as opposed to good people) in Ming China were hereditary fisherfolk whose ancestors were said to have fought the first Ming emperor when the previous dynasty was collapsing. In medieval Catalonia, lords had the *ius maletractandi,* the right to abuse their serfs, because, it was said, their peasants' ancestors had refused to help Charlemagne repel the Muslim invaders and had converted to Islam.

Michael J. Casimir of the University of Cologne studies "wandering peoples," whose members live by moving around among farming peoples, offering goods and services and facing a great deal of hatred. He surveyed the legends of such human kinds as the gypsies of Europe, the tinkers of Ireland, the Gadulia Lahar of northern India, the Inaden of Niger, the Mawken of Southeast Asia, and the Waata of East Africa. All, he found, had similar legends about their origins. Their ancestors had been free, or rich, or proud; at the very least, not despised. Then the ancestors had committed a sin. (Incest, adultery, disrespecting God or Muhammad, forging the nails of Christ's cross, refusing alms to a holy man, were among the transgressions.) As a result they had been punished or cursed or at least obligated to live as they did. The extraordinary consistency of this shape in legends among many different peoples on four different continents suggests, Casimir thinks, that something universal in human psychology is at work. In the actions of ancestors comes an explanation for the painful state in which they find themselves.

The human-kind signal sent by a supposedly lesser human is that he will not or cannot behave correctly. That puts the unconscious cheat detector on alert, as there can be no good bargain with someone who does not follow the rules of trade. Sometimes this message is explicit: "they" don't know how to behave properly.

When the historian Emily Honig witnessed a jostling, shoving, unruly mass on a Shanghai bus, she was assured the people involved weren't regular Chinese; they were from Subei, what did she expect? This notion that those people, over there, don't follow normal rules is linked to sex. ("They" engage in sexual practices that we do not, so they literally aren't playing by our rules.) It's also linked to language. (There are rules for correct speech, which we know and they don't.)

Described out of an anthropology text, this sort of symbolic maneuver can seem transparently ludicrous. For years Korea's paek-chong, for example, could have only personal names, not family names. When they were permitted such names, they had to be words with unpleasant associations to Korean ears. (Similarly, twentieth-century Turks forced Armenians to take last names with pejorative connotations.)

Still, "They are less than human" is also a common claim in twenty-first-century political rhetoric. In mid-June of 2003, the Associated Press transmitted a gruesome photograph of Palestinian men carrying a charred severed arm from a car that had been hit by an Israeli missile. Within a few hours, the photo was posted on a politically oriented Web log, "Little Green Footballs," with the caption "These Aren't Savages?" "OK. I'm sorry to post a photo like this," wrote the blogger, "but it's time to put an end to the denials that Palestinians pull body parts out of missile-struck cars with their bare hands, and the accusations that I'm somehow a racist for pointing it out."

Racist, no. But enjoying the dubious kick of rhetoric that buzzes mental codes: "We are complete human beings, they are lesser (savages)." The ancient methods work today as well as they did in ancient times.

Here, for example, is Rush Limbaugh, the talk-radio star, stigmatizing Iraqis who were abused by U.S. troops. I've marked the appearances, in this transcript from 2004, of the coded cues: "They're the ones who are sick. [Diseased] They're the ones who are perverted. [Don't Know How to Behave] They are the ones who are dangerous. [Help Enemies] They are the ones who are subhuman. [Not Human] They are the ones who are human debris [Filth], not the United States of America and not our soldiers and not our prison guards."

Historically, though, a more common place to find this symbol system is in objects, not words. Buildings, streets, signs, clothes, and other artifacts of daily life get used to mark one group of people as lesser members of the human community. Such arrangements speak directly through eyes and ears to mental codes, telling them, "This is not a person to trust."

Some French churches in Brittany and southwestern France at one time had separate, low-ceilinged entrances for the cagots. Cagots could only bring up the rear of church processions; they could not carry knives. Paekchong could not wear the ordinary person's headgear but instead "a crude bamboo hat." Instead of the usual black silk band to tie the hat, they had to use a thin cord. At funerals, common people wore the bamboo, but paekchong were allowed only a mere kerchief. The garment they had to wear all the time amounted to work clothes.

Rules and customs also prescribed behavior. A despised human kind would have occupations that weren't morally respectable for "normal" people: executioners in peaceloving societies, for example, or those wandering tinkers and traders in agricultural regions.

Members of a marked group are addressed without respectful forms of speech or titles. Ancient Greeks and the Mende of Sierra Leone in the early 1900s and American slaveowners all felt free to call much older men "boy." Koreans talked to the paekchong in a similar way.

What is expected of people marked as lesser humans closely tracks what an ethologist would describe as submissive behavior in an animal — eyes down, voice low, emotions hidden. "When I think of the paekchong," one Korean recalled in the 1950s, "I remember a seedy old man, in dirty, tattered clothes, sitting around. When we had some errand, perhaps only to tell our mothers that we were coming home late, we would send him running. He had to bow and scrape, even to punks like me."

The combined effect of architecture, clothing, speech, and behavior all nudge the unconscious mind to think stigma about "those people" is true. These techniques speak in the language of Us-Them codes, making them confirm for the rest of the mind that those people really are "not right." And so the societal rules, which would be hard to maintain by force alone, come to feel like the natural order of things. A child does not simply hear that "those people" aren't quite right; the child *experiences* it with his or her eyes and ears.

Another Korean man recalled how he saw the paekchong as a child: "There were some at our school, but we used to keep away from them. Somehow we felt they were different, inferior to us. They wore different clothes, they spoke differently, their gestures were different, and they looked different. We thought of them as vulgar, unrefined."

Herbert Passin, the sociologist who studied the paekchong in the middle of the last century, noted how persistent these perceptions are. The mind, having learned a code, is reluctant to stop relying on it. So despised groups can get stuck. The association disappears when they stop the practices that trigger disgust or fear, but those feelings persist past their originating circumstances.

Perhaps it's a little like drug effects that outlast the "high": a perceptual taint persists well past the day when its supporting words and deeds are banned. Passin put it this way in 1956:

> Instead of people being polluted by the kind of work they do, the work is polluted by the kind of people who do it. Therefore even today the aura of pollution clings to the paekchong like a wet cloak, even though their traditional occupations are no longer considered degrading. An ordinary person who works at butchering or leather-work is accepted normally; but a paekchong, even if he is not a

butcher or leatherworker, is still considered not a proper person to associate with.

Writing thirty years later, the French anthropologist Claude Meillassoux described the same phenomenon in Mali, where slavery had been officially abolished by French colonial administrators. The traditional categories of servile people had been struck from public records, and descendants of slaves had obtained important positions in society. Nonetheless, they were still perceived through a film of old associations.

"Even today," he wrote, "whatever their social rank, public opinion still attributes to them all sorts of stereotypical defects: greed, dishonesty, lack of moral values, obscenity, and so on. . . . Prejudices are still so strong that some despise all Black Americans because they are all seen as the descendants of slaves. One does not give one's daughter in marriage to a person said to be of slave descent, whatever his social or political position."

The symbolic language of the cheat detector is unconscious, but it isn't hidden. From a sense that Those People aren't playing the game right flows the refusal to let them.

Symbolism that appeals to the cheat detector is not the only mental faculty susceptible to hijacking. Much older on the evolutionary time scale are another set of codes that respond very quickly to particular information, without the involvement of the conscious mind. They evolved to preserve an animal's life and health in the face of danger from predators, poisonous foods, and other dangers.

Paul Rozin found most people have quite powerful feelings about avoiding contamination. Most people, for example, have a visceral disgust against swallowing what has come out of a human mouth. We don't want to touch things that have been in contact with dirt or disease or corpses. That both these reactions are governed by distinct codes is suggested strongly by the fact that we have these reactions even when consciously we know they make no sense. My own spit is harmless to me; the sweater a man died in is not going to kill me. But codes that evolved long before the conscious mind fill me with disgust at these images.

Rozin found that this kind of disgust is transferable to the moral realm. Just as no one wants the dead man's sweater, so no one wants to wear Hitler's, either. (Yes, he asked.) In fact, Rozin's former student and colleague Jonathan Haidt has found that disgust, however triggered, has a single effect. When he presented volunteers with images of spoiled and rotting food while asking them to judge other people's actions, the physically disgusted people proved far more harsh in their moral opinions.

No surprise, then, that linking a human kind to this fear of contamination yields feelings that "they" are not to be invited to dinner — feelings that seem, while people experience them, to be both natural and moral. In the first part of the last century, in public buildings in Brittany, one could see signs that said: "It is forbidden to spit and to speak Breton." Thanks to the cheat detector (which is still working away, even though I'm now talking about a different mechanism), there is also a third emotion present when the contamination emotions are linked to people. After all, those people look much like us. If they are associated with contamination, we feel, unconsciously but strongly, that they have tried to sneak this disgusting trait into our life. Hence we feel anger.

Death and effluvia aren't the only triggers for the contamination emotions: disgust, fear, and anger toward the "bad" people. Another cue is dirt. In the aftermath of Indonesia's violent coup d'état in 1965, the new government designated the victims and their families as unclean. Suspect people found themselves unable to get jobs in the government, education system, and corporate worlds because they could not fulfill a new requirement: an official letter certifying that they came from a clean environment.

Dirt is a threat to health and order. Those who are associated with it, then, are a threat. Children, anxiously learning how to control themselves and others as they grow up, take to the lessons of dirty kinds quite readily. The Rattlers and the Eagles called boys they despised — not only "enemy" kids but also those in their tribe whose behavior jogged their moral emotions — "stinkers" and "dirty shirts."

Despite their ubiquity, though, these fears centered on bodily fluids, death, and dirt have not proven the most effective for stigma.

Human beings have another built-in fear about contamination, one that has proven extremely adaptable to symbolic uses, as well as extremely strong. We fear disease and disability.

The power of this motivation to affect human-kind thinking probably derives from the fact that it doesn't always need a symbol. The fear of death and the notion of a human kind called paek-chong could only be linked by words and objects that bridged the two. But the fear of disease evolved to make us wary of sick humans, long before symbol-use. Connecting, say, lepers and terror of infection requires no mental mediator. As the playwright and historian Charles L. Mee has observed, people who don't know why he walks with a cane (he had polio in the 1950s) react to him with a plain and simple fear: "Little children back away from me when I come near. Grown-ups have learned to repress this response, but children are honestly frightened of what they might catch from me."

From the fear of contagion, reasonable or not, came the fierce impulse throughout human history to exile the disabled and diseased. In medieval Europe, for example, contracting leprosy meant leaving the arena of exchange with other human beings. Lepers were formally separated from the rest of the human race at a church ceremony, whose officiant would recite the rules of their new life. Here is one list of such rules from fourteenth-century Paris:

Item, I forbid you to ever enter the church, the market, the mill, the public square, and any company or assembly of people. Item, I forbid you to wash your hands or other necessary things in any fountain or stream and if you wish to drink, take water with your cask, or some other vessel. I forbid you to walk about except in leper's clothes, and to walk barefoot anywhere except in your own house. I forbid you to touch anything you wish to buy, except with a stick or rod. Item, I forbid you to enter taverns or other houses if you wish to buy wine. Let wine be put in your mug. Item, I forbid you the company of women other than your own. Item, I forbid you to speak with anyone unless you be downwind of them, and I forbid you to walk along narrow paths unless no one will meet you. Item, I forbid you in walking a narrow path to touch anything at the side unless you wear gloves. I forbid you to touch children or to give them anything. I forbid you to eat or drink in any company except that of lepers.

Sickness still entails isolation. Much as the rational mind knows that cancer and emphysema are not contagious, other mental codes urge us away. Meanwhile, the sick person is removed from life's usual trade of news, favors, and goods. To a brain attuned to reciprocal exchanges, such a person feels less alive. If Paris and other twenty-first-century cities now lack ceremonies for isolating the sick, the emotional atmosphere has not been altered by the centuries.

Howard Markel, a physician and medical historian, took note of this when he described his life taking care of his terminally ill wife:

> Even a disease as "socially acceptable" and noncommunicable as cancer has the potential to frighten healthy people away. Caregivers of the ill, I learned firsthand, also complain of isolation from the so-called healthy or normal world. Friends, relatives, and colleagues frequently avoided both of us, especially as Debby's illness progressed. . . . Entries from the daily diary I kept during those months are filled with envy for those who were healthy, feelings of intense yet misdirected anger, and the sense of being "quarantined," cut off entirely from normal human society simply because I was the husband of a dying woman.

If people were purely rational creatures, such shunning would not take place. Seeing that all human kinds are answers to particular questions, they would see a woman as a cancer patient only when that category was relevant; at other times, they'd place her in human kinds like "mother," "voter," "work colleague." Mental codes for self-preservation alter the picture, promoting the ancient strategy that evolved long ago among our ancestors. Don't go near the sick; you might catch it. And don't waste time with people who cannot engage in the trades of communal life.

Combating this requires the conscious mind to work its top-down effects on the rest: to think, perhaps deliberately, how many other human-kind categories apply to the sick. The disability-rights movement reminds us that disabled people are good workers (reciprocity again) and that they're fellow citizens, fellow parents, and so on.

Some in the movement refer to the rest of society as "temporarily able" — a rhetorical reminder that their human kind eventually includes almost everyone.

However, the opposite rhetoric is also possible: depictions of human kinds as diseased in body or spirit, in which language and imagery replace actual sickness as the trigger for a fear of contamination. In medieval Europe, heresy was called a disease of the soul. In this more psychologically oriented era, we say — quickly, easily, without thinking — that practices and people we dislike are "sick." In the 1950s, the prominent American psychiatrist Francis J. Braceland called rock-and-roll music "a communicable disease."

One need not be an expert in health to use the stigma of illness. The American novelist and essayist Wallace Stegner once wrote a passage about a human kind he disliked and distrusted — people who move around; the sort of person who isn't attached to a single place. Such a person, he wrote, doesn't conserve or build; he just uses things up and moves on. And worse yet, Stegner adds, instinctively reaching for the imagery of They Are Diseased, this person "even seems to like and value his rootlessness, though to the placed person he shows the symptoms of nutritional deficiency, as if he suffered from some obscure scurvy or pellagra of the soul."

People with power are often quick to capitalize on the mind's innate fear of sickness. Often, they extend markers and practices associated with the sick to other despised groups. Cagots, like lepers, often were forbidden to touch food directly. In some parts of medieval Europe, direct contact with food was forbidden to Jews as well. Meanwhile, in premodern Korea, paekchong were not allowed to buy fresh fish in the markets. In many places, outbreaks of plague, smallpox, cholera, and other illnesses are blamed on some sort of bad kind — perhaps an ethnic group, perhaps some human kind whose practices have supposedly brought on the illness.

Then, too, methods of separating and isolating the despised human kind from other people are justified as measures to protect physical health. Isolation adds another level of convincingness to the rhetoric, because people who do not engage in reciprocal relationships can easily be imagined as takers who don't give back — parasites, who prod our fear of being cheated and our fear of contamination too. Daily practice teaches the unconscious mind what words teach the thinking self: there is something wrong with that kind of person.

Modern versions of such practices are still justified, speciously, as health measures. This strategy remains as powerful for us in the twenty-first century as it was in the twelfth. Markel studied quarantine practices and policies in the United States and found that every new group of immigrants was labeled, by words and by practice, as a health menace: "The nationality of 'undesirable' immigrants has changed over time in the United States but their association with disease, either real or perceived, has not."

A harsher way to associate a human kind with disease and disability, however, is to eliminate the symbol stage of the process. People fear a disabled person; societies accordingly have used mutilation as a punishment. People easily fear unusual-looking people. Found all over the world, then, are punishments like tattooing the face, cutting off an ear, shaving the head.

Whole populations, too, have been deprived in such a way that they are, in fact, more unhealthy than other people. They leave even a well-intentioned observer feeling that the stigma attached to Those People is natural and true.

Neither the paekchong nor the cagots exist anymore. As I've said, they were not massacred; they were redefined. Both were real, stigmatized human kinds, whose members lived apart from the rest of society and were supposed to marry only each other. Both endured for hundreds of years. Generations of ordinary people learned that these groups were strange, unclean, and unworthy. Nonetheless, their kinds — and their stigma — disappeared. The legal status of cagot was slowly done away with in the seventeenth and eighteenth centuries, and the tradition was almost dead in practice by the end of the nineteenth. Around that time, the legal status of paekchong was eliminated in Korea. Though prejudice lingered for a few decades, as Passin found, it's no longer a part of Korean life.

As convincing and long-lasting as stigma can be, it's still a matter of thought and feeling — the ever-changing electrochemical patterns in ever-changing human brains, engaging one another in ever-changing relations. So stigma isn't forever. This may be easier to see in the realm of intimate relationships, where the same stigmas come and go easily, as part of the ebb and flow of life with other people.

Life with other people is a constant drawing in and casting out — as if our individual relations were a playful parody of human-kind codes. A speaker of American English, for instance, might say "he's in the doghouse" (They Are Animals), or "I'm on her shit list today" (They Are Filthy), or "When your father gets home, you're dead meat" (They Are Linked to Death). The next day, human nature being what it is, the poisons no longer apply. Relationships among human kinds are not different. They too must change.

So despised groups may disappear as the mental map that includes them vanishes from mind after mind and those who fit the category are simply seen as something else. Despised groups may persist but be undespised, as have the Irish immigrants to North America in the beginning of the twentieth century or Chinese immigrants at the end. A human kind may pass through a period of stigma, leave it, and reenter it (as did the Jews of Europe over the past two millennia). The brain is always in mental motion, always checking its code against its circumstances.

This also means, though, that human kinds that were not stigmatized can be turned into despised groups, by the application of these techniques. As a spoiled identity can be unmade, so it can be made.

In the early 1990s Emily Honig, the historian who studies Chinese ethnicity, documented the creation of a new, stigmatized human kind in and around the city of Shanghai. Since the late nineteenth century, the city had been taking in immigrants from the northern half of its region, the Subei area. "Mostly refugees from floods, famine or war in their home districts," Honig explains, "Subei people did the jobs in Shanghai that were the least lucrative and the least desirable. They dominated the ranks of unskilled laborers — rickshaw pullers, dockworkers, construction workers, night soil haulers and garbage collectors, barbers, and bathhouse attendants."

As I've mentioned, many laws and traditions seek to stage-manage experience, so that daily life confirms the beliefs about human kinds that suit people with power. However, people also have experiences that are not managed by cultural or political authority. Subei people, though visually indistinguishable from other Chinese, did speak differently than their southern cousins. Attuned as humans are to language as a marker, that difference was enough to make them feel like a separate kind. Just walking about and noticing that all the garbage collectors seem to have the same kind of accent was enough to trigger connections between fear and that particular human kind.

Subei people were indeed associated with occupations that prompt unease about contamination, and the seeds were in place for their being defined as a distinct and despised human kind. But, Honig explains, that was not enough. Making the link between their work and their supposed nature as Subei people required people motivated to make that link.

Honig finds those motivated people in the history of a classic political struggle: a fight by different groups over resources.

Shanghai for the last 150 years has been overwhelmingly made up of immigrants. Honig believes people from south of the Jiangnan river magnified their differences with those from the region to its north, in order to claim the status "native" for themselves. The resources at stake were largely symbolic and emotional, exactly the things that matter to human beings, who live on a map of human kinds: What sort of food would be served in restaurants? What style of opera would be presented and supported? Who would feel like Us, and who would feel like Them? "In Shanghai, it was migrants from Jiangnan who ultimately won," Honig writes, "having defined Shanghai culture as one derived in large part from their own traditions."

Recalling Muzafer Sherif's point that human kinds arise from the relationship between observer and observed, you could predict what would happen next. Traveling for her work in the early 1990s, Honig encountered many forms of They Don't Behave Right. She was told that Subei people were the ones pushing and shoving on Shanghai's crowded buses. She heard the common insult, "Ignorant like a Jiangbei." A residence manager described one of his tenant families' constant quarrels: "That is why we don't want our children to become friends with Subei people — they seem nice on the surface but underneath there are always these kinds of problems."

When a fellow train passenger she was speaking with did not know the capital city of the United States, other riders jumped in to "explain" that he was from Subei. An acquaintance of Honig's, talking about a man involved in extramarital affairs, said, "He was from Subei, of course."

The feeling that Those Others don't play the same game extended to language too. For instance, people from Yangzhou, a Subei city, would insist to Honig that their town should not be lumped with that wretched Subei region. "People from Yangzhou know how to speak well," said one man from there. "Our speech is very careful and soft, while theirs [people from Yancheng] is very crude — wawawawawa."

Honig also encountered the imagery I've called They Are Filthy: "Dirty like a Jiangbei" is another common Shanghai phrase. There was also "Jiangbei swine," with its connotation of They Are Animals. She was also assured (They Help Our Enemies) that the Subei people had helped the Japanese during World War II.

People even told her that Subei people had low, comical taste (They Are Lesser Humans). "Jiangbei women," according to local authors of a report in the 1930s, "like to wear red and green silk clothes, embroidered shoes, pink or red stockings, and other brightly colored clothes," but women from south of the river "always wear more tasteful blue, black, or gray colored garments."

In sum, this spoiled identity, originating out of local conditions as they met the changeless shape of the human mind, turned into a human kind that, Honig argues, meets all the definitions of an ethnic group.

As with any other ethnic identity, this one is assumed to be passed on from parents to children. That it was created out of political and economic circumstances is forgotten. "Even in Shanghai today," Honig wrote in 1992, "it is not only the sons and daughters of workers of Subei origins who are shunned as marriage partners, but also the sons and daughters of officials of Subei origins." Marriage introduction bureaus that started up in the mid-1980s often find "anyone but a Subei person" or "will refuse a Subei person" written on the forms people turn in.

The Communist soldiers who took Shanghai in 1949 were largely from Subei, so Subei people are no longer at the bottom of the class hierarchy. In fact, the former president of China, Jiang Zemin, is from Subei. Yet discrimination persists. Jiang was mayor of Shanghai at the time Honig was doing her research. She tried to see him. But her research assistant made the mistake of saying Honig was an American scholar studying the history of the Subei people. "The mayor's secretary, obviously determined to protect his reputation, retorted, 'What makes you so sure the mayor is from Subei?!'"

Twelve

Don't Be a Stranger

The stranger is blind, even though he have eyes.

— HAUSA PROVERB

For when men cannot communicate their thoughts to each other, simply because of difference of language, all the similarity of their common human nature is of no avail to unite them in fellowship. So true is this that a man would be more cheerful with his dog for company than with a foreigner.

— ST. AUGUSTINE

I was not an American; I was not a man; I was by long education and continual compulsion and daily reminder, a colored man in a white world; and that white world often existed primarily, so far as I was concerned, to see with sleepless vigilance that I was kept within bounds.

— W.E.B. DU BOIS

This is a place where the simplest things are hard. Push the office door to open it, and you hit your nose. Around here, they pull doors open. You think you'll eat lunch in a restaurant at 3:00 P.M., but around here no place is serving. You think you can get a sandwich to carry along as you go, but here no one has heard of take-out. You try to explain it, but your command of the language is not good. They think you want to steal their plates and look at each other and roll their eyes, as they would at a child or a lunatic.

Tonight there's a social occasion. You have to give one of the natives a present. You brought a travel pillow. Here we go; people pass it around, squeezing the grainy, yielding insides. One woman asks, What's inside it?

Uh-oh. Buckwheat husks are inside it, but you don't know the word for those, not in this language. The best you can think of is a Russian word for the cooked variety, and though the steamy mush is not much of an approximation for the crisp husks inside the pillow, and though you have no idea if they even use the word here, it's the best you can come up with. And so you say, it's kasha. Well, sort of. Like kasha.

Interest drains from the questioner's pretty face, and she looks away from you to nothing in particular, because you're speaking nonsense. You too look away at a spot on the blank wall, feeling, perhaps, that the dead-end disappointed air of this little conversation is your fault. Or you may be one of those belligerent travelers, the kind who thinks, What the hell? They never heard of kasha? What's the matter with these people? Either way, you are, through no fault of any of these perfectly kind and polite people, now miserable. You cannot show them what you are; they can't tell you how to connect. This is a dead zone.

If intelligence is knowing the right thing to do, you can't be intelligent in such an encounter. You don't know what the "right" word, or gesture, or direction is — and cannot understand when people try to tell you. Nor can you learn from your actions. You might be able to tell from people's reactions if you have done or said the wrong thing, but without knowing their rules for life or the words they use to express them, you can't correct yourself.

The mind reads an instance of not knowing the rules — for language, for lunchtime, for door opening — as code for important facts about your status among the human kinds. It appears to work in the same way as that process that turns black-and-white shapes on this page into words and ideas in your head.

While some parts of your mind perceive shapes in the light, your language areas code those shapes as representations of other, invisible things — including the concepts "black" and "white" and "shape." In the same way, there are parts of the mind that know a person who does not speak your language is neither stupid nor hostile nor disrespectful. But the Us-Them code is not concerned with any of that. It seeks and finds just the cues it needs for its work. Human communities, of any sort — neighborhoods, sports teams, markets — work because their members have learned shared rules. They understand each other. A person who cannot understand or make himself understood, then, feels like someone who is too hostile, too stupid, or too childish to join. If a Frenchman is a man, Mark Twain wrote in *Huckleberry Finn,* why doesn't he *talk* like a man?

The great Italian essayist and novelist Primo Levi, making his way home after liberation from Auschwitz, met this sentiment in the person of a Russian soldier he encountered:

> The fact that a man, an adult, cannot speak Russian, which means he cannot speak, seems to him to smack of insolent arrogance, as if I had flatly refused to reply to him. He is not ill-intentioned, in fact, he is prepared to give me a hand, to raise me from my guilty condition of ignorance; Russian is so easy, everybody speaks it, even children who have not yet started to walk.

Such is the soul-wearing state of foreignness — not knowing the words, not knowing how to behave. French has a word for it, *depaysement:* decountrification. Words and deeds are what make you real to other people and reveal you to them. Not knowing the words, not knowing the deeds, you become a living shadow, alive but ignored for long stretches, like nobody's dog. Unable to take part in reciprocal exchanges that create and confirm dignity, you feel invisible. The anthropologist Clifford Geertz, for instance, describing his first days in Bali, wrote: "As we wandered around, uncertain, wistful, eager to please, people seemed to look right through us with a gaze focused several yards behind us on some more actual stone or tree. Almost nobody greeted us; but nobody scowled or said anything unpleasant to us either, which would have been almost as satisfactory."

Missionaries, journalists, and workers in nongovernmental organizations have described this state of mind too. Usually, though, it is a forgotten stage, hidden behind a bland phrase like "learning our way around" or "settling in." The mind, structured to remember *something,* has a hard time remembering the shape of nothing. One successful conversation in a strange land makes a brighter trail in the memory circuits of amygdala, temporal lobe, and cortex than a week of blank stares.

You might say this is not remarkable, compared to other life experiences. After all, those first days in a new country, or a new town, or a new job, are a little awkward. After a little while, you get your bearings, you get a feel for things, you start to know your way around. You are learning the ropes.

Unlike ropes, though, people must decide if they're willing to be known. When stigma blocks the desire to cure that foreign feeling, they're inclined to magnify its effects instead. If they believe and trust the alienating feelings and enforce the practices that give them a physical confirmation, then the stigmatized person is kept outside that arena where the game of life is played.

That happens a lot. In many societies, people have been locked into foreignness by practices that give them no way to escape. In his magisterial cross-cultural study of slavery, the sociologist Orlando Patterson notes that slaves were always defined as foreign, not as members of the society they served. Often they literally were foreigners, people born and raised elsewhere, then captured in war.

At other times and places, among the ancient Aztecs, the Egyptians, and the Chinese, the slave was an insider, a regular person who had fallen from good status. With this in mind, Patterson doesn't agree that slavery died out in Western Europe by the 1400s. Yes, he writes, Europeans had stopped bringing captives from other lands into their domains to be slaves. But the casting out of people into foreignness by sending them to the galleys continued until well into the nineteenth century. This practice endures in many countries, where one of the consequences of serious crime is being cast out of politics. In those countries, people convicted of crimes can no longer vote.

Stigma makes people aliens in their homes. It leaves them unable to speak the right words or do the right things, so that they are unable to take part in the tit-for-tat among equals that creates and confirms dignity. The foreigner doesn't participate in all the exchanges of favors, of information, of threat, which make people seem human to one another.

Being made foreign is like some nightmare trip that never ends, with no ticket home, no hotel, no passport, and no consulate. Stigmatized people have often observed that this deprivation is at the heart of the laws and conventions that poison their lives. In 1975, the South African activist Stephen Biko told an apartheid-era court that "the black man must reject all value systems that seek to make him a foreigner in the country of his birth and reduce his basic human dignity."

For people trapped by authority and tradition, feeling foreign is not a passing mood; it is a state of mind they have to escape if they are to feel like people. Desire to lose that feeling is at the root of politics — the reason to join and defend such multiperson creatures as states and mass movements. "This is what it all comes down to: Not to be foreign," wrote the novelist David Grossman about the meaning of Israel for Jews. "To belong. To be a partner with equal rights and obligations, a native and organic part of this great body." The same yearning occurred to James Zogby, president of the Arab-American Institute in Washington, when he testified before the U.S. Congress about the discrimination he experienced at airport security checks. "I mean," he said, "we want to be included and fully respected as American citizens."

Foreign feeling is a big problem for the mind. Being seen as human means being seen as someone who knows what to do, who can give and receive love and hate, respect and disrespect. If you can't do that, you're not there.

A child psychoanalyst, Selma Fraiberg, noticed this blankness in her own behavior, when working with blind babies. She and her colleagues loved their charges. They talked about them "the way proud parents do." Yet in their interactions with the blind, the staff felt something was missing: the sense of unconsciously shared rules, of playing the same game. In contrast, Fraiberg wrote, when a sighted child visits, "there is spontaneous rapport and we trot out our repertoire of antics with babies. We are back in the tribal system where the baby plays his social game and we play ours."

Looking into her heart to find a feeling like it, some more common yet similar emotion that she could share with the reader, Fraiberg hit on this:

> If one has worked very largely with blind babies for many years, as we have, the encounter with a sighted baby is absurdly like the experience of meeting a compatriot abroad after a long stay in a country where the language and customs are alien. The compatriot, who can be a perfect stranger asking directions, is greeted like a friend, his regional accent and idiom are endearing, and with nothing more in common than a continent two strangers can embark upon a social exchange in which nearly all the tribal signs are understood and correctly interpreted.

While babies without the right cues can fail to connect with their parents, total strangers can feel a perfect bond, if each finds the right signs in the other — the ones that indicate that this unfamiliar person knows how to be and knows what to do. In fact, a stranger with the right code can be better than a friend without it. More than one veteran of combat has noticed this.

For instance, Paul Moore wrote of his return from combat in World War II: "Many of us felt at sea those first few months. Even if we had definite plans, the world we were entering did not seem real. If I saw a Marine at a bar, I still would leave my friends, rush over, and shoot the breeze. It was like meeting another American when traveling in the Gobi Desert."

As I've already mentioned, these feelings of Usness and Themness are not naturally permanent. Veterans don't usually abandon their families to live with other veterans. (Though that does sometimes happen.) Foreignness for most of us is a sensation that comes and goes, as we cycle through the human kinds that are relevant to our immediate needs. Even a little foreign feeling, though, can make you empathize with stigmatized people, whose natural escape routes have been cut off.

The playwright and historian Charles L. Mee, recovering from polio when he was fourteen, was glad to get back to his suburban family. Yet he also recognized that he was now, somehow, with his crutches, an alien. That led his thoughts to other Americans, whom law and custom aimed to keep in a state of alienation without respite. He remembers watching television, with its images of happy, "normal" households: "This world seemed so foreign to me, and at the same time so familiar; actually, in many confusing ways, this version of the close-knit happy family, secure in the possession of the basic consumer durables, described my life. But at the same time, in some way I couldn't put my finger on, I knew this was not my world at all. I thought: Oh, I think I know how *Negroes* feel."

Of course, Mee's situation was different from that of African Americans in a segregated United States. He had some control over how much alienation he would experience. He could choose whether to come across as other or as one of us to his neighbors, by either emphasizing or ignoring his disability. How much difference does it make when people cannot choose to escape stigma so easily — when they are instead forced to live in it, reminded by tradition, habit, art, and law that they are not part of Us?

Short answer: a lot. Thanks to the last few decades of research on the connections between emotions, stress, and health, there is now abundant evidence that stigma is physically bad for people. It shortens their lives, lessens their abilities, and increases the allure of false consolations, like drugs and drink, that do harm. Because we have a human-kind faculty, there is a direct link between the practices and symbols of stigma in a society and the bodies of people who must live with those practices. Stigma drives up blood pressure, scrambles sleep, and increases your chances of dying young. Its effects are transmitted to the next generation too: a stigmatized mother is under stress, and a stressed mother is more likely to give birth to babies with physical and emotional difficulties.

Some of the research that explores these links has been aimed at curing victims of particularly brutal trauma. Other studies have tried simply to map mind-body links. Both kinds of work point in the same direction: the emotions of Us are good for you, and their opposite, the emotions of not-belonging, are literally toxic. A victim experiences that effect as stress, strain, and grief. A lab measures it as patterns of blood flow or neural firing in the brain, or as changes in levels of hormones and neurotransmitters. These are different measures, at different levels of explanation, for the same wound.

People who live their whole lives in stigma are often silent about it. There are more records from people forced out of their human status, who saw what they had lost and described it: free people made into slaves; well-off people thrown into poverty; "respectable" citizens who found themselves in prisons. And people who found themselves abruptly recategorized by political change.

First, in their stories, comes shock. You are the same today as you were last week, the same as you were when you spoke, person to person, to a neighbor. Now the neighbor ignores you, spits on you, wants to set fire to your home.

When a man is cast into slavery, says Homer, he loses half his *arete*, his human capacity and merit. After he had been worked over by a "slave breaker," Frederick Douglass recalled, "I was broken in body, soul, and spirit. My natural elasticity was crushed, my intellect languished, the disposition to read departed, the cheerful spark that lingered about my eyes died; the dark night of slavery closed in upon me; and behold a man transformed into a brute!"

A confident person's natural elasticity is a consequence, like any other state of mind, of chemical and electrical signals that travel between the brain and the rest of the body. Those signals fly in both directions. Brain "tells" body to relax or prepare for a fight, for example; body tells brain what thoughts and feelings are possible, given its physical state. An exhausted, frightened body usually won't permit its brain to feel joyful and confident; a brain consumed by fear won't signal its body to stand up tall and proud. As a person ages, these messages shape the paths on which they travel. Like a country road that widens over the years into a superhighway, the path to a strong and frequent emotion gets easier to take; conversely, the way to a seldom-felt emotion gets slow and difficult, like a potholed street no one drives down.

Still, there's a big difference between the way a body changes and the way a brain does. While the body is partly shaped by the world around it — muscles growing as they lift things, skin tanning in sun-light — the brain is responding to itself.

This insight is recent. When research on emotional stress began in the 1930s, the focus was pressure from the physical world. Walter Cannon, the Harvard physiologist who first applied the word *stress* to biology, took the term from mechanical engineering, where it de-scribed the distorting effects of strain on girders, bridge cables, and the like. Hans Selye, the University of Montreal biologist who mapped the injuries of stress and popularized the word, also intro-duced mechanical analogies to explain it.

It was the next generation of stress researchers, when they ex-plored the heart-pounding, skin-tingling, gut-wrenching feelings of the "fight-or-flight" response (a term Cannon coined), who turned inward. They found that the most important causes of fight-or-flight effects are not objects or events, but *thoughts.*

Fight or flight is an emergency-response system that evolved to respond to physical dangers. Bruce McEwen, a neuroendocrinolo-gist at Rockefeller University, has pointed out that this system is very old in the history of life; the human version is not much different from a salmon's. In people, though, the fight-or-flight system, at-tuned to physical danger, is not always in charge.

Unless you've had a most atypical life, you probably haven't spent your most stressed hours fighting physical dangers. It's more likely your stress comes from thoughts about where you stand with other people — in office, home, neighborhood, and society. You have probably worried about holiday spats, sibling rivalry, meeting your deadlines, looking foolish in front of your coworkers, or getting fired for a lot more of your hours on earth than you have spent flee-ing bears or floods.

So your stress response is not guiding your "upper" mental capac-ity. Quite the opposite. The part of your mind that imagines tomor-row, that remembers the election of 1999, that traffics in symbols like the flag or the Eucharist is often guiding your stress response. The difference was summed up in the title of a book by another pioneer in the field, McEwen's former student Robert Sapolsky: *Why Zebras Don't Get Ulcers.* Most animals feel stress when they sense danger. Humans feel stress when they *imagine* danger.

For primates that live in groups — including most monkeys and apes as well as *Homo sapiens* — one of the greatest dangers imaginable is exile from that source of comfort, safety, and knowledge. In such a band, notes the biologist Richard Wilkinson, of the University of Sussex, our ancestors lived all their lives. "In a world where people's survival depended not on money in the bank but on their social bonds, social exclusion would inevitably be highly aversive," he writes. "If you are excluded from the cooperative group, you risk being victimized or preyed upon." The imagined dangers that trigger the stress response most intensely are those that threaten your sense of belonging. As Jonathan Shay puts it, "the body codes social recognition and acceptance as physical safety."

The fight-or-flight response evolved millions of years ago. It was a simple code for translating the perception of danger into readiness for action. As McEwen says, this response shifts energy from long-term needs, like reproducing, learning, resisting disease, finding mates, getting food, and digesting it. Those goals are set aside in favor of responses that make the body ready to run or fight.

First, a brain structure called the hypothalamus signals the adrenal glands, on top of the kidneys. The glands respond with the body's equivalent of an air-raid siren. They secrete hormones — substances that travel all over the body prompting cells in many different places to act.

One of these, adrenaline, causes many of the fight-or-flight sensations that reach the conscious mind. It prompts the brain stem to signal various organs, via its direct links to eyes, salivary glands, larynx, heart, lungs, intestines, kidneys, and genitals. The heart speeds up, going from perhaps 50 beats a minute to 100, or even 150 (so blood can reach the muscles you need to run or fight); bronchial tubes open up in the lungs, so that more oxygen reaches the brain (causing that feeling of sudden alertness and clarity); the hair may stand on end, because blood vessels near the skin have tightened (to prevent too much bleeding if you are injured); the gut churns (you might need to evacuate their contents to lessen your weight as you run).

Hormones act as neurotransmitters in the brain. Adrenaline makes the cells that code for memories work harder, creating those flashbulb recollections and crystal-clear images of dangerous experiences. People given an adrenaline-blocking drug in one famous study were unable to recall a tragic story any better than a bland one — unlike the comparison group, who remembered the sad story much better. Conversely, people given an injection of adrenaline when they look at a series of pictures remember what they saw more clearly. The brain also responds to adrenaline by releasing natural painkillers, the endorphins. If you are to flee or to fight, you do not want to be sensitive to every scratch.

A few seconds after this first biochemical scramble comes another set of responses, involving the hypothalamus, the pituitary gland, and the adrenals. (It's called the hypothalamic-pituitary-adrenal axis, or HPA.) The hypothalamus puts out corticotropin-releasing factor, a chemical signal to the pituitary gland, nestled just below. The pituitary releases adrenocorticotropic hormone, which tells the adrenal glands to switch from releasing adrenaline and instead put forth a second hormone, cortisol.

Cortisol has effects all over body and brain, all following the logic of emergency, which puts "right now" ahead of the long view. Throughout the body, cortisol frees up glucose, the sugar that fuels brain and muscle activity. In the immune system, it signals white blood cells to get stickier, the better to clot a wound, and to gather near the skin and in the lymph nodes, where they'll be needed most if the body should suffer injuries. (McEwen, who figured this out with his colleague Firdaus Dhabar, calls it "stress induced trafficking.") For the brain, cortisol triggers supplies of extra glucose.

Cortisol also acts as a brake on the effects of adrenaline. It converts released "fuel" back into sugars and fats. It also triggers a set of events in the brain that make you yearn to replace the fuel you lost — in other words, it makes you hungry. Promoting the storage of fuel, it also converts some protein in muscle and bone to fat, and it steals minerals from bone.

What this adds up to, McEwen argues, is that stress is a natural balancing act between immediate needs and those of the long term. Adrenaline is essential in a crisis, for example, but too many sudden increases in blood pressure cause small tears in blood vessels; after the body repairs these with plaque of cholesterol, the result is impeded blood flow — and the risk of heart attack or stroke. So too the sympathetic nervous system also readies the body for fight or flight; other nerves — the parasympathetic system — do the opposite, sending signals to slow the heart rate, keep digestion moving, and relax.

Cortisol illustrates his point. Too much of it, too often, has effects that are like a bad parody of its benefits. Over time, it causes the thymus, that source of immune-system white blood cells, to shrink. If you are being chased by a bear, after all, your body should not be devoting too much energy to keeping your immune system ready for that cold you might catch next winter.

Long term, cortisol also prompts the body to store too much fat. (In fact, the ratio of waist to hip is now sometimes used as a measure of how much stress a person has experienced through life.) Too much cortisol for too long can interfere with bone formation. And too much cortisol damages the hippocampus, that crucial part of circuits that relate different experiences to one another.

London taxi drivers, who must learn detailed and complicated maps for navigating around their city, have larger hippocampi than their fellow citizens. Some studies have found, conversely, that people who have suffered severe traumas, like child abuse or wartime breakdowns, have smaller hippocampi than comparable people who did not suffer. In other words, stress may have the opposite effect on the hippocampus from that of steady effort. Apparent shrinkage also has been found in people who have suffered from chronic depression. Not all of these people were depressed at the time that Yvette Sheline and her colleagues at Washington University did the study. But the extent of hippocampal shrinkage was proportional to the amount of time they had been depressed in the past. "Under severe stress," McEwen writes, "the brain is quite literally withdrawing, showing a slight amount of cognitive impairment but protecting itself to fight another day."

Stress responses, then, are good for short-term emergencies and bad as a way of life. If, as I have been arguing, stigma is a cause of stress, then stigma as a way of life will turn out to be a cause of ill health. And the effect will be a direct consequence of stigma itself, not an indirect result of it. In other words, it will turn out that people on the bottom of society's hierarchy, who die younger and endure more illnesses, will suffer because they *perceive* themselves at the bottom — not just because they can't afford doctors or good food or safe housing.

In fact, this is exactly the case, and epidemiologists have been surprised at just how big the effect is. In the early years of research into why poor people are less healthy than the rich, Wilkinson and his colleagues looked to housing, diet, air pollution, and the like for the cause. But physical circumstances were not the explanation. As he put it, "We assumed that the key relationships were between people and things." Instead, he says, the key is relations between people and people.

Human beings who perceive themselves to be friendless outsiders, at the bottom of a hierarchy, suffer severely from the effects of chronic stress. There are greater risks for long-term health, like exposure to dangerous chemicals. But few people work with dangerous chemicals. In contrast, Wilkinson writes, "A large proportion of the population are exposed to the difficulties of subordinate social status and poor social networks, so the combination of high proportion of the population so exposed, and big differences in risk, make these extremely important risk factors."

People who perceive themselves to be at the bottom of the social ladder score higher on the standard medical markers of stress. They have higher levels of cortisol in their blood and saliva. They have a lower ratio of waist circumference to hip circumference, an indicator of the presence of abdominal fat, which constant stress promotes; they have higher blood pressure and higher rates of cholesterol, heart disease, and stroke. They also have higher incidences of anxiety and, especially, of depression.

Studies of large populations are good at exploring relationships among traits and describing how strongly one is tied to another. For example, recent research has shown that people who think they're low in status are much more likely to suffer stress-related health problems. And it turns out that people's perception of their status, not poverty or lack of education, is the important element. If you rely upon a person's income or schooling to make a prediction about her overall health, your odds of being right are not as good as they would be if you relied instead on how she ranks herself among the human kinds.

However, a link between two measurements does not reveal which is cause and which is effect. Galton's great successor in the establishment of modern statistics, Sir Ronald Fisher, spent many years arguing that smoking did not lead to cancer. After all, the data that could establish such a link could also support the opposite idea: that people prone to cancer were drawn, because of their unusual lungs, to take up tobacco. (In fact, this is what Fisher believed.)

If an absence of we-feeling is associated with stress and ill health, then, that doesn't prove that stigma causes ill health. It could be the other way around: Maybe people prone to ill health get stressed easily, which makes them less able to succeed, so that they end up at the bottom of the ladder.

Sorting that out requires a different kind of evidence, which doesn't rely on correlation. As with the link between smoking and lung cancer, the stigma-to-stress-to-ill-health chain has been established by studies of particular individuals over long periods of their lives. These studies tracked people who started out with typical health and stress measures, followed them through low-status situations, and measured the rise in their blood pressure, cortisol levels, and cholesterol rates. That's the work that makes clear the causal link. The problem is not that less healthy, less capable people gravitate to low-status work; rather, low-status work makes people sicker and less capable.

Since 1967, Sir Michael Marmot and his colleagues at University College of London have been studying civil-service employees, relating their health measures to their work lives. Measures of stress-related ill health increased as they went down the ranks of civil servants. Top-ranking administrators had the lowest blood pressure; bottom-ranking clerks had the highest. The difference wasn't due to varying levels of care. Habits like smoking and drinking didn't account for most of the effect, either. High-ranking smokers still lived longer and felt healthier than low-ranking smokers, and low-ranking teetotalers had worse health measures than high-ranking ones. Marmot found that the lowest-level bureaucrats were four times as likely

to die of a heart attack as those on the top rung of the office pecking order.

You might think these status differences were all consequences of
nonpsychological factors. After all, stigmatized people — gypsies in
Eastern Europe, African Americans in the United States, untouchables in India — often are poorer and less educated than their fellow
citizens. Lacking information about medical matters and money to
pay for health care would lead to a less healthy life.

If this were correct, though, scores on health measures like blood
pressure and cortisol levels should depend on material conditions:
People with medicine cabinets and family doctors should be better
off than people who lack these amenities, no matter where they live.
In fact, this is not always the case.

For people who aren't in abject poverty, material advantage
doesn't correlate with measures of health and stress. People who see
themselves at the bottom of a rich society are in worse shape than
those who see themselves at the top of a poor one. This is one of the
reasons that measures of overall health don't favor the wealthiest societies — why the people of Greece have lower incomes but longer
life expectancies than Americans. If you want low cortisol levels and
a healthy outlook on life, you're better off being in the elite of a
poor nation than trudging off to a no-respect McJob in a wealthy
one.

About ten years ago, Nancy Adler, of the University of California in
San Francisco, began trying to incorporate status perceptions into the
study of public health. She shows her research subjects a sheet of paper
on which is printed a ten-step ladder (it's called the MacArthur Scale of
Subjective Social Status). She asks the volunteers to imagine that the
ladder represents their society and asks them to mark where they
would place themselves. Correlated with psychological tests and
physiological measures of stress and health, the ladder can be used to
see whether the women's self-perceptions are connected to stress-
related health problems.

When Adler, a health psychologist, gave the ladder study to 150
women who were participating in a medical study, the results were
clear. Self-placement on the status ladder was a better predictor of

health than the objective measures of social standing, like income level and education. The higher a woman placed herself on the status ladder, the smaller would be her waist–hip ratio, the lower would be her base cortisol level, and the less likely she was to be extra sensitive to cortisol's effects.

The results of psychological tests were even more striking. The higher the women placed themselves on the ladder, the lower they scored on measures of chronic stress; the less they described their lives as stressful, the less often they reported dealing with their problems through excessive drinking, going to the movies too often, or engaging in other forms of head–in–the–sand escapism. The higher on the ladder they rated themselves, the more likely they were to say they felt in control of their lives and the more likely they were to say they coped with problems by facing them head-on.

These findings point to a link between medical measures of health and psychological measures of attitudes toward life, relating them both to perceptions of low standing in society. I think it's reasonable to call those perceptions a form of Themness — a recognition that human kinds all around you are run by and for people who don't include you.

What about Themness makes it unhealthy? Part of the answer is suggested by work on animals and their "pecking orders."

As the name implies, the first scientist to discuss pecking orders worked with chickens. It was a German biologist, Thorleif Schjelderup-Ebbe, who coined the term *Hackordnung* to describe the predictable pattern he saw in the hen yard, where a "top" bird pecked but was never pecked, a bottom animal was pecked but never pecked, and all the others fell in between. (Political journalists imported the term into their work in the 1950s, which is how it became part of American common sense.) Many group-living animals have such orders, sometimes permanently, sometimes only when they're fighting over food or mates.

If the lives of hunter-gatherer groups are any indication of the way all humans once lived (which seems a pretty good bet), then it is important to note that these people do not live by pecking orders. Hunter-gatherers are strictly egalitarian. In fact, as the anthropologist

Christopher Boehm has reported, such groups tend to practice what he calls "counterdominance" — the group gangs up on anyone who is too strong, too scary, or too full of himself. People's pecking orders have to be imposed.

Human nature gives a single shape to the practices that do this imposing, no matter where or when they take place. The same stigmas recur all over the world. In 1975 the French anthropologist Michel Izard coined a term to describe these customs and practices. In the precolonial West African society he studied, he noted that the slaves were people who had been captured in war. As losers of the battle, they were already dead, without the attributes of living human beings. Physically alive but without any of the attributes of a human, the slaves lived in a condition of "social death."

Some years later, the historian Orlando Patterson of Harvard proposed that the concept of social death was an element of all slave systems throughout history. In Patterson's wake, researchers in other fields saw that the imposed foreignness of social death applied to other human kinds besides slaves. Historians applied it to heretics under the medieval Catholic Inquisition. Others noted how well it described the experience of people trapped in Nazi codes for human kinds. Social death is, as Lawrence Hirschfeld said of racial categories, "easy to think with."

The term is a good one for imposed, irrevocable foreignness, for removal from the human community where all the back-and-forth exchanges of life take place. In fact, the concept of free people, now an abstract ideal, was originally a distinct human kind: the free were those who were born and developed together, in the networks of social life. "This membership," as one scholar has put it, "confers a privilege which is unknown to the alien and the slave."

To the rational parts of the mind, separation from the life of emotional and practical trade makes life difficult; to human-kind faculty, it's a catastrophe. Victor Klemperer, whose diaries recorded his precarious life in Nazi Germany as a victim of its racial laws, described the sensation when he was jailed and not allowed to keep his belt: "What good is philosophizing about the inviolability of one's inner moral dignity? I experienced the misery of my trousers falling down as the most extreme humiliation."

So people are affected by the signals of Themness, in a way that a creature without a human-kind code would not be. This might explain why the Nazi regime, bent on exterminating the Jews of Europe, also took the trouble to make certain they would not have pets. And why an aristocrat of the Fulani people of West Africa, finding himself a slave in eighteenth-century Mississippi, would not be practical and accept a haircut. To be shorn of his long locks was to lose his membership in humanity — not just his status as a prince but the world in which his hair meant something. He struggled so hard to avoid the shears that he had to be knocked down and tied to a tree.

The patterns that Patterson found in the rites and symbols of slavery are just the ones that would impress the mind's mental code for Us and Them. All the signs that tell the mind it belongs to a community of true humans, fit to trade favors and make bargains, are removed by the rituals of enslavement.

The ceremony of entrance into the socially dead state was a universal feature of slavery, Patterson found. The slave made a symbolic gesture of rejecting his community — exchanging the clothes that mark his place among the human kinds for those of his master's people, for instance, or placing his head in the master's hands. The name by which he was known as a full human being was taken away.

Often, too, a slave was marked: a shorn head is "found in the great majority of slaveholding societies," Patterson observes. The slave might be branded, tattooed, required to wear something, and forbidden to wear another — a mark of social death that no human mind can miss. Victor Klemperer, in his diary, records the first day that he is obligated to wear the Nazi-imposed yellow star for Jews: "I am shattered, cannot compose myself."

The ceremonies Patterson describes have a more-than-passing resemblance to Primo Levi's description of how he and his fellow deportees were processed at Auschwitz: "Nothing belongs to us anymore; they have taken away our clothes, our shoes, even our hair; if we speak, they will not listen to us, and if they listen, they will not understand. They will even take away our name; and if we want to keep it, we will have to find in ourselves the strength to do so, to manage somehow so that behind the name something of us, of us as we were, still remains."

If social death is created by manipulating a human-kind code of the mind, then it should not be surprising that its symbols and practices appear in widely separated times, places, and situations — including the kinds of trauma that therapists and doctors try to cure. That's the principle behind a recent movement to apply the concept of social death to help victims of torture, abusive homes, cults, kidnappings, and terrorist attacks.

In a way, this new field is an inverted mirror of the ancient work of stigmatizers. Where slave masters and inquisitors created social death, the therapists try to undo it, with many of the same tools — words, actions, commands, organized behavior. They too want to speak to the Us-Them code, in the special language it understands. But where the rhetoric of stigma tells the victim "you are one of Them," the therapists speak of rejoining the human community and of restoring connection and trust. In other words, they speak of Us.

Jonathan Shay is a Massachusetts psychiatrist and writer who works with troubled American veterans of the war in Vietnam. His clients all suffer from what contemporary psychiatry now calls post-traumatic stress disorder. (In earlier wars, it was "shell shock" and "combat fatigue.") Years ago, he read Patterson's accounts of slavery and saw a connection with the experience of his veteran patients. After all, as Shay has written, in war each side is attempting to break the will of the other to fight. "The mind, the heart, the soul of the combat soldier become the focus of competing attempts to enslave." And no modern soldier is free to decide to quit; all, whether they wish to be there or not, are captives, and a combat soldier who runs away from the enemy faces the same fate as one who runs toward them: capture, confinement, possible death.

"The front line is thus a narrow zone of fear and death lying between two prisons," Shay has written. But social death, he told me, is a concept that applies far beyond the realm of the military. The trauma of being cast out of the human community is a physical event, an injury done to brain and body that does not differ depending on politics, religion, or the scale of the crime: an abused spouse's experience may be "smaller" than a political prisoner's numerically — if she's her tormentor's only victim — but it certainly isn't physically or psychologically less destructive. Shay's clients, Greek slaves, the prisoners of Auschwitz, and women kidnapped and forced into prostitution have all been through the same biological experience. What Shay calls "complex post-traumatic stress disorder" is the result of social death.

This list finds parallels in experiences of social death that are not called slavery — the reclassification of human kinds by modern societies, as Nazi Germany did to "non-Aryans" and Khmer Rouge Cambodia did to the people of its cities. However, it is also striking how well it fits more temporary transformations, which are a part of gentler lives in modern democracies: experiences as entering a prison, starting boot camp in military service, or being hazed to join a fraternity.

If human-kind perceptions are always under revision, responding to our shifting circumstances — with ever-changing answers to ever-changing questions posed by life — then they won't be permanent. To lock certain people into only one category, authorities must artificially arrange people's experience so that certain perceptions are frozen; even as situations change, these judgments feel permanent, always right and always relevant. And this is how I think of social death. It was not only lack of medical care or fresh vegetables that shrank the thymus glands of those paupers whose bodies so misled medical science. It was unrelenting stigma.

Thirteen

Hazings and Conversions

Now I see myself as a slave without being painted and no feathers attached to my head, my arms, around my waist, as the important people of my country are decorated, then I want to be dead.

— TUPINAMBAN SLAVE, SEVENTEENTH-CENTURY BRAZIL

"One is stripped of all civilian possessions except for what would fit on the small shelf of a narrow locker," the sociologist Pierre L. van den Berghe wrote, years later, about an experience he called "one of the most traumatic of my life." In a few hours, the marks of his membership in the human kinds he cherished — contact with people, his hair, his clothes — were taken away. His thoughts were no longer his own. They were now occupied with learning the rules that enforced his status as a nobody: rites of obedience to superiors, rhythmic group movement, the eight-digit number that had replaced his name.

The experience was basic training at the U.S. Army's Fort Ord, near San Francisco. The recruits had arrived with all manner of humankind codes and all sorts of loyalties from their civilian lives. (Van den Berghe served in the 1950s, when conscription was still in place, and the U.S. Army drew soldiers from all economic and regional groups.) The Army needed to put a new human kind — soldier — into the recruits' thoughts and feelings. More important than teaching them how to clean a gun and salute was the lesson that they belonged to this kind and that being part of it was more important than the other tribes to which they belonged. Without this "unit cohesion," armies can't fight well, because a warrior's strongest motivation has always been the welfare of his comrades. (Soldiers say loyalty to the comrades they live with and fight with is their strongest motivation.)

A deliberate plan to erase and replace a person's human-kind map is not modern. Almost all people go through "rites of passage," in which they are moved, forcefully and sometimes forcibly, from one human kind to another. These rites often organize their participants in ways that convince them that their new group is real, along the lines that Donald Campbell sketched. Participants groom and dress alike (as in the shaved heads of monks or new troops) to enhance their perceived similarity. They live and work together, apart from the rest of society, which tickles the mind's penchant for noticing which people are always near one another. This also enforces the thought that the group contains only those who belong and that any outsider will be ejected. New members live, work, and often suffer as a single unit.

When a whole building full of recruits is punished for one person's misdeed, everyone is forced to perceive that they share what Campbell called a common fate. Their marches, dances, chants, and other movements show the coordination of action that he called "good figure," another prompt for the mind to see people as a single entity. And finally, the new recruits — be they soldiers, nuns, prisoners, cult members, or medical residents — learn a specialized jargon. (Often, as van den Berghe points out, there are two, the official language of the institution and the talk of the ordinary grunts in the field, trying to get by.) The special language shows its speakers and all outsiders that information passes more quickly inside this human kind than outside it.

However, it's not just perception that must be rearranged to make a new tribe. Emotions must be changed as well; this new group wants not just your recognition but your loyalty. It is supposed to replace or at least take precedence over your old ones. And emotions don't respond to reason. They listen to the body and its day-to-day experience. If my goal is to take people of many different human kinds and make them one, then I'm going to need to inflict a little social death.

That may be why the features of training and initiation, both traditional and modern, have recognizable parallels to the creation of slaves. There is often isolation, in an unfamiliar place. Removal from friends, family, and familiar habits is a message to the human-kind faculty: Your old sense of Us and Them no longer applies. Like a child or a foreigner, you must learn how to feel right in this new environment, by learning how to play the same game as the natives. (The metaphor of becoming a child again is sometimes explicit, as in the Christian notion of being "born again" at baptism.) The loyalties by which you navigated have no use here. Added to the stress of learning a new code of human kinds often is sheer physical fatigue. New arrivals work hard and don't get to sleep enough.

Even as the mind is learning that old codes will not make it feel safe anymore, the body is getting the same message: we're in trouble. The effect is pressure, from "above" in the mind and "below" in the muscles, to forget the old human kinds and learn the new one. The mind seeks a new mental map that will bring back feelings of safety and security. The authorities provide that pattern — a set of representations that suits them.

This social death, though like the one Patterson explored, lacks one of the necessary traits he defined: it is not permanent. Those who endure it will leave it behind, but not for a return trip to their old place in life. Instead, they will become a different kind of person: a good soldier, a pious monk, a fraternity brother. The way out is to become part of this new Us.

There is nothing new or modern about susceptibility to these techniques. They're outlined in the manuals of Europe's medieval inquisitors. They're also in anthropologists' accounts of rites of passage. The likeliest explanation for their ubiquity is that they work on the human-kind codes found in every mind. Other parts of the mind can even watch the process, bemused to realize that it's working — because the human-kind code is its own separate system.

Paul Moore, a U.S. Marine in World War II, described one part of himself watching the other respond to manipulation. "I must say," he wrote in his memoirs, "that when the band sounded off with 'From the halls of Montezuma' I felt a surge of pride and joy, marching smartly with my rifle on my shoulder, the Marine Corps flag and Stars and Stripes waving in the breeze up ahead. I could understand how the young men of Germany became Nazis."

If you concentrate only on the disastrous effects of stigma, it's easy to forget that the temporary social deaths of initiation are not always bad. Many people welcome the emotional battering that tells them they are not a part of humanity right now. Like the poet John Donne, inviting God to "batter my heart," they want to be remade. This experience of giving yourself over to a new human kind can be a tool for making yourself better. In fact, the harsher an initiation is into a fraternity, sorority, or other such club, the more people value their membership. Moore, for one, was grateful that his code of human kinds had been rebuilt; he wanted to fight well and knew he had to be changed. "When I saw my first bodies and faced fire for the first time," he wrote, "I was thankful that I was no longer a sensitive, protected preppy."

This moral ambiguity of human-kind codes creates a political problem that has never been solved. A healthy society can't condemn the techniques that make enemy soldiers effective, because those same techniques have formed its troops. Loyalty to one's kind, too, is double-edged. Such loyalty preserved the South African statesman Nelson Mandela's resistance to apartheid through twenty-seven years in prison. The same form of loyalty, though, kept Kim Yong Su, a captured soldier, in a South Korean prison for the same term — twenty-seven years — during which he could have changed his mind and walked out a free man. His cause was North Korean Communism.

There is a difference between good and evil purposes; but that difference is unknown to the human-kind code. Wanting to join, wanting to be altered, wanting to be made, through our human-kind emotions, into someone new — these urges are a part of human nature and no political program can succeed by condemning them. The human race has to live with the danger that they will be misused. It might, in fact, be more useful to think of the dark side of training as a perversion of a perfectly natural aspect of life: the desire to join human kinds that we admire.

Nonetheless, we are descendants of people who were allergic to such pecking orders, and our bodies still are. As I've mentioned, animals at the bottoms of pecking orders show all the biological and behavioral signs of severe stress. In experiments on rats, some of the animals at the bottom simply drop dead. "Social hierarchy," writes Richard Wilkinson, "is the human equivalent of pecking order or dominance hierarchy. Though institutionalized to minimize open conflict, it is nevertheless a ranking based on power, coercion, and access to resources regardless of the needs of others."

That people are highly attuned to pecking orders has been established by many lines of research. Studies of people who are worked hard and deprived of control show a sharp drop in their levels of testosterone, a hormone that in both men and women is associated with feelings of confidence, aggressiveness, and zest for life. (In one study, six days of irregular sleep, little food, and heavy exercise so reduced testosterone levels in twenty-one Norwegian military cadets that their beards stopped growing.) James M. Dabbs, a University of Georgia biologist, found that simply losing a tennis match caused levels of testosterone in the losers' blood to fall. The hormone is so sensitive to the Us-related emotions that, Dabbs found, you don't even need to play the tennis match to be affected by the score. Sports fans whose team loses also experience a drop.

However, it isn't just pecking-order losers who suffer, as Robert Sapolsky has pointed out. For decades, Sapolsky studied social stress in a troop of wild baboons, which, unlike people, *always* establish a pecking order when they live together. By taking blood from tranquilized animals and analyzing the tissues of dead ones, Sapolsky was able to measure the amount of stress each animal was experiencing over time. And on all measures, he found, the top baboon was far more stressed than those who were not too far below — the ones who were not at the bottom, but who weren't worried about defending the throne, either.

What is especially stressful to a troop of primates — be they baboons, monkeys, or people — is the uncertainty of testing to establish a pecking order. Sapolsky was horrified to learn a few years ago that U.S. government rules for housing experimental rhesus monkeys were going to be changed to require a social hour, where the separately caged animals could spend time in one big room. That would be "a good way to give a monkey a heart attack," he says. At each meeting each and every animal would be a complete foreigner and would have to find its place. Once the pecking order was established, they would be taken back to their separate cages, forget the rules, and start from scratch again the next day. Primatologists managed to get the rule quashed.

Aside from status trouble, the other source of toxic stress, according to work on animals, is what Marmot has called "lack of control over life circumstances" — the feeling that you cannot figure out your own reliable rules for life (either because those rules are made by others or because you're in a chaotic situation in which there aren't any reliable patterns to be seen). One experiment involved rats who learned that, once they heard a tone, a particular part of their cage would get a mild electrical jolt. The animals soon learned to move to the other side as soon as they heard the sound. Then the experimenters made nonsense of the rule. The rats would move to the safe place and get shocked anyway. Soon afterward, they gave up moving at all. Even when the rules were restored, they still just huddled and stared rather than taking action to avoid the shock. They had learned that they were helpless. They were pretty sad to see, huddling in terror, taking no action to save themselves. They also showed every biological sign of severe stress.

Stigma tells its victims they are at the bottom of a pecking order because of a condition they cannot change: their membership in a supposedly fixed human kind. However, as I've mentioned, these effects are easy to reverse; people who are suffering from Themness can be cured by we-feeling.

First, stigma must be imposed and reimposed constantly because its victims will be quick to ignore it if they can — after all, they want to live. Second, no matter how thoroughly stigma is imposed by law and custom, its victims will resist. They have the means: Any human being can see herself as a member of thousands of human kinds, so why see yourself as part of one that is stigmatized? And they have the motive: the body wants to persist, in good health; the brain wants to thrive; the mind avoids unnecessary suffering.

One form of resistance to stigma has emerged in some of the

work Nancy Adler has been doing with her ten-step ladder. It turns out that there were considerable differences among women who were, objectively, of the same status: some placed themselves higher on the ladder than others. They were, in essence, using their human-kind faculty to improve their perceptions of themselves. Where some of the volunteers ranked themselves by job or education, others were perceiving themselves in other human kinds, whose status was higher. They might be church deacons, for example, rather than cleaning ladies, or political activists rather than college dropouts.

As he reckoned with his polio, Charles Mee saw clearly that he had to resist being placed in the category "polio victim"; he thought and felt that resistance was a matter of life or death. He fled occupational therapy, where he would have been taught some simple trade, suitable for his supposed kind. He writes: "The child who accepted the stigma of being 'not like other children' very often found himself on the road to withdrawal from the society of normals, to isolation, and, in time, to bitterness and anger and self-hatred." Mee insisted on being, as much as he could be, a "normal" kid.

One realm in which people express resistance to stigma is the world of clothes and fashion. In medieval Europe, many despised kinds (soldiers, wandering minstrels, and criminals) wore special clothes: multicolored, or "pied," or dagged — slitted along the sleeves. (The stereotype has been preserved, long after the actual tribes disappeared, in the fairy tale of the wicked pied piper.)

The association of brightly colored, eye-catching clothes with stigmatized groups is quite likely due to the mind's human-kind faculty. It's hard to see how else this link could be present in Europe five hundred years ago, where, one scholar writes, "all bright and too tight became a commonplace image of infamy," and also in the minds of Chinese residents of Shanghai in the 1930s, who believed that only Subei women wore bright, loud clothes, not like the tasteful dresses of other women.

In any event, the association of loud clothes with officially stigmatized people does not always work the way the authorities wish. After all, human-kind thoughts are ever-changing. People who are officially dubbed loose and low class can look kind of cool to people who aren't in charge — for instance, young people. What we know is that in medieval Europe, as in twenty-first-century America, authorities were vexed to see disreputable "lowlife" clothing adopted by regular people.

Medieval youths slashing their sleeves to imitate street toughs might sound familiar to parents in suburban America who find that their teenagers want to dress like inner-city "gangstas." The son of a lord or burgher in fourteenth-century France dagged his respectable clothes to look more like a common foot soldier or thug; in the United States today, many a lawyer's son and doctor's daughter adjust their clothes to look more like what a prison inmate would wear. "You make your pants baggy," Oscar Rodriguez, a twelve-year-old seventh grader at the School of the Incarnation in Washington Heights told a *New York Times* reporter. "You put them down low, and you put your shirt over it so they don't see your boxers or anything. Then you tie like a belt around it to hold your pants up," he said, but added, "You get into trouble anyway."

You get in trouble, because authority wants to keep control of the meaning of these signs of stigma. In medieval Europe, the elite wanted pied clothing to stand for a despised kind of person and a despised way of life. So they inveighed against fashion. In 1272, in Germany, one Berthold of Regensburg preached this: "You are not satisfied that almighty God has given you a choice of colors such as red, blue, white, green, yellow, and black for your clothing. No, in your arrogance you have cut your clothes into pieces — here putting red in the white, there yellow in the green, another is striped; this one motley, that dark brown. . . . This arrogance never ends, for as soon as someone discovers a new fashion, all of you must try it!" In the contemporary United States middle-class parents don't want their children to dress in the no-belt, no-shoelace fashion that they associate with prison inmates. Bring on the school uniforms. What irritates the authorities is not that people might join a despised group (who'd want to?) but rather the prospect that the sign, which gives them power, will lose its stigma. Tattoos in North America have gone through this process in the last forty years, as I've already mentioned.

So stigma as an institution is not just a matter of creating stereotypes and maintaining people's belief in those stereotypes. The same conventions that make a stereotype seem true to the onlooker also have an effect on the mind and brain of the *target*. The traditional methods of stigma that appear across many times and societies are those that efficiently do both kinds of work. These practices make onlookers believe that the target people are "not our kind" because of their looks and behavior. And the same practices also make the targets more likely to be the sort of people the stigma predicts. If your kind is *never* treated fairly, what sense does it make to put off today's pleasure for a better reward next month? Why count on the future when you see the rules changed or ignored every day? Why, in particular, should you keep promises made to those who make no promises to you? Stigmatized people often are said to live in the moment, while the rest of their society says they "lack character" and let themselves be ruled by their emotions.

Similarly, if your human kind is not allowed to keep the results of its labor, you have little incentive to work hard. So you don't. And so your oppressors say your kind is lazy. Then, too, if your kind is not given leisure to think about needs beyond survival, you might not be very interested in philosophy or math and might discourage such interests in your children; they will need every ounce of energy for practical pursuits. And so you and yours will confirm the stigma that your kind is unrefined and stupid.

In other words, stigma has an aspect of what the sociologist Robert K. Merton called a self-fulfilling prophecy. Generation after generation of people have been confined to stigmatized human kinds, stopped by law and custom from applying less damaging categories to themselves. It's hard to believe that this would not have some effects.

For example, in 1860, men designated as black in the U.S. averaged two inches shorter than the average white man — just the sort of real, measurable difference between two human kinds that "race realists" might use in their arguments. That difference in height was the consequence of stigma. It was an effect of stress, grief, overwork, and inadequate nutrition. Today, 140 years after the abolition of slavery and 50 years since the civil rights movement began, the average height of black and white men in the United States is the same.

That change hints at the reason stigmas are not always self-fulfilling.

As Sherif pointed out, human-kind codes derive from the perceived relationship between two human kinds. Naturally, then, as relationships among groups change, stigmas that no longer "fit" will cease to feel right. Slavery was banned and the civil rights of African Americans guaranteed by law because enough whites could be persuaded to see nonwhites as part of shared human kinds — as fellow believers in a just God, for example, and as fellow citizens of the same nation.

In other words, stigma can be undone because human beings are so good at seeing each other in multiple, overlapping human kinds. No one is a member of only one human kind ever, not in his own mind and not in the mind of anyone who looks at him. Accordingly, no stigma is ever perfect in its action; ordinary people, as they lead their lives, see one another in many different ways, some of which are free of stigma altogether.

This is why stigmatizing practices aim to narrow people's perceptions and to limit the kind of experiences they have with one another. The human-kind imagination is ever ready to see alternative codes of a situation; it is quick to think that the woman who just got on the train — even though she speaks a different language, and follows a different religion, and has no watch or cell phone — is a mother, just like me. Stigma prevents that moment of remapping. Its rules starve the human-kind imagination; they aim to prevent anyone from seeing the stigmatized as part of any human kind except the bad one. And this is a common aspect of rules for slaves, low castes, new initiates into religious orders, new prisoners, recruits in basic training.

Such practices forestall moments in which a woman might look at her slave and feel "We are both mothers," rather than "We are two entirely different kinds of person." Stigma prevents alternative kinds from becoming visible in ordinary experience. Yet this multiplicity of human kinds is still available, to onlookers and to the stigmatized. Most stigmatizing rules get violated, forcing the authorities to reimpose them.

Of course, this flexibility of mind is also available to the stigmatized. They use their ineradicable freedom to code the human kinds in many ways in order to recast themselves and their kind. That sort of remapping is at the heart of resistance to stigma, which I've described.

Resistance by recasting has been documented by historians and sociologists in many times and places. The more thoroughly people are hemmed in by strictures of stigma, the more their true beliefs about human kinds take place out of the view of those with power. As the political scientist James Scott of Yale has written, for stigmatized people, "the more menacing the power, the thicker the mask."

Oppressed peoples tell one another folktales about heroes who behave just like the frightened, humble sorts that masters expect — in order to get their way by craft and stealth. The tales reflect real strategies, Scott says, for "the active manipulation of rituals of subordination to turn them to good personal advantage."

If a stigmatized person can't redefine himself as a member of some other kind, then he redefines the kind in which he is trapped. The slave considered lazy by masters is actually crafty, saving himself from their will. The submissive wife who seems to bow to her husband actually runs the household. Terms that are supposed to connote stigma are put in a new context. Black is beautiful. We're queer, we're here, get used to it. Scott quotes an Ethiopian proverb: "When the great lord passes, the wise peasant bows and farts."

This kind of resistance, though, has a double edge. It defends against ill effects of Themness; however, it depends on the same human categories as the stigma it fights. True freedom from stigma does not depend on simply changing the terms applied to your human kind; rather, it consists in your freedom to ignore that human kind in favor of other categories for people.

The body tries to keep itself alive and healthy, and so it steers your mind away from human-kind ideas that depict you as helpless, statusless, or both. Physical well-being is undoubtedly one of the reasons that the mind naturally tries to find alternative ways of viewing the self on the map of human kinds. Slaves reimagining themselves as a Chosen People, a member of a stigmatized minority redefining herself as a doctor or a cop — by such redefinitions do people resist stigma and preserve, for themselves and their children, room to live and flourish as human beings. Redefining your human kinds is the most basic form of resistance. Each of us can do it, as did some of Nancy Adler's research subjects. But the most convincing signs of a human kind are the ones we can see, hear, and feel in the bodies and actions of others. So psychological resistance to oppression looks for confirmation, help, and allies.

That's where the personal becomes political. Social movements start by proposing new human kinds to persuade even those who benefit from the old ones. Don't think in terms of race, argued the American civil rights movement; we are all God's children. Sometimes these movements succeed. Official codes of the human kinds get redrawn. Segregation ends. Equal opportunity for women becomes an official goal of society. Understanding the human-kind code lets you see the links: how a biological need for health helps drive a psychic need to escape stigma, which helps drive a political need to change society.

Not surprisingly, perhaps, among the people with an unusual talent for redrawing mental maps are politicians. After all, they must recruit and maintain interest groups in order to have people to lead. So they must either reinforce existing boundaries and harp again and again on the one grouping that they wish to promote, or they must be adept at getting people to imagine themselves in a new kind of Us — as warm and safe as the old, but somehow better.

A memorable example of this kind of rhetoric of redrawing is the speech Robert F. Kennedy gave to a shocked crowd on the night that Martin Luther King Jr. was assassinated. At this volatile moment, Kennedy, a rich white man, a senator, and a candidate for the presidency — a privileged insider — reimagines the code of human kinds to place himself with the African Americans who are listening to him. He imagines an Us that consists of the category "those who have seen someone they love assassinated." Our mental codemaker is not designed for stigma. It licenses slavery and genocide only when it freezes perceptions with fear; it can turn a peaceful town into a burning ruin. But that codemaker, part of our human nature, also permitted Kennedy to say these words and the crowd to accept them with respect:

For those of you who are black and are tempted to be filled with hatred and distrust at the injustice of such an act, against all white people, I can only say that I feel in my own heart the same kind of feeling. I had a member of my family killed, but he was killed by a white man. But we have to make an effort in the United States, we have to make an effort to understand, to go beyond these rather difficult times.

Fourteen

The Heads on the Poles

I wish I could report otherwise, but scientists need their heroes and heads on poles as much as any other human group.

— DAVID SLOAN WILSON

One of the most striking traits of the inner life of a crowd is the feeling of being persecuted, a peculiar angry sensitiveness and irritability directed against those it has once and forever nominated as enemies. These can behave in any manner, harsh or conciliatory, cold or sympathetic, severe or mild — whatever they do will be interpreted as springing from an unshakable malevolence, a premeditated intention to destroy the crowd, openly or by stealth.

— ELIAS CANETTI

June 6, 1997. The annual meeting of the Human Behavior and Evolution Society in Tucson is coming back from lunch to hear a plenary address. A tall, thin, sandy-haired man with an eager smile is at the podium: John Alcock, a professor of biology at Arizona State University. The conference brings together scholars, writers, hobbyists, and cranks whose shared conviction is that evolutionary principles can and should be used to explain why people act the way they do. Most speakers at the five-day meeting get twenty minutes, on a program shared with several others. As a plenary addresser, Alcock gets the entire hour and the attention of the entire group. His topic is unusual — not a principle or theory, or review of some crucial question. His title is "Unpunctuated Equilibrium: Evolutionary Stasis in the Essays of Stephen Jay Gould."

Gould, of course, was the Harvard paleontologist who is famous as an essayist on topics biological, particularly those having to do with evolution. Within his field he is well known for a controversial theory that evolution moves in fits and starts, not smoothly (that's "punctuated equilibrium"). Outside his academic milieu, among interested laypeople who make his books best sellers, he was known for thinking that much about evolution can't be explained by general principles — not even those of natural selection. In general, he held, living things are the way they are and do the things they do because they are adapted to their environment. But many of the particulars are accidents. For instance, a family may carry a mutation that causes their children to have an extra fold of skin under their eyelids. If this feature is considered attractive and desirable, the trait could spread so that, many generations later, millions of modern descendants have this "epicanthic fold." (This example is mine, not Gould's, by the way.) Such an outcome would be an instance of evolution, but not of adaptation to an environment. Rather, it would exemplify sexual selection: like the peacock's tail, the epicanthic fold would have arisen by accidental mutation and then spread because it was considered pleasing in a mate.

Some doubt this and claim that the epicanthic fold arose as an adaptation to life on the snowy, windy steppes of Asia. But, as the science writer Steve Olson has explained, this assertion is debatable. After all, many peoples have lived on snowy, windy steppes for a long time without looking like East Asians. And that's not because epicanthic folds are rare. Many newborns of all ethnicities are born with one, though it often disappears later. If the trait were adaptive, then it should be found in the environments where it helps. And it shouldn't be found in, say, hot deserts. But it is: many !Kung in the Kalahari Desert have this feature too.

Gould's frequently made point is that it is far easier to *imagine* a trait is adaptive than to prove it, so refusing alternative explanations is a mistake. He pointed out that male nipples are a side effect of the basic human body design, for example, so asking why men have nipples is pointless. That would be like seeking the purpose of spandrels, the triangular spaces between arches in a cathedral. Spandrels have no function; they are a consequence of the shape of arches. (Gould and his Harvard colleague, the geneticist Richard Lewontin, made the spandrel argument in a paper that is either famous or infamous, depending on your intellectual loyalties.)

The people at the Human Behavior and Evolution Society meeting don't want to hear about accidents. They want principles, whose operations can be relied on, whatever the messy details. And one of those principles is that everything in life has a function (or, at least, is best understood if thought about as if it had a function). They ask and try to answer such questions as "What is grief for?" Gould did more than refuse their idea. He attacked it, ferociously, ever since his Harvard colleague E. O. Wilson launched their movement with his book *Sociobiology* in 1975. For decades, Gould ridiculed colleagues who thought Freud, Marx, and Wittgenstein could be swept aside by Darwin.

He is not alone among scientists. In 1999, the anthropologist John Tooby, then the president of the Human Behavior and Evolution Society, warned fellow Darwinians that Gould's arguments "have won the hearts and minds of large numbers of neuroscientists, biomedical researchers, anthropologists, psychologists, linguists, and even a substantial number of non-evolutionary biologists." Much more frustrating to the sociobiologists, Gould had a platform: his essays were published every month in the magazine *Natural History*. Then they were collected into well-reviewed, big-selling books. Most Americans interested in evolution saw Gould as its spokesman. He was, after all, famous enough to rate a guest appearance on *The Simpsons*.

And so, here in Arizona, I learn that the people Gould called "Darwinian fundamentalists" hate him — enough to spend forty-five minutes here, snickering and applauding as Alcock tears into Gould's prose style ("demonstrations of erudition — foreign phrases, poetry — irrelevant to the intellectual arguments but widely regarded even by his critics"), his manners ("branding the opposition with denigrating labels such as 'pop science,' 'pop psychology,' 'cardboard Darwinism,' or 'fundamentalist Darwinians' ") and his think-ing about adaptationism. Alcock ends with one arm extended, fist clenched, calling out, "Long live the adaptationist program!" to ap-plause, laughter, and cheers. The society's newsletter later reports that many in the group agreed with the sentiments of member J. Philippe Rushton: this address is "an emotional high point" of the meeting.

As I sit in the raucous audience, I find myself thinking of the fes-tival of hate described in George Orwell's novel *1984*, when a crowd assembles to look at images of the regime's official enemy, Goldstein. Orwell would grasp what's happening here, I think. What Darwin would make of it is hard to imagine.

As the applause dies down, and audience questions start, one of the first hands up belongs to a man who calls the show undignified and embarrassing. But this crowd is not with him. You have to under-stand, several attendees tell me later, how frustrating it is, how much harm Gould has done, what a hard time I get in my department.

It's a fair point, as far as it goes. Tribal flag-waving isn't confined to the Human Behavior and Evolution Society, and in their early years especially, people interested in these ideas encountered plenty of close-minded, how-dare-you scorn. In 1980, for example, the an-thropologist Clifford Geertz began a book review with these words: "This is a book about the 'primary male-female differences in sexuality among humans,' in which the following things are not discussed: guilt, wonder, loss, self-regard, death, metaphor, justice, purity, intention-ality, cowardice, hope, judgment, ideology, humor, obligation, despair, trust, malice, ritual, madness, forgiveness, sublimation, pity, ecstasy, obsession, discourse, and sentimentality. It could be only one thing, and it is. Sociobiology."

Thump! But what does this put-down actually mean? Basically, that you can't say anything about sex without talking about all these important topics because . . . well, you just can't! It is not, really, an argument. Instead, it's a bit of Us-Them stigma: Sociobiologists aren't thinking right. They Don't Know How to Behave.

In a sense, then, Alcock's talk was payback, in the same Us-Them coin. He was saying that Gould did not think, write, or research in the proper way. Alcock's was an hour-long exhibition of the same stigmatizing imagery. I was reminded of it a couple of years later, when the anti-Gould writer Robert Wright published an essay arguing that Gould's views encourage creationists to undermine evolutionary science — effective rhetoric because it is a form of that old standby of stigma, "They Help Our Enemies."

The fierce and focused anti-Gould screeds are a nice example of how readily ideas spawn human kinds. At first, an idea defines the trait (we are the people who believe in the adaptationist paradigm; they are the ones who don't). Human-kind feelings kick in and the idea becomes the banner we wave to rally those feelings and the shibboleth used to test other people's commitment.

At the same 1997 HBES conference, I sat next to a prominent Darwinian author who wasn't pleased about the choice of that night's speaker, a well-respected scientist. "I'm not sure what he's doing here," said the writer. "Some of the things he says aren't consistent with evolutionary thinking, really. Sometimes they sound like the sort of thing . . ."

Would he mention the Evil One?

Yes.

". . . that Stephen Jay Gould would say."

Gould died in 2003, depriving the evolutionary psychology movement of its focal demon. Away from the subject of Gould, that movement is, in any event, divided into many different persuasions. Yet the "ev-psych" people's air of resentment persists, even after Gould's death. Many of their papers, articles, and books still use the rhetoric of a persecuted people: we are ignored, we are misunderstood, we are deprived of grants and lab space.

Once an idea has become a banner, it's no longer free, in either sense of the word. It can't be used without cost — citing it cuts you off from people who refuse to join the human kind that the idea represents. And the idea itself is not free: it can't go where it pleases. If you change your mind, your human-kind code tells you that you're betraying your brothers in the fight. This may be why intellectual life crackles with the language of loyalty and treachery, of who is with Us and who is with Them. Certainly, the Alcock talk made clear that evolution-and-behavior thinkers ("Darwinians" to their friends, "evo psychos" to enemies) have become, in the eyes of both friends and enemies, a human kind.

That leads to a complicated way of life — having your theory both explain *and* exemplify human behavior. It would be nice to report that the evolutionary psychologists avoid getting into self-conscious tangles about that. But they march right into the hall of mirrors. I've seen them give talks on how to cope with a rough boss by treating him like a dominant chimp and advise friends and relatives to take adaptive mates. (Older women and younger men? A no-no.)

Yet evolutionary psychologists' tribalism says nothing, one way or the other, about whether the idea that rallied them is *right*. Their thinking has won over scientists and laypeople during the past quarter century because it cuts through the fog of details to get at the root question: Why are our minds the way they are?

The Darwinians look for what the late evolutionary biologist Ernst Mayr defined as "ultimate causes." That is, not how a trait or behavior works, or which parts of the brain it recruits, or how we know it is there, but a question from a different level of description: *Why* does it exist? That's what distinguishes their level of analysis from the ones that look at "proximate" causes.

Here is the difference: if, like most people, you can see colors, the proximate causes include the rods and cones in your eyes, the architecture of your optic system, the many codes in your brain that process signals from your eyes. The ultimate cause, in contrast, is whatever evolutionary pressure required that humans see color — as do flies and sparrows, but not dogs and cats. When you can say what *ultimately* causes some trait, goes the argument, then you put together many separate pieces of knowledge — rods, cones, neurons, brain regions, paintings — into a complete picture.

For human-kind problems, that's an attractive prospect: a way to make all this data — about DNA being copied, and molecules crossing cell membranes, and hormones surging, and stressed-out office clerks, and summer-camp cultures, and the rise of Hitler — really fit together. Perhaps research on politics can fold neatly into work in psychology, which in turn can fit neatly into work in biology. At the moment, many of the theories and procedures used in one field don't match those used in others. Sometimes, they even contradict one another.

For example, when evolutionary biologists theorize about traits like color vision and self-sacrifice, they picture a single gene. However, geneticists hold that most behavior depends on interactions among many different genes. Or, to take another case, the concept of "French culture" might be a powerful force to an anthropologist, who assumes it can cause people to act in particular ways. But a psychologist can spend his or her career looking for the sources of behavior in human nature and the particular circumstances of a person's life, and not think about culture at all. Ask a different question, you get a different answer. Scientists who try to connect various modes of knowledge sometimes find themselves stumbling over differences in the way their separate disciplines interrogate the world.

A lot of social-psychology research is premised on the idea that injustice and injury can be cured or prevented. That was why Theodor Adorno was looking for authoritarian personalities and why Gordon Allport wanted to understand the nature of prejudice. I wasn't surprised, then, when I watched a social psychologist draft a statement describing how the amygdala was "the culprit" in racial perceptions.

Neuroscience belongs to a different tradition. Much of its work is done in hospitals and medical schools, where equipment like PET scanners and MRI devices is located (and researchers work odd hours, at times when the machines aren't being used for patients). When neuroscientists talk to outsiders (writers like me, for instance, or, more important, people who might donate some money for research), they sound like doctors. Parkinson's disease or spinal injury is a much more likely topic at a neuroscience meeting than ethnic violence. The preferred level of analysis is Everyone — "the brain" and "the mind." It's a medical model of doing good — curing physical ills, not social ones.

One of my acquaintance's neuroscientist collaborators pounced on that word, *culprit*. The morally significant word that felt right to the psychologist was a red flag to the brain scientist. The term had to be changed, she told me. (It was.)

The difficulty is not that one field is right and the other wrong, any more than that today has to be either Thursday or April 16. Rather, the problem is that science, unlike a calendar, doesn't neatly lay out the relationship of each viewpoint to the others. There is a biochemistry of protein making, whose theories and methods do not neatly align with those used to study the molecular biology of genes, a field which does not neatly line up with the biology of human bodies, which does not neatly line up with the psychology of the mind, which does not neatly line up with history, anthropology, sociology, political science, "best practices," "management science," or any other organized body of knowledge about human kinds. The Darwinians are certainly right that answering the "ultimate cause" question about human tribes would help make connections. It would reveal how knowledge at one scale (for instance, the cell) relates to knowledge on another (the nation).

After all, in studying human kinds, researchers — whether or not they agree with the sociobiological program — are mixing anthropology with biochemistry, brain scans with psychology. Darwinians are rightly exasperated when they encounter unthinking banner waving: The self-satisfied and often ignorant cry that "you can't say insect behavior has any bearing on American politics!" As the evolution crowd says, this is not a self-evident truth. The satisfaction of defending "our" familiar knowledge against alien ideas has no relationship to the question of whether those ideas are right.

Still, many Darwinians are at the opposite extreme; their claim is that communication among the sciences can be, will be, perfect — that politics will fold into anthropology, which will fold into biology, which will fold into chemistry, which will fold into physics, in a neat, consistent framework. Many scientists doubt this heartily.

To see why, consider the human kind we call dyslexic. At the psychological and social levels of analysis, dyslexics are a real human kind: they're schoolchildren (and adults) who don't perceive words as most people do. The condition was first described at the end of the nineteenth century as a form of "word blindness." Today's view is that dyslexia is a consequence of the way brains interpret phonemes, the chunks of sound that are building blocks for words.

Dyslexia, like almost all traits, must result from interactions among many different genes. Nonetheless, one need not know which genes in order to figure out how important heredity is to the condition. Research began in the 1950s, with comparisons of fraternal and identical twins (Francis Galton's idea again), and more recent statistical studies suggest that part of what makes dyslexia happen is a consequence of inheritance.

Levels of analysis are largely independent of one another, so work at one level can take place before another is even known. When Gregor Mendel worked out the principles of heredity in the 1850s, for example, he used pea plants in a garden. DNA would not be described for another century. He did not know how the patterns of inheritance he discerned were made. Biochemistry and molecular biology arose only after he died.

Nor could he speculate about *why* pea plants would come in different heights, with different-colored flowers. That kind of delving into "ultimate causes" is the realm of modern evolutionary biology — the fruit of the "new synthesis" in biology that arose by combining Darwin's principles for natural selection with Mendel's for the workings of inheritance.

So there are a few distinct levels of analysis at which dyslexia can be studied. If you could take an elevator up through them, you would pass (to name a few): level 1, the molecular-biological (the making of proteins from a DNA template); level 2, the information-gene (alleles on different chromosomes that correlate with signs of dyslexia); level 3, the neurobiological (how brain activity in dyslexics differs from that of nondyslexics); level 4, the medical (how to tell if someone is dyslexic and what to do); level 5, the cultural (do we stigmatize dyslexics?); and level 6, the evolutionary (why evolution produces dyslexics).

When researchers study anything, they only use concepts from their discipline's level of analysis. In this way, many different ideas are applied to "the same" things. This is one reason that scientists, though they have completed a map of the human genome, cannot say precisely how many human genes there are or what they all do. At level 1, they see a tightly packed spring of deoxyribonucleic acid. At level 2, that molecule is divided into sections that bear information, and the rest is so-called junk DNA (a label that may fade as biologists establish how important that "junk" is). When you hear that people have a "gene for" something, you're at level 4, which defines what that something is (eye color, tallness, intelligence, propensity to divorce).

Up at this level of analysis, the gene is no longer a chemical or biological thing. It's a unit of information. At Level 6, it's not even that — it's just a way of labeling the source of some interesting trait, like fur or keen eyesight, in an animal's body, which evolutionists call the phenotype. (This distinguishes it from the genotype.) That trait may be rooted in a single gene or 13 or 130. At this level of analysis, you don't need to know, as Oxford's Richard Dawkins has explained: "In our Darwinism we postulate that there are genes for this and genes for that. We just leave the embryological causal link between genes and phenotype as a black box. We know that genes do, in fact, cause changes in phenotypes and that's all we really need, in order for Darwinism to work."

Of course, Dawkins didn't *deny* genes are chemical. He's not ignoring how genes-as-information work. His point here is that neither the molecule nor the information content of a given gene will answer *his* kind of question. His requires a different mode of thought. Again, think of a calendar. A single day in 1941 was simultaneously Wednesday, March 26, and the birthday of Richard Dawkins. So too *gene* can be a molecule in one lab, a unit of information in the office down the hall, and an evolutionary black box in the classroom one flight below.

The unsettled question about these different realms is their relationship to one another. At one end of the spectrum of opinion, there's the supposedly postmodern fuzzy-wuzzy notion that the levels of analysis have no connections at all. Can't be right: the history of science is too rich in cases of concepts and experiments from one level solving problems at another. For instance, the mathematics of impossible worlds, where the problems run to how best to pack ten-dimensional spheres, has turned out to be useful for pushing data through fiber-optic phone lines. The quark, first conceived at the mathematical level as a convenient entity for making equations come out right, is now considered a physical thing that experimental physicists can pursue. In the realm of mind and body, an analysis of your blood at the biochemical level, by revealing cortisol levels, can tell investigators something about you at medical and psychological levels of analysis, namely, how much stress you habitually experience.

Now, jump to the opposite extreme: the claim that science *already* fits wonderfully together. That too must be wrong. For example, the concept of psychological stress is changing. (That's one reason Bruce McEwen entitled his book *The End of Stress as We Know It*.) Yes, twenty years from now, a person given an impossible deadline at work will still experience a rise in cortisol. But will that person's inner experience, the feeling that accompanies that rise, be called stress or allostasis or some term not yet invented? Or will the feeling still be called stress but cortisol no longer used to measure it? I don't know. Neither does anyone else. Science changes with each passing day.

A safer approach to the relationship between levels of analysis is reliance on probability. Theories that agree on several levels are more *likely* to make good predictions and lead to further work than theories that contradict each other. This is what E. O. Wilson means by *consilience* — reassuring agreement at all the levels of description.

The problem is, new work is always under way at each level. So the probabilities among relationships are constantly shifting. For example, psychologists' move in the last few years to classify depression as a physical illness prompted new research into its biochemistry. Conversely, discoveries about the biochemistry of substances like serotonin and dopamine will likely force changes in the disorders now termed depression. Psychology and biochemistry inform one another; but neither *determines* what is done in the other. That they agree today, then, doesn't guarantee the two fields won't part ways in the future.

Perhaps it's clearer to say only that work at one level puts limits on others. Genetic analyses in the Balkans show how different ancestral populations arrived and migrated through the region. But the genetic markers used by biologists do not match the political boundaries that today divide Serbs, Croats, and Bosnians into supposedly separate peoples. So the genetic level of analysis places a bound on what can be said about the scientific validity of the human kinds called Serb and Croat, which were formed at the cultural and political levels.

This still leaves plenty of room for levels of analysis to be independent of one another. For example, if, in some future epoch, the human kinds Serb and Croat were to vanish and become as dead as Hun and Visigoth are today, that would not mean work on their genes had become meaningless. Population-marking patterns in DNA is a concept that doesn't depend on cultural or psychological beliefs. In the future, when dyslexia gets redefined as a human kind, the genetic work on it won't perish. There will still be identified genes, at particular locations on particular chromosomes. But such "genes for" dyslexia may be renamed as genes for three different disorders with three new labels.

This is why science is reliable, portraying a real universe *outside* our heads, *and* ever-changing — because the concepts we apply to that world are *inside* our heads. So DNA is real; genes are real; dyslexia is real. Nonetheless, the day probably will come when no one talks about dyslexia, and the "genes for" that condition will be considered "genes for" something else.

In the face of change and uncertainty about these questions, Gould advocated a live-and-let-live approach that he called "pluralism." It's an outlook of scientists who do not believe, at least not yet, in the unity of knowledge — a willingness to allow that different questions have different answers and that your problems change with your circumstances.

This is the way most people live their lives — with different thinking for different purposes. Pilots know why airplanes stay up or fail to; yet, Leon Trotsky once observed with disgust, many pilots he knew carried a rabbit's foot or some other good-luck charm. Why be as narrow-minded, as dead to the realities of the human psyche, as Trotsky was? There is more than one question a human being can ask; there always will be.

Pluralists believe that this approach isn't just for daily life. It's also their philosophy for science. Their notions are not unique to the "soft" disciplines or to biology. The paleontologist Niles Eldredge once began a lecture to a group of mathematicians and physicists by remarking that they probably didn't have the kind of raging controversies in their fields that evolutionists had. In math and physics, he figured, people probably agreed on the fundamentals. The response was a gale of laughter.

Peter Galison, the physicist and historian of science at Harvard, stresses the principle of multiple forms of knowledge throughout his history of modern physics, *Image and Logic*. A mainstay of research from the mid-1930s to the mid-1950s was the capturing of a subatomic particle's track in the emulsion of a photographic plate, which they then called "ionography." What this technique was, Galison observed, depended on who was using it: "To some practitioners of the art (those coming from photography) it was an exploration of the fundamental processes of atomic, crystalline, and gelatinous materials. To cosmic ray physicists ionography was a probe of deep space, to nuclear physicists it was a look into the basic bits of matter, to the geochronologist it was a probe of the unimaginably distant past." This variety of interpretations, Galison believes, wasn't a problem; it was good for physics to have these disparate answers rubbing up against each other.

In biology, scientists who see genes as information or conceptual tokens sometimes irritate those who work with genes as chemicals. "The Ev Psych people talk about genes, but they don't know genetics," the geneticist Jonathan Marks once said to me. And both kinds of gene-centered scholar annoy those who look at whole animals and their traits. ("Annoy" might be putting it mildly, actually. E. O. Wilson, evolutionary theorist and nature lover, has written at length about his feud with James Watson, who, as codiscoverer of DNA, not surprisingly wanted to steer biology to the molecular level of analysis. During the 1950s and 1960s, when both men were at Harvard, Wilson writes, "I found him the most unpleasant human being I had ever met.")

Yet Wilson hails Watson as a valuable enemy. The different camps in science stimulate and correct one another. Disunity, that constant struggle of different traditions, in the absence of some ultimate Truth to settle everything, is what makes science strong and lively.

Does this mean that all answers are equal — that my rabbit's foot deserves as much respect as Newton's theory of gravity? Of course not. Some answers are *better* than others: for instance, science can get a human into orbit, and the rabbit's foot can't. If the question is how can we send people to the moon and bring them back, then clearly engineering must beat the furry foot. Of course, some questions are more important than others. However, if the question of the moment is how to get the pilot to start the plane, engineering might be less handy than a magic charm.

In other words, you have to judge an answer by the question it addresses. Saying "engineering is better than belief in charms" is meaningless until you can say what engineering is better *for*. Pluralism is not the absence of standards; it's just the recognition that standards are created by the problems, which are set by human beings. The human context of any question — who is asking it? why are they asking it in that way? — has to be taken into account.

The opposite of pluralism in science is a belief that, ultimately, context doesn't matter. In the long run, goes the argument, the human race will find that all the levels of analysis fit together. In such a future, the study of politics would fold neatly into the work on psychology, which in turn would fit neatly into the work on biology. Some scientists, including E. O. Wilson and the physicist Murray Gell-Mann, believe that such folding is bound to happen. Reality is out there, waiting to be discovered, and we get to the same results, no matter who does the work or where they begin.

The clearest contrast between these two philosophies is in their view of the future. One of the few predictions a pluralist can make about people in 3010 is that they will look on our science as a collection of mistakes, missed opportunities, and lucky guesses. Our great-great-great-grandchildren will wonder how we ever believed nonsense about quantum gravity or brain biology. They will wonder why we missed what is so easy to see in hindsight, and they'll admire the few investigators, here and there, who caught a glimpse of the "right" path. They might appreciate that their science was made possible by ours, but that's not the same as thinking ours is right. Those future people will be, in short, like the evolutionary theorist who once told me he didn't want to participate in an interdisciplinary seminar, which had been set up to read the founding texts of different academic fields. He didn't need to give any precious class time to Darwin's *Origin of Species* because, after all, "Darwin was wrong about a lot."

An antipluralist, by contrast, must believe that today's science will endure forever. After all, if science is steadily uncovering Truth, then yesterday's insights must be just as sound as today's. Once right, a scientist must be right for all time.

The English astrophysicist and science writer John Gribbin is an antipluralist. "There will never be a successful description of the Universe which says that Einstein's theory is wrong in any of the areas where it has already been tested," he writes. "It is a factual, objective truth that light gets 'bent' by a certain amount when it passes near a star like the Sun, and the general theory will always be able to tell you how much it gets bent."

This is true; but the day will come when no one wants to know how much light gets bent because scientists will be working with a different framework of knowledge, asking different questions instead. That's the nature of science. As the physicist Rob Myers of the Perimeter Institute of Canada once said, "General relativity is an amazing theory in that it predicts its own demise. Einstein's theory is telling you it can only bring you so far and then you're going to need a better theory to understand how physics proceeds from there." In science, certainties do not last.

In the mid-nineteenth century, for example, enlightened doctors believed that disease was caused by noxious vapors called miasmas, concentrated at low elevations. In 1849, this theory was used to forecast rates of cholera infection in different parts of London. The predictions were excellent: they closely matched actual rates, in a great vindication for miasma theory. Nonetheless, because Louis Pasteur and his successors established the germ theory of infection, no one today asks miasmal questions.

If Gribbin thinks the future will be different, he isn't saying how. He claims, grandly: "It is because there are ultimate truths out there that science hangs together so well." A clear and deeply felt conviction, but not a scientific one.

If you could only look at the stars through a single telescope, you would never find out if the scope is out of focus, because you'd have no other way to see the sky. Science is that telescope; we can judge if it is operating well, but we cannot verify that it sees ultimate Truth. As the philosopher Hilary Putnam of Harvard once pointed out, when you talk about a "real world" that exists outside of your knowledge of the real world, you literally don't know what you're talking about. Since we have nothing but science with which to check science, claims about absolute certainty are leaps of faith, not reason.

In their daily work, many scientists cautiously stick to one level of analysis. Their experience has taught them that useful knowledge — like diagnoses that actually cure people or teaching strategies that help children learn — usually arises when questions from one level are answered at the same plane. When your child's doing poorly at math, you don't spend your time studying the subatomic particles that make up the atoms in his body. When you need to understand those particles for physics class, you don't read a biography of E. O. Wilson, even though he is made of quarks. If you ignore this principle you end up confused, trying to settle one kind of question with an answer framed in the wrong terms.

This confusion swirls around the problem of human kinds because there is no consensus about which levels of analysis are right for it. If you want to know why Johnny can't read, you won't study quarks, and you might study the neuroscience of reading; but if you want to know why Johnny's kind of people are not reading as well as Janey's, you study . . . what? Genes? Neuroscience? Psychology? History? Do you accept that Johnny's kind is even the right category to look at? In the absence of a standard, discourse about human kinds is a jumble.

One tempting escape route is to ascribe the precision of work at one level of analysis to another. For example, take the claim that personality traits, like neuroticism and excitement seeking, can be linked to specific genes. Several teams of researchers made claims like that in the late 1990s, naming several genes that carry instructions for making dopamine receptors in brain cells. That genes for the receptors can be found at a particular spot in human DNA is a biochemical and genetic-information fact. However, the same precision does not attach to the idea that there is a kind of person who craves novelty.

That's because the human-kind concept is not biochemical or genetic. It was made at the psychological and cultural levels of analysis, where matters aren't as defined. Some psychologists, noting how people change with their surroundings, don't believe a trait like novelty seeking holds constant throughout life. To them, working at their different level of description, the news that gene D4 has been mapped in a lab does not mean that novelty seeking can be. And, in fact, the difficulties of bridging the levels make such studies hard to replicate. One recent analysis of the novelty-seeking studies found no link between the targeted genes and the proposed personality trait. And a broader examination of studies on gene-personality links in general has concluded that none demonstrate a valid connection.

A similar precision-mongering fuels the fad for ethnic genetics. At the genetic level of analysis, scientists are tracking how different ancestral populations moved about the earth. They can do this because even though all populations have essentially the same genes, particular versions of each gene tend to crop up at different frequencies in different populations. And genes often get inherited in bunches, called haplotypes. By tracing a haplotype — a particular combination of particular versions of genes — geneticists can track ancient migrations.

So, for example, geneticists have established that among the ancestors of Ashkenazic Jews were some men who were also ancestors of non-Jewish Eastern Europeans; Ashkenazic populations carry a haplotype much more commonly found among Eastern Europeans today, a haplotype that other Jewish populations don't have. Geneticists also established that large numbers of men descended from the *kohanim,* ancient Judaism's priestly caste, share a haplotype rarely seen in other populations. On the other hand, genetic research has also shown that another priestly caste, the Levites, have in their genome some genetic material contributed by non-Jews.

All well and good for science. It's by such markers that the movements of different ancestral populations are understood. But trying to use this science to determine who today is a kohanim would be a bad idea. Some 30 percent of kohanim lack the marker. And there are other peoples besides the Jews who have this genetic pattern in abundance: Palestinians. Such markers are real and important information about the history of populations; but they come from the genetic level of analysis. They can't tell you who is or isn't a Jew because the concept of the Jewish people comes from the cultural level of analysis.

Still, there are times in science when levels of analysis start to bump into one another. Then the problem of how they connect becomes unavoidable. This is where the sciences of mind now stand. Findings from one level, for example, that certain chemicals increase the amount of serotonin available in the brain, now have practical consequences at other levels: depressed people who take those chemicals in pill form often feel better. When a medical school's MRI equipment is used to investigate how white students' amygdalas react to African American faces, then the biomedical, neural, and social-psychological levels need a common language. Despite the Darwinians' trumpetings, that quest is not over. It has barely begun.

Fifteen

Species of Darwinism

Science is fragmentary and incomplete; it advances but slowly and is never finished; but life cannot wait. The theories destined to make men live and act are therefore obliged to pass science and complete it prematurely.

— EMILE DURKHEIM

Darwinism addressed the mystery of human kinds early: Charles Darwin himself was intrigued. By his principle of natural selection, only the more successful organisms should succeed in having off-spring and perpetuating their traits. This was the "survival of the fittest," a phrase coined by the philosopher Herbert Spencer, before Darwin published the theory of evolution. To Darwin, however, it was obvious that creatures often made themselves less fit so that others could do better.

Honeybees sting enemies, which is good for the hive but bad for the stingers, which die. A bird that sounds an alarm about an approaching cat helps other birds but draws the cat's attention to itself. This is altruism in its biological sense — reducing your fitness in a way that boosts someone else's. In the human universe, of course, there are even more examples. In fact, moral codes are almost entirely about restraining that impulse to maximize your fitness, as the

Darwinians put it. Ethical behavior restrains the individual's desires for the sake of fairness, kindness, and the rights of others.

Darwin saw that pure and simple natural selection, acting on each individual creature, should stamp out this kind of behavior. Nonaltruists, who were not giving up any advantages, should live longer and have more offspring than self-sacrificing animals, until, eventually, altruistic behavior disappeared. He reasoned that natural selection must work on whole groups, not just individuals. Of course this would be true of people as it was of other creatures.

"There can be no doubt," he wrote, "that a tribe including many members who, from possessing in a high degree the spirit of patriotism, fidelity, obedience, courage and sympathy, were always ready to aid one another, and to sacrifice themselves for the common good, would be victorious over most other tribes; and this would be natural selection." He did not take up the question of what a tribe might be. (Apparently, like his cousin Francis Galton, he thought that self-evident.) That would prove to be a problem later, but at the time, the idea that actions could evolve "for the good of the group" took its place among the foundations of evolutionary biology.

Forty years ago, though, the evolutionary facts were rearranged into a new framework. The rearranger was George C. Williams, a biologist who, after attending a talk about adaptation for the good of the group, decided that he would rather quit academia than work in such a woolly-headed field. Instead of going to General Motors, Williams drove out the heretics. He zeroed in on that "tribe" problem — the difficulty of defining this "group" that evolution can act on.

Is it the species? Problem: the definition of a species is not entirely settled in biology. (As you might expect, there are good-enough concepts at each level of analysis from biochemistry to high theory, but they don't line up perfectly.) Anyway, the idea that a soldier in Indonesia gives his life for the good of Homo sapiens in, say, Norway is logically suspect, to say the least. Try some other candidates for a community, like a flock of starlings. What if they disperse for a few days? Do birds of a feather, who do not flock together, still make a flock? Groups as they were conceived by his field, Williams showed, were vague, ephemeral entities. Evolution could not act on things that winked in and out of existence, nor upon things that exist on Wednesdays and Fridays but not on Thursdays. "There are no communities, really," Williams once said to me. "They're so temporary and ill-defined."

Even individual people, though much better defined, weren't going to pass muster as units of selection, Williams says. After all, it is not an individual Joe or Jane that moves down the generations, but a trait — blue eyes, or a propensity to like the taste of sweets. The only entity that was permanent and stable enough to be the target of selection, Williams proclaimed, was the information in DNA — what I've called the *information gene* (because, obviously, the chemicals in your body, those particular molecules in particular you, are not going to outlive you).

A few years later, Richard Dawkins proclaimed that natural selection worked only through the "selfish gene," whose only drive was to make copies of itself. In this view everything that looks like altruism, biological or moral, is genetic self-interest, seen through a gauze of misunderstanding. After all, our human-kind codes shape our perceptions. We see altruism everywhere because our minds are built to see it. But it isn't really out there. "Scratch an altruist," wrote the biologist Michael Ghiselin in 1974, "and watch a hypocrite bleed."

This left a problem: how evolution gets from selfish gene to selfless (if hypocritical) person. The answers that the selfish-gene school proposed are the core of today's evolutionary psychology. These are principles that, the new Darwinians believe, will prove to be context free — explanations for human thoughts and feelings that will be true in all times and places. This is the faith that Gould derided as "Darwinian fundamentalism."

As his opponents pointed out, this name-calling invited you to notice the tribal-banner aspect of these theories and ignore their other aspect: their merit. If Darwinism, like "free trade" or "affirmative action," is a marker of identity, it is also a set of ideas that convinced many biologists and guided their work.

The first of these key concepts was published a year after Williams's assault on the notion of group selection, by the late evolutionary biologist William D. Hamilton of Oxford. Though theoretically rigorous, the work had its origin in Hamilton's reflection that he would sacrifice more for his brothers than for his friends. This kind of loyalty to relatives had been remarked on by the English biologist J. B. S. Haldane some thirty years earlier when he was puzzling over altruism. Asked if he would give his life for his brother, Haldane replied he would sooner die for "three brothers or nine cousins."

Hamilton saw that selection at the information-gene level could explain this behavior. At that level of analysis, relatives share genes in a way that can be described precisely. In the framework I suggested in the last chapter, that is a different situation from level 1 (no actual molecules of DNA in a father and son are shared because they are in separate bodies). It is also different from the view at level 4, where we can recognize family traits (like "the Smith men are all silent, steady types") without knowing how (or if) genes are involved.

At the information level of analysis, a gene is not confined to a single body. (Different people can all carry a copy of the same information.) And the rules of heredity, which tell exactly how many informational genes are shared among family members, work without regard to what those genes do. Even if a Smith son is noisy and capricious, you can still be sure that he got roughly half his genetic information from his father and half from his mother.

So Hamilton applied this precision to the problem of altruism. If two brothers share genetic information and one dies so the other may live on, the fitness of their shared genetic code has not been reduced at all. The information survives. Even sacrificing your life will not reduce the fitness of the genetic information in you, if your sacrifice increases the fitness of others who carry copies. Using the rules of heredity and simple math, biologists could make predictions about how relatives would act to enhance this shared "inclusive fitness."

Inclusive fitness solved many puzzles about altruism among animals. The concept explained, for example, why bees die for the colony. (Worker bees are near-clones; almost all the genetic information in a sacrificed bee lives on without it.) It makes good predictions about parenting and kin relationships in many different species and prompted new work on human behavior. The psychologists

Martin Daly and Margo Wilson used it as the basis for a reexamination of family violence, in which they found that children were far more likely to be murdered by stepparents — nonrelatives — than by genetic kin.

On the other hand, some attempts to apply kin selection to human kinds were silly. One paper puzzled over why people care for their pets. (After all, you share more genes with your worst enemy than you do with a cat.) Robert Wright scratched his head over the problem of soldiers dying for nonrelated comrades. And one scholar proposed, in all seriousness, that police departments and the military consider deploying siblings together because they would be more likely to watch one another's backs.

For these writers, kin-selection theory is a lovely way to banish the individual mind, with its messy, changing thoughts and feelings, from the question of human-kind behavior. In that they're not unlike a separate group of kin-obsessed thinkers, who want to use genes to justify cultural beliefs about race and ethnicity.

In the work of this school, the Darwinian search for principles that are true forever keeps company with the human-kind code's urge to believe in what we see. Today's ideas of race, these thinkers say, are true. This is the stance of "race realists" like the molecular biologist Vincent Sarich of the University of California, his coauthor Frank Miele, and J. Philippe Rushton of the University of Western Ontario.

Rushton argues that people prefer their own race or ethnic group for company because those in each group are more genetically similar to each other than they are to outsiders.

Moreover, he says, these race categories really are, as a matter of science, the sort of concepts that we feel them to be — valid answers to important questions you can ask about a person. According to Rushton, racial difference is everywhere. He says that yellow people are smarter than white and white are smarter than black. He also reports that black Africans and their descendants use a child-rearing strategy that requires many offspring, each of whom gets little parental care (like frogs and fish), while whites incline to a strategy of few offspring who each get a lot of care (like many birds).

This is not an argument much favored by most Darwinians but it does have a strong emotional content. It is certainly effective for triggering stigma. It's code for They Are a Lesser Kind of Human (less intelligent, less caring as parents). Most of the Darwinian behavior people, including Tooby, reject it outright.

They do that not because they think it's immoral to encourage racism. (That line gives Rushton an opening to claim that he is simply telling hard truths that liberal academics don't wish to hear.) Rather, they fault his science, including his attempt to collapse levels of analysis. For example, Rushton assumes that similarity at one level is the same at all the others: if people say they belong to one race (the level of culture) and have similar amounts of melanin in their skin (the level of individual bodies), then he expects that they will also have similar brain activity (the neural level) and that this will be based on similarity at the level of the gene. Many, if not most, of the evolution-and-behavior people say that this is not so, because "similarity" at one level doesn't translate to any other.

If it did, a person's skin color would always tell you his race. But the history of light-skinned American blacks "passing" for white was possible because the two levels of analysis are not in sync. If the levels lined up, a DNA sample would tell you for sure what cultural race a person was. (It doesn't.) Similarly, Rushton offers statistics to show that black people have smaller skulls on average than whites. He then claims this supports his argument about the relative intelligence of the races, because a smaller skull implies a smaller brain. But the evidence for a connection between brain size and intelligence is not there. Women's heads are generally smaller than men's, but women do not score lower on intelligence tests.

Moreover, any human kind's average scores on those tests turn out to be — surprise, surprise — sensitive to stigma. For example, ethnic Koreans in Japan find themselves treated as outsiders in many subtle and unsubtle ways. They score less well than Japanese people on IQ tests. But the test results of Koreans in Korea are equal to those of Japanese. Which IQ scores should be the ones related to the average volume of a Korean skull?

Remember, too, that IQ tests were invented about one hundred years ago. It's a leap to project those results back in time — to say, in effect, "The people of Group X have these scores on a test; there-fore, people who lived five hundred years ago, who called themselves X, also would have scored the same way." In fact, we can't know what Leonardo da Vinci or Plato would have scored on an IQ test for the simple reason that the test and the framework to make sense of it did not exist in their time. What to do?

The easiest thing to do is not to worry about it. That's the ap-proach of Kevin MacDonald, a psychologist at California State Uni-versity, Long Beach, who holds that Jews are genetically, physically, and culturally distinct — distinct on all levels of analysis, then — from the rest of the human world. One of his arguments is that the IQ scores of Jewish people are higher, on average, than those of non-Jews. As that is true now, MacDonald assumes it was true in the days of Maimonides and King David. "Because of Jewish within-group cooperation as well as eugenic and cultural practices that have resulted in an average IQ of at least 1 standard deviation above the Caucasian mean," he writes, "Jews are highly adept at achieving their goals." The whiff of stigma is hard to miss in this passage: Smarter than Us, as I've mentioned, is not so different from Dumber than Us. Both say these people are outside the rules of our game, in the realm of Them, with the animals and the demons.

A more benign jumbling of different levels of analysis occurs in the work of Jon Entine, a television producer and journalist who claims, like Rushton, that only political correctness and postmod-ernism stand in the way of everyone realizing that genes, bodies, and human kinds line up neatly together. In his best-selling book, *Taboo,* Entine argued that racial differences in sports ability were real, im-portant, and genetic. (The "taboo" is supposedly against speaking this sort of truth.)

In *Taboo* Entine offers heaps of statistics to show how black and white athletes are different. Blacks have won the most Olympic me-dals in long-distance racing, while whites have won in weight lifting. He's right. However, he is wrong to assume that race, a category that we work with at the cultural and political levels, can be derived from the genetic level.

The geneticist Jonathan Marks of the University of North Carolina has pointed out the reason: The cultural races we can see at the Olympics are creations of history and politics; they do not match the patterns in the genes. At the level of genes and haplotypes, scientists sort human beings into hundreds of populations and subpopulations. Looking at human populations on this genetic level, you would not see "black runners" winning all those medals. You would see runners who were all descendants of particular populations, each one too local to match our idea of races.

Entine himself notes this in those parts of his book where he breaks down the human kind "black athletes." In describing the remarkable accomplishments of Kenya's best runners, Entine writes that three quarters of them are from the Kalenjin ethnic group; half the Kalenjin are from one tribe, the Nandi. He admits a famous running school in the region has a part to play in this record but asks why it's so terrible to propose that this kind of human being also has genes that help members in feats of running.

It's not so terrible. But the "black race" encompasses far more people than the Nandi. A citizen of Cameroon or Alabama, though culturally classed as a black person, might not have those East African runner genes. What's left, then, of Entine's claim that it is "blacks" who dominate running? He has jumbled genetics-level population groups with human kinds we use in daily life, from the political-cultural level of description.

The "black race" includes populations of superb runners and populations of nonrunners. In North America, the black race includes millions of people with many genes inherited from white ancestors. So this race is certainly real at the political and cultural levels; at the genetic level, though, it doesn't exist.

The leaders of the evolutionary psychology movement would be glad to disown race realists and ethnic Darwinists if they could. John Tooby has written: "Kevin MacDonald is not remotely an evolutionary psychologist, any more than B. F. Skinner was a Freudian psychoanalyst, or *Social Text* the leading physics journal of our time."

But Darwinian approaches to behavior, including Tooby's evolutionary psychology, can't be so easily detached from the ideas of

Rushton, Sarich, or MacDonald (a former editor of the newsletter of the Human Behavior and Evolution Society). This is because the mainstream Darwinians share the assumption of the fringe thinkers: that certain human kinds are objectively real, as determined at the genetic level of analysis, and that these human kinds predict how people will act.

Consider the Darwinian claim that you will be more likely to sacrifice for a sibling than a friend (because you share more genes with the relative, never mind your beliefs or experiences). This says the human kind called "kin group" is real and consequential and doesn't depend on circumstances or on who is observing it. Similarly, some Darwinians claim that genetics can predict your proneness to religious mysticism or divorce (again, never mind your circumstances).

Once they accept the idea that certain human kinds are objectively real in all times and places, Darwinians have no way to shut the door against "race realists" and ethnic stigmatizers. If some human kinds can predict behavior, why not the ones *they* propose? Others can bring in cultural, psychological, or even neural information to point out that all human kinds are in the minds of those who perceive them, and that human kinds change over the course of history. But if you're a Darwinian, you've committed yourself to the idea that subjectivity and history can be factored out.

Many neuroscientists and psychologists are skeptical about Darwinian theories for exactly this reason. They think it's unwise to try to explain human action by ignoring the mind. For questions involving human kinds, it's obvious that the brain can't be ignored in favor of the genes.

It's psychological kind, not genetic kin, that matters most to the mind. If the message of the human-kind code is contradicted by the genes, then the genes lose. Among the oldest illustrations are religious texts. One is the story of Abraham, who puts his standing as a man of God above his fatherhood and prepares to sacrifice his son. People cast out and even kill relatives every day. It is easy, once those relatives have become bad people, no longer worthy members of our kind. Brothers kill a sister for dishonoring their family. A gay man comes out to his parents and discovers they have stopped speaking to him. The point here is not, of course, that people *never* value kin ties;

it is that kin ties won't *inevitably* predict behavior because something else is in the game: the believing, feeling, experiencing mind.

Meanwhile, of course, the better side of human kind-mindedness is also in evidence: soldiers do die for comrades who are not relatives; adoptive parents rear children who aren't kin; and don't forget those pets. "Who is your brother?" asks a Bedouin proverb. The answer: "He who is useful to me, and to whom I am useful." In fact, most scientists agree that our ability *not* to obey kin-selection rules is one of the great mysteries of human behavior that has to be explained. Economists once assumed that people act to maximize profits for themselves and their close kin. But real humans, in experiments as well as in their day-to-day behavior, are much more concerned with being fair and cooperative than they would be if they were just looking out for number one and family. How could such altruism for nonkin have arisen and been maintained? Why weren't such nice-guy ancestors overwhelmed by the imperatives of the selfish gene?

Many Darwinians have an answer for that. It's a powerful theory that frees them from the conundrums of trying to explain human behavior by kin selection.

It was supplied by the anthropologist Robert L. Trivers of Rutgers in the 1970s. Trivers's idea is a principle he dubbed "reciprocal altruism" — basically, you scratch my back and I'll scratch yours. The cost of putting yourself out for my benefit is not so terrible, *if* you can be sure that I will return the favor. A bunch of altruists should, in fact, live longer and raise more offspring than the self-interested. The catch is that almost everyone in the game had to play nice. Too much cheating by the selfish makes altruism a self-defeating strategy.

Biologists have feasted on this idea for three decades. It was clear, made sense of the facts, and — most important — suggested experiments that could actually be done and published. Reciprocal altruism has been used to explain activity among animals from ants to vampire bats (who share their blood meals with unsuccessful hunters, knowing they'll be repaid some other night when they come up empty). Reciprocal altruism seems to be the bridge between the selfish gene and the selfless person.

Trivers stipulated a few conditions that had to obtain for this strategy to work. For people to live by exchanges of self-sacrifice, they must have frequent contact. (I cannot count on you returning a favor if we'll never see each other again.) They'd also need to act differently toward a cheater than toward one who is playing the game nicely. And they would need to be able to keep track of which actions belong to which actor. When you don't return the favor, I need to know that I didn't get paid, and I need to know that the deadbeat is you, not someone else.

That's the ultimate cause that Darwinians propose for the cheat detector that I mentioned a few pages back. The idea is that evolution shaped the human mind to be alert to rules and exhanges among people, resulting in a mental faculty dedicated to that job alone. The English science writer Matt Ridley described it succinctly: "It treats every problem as a social contract arrived at between two people and looks for ways to check those who might cheat the contract. It is the exchange organ." And, in fact, Tooby and his colleague (and spouse) Leda Cosmides have found evidence that people have a much easier time solving logical problems when they are described as rules for people's conduct. Elsewhere in Trivers's wake, anthropologists reconsidered the meaning of gossip and of honor and reputation. Being tuned to reciprocity makes us interested in other people's behavior — will they cheat? — and concerned about how people see us. Brain codes for reciprocity are a good bet.

In the world's few remaining societies that live by gathering plants and hunting wild game, hunters share their kills with scrupulous fairness. Hunting, after all, involves luck as well as skill — you can't count on always making a catch. And even the hungriest family can only eat so much at a sitting. For this reason, as Ridley puts it, nomadic hunters find that the best place to store meat for the future is in the minds of other people. They're said to live, as an aid worker I met in Haiti described his peasant neighbors, in these terms: "You always give of whatever you have, because some day when you've got nothing someone else will give to you."

Evidence for the primacy of reciprocity also turns up in historical accounts, sometimes surprisingly naked. You might expect that medieval Catholic Europeans would have venerated their saints without exception. But the patron saint of a village who failed to give good return could be fired. In a ritual called the humiliation of saints, the nonperforming holy one's statue would be removed from a church and buried, to make way for a new patron saint — one who, one presumes, would be more attuned to the mind's demands for reciprocity.

If the mind has a code for reciprocal altruism, that would account for the high value people seem to place on it, and possibly for a lot of their face-to-face niceness with one another. No need for intellectual acrobatics to explain why a soldier would die for an unrelated comrade, leaving his children fatherless. Perhaps, as the biologist Richard D. Alexander of the University of Michigan suggested, "indirect" reciprocal altruism predicts that the soldier's emotions of loyalty and his care for his reputation among his comrades can come to count for more than his genetic stake.

However, favor trading among people who know each other well can't produce large nations, religions, armies, social movements, and other important, life-and-death human groupings whose members never meet. My fellow feeling for the people of New York City does not depend on every one of us taking turns doing each other's dishes. Nor can my reputation precede me among all those eight million people, so indirect reciprocity won't apply either.

For a city or a nation to exist, its members must be good at satisfying their need for reciprocity with *symbols,* not actions. As I learned in the wake of the September 11 attacks on the city, strangers here assumed we could trust and depend on each other because we gave signs of trustworthiness, signs of belonging.

That raises two problems for the reciprocity idea. The first is a matter of scale: How can people form themselves into entities made up of thousands, millions, or even hundreds of millions?

One way to address that issue has been outlined by the anthropologist Robert Boyd of the University of California at Los Angeles and his frequent collaborator, Peter J. Richerson, a biologist at the University of California at Davis. The pair propose that human kinds let people use *rules* to substitute for personal knowledge of others. In other words, while I trust a familiar neighbor because I know him well, my trust for a fellow American is based on knowing that she and I share the same rules. That's what being in the same human kind tells us. In their work on what they call our "tribal social instincts," Boyd and Richerson suggest that the code creates a deep-seated urge to conform to the people around us. That's how we assure one another that we are all "playing the same game," to use a phrase of the anthropologist Fredrik Barth.

"At least in all the models we made, reciprocity kinds of mechanisms break down rather quickly as a function of group size," Richerson told me. "So it does take, we argue, something like this cultural group selection mechanism" to explain large-scale cooperation.

As humans grew in numbers after the last Ice Age, Boyd and Richerson argue, diverging bands would have reason to keep clear of each other: only "our people" would show, in their language and habits and clothes, that they were playing life by "our" rules. Tribes competed for the same hunting grounds and food sources, so each would have every incentive to develop rules for its members alone. By setting local "rules for the game," culture would channel the mind's ability to team up with anyone. Instead, people would grow up learning to team up with the *right* ones. And we learn to tell the right ones by looking for *signs* of rightness: language, looks, movements. That's how we can have millions of people all taking part in a nation or a religion, treating total strangers as trusted familiars.

Still, there is another problem posed by huge human kinds besides sheer size. They are not just populous; they are also varied, overlapping, and highly changeable. Consider this hypothetical story: A man is speeding in his car. A cop flags him down and approaches. As he rolls down his window, the man makes a sexist remark about women drivers. He looks — uh-oh — the cop is female. She's also African American, and so is the driver. He now tries to talk her out of giving him a ticket. Does she treat him as a civilian, a black person, or a man? In other words, does she behave as a cop, a black person, or a woman?

I don't know. Neither do you. That's the point: people have many possible human kinds to use when they encounter one another, and often you can't be sure which one a person will see as relevant.

Darwinian theorists, if they are to come up with experiments and insights into the workings of the mind, have to deal with this variety. How did the codemaker evolve to recognize those symbols? And what does that evolution tell us about its shape? Researchers are split between two schools, which make different predictions and have different consequences for the levels–of–analysis problem. Call them the "specialist" and the "generalist."

The specialist line is that human-kind codes evolved for work that can be defined narrowly. So, the codemaker has default settings — a particular range of cues, which best fits one particular function. In this view, we have a template for a human kind. Others are convincing because they remind us of the basic model.

In the view of the University of Pennsylvania anthropologist Franciso Gil-White, for example, this default setting is the ethnic group. That, he argues, is the fundamental human-kind code, from which other groupings, like race, nation, and religion, must draw. He believes the evolving human mind, pressed for a way to manage the problem of reciprocity, adapted an already-existing mental code for a new purpose. Specifically, Gil-White proposed that people's sense of ethnicity is built on their sense of how plants and animals divide into species.

People don't think caterpillars are a different species from the moths they become; they don't expect that a cat raised by wolves will become a wolf. Their sense of what it means to be a kind of creature is not based on appearances, but on a sense that, beneath appearances, there is an essential, unchanging, underlying nature. And that's how Gil-White's research subjects in Mongolia talked to him about ethnic groups.

The alternative evolutionary idea, which I've called the generalist model, is that there is no default human kind for the codemaker to prefer. Instead, generalists believe, the mind evolved to scan other people for clues about who is allied with whom. The code evolved from a general-purpose tracker of coalitions (Who can I work with around here? Who is against me?), which can be found in simpler forms in most animals that live in groups, from dolphins to bats to monkeys.

As the human brain got larger, more and more capacity could be devoted to this coalition-tracker, so it got linked to the symbol-using parts of the mind. Once that happens, the coalitional code is no longer confined to real people that its owner could see. It could imagine favor trading and alliances with others, even if they were distant, if they bore the right signs. So was born the human-kind faculty as we know it — races, ethnic groups, nations, religions, political parties, militaries, and on and on.

On the one hand, if the specialists are correct, then the human-kind codemaker has implications for other levels of analysis — especially political implications — that are different from the generalist model's. After all, if ethnicity is the default model for human kinds, everyone will tend to see ethnic groups everywhere. New groupings, if they are to succeed, will have to fit that template. Appeals to your reasonable self-interest or your moral commitments will never carry as much weight as appeals that feel ethnic.

On the other hand, if the generalists are right, then no particular grouping at the political-cultural level is bound to impress the mind more than any other. In politics, this would mean that people have no innate bias for an ethnic, or ethnic-feeling, understanding of their world. It means other arrangements can give them just as much we-feeling.

Henri Tajfel's work fits the generalist line. That's why a number of scholars, including Gil-White, disdain it. They hold that Tajfel groups have no resemblance to any real human-kind experience. Sorting is one thing, Gil-White says, but real groups involve stakes for those who are in them.

Tajfel's work dovetails with a generalist theory that people's human kinds are the result of looking for coalitions — anywhere, with anybody. For example, work by Gil-White's Penn colleague Robert Kurzban also produced Tajfel-style loyalties when he arrayed his volunteers into the "Yellow Team" and the "Green Team" and had them compete.

More recently, working with his mentors Tooby and Cosmides, Kurzban devised an experiment that I think pits the specialist and generalist claims against each other. The researchers asked their volunteers (undergraduates at the University of California at Santa Barbara) to look at eight photographs, each of an ordinary-looking young man or woman, all of whom were wearing the same gray jersey. At the same time, each volunteer read a sentence on a computer screen. The sentences were all about group conflict — "They were the ones who started the fight!" and the like, arranged to make it clear that these eight people were split into conflicting pairs.

Then the students were given a "distractor task" to get their minds off the subject. After that, the experimenters asked the students to recall which sentences went with which photograph. The distraction guaranteed that this would be difficult and would force the students to rely on their "feel" for their situation — in other words, to trust the unconscious workings of their human-kind codes rather than their conscious memories.

According to the racial categories used in North America, the students in the photographs were either black or white, and as Kurzban expected, his experimental subjects tended to correct what they knew to confirm that human-kind map. Even though the two sides in the fictional fight were racially mixed, in their answers the students tended to pair blacks with blacks and whites with whites.

However, in his next experiment he showed photographs in which there was another human-kind indicator. Same students, same sentences, same jerseys — except now, thanks to Photoshop, each shirt was either yellow or green instead of gray. That way, the volunteers had two color schemes to take in: black or white skin, yellow or green shirts. The sentences they heard implied the conflict was actually between the Yellows and the Greens, not the blacks and the whites.

If the brain's human-kind code has a default setting for indicators of ethnicity, those shirts should have made little difference. The connection they hinted at should have been nothing compared to the perception of racial difference — which, after all, is an easily perceived difference that Americans learn very young. But if the shirts did affect people's sense of who belonged together, that would support the generalist case: even a brand-new, never-before-seen hint of a bond among people would have registered in the same way as skin color.

The shirts made a big difference. Most of the experimental subjects had no difficulty picking up the hint that this argument was structured by shirts, not skins, and that is how they recalled it. As Kurzban, Tooby, and Cosmides summarized the work when it was published in *Proceedings of the National Academy of Sciences:* "Despite a lifetime's experience of race as a predictor of social alliances, less than four minutes of exposure to an alternate social world was enough to deflate the tendency to categorize by race."

So perhaps an "ultimate cause" explanation for human-kind thinking is coming together. The selfish gene creates self-sacrificing people because reciprocal altruism succeeds in the long run. The mind is set to make sacrifices for those who will, in turn, return the favor. The human-kind code is so powerful because it tells you whom to trust for that kind of trading; in other words, whom you can trust with your genes. This is why it triggers such strong emotions. Meanwhile, the thinking, classifying, symbol-using power of the human mind makes this codemaker different from the ones that animals use in their prides, flocks, and herds. The human version is more flexible; it offers a way to treat *any* human being as either one of Us or one of Them. And the human version can perceive a continuum of Usness and Themness, rather than a simple on or off choice.

Could this be the framework that connects all the levels of analysis? Many scientists aren't so sure. They have doubts about the overarching claim that is supposed to make it all cohere: the idea that evolution only works with the selfish gene. In fact, Boyd and Richerson believe this is not so. The only way tribal instincts could reward our ancestors, they say, is if those ancestors were competing for advantage as Darwin imagined — as tribes, not just as individuals.

That's heresy to the "selfish gene" crowd, but it has important advocates, including Hamilton and David Sloan Wilson. Wilson (no relation to E. O.), a theoretical biologist at New York's Binghamton University, believes selection does indeed work on groups as well as genes. Wilson disagrees with George Williams's famous dictum that a group is too fuzzy and temporary for the workings of natural selection. (In fact, Wilson was so taken with his insight that, as a young grad student, he charmed Williams by trying to get him to change his mind with a personal visit — it was like an atheist giving his idea a best shot in a talk with the pope.)

The reason tribes, groups, and communities seem too vague for science, Wilson says, is only that they've been defined in a confused way. Science, he argues, should not be using definitions taken from the political, cultural, or psychological levels of analysis to theorize about human kinds.

Wilson wants evolutionary theory to start from scratch, with a group concept created at its own level, for its own purpose. His argument is this: theorists study traits that affect fitness. Groups, then, should be defined as everything that shares a given trait. Nothing more, nothing less. If the trait is a willingness to sacrifice oneself, then you study the group made up of all the self-sacrificers. You don't worry about whether that group crosses other kinds of boundaries, coined at other levels. You don't ask if Americans are less altruistic than Tibetans. You look for altruists, wherever they are.

The commonsensical ring of this idea masks its revolutionary aim. Where selfish-gene theories need to reduce all the levels of analysis to the information gene, Wilson's theory lets all levels of analysis coexist. He proposes that all scales, from chemical genes to whole ecosystems, share a common evolutionary principle: If they manifest a trait that can be subject to natural selection, they will evolve.

He does not insist that the boundaries of trait groups match the ones we use for nonevolutionary reasons. Some trait groups cross our cultural boundaries: The world's self-sacrificing people are distributed among many nations. Some trait groups cross the species boundary. Within your gut, for example, are billions of microbes without whose activity you could not digest your food. Cell for cell, there are about as many of "them" as there are of "you," and they need you as much as you need them. With these bacteria, of course, you don't share a shred of DNA. To Wilson's way of thinking, though, you and your guests are a coevolving group.

Going deeper, he notes, even your genes are not a harmonious team. Some of them got into your inheritance by "cheating," using chemical tricks to make sure they were copies from your parents' DNA into yours. Your genes are not a smoothly functioning unit; they are fractious, contradictory competitors, as Hamilton once observed. "As I write these words," he wrote, "even so as to be able to write them, I am pretending to a unity that, deep inside myself, I now know does not exist. I am fundamentally mixed, male with female, parent with offspring, warring segments of chromosomes that interlocked in strife millions of years before the River Severn ever saw the Celts and Saxons."

To Wilson's way of thinking, this means that even as some trait groups cross our usual definitions, others exist within them. You are a coherent individual at some levels of analysis, but not at all. You have competing groups inside you as well as outside.

This framework offers an evolutionary theory without the problems of selfish-gene reductionism. It is not a problem for "multi-level selection" if self-sacrificing people in a military unit are not genetically related. Gene sharing is not the trait that defines their group; altruism is.

David Sloan Wilson, I think, shows how the quest for an ultimate cause need not run afoul of the levels-of-analysis problem — and how an evolutionary explanation of our human-kind code need not come down to selfish genes. It's probably no coincidence that he often had a friendly word or two for Richard Lewontin and even for Stephen Jay Gould. When Wilson was host of the Human Behavior and Evolution Society's annual conference in 1992, in fact, he even tried to invite Gould to speak.

"I thought we would hear him out, and then all go out and get a beer and talk about these issues," Wilson told me. But hotter heads prevailed; Gould was never invited.

Conclusion

Doubt is not a pleasant condition, but certainty is an absurd one.

— VOLTAIRE

The brain's response to the ever-changing flow of experience is also ever-changing, so the sense that our categories are solid must be an illusion. They are, instead, the aftereffects of a meeting between mind and world — as are all thoughts and perceptions.

To put it in grammatical terms, we imagine ourselves in a world of nouns, like "France," "the Muslim world," or "old people." But the mind's environment is a world of *verbs* — perceiving, feeling, and thinking. Categories are like adverbs that color experience. Lawrence Hirschfeld has described the difference this way: "To some extent, then, it is incorrect to talk about race at all, even in quotation marks, if we intend by the term distinct and corporate groups of people. Rather we should talk about the way conduct and cognition are racialized."

Perhaps a true science of human kinds will not traffic in everyday language at all. When a future kind-scientist from Los Angeles walks down a street in Paris, taking in the sight of various people, perhaps she won't think, "These are French people, doing typically French things." Perhaps instead she'll think, "I am having an experience that is, at this moment, 75 percent colored by French-American differences, and 12 percent by black-white differences, and 13 percent by male-female differences." And so on.

This is where research on mind and brain is pointing — away from human kinds as objects or laws, toward human kinds as mental experience. It is a change long anticipated by some social psychologists. Decades ago, for instance, Henri Tajfel said, "Groups are processes, not things."

Still, folk-psychological human kinds are not going to disappear any time soon, for a number of reasons. One is that talking about human kinds as mental experiences is incredibly hard. We aren't structured to think of nations, tribes, and races as ever-shifting creations of subjective experience. Speaking of them in that way is cumbersome and slow. Many of the words we need don't yet exist.

Second, and more important, millions of people all over the world don't have the freedom to speak about human kinds in this fluid, subjective way. They are trapped, for political and economic reasons, in human-kind schemes to which they have not consented and which do them harm. Treating human kinds as if they were *only* subjective mental states slights this problem of injustice. A white person and a black person in today's New York City can agree over coffee that race is "all in your mind." But when they leave Starbucks and raise their hands to hail a taxi, the white person is more likely to get a cab. In that moment, race is as real as gravity.

So in understanding the mind, you can't forget the world. You're stuck with the human kinds that people believe in now, however well you can explain the origins of those beliefs. The new science of human kinds won't undo politics.

But then, who said it needs to? I think often of George Lakoff's important warning: Ask a different question, get a different answer. There is no final answer about the nature of human kinds — no way of saying that races or national characters or personalities are "real" or "constructed." Race is real in some times and places and situations, and not in others. The way to a better understanding of human kinds — and thus to better politics and a better life for all of us — is not to take sides in the old argument. It is, rather, to ask better questions. And I have a few candidates.

One is the problem of reconciling the slippery flexibility of individual consciousness with the long-lasting identity of the human kinds we perceive. Brain and body are in constant motion, and so is the mind. In the course of a day, I can pass through dozens of human kinds. I can feel and act American among a gaggle of foreign tourists; then feel and act like a New Yorker when talking to a Texan; then feel and act male when talking to a woman. In the course of a single conversation with a colleague, I may sense myself in all three of those human kinds, and half a dozen more.

The problem is not simply that human kinds pass kaleidoscopically through your mind. Human kinds also change, as a consequence of that passage. Concepts are affected by the way we think about them and use them. In this, human kinds are like memories. When I experience a memory, I feel as if I am taking an unchanging record of the past off its shelf. But what is happening in my brain is the creation, here and now, of a new version of that past experience.

In the same way, each time I make use of the human kind New Yorker, I am re-creating it, and so the category "New Yorker" that is in my mind this morning is probably different, subtly, from the same category when I thought about it two weeks ago.

Every description of a human kind — every statement like "Muslims are peace loving," "the Chinese peasants are hardworking," or "Californians are casual" — is also an act of persuasion. If I say it and believe it, and then you hear me and believe it too, then the human kind we're talking about becomes more like what we say. In our minds, anyway.

No doubt this explains why human kinds can appear to change over the centuries, so that many Europeans no longer believe that Spaniards are severe and grim, Turks dignified, and Greeks frivolous, as they apparently did in the time of David Hume. But what explains why human kinds *endure?* Something about the way human experience is organized causes us to desire that these products of our ever-changing minds be permanent. If this hasn't been addressed in a lot of research that touches on human kinds, it's probably because the people who study subjective experience don't communicate often with those who work on objective facts about nations, religious communities, and other human kinds. But that's changing.

Part of the answer to this question — what makes human kinds feel so permanent? — probably lies in the double nature of codes. Just as these letters are both fixed chemicals arranged on paper and a sequence of words, so anything that conveys a code is both itself and the thing it represents. In the case of human kinds, people themselves often are the objects that carry the code: any American you can meet will be both himself, Joe Smith, and a pointer to the general concept called "those Americans." Somehow, human beings can and do learn to forget that the code is represented by living people. They can learn to look at others and see not human beings — particular Joe Smiths — but *only* symbols. This makes it easier to think of "the Americans" as an unchanging real object in the world. But it also makes it easy to think of killing particular Americans because of what America does. Most people would hesitate to injure or kill a particular flesh-and-blood person; we rip up symbols easily. So the second open problem about human kinds will be figuring out exactly how this mental code causes us to see people *only* as symbols of a category. What about the human-kind faculty that permits us to forget the doubleness of code — to forget that people are people?

Sorting that one out will require a detailed description of kindsight in mind and brain. Which brings me to the third open question: Is kind sight best thought of as one faculty or many? My guess is that it will be broken down into many different, independent processes. For instance, we have a capacity to cooperate and get in sync with other people ("in the same boat" capacity); we have a capacity to believe that other people are part of Us even if we have never met them (essentialism); we have the capacity to organize ourselves around any reliable distinctive sign. Then too we have the tendency to think people's behavior stems from what we perceive them to be, not what they perceive to be happening (attribution error). We have the capacity to see other people as not-human. In our day-to-day talk we sound as if all these codes are the same, but they aren't.

Which leads me to the fourth open problem: sorting out the difference between a human kind as a cause and a human kind as an explanation. Explanations come to mind after an event, as when we say, "Ethnic hatred was one of the reasons that Yugoslavia fell apart." Explanations are in our minds. On the other hand, causes are forces that really exist in the world, whether we know it or not. To say that "ethnic hatred" caused Yugoslavia to fall apart is to claim that ethnic hatred actually made something happen. Though it's obvious that these are different ways of thinking about human kinds, most people slip from one to the other without noticing. And so we're susceptible to thinking that after-the-fact explanations are before-the-fact causes.

I think these four issues — how does the ever-changing mind relate to unchanging institutions? how can people be seen as *only* tokens of their human kinds? how many different, separate processes make up kind sight? and how should we understand human kinds as causes and explanations? — will turn out to be the crucial ones for research on problems of war and peace, tolerance and prejudice. In the meantime, a lot of the more familiar questions that science has been asked to answer about human kinds will probably disappear. They will turn out to be unanswerable because they don't make sense. To ask, as people do, if the black, white, and yellow races are real is to confuse levels of analysis beyond hope of an answer. You might as well ask science to tell you if apples are good.

The missing term, in both cases, is the purpose of the question. Apples are good snacks, poor building materials, and extremely inadequate spaceships. In the same way, the notion of a white race was indisputably real under the Jim Crow regime of the United States or the apartheid regulations of pre-liberation South Africa. It is not a meaningful concept for describing population shifts around prehistoric Eurasia because no haplotype for whiteness can be tracked. And it is a lousy candidate for medical purposes, because it's so vague. Neither question — are apples good? are races real? — can be answered without a context.

Well, so what? Points about the nature of knowledge aren't compelling to most people outside the small circles that are interested in epistemology for its own sake. What impact on everyday life can these observations have, anyway, when they predict that human beings will always use their human-kind maps? People will go on deciding that this ethnic group is clannish and that one is smart, or that people from this region are dumb while those others are fast talkers, and so on and on. Astronomy's current account of the earth's orbit lets us accomplish much more than the ancient notion that we're the center of the universe. But there are times in life when we still speak of "sunrise" and "sunset," and no harm done.

Yet I think mind science will have an impact on problems like racism, war, and prejudice. It will be felt in between the high reaches of theory and the ticktock of everyday life — in the realms of politics, culture, and public policy. Those are the areas in which human-kind beliefs affect people's lives.

The legal system, for example, has the power to impose stigma. It can pull you over for speeding, curtail your freedom of movement, and take away your right to vote. These create short-time, medium-time, and long-time versions of the same experience: being removed from the stream of regular people — cast out of Us and made one of Them.

With all the evidence that stigma is powerful and dangerous and the historical record showing how it has been put to such bad uses in the past, the law should be careful about invoking human-kind emotions. Yet there are legal scholars, lawyers, and judges who think stigma is a fine tool for the legal system to use. They are all for "shame punishments" like chain gangs, prison cams, and license plates that tell the driver's crime to the world.

A better argument is that stigma — as a historical phenomenon and as a psychological and medical experience — is far too dangerous to invoke. Stigma is, as Martha Nussbaum of the University of Chicago elegantly points out, inherently counter to the spirit of law because it acts on irrational, unconscious parts of the mind. An understanding of how human-kind psychology works shows why shame punishments are a terrible idea. These are devices that the law should not use.

The second arena in which law invokes human-kind judgments is in the area of enforcement. The police want to catch not Muslim criminals or African American criminals but just plain criminals — a distinct human kind that doesn't line up perfectly with any other. Yet an argument has been made that some kinds of associations, though not perfect, are good enough. In other words, the cop who is more suspicious of young black men in an SUV makes the argument that young-black-maleness is a good enough proxy for the real trait that matters, which is criminality. Not perfect, yet not completely wrong.

But "folk sociology" is not a good instrument for finding criminals. First, because it's largely unconscious, this code can't be separated from unintended effects. As the Implicit Association Test suggests, even people who sincerely believe they are free of prejudice may find their human-kind faculty saying something different. It works in its own way, looking for its particular cues in the world. We can't entirely control that mental process, any more than we can control most others; for instance, you can't decide not to see these words as words. We can control how the rest of the mind treats the human-kind code's message. Given what's known about the mind, people should be skeptical of ethnic profiling. After all, as the U.S. Customs Service discovered, it doesn't work as well as other techniques.

Last, the law protects "us" — citizens of a particular nation, law-abiding members of a community. The philosopher Peter Singer claims that concern for others' rights has been steadily expanding through human history, from early days of focus on the immediate family out to the clan, the tribe, the whole people, and finally the entire human race. This abstract and unemotionally involving idea of "all humanity" is, in theory, the basis for a universal law already: the UN Charter holds that each and every one of us has the same basic human rights. Understanding our human-kind faculty makes it clear that humanity probably will never reach the ideal state in which all people are equally concerned — nontheoretically — with the rights of all others. For good and for ill, *Homo sapiens* is inescapably a tribal animal.

This doesn't mean the ideal is not to be aimed at. Many beautiful and important human institutions are based on ideals. It's an excellent use of the human-kind faculty to posit some perfect state that is what Our Kind wishes to achieve. We fail; but without the ideal of the perfect marriage, the perfect citizen, or the perfect state, how could we realize the imperfect versions with which we live? What a clearer understanding of the human-kind faculty might help with, I think, is predicting the hurdles that human nature throws on the path toward perfection.

Another area where human-kind categories matter is medicine, where racial, ethnic, religious, and cultural categories are in use every day. Some doctors, like some cops, defend the practice on the grounds that "it works." But it doesn't always, as the white patient whose sickle-cell anemia went untreated, or the black patient whose ulcer was mistaken for sickle cell, could both attest.

It seems clear now that research at the biological levels of description is never going to confirm categories created at the historical and cultural levels. Scientists draw boundaries among people with haplotypes and other genetic markers, but these boundaries do not match the ones we cherish — for races, ethnic groups, nations, and extended families. The groupings we see arise from psychological and cultural levels of analysis. They're the product of our human-kind faculty interacting with our experience. That makes them a different kind of knowledge than those used at the molecular or genetic level of analysis.

This point is not controversial when it's made about other faculties that get us through life, for example, eyesight. Your eyes and visual system evolved to see the things that mattered most to your ancestors, like food, danger, and other ancestors. You can't see bacteria because your ancestors did not need to. Thus many centuries of human history passed before the germ theory of disease was accepted around the world. People found it hard to believe they could catch a deadly disease from something they could not see.

Yet people want to avoid getting sick and did so long before the germ theory came along. Evolution had provided other defenses — certain sights (and smells) prompt disgust, which makes you avoid their source. And tradition provided folk wisdom: diseases are caused by catching a chill, by the influence of the stars, or by miasmas.

Innate reactions like disgust and the traditions of folk medicine were not ineffective. As I've mentioned, the miasma theory of disease made pretty good predictions in the nineteenth century. The germ theory triumphed because it made better predictions and explained more. But the important point is this: even though the scientific account of disease doesn't completely contradict our instincts and traditions, it doesn't completely confirm them. It's *different*.

And this is what we should expect, given that all our perceptions and concepts refer to a single reality. We have psychological and cultural codes in our minds, guiding us to avoid disease. They work, more or less. So they correspond in some ways with a scientific account of disease. For example, innate capacity to learn disgust tells most people to shun rotting food. That aligns with a biological-level account of all the nasty bacteria growing in the rotting food. In other ways, though, our instincts and traditions don't line up with biological knowledge. Most people don't clean kitchen knives and sponges enough to avoid spreading bacteria from one food to another because, well, they feel clean, and we can't see anything. Many shun people with noncontagious diseases, too. Remember the test subjects who didn't want to wear Hitler's sweater, though biology told them they couldn't catch Hitlerness.

In other words, our rules of thumb for getting through the day-to-day world, those beliefs some scientists call folk physics, folk biology, and folk psychology, have some relationship to scientific accounts of the world but not a perfect one. And the more those scientific accounts develop, the less they resemble the world we evolved to see and the mental maps we use to see it. So we should no more expect medicine to confirm the human kinds we believe in than that it should confirm folk physics or folk biology. If I begin with the assumption that blacks and whites are different, and then go looking for measurements that reflect that difference, I will find them. If I begin with the assumption that owners of SUVs are different from owners of minivans, I will find measurable differences between those two groups too. (In fact, somebody did.) Same with "science fiction fans" and "people who don't like science fiction." Human beings have so many points of similarity and of difference that a line can be drawn between any sets of people, at nearly every level of description, from their molecular biology to the political opinions they express.

Race-realist academics, race-profiling doctors, and other writers offering supposedly taboo truth about ethnic and racial categories are making a special claim: that the rule-of-thumb human kinds of our psychological and political levels of analysis match the categories of molecular biology, genetics, and neuroscience. Their argument is, essentially, (1) Look, we all know that races and ethnic groups are real at the level of politics and culture; and (2) they must be real at the level of molecules, genes, cells, and organs, too.

About the first point very few people would disagree. As we've seen, at the political and psychological levels, once a human kind is believed in, it has consequences for the people placed in that category. Racial and ethnic groups are real the way money is real — because people believe they are and act on their beliefs.

The nub is the second point. There is no reason to believe that categories at one level of analysis must line up with categories from another. The value of the dollar bills in my pocket is a consequence of political arrangements and people's beliefs. It doesn't derive from other levels of analysis. If I burn that dollar bill, atoms of carbon in it will fly off, but they won't be different from the carbon atoms in a euro or a yen. The physics of atoms is unaffected by whether the atoms happen to be in currency. The two levels of description don't meet.

So it's never a good idea to try to pour science into molds made by unscientific means. We should not look to science to tell us the truth about Japanese genes or why white men can't jump. Japanese and white are not the same *kind* of concepts as genes and never will be. Assuming that there's some special truth attached to the human kinds in which we believe today is no more likely to work in the political arena than it will in law or medicine. After all, if your politics is based on "scientific facts" about a particular group of people, what happens to such politics when the scientific facts change?

A while back I mentioned a distinct, physically real human kind: people who, according to medicine a century ago, had abnormally large thymus glands. As we saw, they turned out to have normal innards. The doctors were misled because their examples of the human body came almost exclusively from the ranks of stigmatized people. And stigmatized people, because they are stigmatized, have smaller immune-system glands and larger stress-related glands. By the time better categories came along, thousands of unnecessary cases of thyroid cancer had been created by useless radiation treatments based on the older beliefs.

The nature of human kinds is all there, in that story. The way these categories change over time, even though we feel they are eternal. The way they have real consequences, even if we later learn they were not a good match with reality. The way they cause physical changes in people, like those shrunken glands. That leads us to put cart before horse, and imagine that the physical change caused the category, instead of the other way around. And, finally, the way mistaken, unjust, senseless, and cruel human-kind judgments will be included in textbooks and lectures and endorsed by smart, confident, educated people.

The moral of that story, I think, is simple: the code is in your head, where you make and remake your version, every day. Human nature shaped that power, with its special opportunities and vulnerabilities, but it's you who wield it. Your human-kind code makes nothing happen, for good or ill, unless you choose to act. Ethnic tensions, religious strife, political conflict, clan rivalries, and the like have never harmed anyone and never will. *People* do the harm.

In other words, the Us-Them code does not own you; you own it. This power to believe in human kinds, and to love or hate them, is part of your human nature. You could think of it as a set of buttons and levers, built in to your mind. You didn't choose the control panel, but you can decide how to live with it. Push your own buttons and pull your own levers, for instance. Or look away, and let someone else — the politician, the propagandist, the ethnic chief, the family patriarch, the radio loudmouth, the priest, the hack writer — do it for you. Human kinds exist because of human minds. They're in your head, bound to your fears and hopes, your sweat glands and your gut. But how you choose to live with them is up to you.

Acknowledgments

"What terrible moments does one feel," wrote Alexander Pope, "after one has engaged for a large work! In the beginning of my translating the Iliad, I wished anybody would hang me, a hundred times. It sat so heavily on my mind at first, that I often used to dream of it, and do sometimes still."

This is no *Iliad,* but I know the feeling. What brought me through those terrible moments was the help, encouragement, and patience of many generous people. Thanks to them, I've also known the not-terrible and the exhilarating moments of a "large work."

From the outset, my agent, Sloan Harris, believed in this project and did everything right.

I was outrageously fortunate in editors at Little, Brown. First, Jennifer Josephy bought the book with enthusiasm. Sarah Crichton, editor and publisher, guided it well, as did her successor, Michael Pietsch. Deborah Baker focused and defined the project. Pat Strachan brought it to its published form, much improved by her intelligent and gracious attention. As the manuscript turned into a book, Helen Atsma's assistance was invaluable. I thank Wendy Jacobs for meticulous copyediting and sharp reminders about the sensitivities of this topic, Kathryn Blatt for her careful proofreading, and Peggy Freudenthal for her patience and perfectionism.

Three institutions gave crucial help too. The New York Public Library, in the person of Wayne Furman, gave me a perch in the venerable Allen Room, where (I was reminded whenever I heard the afternoon tour go by) so many great books were researched and written. The Corporation of Yaddo provided several weeks of idyllic working conditions. The Marine Biological Laboratory in Woods Hole, Massachusetts, bestowed a generous fellowship, which let me tag along with the students and instructors of Neural Systems and Behavior course, class of 2002. Directors Catherine Carr and Rick Levine let me spend the summer with a crew of brilliant, sleepless neuroscientists.

For reading the entire manuscript and suggesting improvement, I thank Jonathan Shay, Derek Bickerton, Cynthia Hughes, Rebecca Steinberg, John Horgan, and Gabriela Ilieva. Thanks too to those who took the time to look over sections: Otto Adang, Peter Galison, Robert Kurzban, Peter Richerson, Lawrence A. Hirschfeld, David Sloan Wilson, Don Beck, Robert M. Sapolsky, Robin Marantz Henig, Frans B. M. de Waal, Jamie Arndt, Nancy Adler, Wemara Lichty, and Jonathan Haidt. I'm grateful to J. M. G. van der Dennen for a copy of his study of ideas about warfare; to Gary Taubes for a suggestion about Type-A personality research; to Kate Dailey for research assisstance; and to the late Jeanette Wakin for pointing me to the history of religious conflicts in medieval Europe.

Finally, thanks for their forbearance to the people who sacrificed the most. To write this book about how much human beings are shaped by company, I had to forswear it. I chose that isolation, but people close to me didn't, and they put up with missed dinners, long absences, trance-like silences, and other book symptoms with stoicism and affection. The people closest to me supported this project, materially, intellectually, and emotionally: Jean-Jacques Berreby, Mary Ryan, Alexandre Berreby, and Beverly Bergman. None ever suggested that perhaps it all wasn't worth the price. I'll miss this work (I dream of it still), and I, too, came to think the terrible moments were worth it. I hope they agree.

Notes and References

EPIGRAPHS

vii **so we did the work.** John Beeson, *A Plea for the Indians* (1857; Reprint: Ye Galleon Press, 1982). Beeson, who quoted this man, was himself an eyewitness to the slaughter of Oregon's native peoples in the 1850s.

vii **he was still one of us.** Associated Press, "Oregon Bids Farewell to 'Free Willy' Star," February 21, 2004. As the headline suggests, Keiko wasn't just "one of us"; he was a celebrity.

INTRODUCTION

3 **(and at hatred too).** For new ways neuroscience is hooking up with political science, see Matthew D. Lieberman et al., "Is Political Cognition Like Riding a Bicycle? How Cognitive Neuroscience Can Inform Research on Political Thinking," *Political Psychology* 24, no. 4 (December 1, 2003): 681–704. For neuroscience and economics, see P. Read Montague and Gregory S. Berns, "Neural Economics and the Biological Substrates of Valuation," *Neuron* 36 (October 10, 2002): 265–84. For neuroscientific investigations of moral quandaries, see Joshua Greene et al., "An fMRI Investigation of Emotional Engagement in Moral Judgment," *Science* 293 (2001): pp 2105–8.

3 **not "what we eat"?** For example, the writer Tété-Michel Kpomassie reports that Inuit villages were seal eating, caribou eating, or fish eating. In the Thule region of Greenland, he writes, in a year of few seal but plentiful fish in nearby waters, some seal-eating Inuit starved. See Tété-Michel Kpomassie, *An African in Greenland* (New York Review of Books, 2001), p. 125.

3 **they never saw?** Andrew Jacobs, "The Struggle for Iraq: The National Mood; Shock over Abuse Reports, But Support for the Troops," *New York Times,* May 8, 2004.

3 **never seen the place?** Associated Press, "Murder Inspires Wave of Dutch Attacks," November 10, 2004.

3 **other kind of people?** Thomas J. Lueck, "Orthodox Jews in Brooklyn Burned Banned Wigs," *New York Times,* May 17, 2004, p. B3.

4 **mug turns into tea.** Noam Chomsky, "Language and Nature," *Mind* 104 (1995) p. 1.

4 **mean by 'ethnic group.'"** Francisco Gil-White, "The Study of Ethnicity Needs Better Categories," an unpublished paper available on Gil-White's Web site: <http://www.psych.upenn.edu/~fjgil/Connor.pdf>.

5 **time pressure they felt.** John M. Darley and C. Dan Batson, "From Jerusalem to Jericho: A Study of Situational and Dispositional Variables in Helping Behavior," *Journal of Personality and Social Psychology* 27 (1973): pp. 100–108.

5 **who thought about Superman.** L. D. Nelson and M. I. Norton, "From Student to Su-

perhero: Situational Primes Shape Future Helping," *Journal of Experimental Social Psychology,* in press.

6   **too little on situation.** Lee Ross, "The Intuitive Psychologist and His Shortcomings: Distortions in the Attribution Process," in *Advances in Experimental Social Psychology,* vol. 10 (Academic Press, 1977).

6   **personality traits for everyone.)** The peculiar history and widespread effects of personality testing are described in Annie Murphy Paul, *The Cult of Personality: How Personality Tests Are Leading Us to Miseducate Our Children, Mismanage Our Companies, and Misunderstand Ourselves* (Free Press, 2004).

6   **not cheat on a spelling test."** Quoted in Jeffrey Rosen, "Jurisprurience," *New Yorker,* September 28, 1998, pp. 34–39.

6   **abused their charges.** Craig Haney, Curtis Banks, and Philip Zimbardo, "Interpersonal Dynamics in a Simulated Prison," *International Journal of Criminology and Penology* 1 (1973): 69–97. Reports about this experiment were the basis for a 2001 movie, *Das Experiment,* directed by Oliver Hirschbiegel.

      Today, in the wake of scandals over the abuse of detainees in the war on terror and the conflict in Iraq, the debate over the "Stanford prison experiment" rages on. Does it prove that anyone can become abusive in a prison setting? Some psychologists say so. Others argue that this notion excuses the abusers, and their superiors, who let them do wrong. See Susan T. Fiske, L. T. Harris, and A. J. Cuddy, "Social psychology. Why ordinary people torture enemy prisoners," *Science* 306 (2004): 1482–83, and, for a counter-argument, Raj Persaud, "Abuse of prisoners at Abu Ghraib," *Science* 307 (2005): 1873–75.

7   **How did I know?** I guess I was working on a principle of analogy, as did European thinkers in the Middle Ages. Cold fluids, like mountain streams and rain, are clear. Hot fluids, like blood and chowder, are cloudy. What I remember best isn't *what* I thought but *how* I thought it: without a trace of doubt.

8   **so do novelists.** For example, Marcel Proust, who describes with great sympathy a character's belief that "in fashioning a work of art we are by no means free, that we do not choose how we shall make it but that it pre-exists and therefore we are obliged, since it is both necessary and hidden, to do what we should have to do if it were a law of nature, that is to say to discover it." The philosopher Richard Rorty quotes this passage in *Contingency, Irony and Solidarity* (Cambridge University Press, 1989), p. 98.

9   **reinvent and reinvigorate it."** Robert M. Sapolsky. "Circling the Blanket for God," in *The Trouble with Testosterone, and Other Essays on the Biology of the Human Predicament* (Scribner, 1997), pp 241–88.

10   **they'd probably be disappointed."** Peter Galison, interview with author, February 1995.

10   **the cosmological constant may be back.** See, for example, Kenneth W. Ford, *The Quantum World: Quantum Physics for Everyone* (Harvard University Press, 2004), p. 246.

10–11   **until geologists decided that they do.** The famous story of Alfred Wegener's theory of continental drift and its journey from ridicule to triumph is told in Hal Hellman, *Great Feuds in Science: Ten of the Liveliest Disputes Ever* (Wiley, 1999), chap. 8.

11   **canceled brontosaurus.** Greg Lichtenberg, a writer, made this point about brontosaurus in the literary magazine *Fence* (vol. 1, no. 2). The paleontologist Jack Horner has described the same sort of revisions for Tyrannosaurus Rex. According to today's theory, the upright skeleton in the American Museum of Natural History that I admired as a child actually is all wrong and had its neck, back, and tail broken. For more on this, see John R. Horner and Edwin Dobb, *Dinosaur Lives* (Harcourt Brace, 1998), pp. 4–5.

11   **not be true.** Joshua Johnson et al., "Germline Stem Cells and Follicular Renewal in the Postnatal Mammalian Ovary," *Nature* 428 (2004): 145.

11   **do much good.** Denise Grady, "Doubts Raised on a Breast Cancer Procedure," *New York Times,* April 16, 1999, p. A1.

11   **adult brains can and do.** Peter Eriksson et al., "Neurogenesis in the Adult Human Hippocampus." *Nature Medicine* 4, no. 11 (1998): 1313–17.

11   **primate species examined.** Elliott Bush and John M. Allman, "The Scaling of Frontal Cortex in Primates and Carnivores," *Proceedings of the National Academy of Sciences of the United States of America* 101, no. 11 (2004): 3962–66.

12   **same color.** G. K. Chesterton, *Orthodoxy* (1908; Reprint: Reformation Press, 2002); see chap. 7.

ONE: "THAT'S OUR BIGGEST DIFFERENCE"

15   **I call "human kinds."** I'm using *human kinds* much as they're defined by Lawrence A. Hirschfeld of New School University, with one difference. Hirschfeld says a human kind is any collection of people that a person recognizes as being "like me" in some fundamental and enduring way. My definition also includes temporary collections of people who don't see themselves — not at first, anyway — as fundamental and enduring. "Passengers on the 8:15 ferry" is a human kind by my lights, though it isn't in Hirschfeld's definition. See Lawrence A. Hirschfeld, *Race in the Making: Cognition, Culture and the Child's Construction of Human Kinds* (MIT Press, 1996), pp. 13, 20.

    The term *human kinds* has also been used by the philosopher Ian Hacking of the University of Toronto. But Hacking's definition is narrower. For Hacking, human kinds are *only* the categories devised since the early nineteenth century by hospitals, schools, census takers, and other designated experts working with statistics and other data. "Child abuser" and "person with multiple personality disorder" fit Hacking's definition of a human kind, but race and ethnicity don't.

    Hacking believes those older ideas are too different from social science–type categories to fit under a single umbrella term. See Ian Hacking, "The Looping Effects of Human Kinds," in *Causal Cognition: A Multidisciplinary Debate,* ed. Dan Sperber, David Prèmack, and Ann James Premack, pp. 350–94 (Clarendon Press, 1995).

    I prefer the widest possible definition because in people's lives the difference between social-science and primeval notions of human kind is blurred. I've heard strong tribal feelings expressed about newfangled, expert-defined human kinds, like "the Attention Deficit Community" or "transsexuals." Conversely, I've noticed people eager to use expert-based, scientific procedures, such as DNA testing, to verify their membership in primeval human kinds; for instance, the *Kohanim,* the traditional priestly caste of the Jewish people. If modern human kinds are utterly different from primordial ones, why can people treat these kinds as if they were all the same? The simplest answer might be the right one for the questions I'm writing about: in the mind, all human kinds *are* the same.

15   **students of Steven Pinker."** A small human kind but not a trivial one. Scientists, as someone once said, are like Tibetan monks: they come in lineages. Scientists get their ideas from working with, for, and against other scientists. In that process, mentors count for a great deal.

15   **do for faraway people.** For example, a survey conducted by the American Animal Hospital Association found nearly half its North American respondents saying they would "spend any amount of money" to save a pet's life. Almost half had taken time from work to tend to a pet. Three quarters said they would spend $1,000 to save a pet's life. See Tralee Pearce, "Resuscitating Rover," *Toronto Globe and Mail,* August 9, 2003. Compare that $1,000 to the average given per household in the United States to all charities each year: $1,600. See Rebecca Gardyn, "Generosity and Income — For Americans, Those Who Earn the Least Money Tend to Give Away the Most," *American Demographics,* December 1, 2002.

15   **and so on and on.** Thanks to Steven Somerstein, Esq., for pointing out this distinction among his fellow veterans.

17   **a political ally, rebuked the clergymen.** For Berlusconi's quotations, see John Hooper and Kate Connolly, "Berlusconi Breaks Ranks over Islam," *The Guardian,* September 27, 2001; for American clergy and for President Bush's comment, see Gustav Niebuhr, "U.S. 'Secular' Groups Set Tone for Terror Attacks, Falwell Says," *New York Times,* September 14, 2001.

18   **in Jesus, and apologized.** Joseph Fried, personal communication, June 8, 1999. This account emerged at the trial, in 2000, of police officers accused of grotesquely abusing a Haitian man, Abner Louima. Fried, a reporter for the *New York Times,* covered the trial.

18   **of cloth," she said.** Marlise Simons, "Mother Superior's Role in Rwanda Horror Is Weighed," *New York Times,* June 6, 2001.

18   **"symbolic species."** See Terrence Deacon, *The Symbolic Species: The Co-Evolution of Language and the Brain* (W. W. Norton & Company, 1998).

21   **bigger than anything else."** Paul Begala and J. C. Watts, *Crossfire,* November 15, 2002; transcript available online at <http://archives.cnn.com/2002/ALLPOLITICS/11/15/cf.opinion.jc.watts/>.

21   **them to act out.")** Nicholas Lemann, "Buffalo Tim," *New Yorker,* May 25, 2004.

22   **that it might rain.** The idea that a concept "licenses" some inferences but not others was proposed by the philosopher Nelson Goodman.

24   **not Isaiah, the polymath.** The story is recounted in Marilynn Berger, "Isaiah Berlin, Philosopher and Pluralist, Is Dead at 88," *New York Times,* November 7, 1997.

25   **nor bones, nor hair, nor skull."** F. Max Müller, *Biographies of Words and the Home of the Aryas* (1988; Reprint: Kessinger Publishing, 2004), p. 120.

25   **life-and-death human kind.** The role of "experts" on Jews — bureaucrats who, once they had that designation, busily found work for themselves — is described in Christopher Browning (with contributions by Jürgen Matthäus), *The Origins of the Final Solution: The Evolution of Nazi Jewish Policy, September 1929–March 1942* (University of Nebraska Press and Yad Vashem, 2004), p. 11.

25   **that gets people killed.** See David Grann, "The Brand," *New Yorker,* February 16 and 23, 2004, pp. 157–71.

25   **over a soccer match.** This war is described in Ryszard Kapuscinski, *The Soccer War* (Vintage, 1992).

25   **risked their lives was the soccer gang.** Otto M. J. Adang, "Systematic Observations of Violent Interactions between Football Hooligans," in *In-group/Out-group Behaviour in Modern Societies: An Evolutionary Perspective,* ed. K. Thienpont and R. Cliquet, chap. 9 (Vlaamse Gemeenschap, 1999).

25   **killed thirty thousand people.** See Alan Cameron, *Circus Factions: Blues and Greens at Rome and Byzantium* (Clarendon Press, 1976). In the "Nika" riots of 532, Greens and Blues fought *together* against the authorities.

26   **person who wears eyeglasses.** George Chigas and Dmitri Mosyakov, "Literacy and Education under the Khmer Rouge," *Cambodian Genocide Program,* 2001); available online at <http://www.yale.edu/cgp/literacyandeducation.html>.

26   **not in itself enough to protect anyone.** Ben Kiernan, *The Pol Pot Regime: Race, Power and Genocide in Cambodia, 1975–1979* (Yale University Press, 1996), chap. 7. For the numbers killed, by ethnicity, see p. 458.

27   **in their territory.** Nancy Ramsey, "Sisterhood in a Floating Powder Room; An Oscar-Nominated Documentary Captures Life aboard the Staten Island Ferry," *New York Times,* February 12, 2004, p. E1.

27   **speechless. Just speechless."** Quoted in Jason Tanz, "Wounded to the Quick by an Affair Gone Astray," *New York Times,* December 13, 2002, p. F1.

28   **dumb as the next guy."** Richard Feynman, *"Surely You're Joking, Mr. Feynman!": Adventures of a Curious Character* (W. W. Norton, 1988), p. 216.

28   **while Asians are.** Margaret Shih, Todd L. Pittinsky, and Nalini Ambady, "Stereotype Susceptibility: Identity Salience and Shifts in Quantitative Performance," *Psychological Science* 10 (1999): 80–83.

29   **to his scorned country."** Cajal is quoted in J. L. Heilbron and W. F. Bynum, "1904 and All That," *Nature* 426 (December 18, 2003): 761–64.

29   **get different answers.** George Lakoff, *Women, Fire, and Dangerous Things: What Categories Reveal about the Mind* (University of Chicago Press, 1987), p. 186.

30   **in early childhood.** Sigmund Freud, *Group Psychology and the Analysis of the Ego.* Trans. James Strachey (1921; Reprint: Norton, 1980), pp. 11–14.

30   **has repressed."** Elisabeth Young-Bruehl, *The Anatomy of Prejudices* (Harvard University Press, 1996), p. 34.

31   **black people more intelligent.** This melanist theory was promoted by Leonard Jeffries, a professor at City College in New York City. See Massimo Calabresi, "Dispatches: Skin Deep 101," *Time,* February 14, 1994.

31   **be *less* intelligent.** See J. Philippe Rushton, *Race, Evolution, and Behavior: A Life History Perspective,* 3rd ed. (Charles Darwin Research Institute Press, 2000).

31   **hostile to Croatia.** This claim was made by the late Franjo Tudjman, president of Croa-

tia at the time, in 1997. It was discussed in Marek Kohn, "The Green Banana Gang," *New Statesman,* December 5, 1997. The implication that citizens of modern Croatia are genetically distinct from their neighbors is false. For example, an analysis of Bosnian and Croatian mitochondrial DNA, performed by Michele Harvey of the University of Washington and her colleagues, found "little or no genetic distance" between the DNA from each group. Harvey described the work in a presentation at the 1997 Cold Spring Harbor Conference on Human Evolution, Cold Spring Harbor, N.Y., October 4–8, 1997.

This doesn't mean, of course, that the peoples of ex-Yugoslavia are completely indistinguishable — just that the variations in their DNA do not map onto today's political map.

TWO: "THERE ARE FEW QUESTIONS MORE CURIOUS THAN THIS"

32   **a guy named Ryan again."** Scott Fornek and Stephanie Zimmermann, "Sex Scandal Drives Ryan from Race," *Chicago Sun-Times,* June 26, 2004.

33   **their common ancestors."** Joseph R. Strayer, "France: The Holy Land, the Chosen People, and the Most Christian King," in *Medieval Statecraft and the Perspectives of History,* ed. John F. Benton and Thomas N. Bisson (Princeton University Press, 1971), pp. 300–314.

33   **variance with their own."** Dante, *Convivio,* I.5.55–66, quoted in Barry Windeatt, ed., *Troilus and Criseyde* (Penguin, 2003), p. 375 nn.

34   **talking about?** This 1925 quotation by Louis Proust is quoted in Mort Rosenblum, *Mission to Civilize: The French Way* (Doubleday, 1988), p. 21.

34   **than a Dane."** David Hume, "Of National Characters," in *Essays: Moral, Political and Literary,* ed. Eugene F. Miller, pp. 197–215 (1777; reprint: Liberty Classics, 1986).

36   **defining a family.** Kurt Lewin, "Bringing Up the Jewish Child," in *Resolving Social Conflicts and Field Theory in Social Science,* pp. 122–32 (American Psychological Association, 1997).

37   **has explained why.** Robert M. Sapolsky, "Poverty's Remains," in *The Trouble with Testosterone and Other Essays on the Biology of the Human Predicament.* (Scribner, 1997), pp. 113–24.

38   **use the energy at hand."** Quoted in "100 Years Ago," *Nature* 412 (2001): 867.

38   **trail that should be abandoned."** J. J. Ray, "If 'A-b' Does Not Predict Heart Disease, Why Bother with It? A Comment on Ivancevich and Matteson," *British Journal of Medical Psychology* 64 (1991): 85–90.

38   **is medically useless.** Michael Myrtek, "Type A Behavior Pattern, Personality Factors, Disease, and Physiological Reactivity: A Meta-analytic Update," *Personality and Individual Differences* 18 (1995): 491–502.

39   **white, male, right-handed subjects.** See Joseph Dumit, *Picturing Personhood: Brain Scans and Biomedical Identity* (Princeton University Press, 2003).

40   **Their descendants are.** See Noel Ignatiev, *How the Irish Became White* (Routledge, 1995).

40   **called *cagots*.** The history of this human kind is described in two books: Françoise Bériac, *Des lépreux aux cagots: Recherches sur les sociétés marginales en Aquitaine médiévale* (Féderation Historique du Sud-Ouest, 1990); Paola Antolini, *Au-delà de la rivière: Les cagots, histoire d'une exclusion* (Editions Nathan, 1991).

40   **ears were shaped.** This is described by an author who remembers cagots from his own childhood: Jean-Emile Cabarrouy, *Les cagots: Une race maudite dan le sud de la Gascogne* (J & D Editions, 1996).

40   **mark on their clothes).** See Ulysse Robert, *Les signes d'infamie au Moyen Age: Juifs, Sarrasins, heretiques, lepreux, cagots et filles publiques* (H. Champion, 1891).

40   **fit the definition.** My list of traits for an ethnic group derives from a number of definitions proposed by psychologists, sociologists, political scientists, and anthropologists. Each discipline tends toward a definition that suits its questions — psychologists focusing more on how an individual perceives someone as belonging to an ethnic group, anthropologists instead looking at how ethnicity organizes people's behavior, political scientists emphasizing how ethnicity is both a cause and an effect in political struggles. There is no universal definition for the term, but there is convergence on the features I mentioned.

For a psychologist's definition of ethnicity, see Gordon Allport, *The Nature of Prejudice* (1954; Reprint: Addison Wesley, 1979), pp. 85–106. An anthropological take is

Fredrik Barth, introduction to *Ethnic Groups and Boundaries,* ed. Barth, pp. 9–38 (Waveland Press, 1969). A politically oriented, "interest-group" definition is in Abner Cohen, *Custom and Politics in Urban Africa* (University of California Press, 1969), p. 4.

40 **simply were recategorized.** Françoise Bériac, *Histoire des lépreux au Moyen Age: Une société d'exclus* (Editions Imago, 1988).

41 **abolished in 1894.** Anders Hansson, *Chinese Outcasts: Discrimination and Emancipation in Late Imperial China* (E. J. Brill, 1996), pp. 13–15.

41 **Korean society."** Soon Man Rhim, "The Paekchong: Untouchables of Korea," *Journal of Oriental Studies* 12 (1974): 30–40.

42 **flying wedge of police.** Solomon Asch, *Social Psychology* (Prentice-Hall, 1952), p. 225.

THREE: COUNTING AND MEASURING

46 **razor blades you buy.** See Malcolm Gladwell, "The Science of Shopping," *New Yorker,* November 4, 1996.

47 **to drive research today.** For twin studies in particular and Galton's life and works in general, I have relied on Nicholas Wright Gillham, *Sir Francis Galton: From African Exploration to the Birth of Eugenics* (Oxford University Press, 2001).

47 **to estimate the degrees."** Quoted ibid., p. 191.

47 **nature versus nurture.** Ibid., p. 192.

47 **portrait of a type."** Francis Galton, *Inquiries into Human Faculty* (Macmillan, 1883), p. 222.

48 **not an individual."** Both quotations in this paragraph are from Francis Galton, *Inquiries into Human Faculty* (Macmillan, 1883), pp. 340–41.

48 **Cleopatra's looks "simply hideous."** Ibid.

48 **and saw none.** Arthur Batut, *La photographie appliquée à la production du type d'une famille, d'une tribu, ou d'une race* (Gauthier-Villars, 1887).

48 **of the invisible."** Ibid.

48 **"portrait of a probability" that Galton had devised.** I learned about Galton's composite photos (and Wittgenstein's interest) in Allan Sekula, "The Body and the Archive," in *The Contest of Meaning: Critical Histories of Photography* (MIT Press, 1989).

48 **any given group of men."** Galton. *Inquiries,* p. 354.

49 **a very curious mixture."**) Ibid., p. 343.

50 **printed numbers" about human beings.** Ian Hacking, "The Looping Effects of Human Kinds," in *Causal Cognition: A Multidisciplinary Debate,* ed. Dan Sperber, David Premack, and Ann James Premack, pp. 350–94 (Clarendon Press, 1995).

50 **his best-known book.** Quetelet's role is described in Sekula, "The Body and the Archive."

50 **and politically desirable.** Quetelet *(Treatise on Man),* quoted ibid.

51 *The Bell Curve.* Richard J. Herrnstein and Charles Murray, *The Bell Curve: Intelligence and Class Structure in American Life* (Free Press, 1994).

51 **normal person. He is not."** Quoted in David Remnick, "The King Leaves the Castle," *New Yorker,* February 17 and 25, 2003.

52 **about real people."** Steven Pinker, *How the Mind Works* (W. W. Norton, 1997), p. 323.

52 **stereotypes are true."** Jonathan Haidt, telephone interview with author, October 2003.

52 **Kampalese-Americans."** Lee Jussim, personal communication.

53 **work on the same principle.)** See Heather MacDonald, "What We Don't Know Can Hurt Us," *City Journal,* Spring 2004. For a counterpoint to MacDonald's pro-screening arguments, see the Electronic Privacy Information Center Web page on passenger profiling: <http://www.epic.org/privacy/airtravel/profiling.html>.

53 **was a member.** Of course, this is shorthand. The computer doesn't think; it simply switches circuits ON and OFF, representing 0 and 1. At a different level of analysis, these 0's and 1's stand for symbols that the software manipulates. One level up from there, the symbols stand for things like "destination" and "when ticket was bought."

54 **with race or religion."** Testimony of Cathal L. Flynn, Federal Aviation Administration's Associate Administrator for Civil Aviation Security, "The Status of Aviation Security Efforts with a Focus on the National Safe Skies Alliance and Passenger Profiling Criteria": Hearings before the Subcommittee on Aviation of the House Committee on Transportation and Infrastructure, 105th Cong., 2d Sess., pp. 12–87 (May 12, 1998).

54   **any level of suspicion."** United States Customs Service, "Personal Search Handbook" (U.S. Department of the Treasury, 1999), emphasis in original.

54   **breakdown by race, nationality, ethnicity, and gender.** Dean Boyd (USCS spokesman), telephone interview with the author, November 1, 2001.

55   **department spokesman described it.** Boyd interview.

55   **and his hands were shaky.** Boyd interview.

55   **it only searched 6,111 people.** Michael Fletcher, "Fewer People Searched by Customs in Past Year; But Changes Yield More Drug Seizures," *Washington Post,* October 19, 2000.

56   **accept its categories.** "Modes of understanding" is a phrase coined by the British philosopher Michael Oakeshott.

57   **a book about homosexuality."** Kramer quoted in Douglas Martin, "C. A. Tripp, 83, Author of Work on Homosexuality, Dies," *New York Times,* May 22, 2003.

58   **then knowledge about them."** Hacking. "Looping Effects."

58   **term *homosexual* in 1868?** I follow the history of the term given in Rictor Norton, "A Critique of Social Constructionism and Postmodern Queer Theory: The Term 'Homosexual,'" 2002. Available online at <http://www.infopt.demon.co.uk/social14. htm>.

59   **any other Adams and Eves."** Larry Kramer, "Why Gay Identity Should Evolve toward a More Complete Culture," *LGNY (Lesbian and Gay New York),* July 6, 1997, p. 29.

59   **they had no history."** Quoted in Will Sullivan, "Sterling Sexuality: Was Yale Patron Gay?" *Yale Daily News,* April 3, 2003.

59–60   **was more cautious).** See C. A. Tripp, *The Intimate World of Abraham Lincoln* (Free Press, 2005).

61   **our words and our species.** On the abundance of homosexual behavior in many species, see Bruce Bagemihl, *Biological Exuberance: Animal Homosexuality and Natural Diversity* (Stonewall Inn Editions, 2000).

61   **parts of Papua New Guinea another.** See Gilbert Herdt, *Guardians of the Flutes,* vol. 1: *Idioms of Masculinity* (University of Chicago Press, 1994).

62   **sex between women.** See Eva Cantarella, *Bisexuality in the Ancient World* (Yale Nota Bene, 2002).

62   **thinking to our own.** For more about this translation process, see Arnold Davidson, *The Emergence of Sexuality: Historical Epistemology and the Formation of Concepts* (Harvard University Press, 2002); and also David M. Halperin, *How to Do the History of Homosexuality* (University of Chicago Press, 2004).
       For a spirited defense of essentialism applied to gay people, see Rictor Norton, *The Myth of the Modern Homosexual: Queer History and the Search for Cultural Unity* (Cassell, 1997).

63   **claims they're arbitrary.** See Catherine Z. Elgin. *Between the Absolute and the Arbitrary* (Cornell University Press, 1997).

FOUR: BIRDS OF A FEATHER

65   **was the category "game."** Ludwig Wittgenstein, *Philosophical Investigations,* trans. G. E. M. Anscombe (Blackwell, 2001), pp. 27–28.

65   **on Wittgenstein's mind.** Ludwig Wittgenstein, *The Blue and Brown Books* (Harper Torchbooks, 1960), p. 18.

65   **chair than *electric chair.*** Eleanor Rosch, "Cognitive Representations of Semantic Categories," *Journal of Experimental Psychology* 104 (1975): 192–253.

66   **any other single symptom.** Ziva Kunda, *Social Cognition: Making Sense of People* (MIT Press, 1999), pp. 33–34.

66   **a two-of-six list.)** The definition is available online at <http://www.behavenet.com/capsules/disorders/dysd.htm>.

66   **makes sense to the perceiver."** Paul Davidsson, "Concept Acquisition by Autonomous Agents: Cognitive Modeling versus the Engineering Approach," Lund University Cognitive Studies 12, ISSN 1101-8453, Lund University, Sweden, 1992. A link to the full text of this paper can be found at this web page: <http://ai.cs.lth.se/papers.shtml>.

68   **important distinctions among species.** Alison Gopnik et al., *The Scientist in the Crib: What Early Learning Tells Us about the Mind* (Harper Perennial, 2000).

68   **a few basic principles.** This view is laid out in Frank C. Keil, "The Birth and Nurturance of Concepts," in *Mapping the Mind: Domain Specificity in Cognition and Culture,* pp. 234–54 (Cambridge University Press, 1994).

68   **out of a burning home."** Barsalou's reference to "ad hoc" categories like "things to take from a house fire" is described and quoted in George Lakoff, *Women, Fire, and Dangerous Things: What Categories Reveal about the Mind* (Chicago: University of Chicago Press, 1987), p. 45.

69   **they're supposed to solve.** This view of the mind was worked out by the pragmatist thinkers William James, John Dewey, George Herbert Mead, and their intellectual heirs. It holds, simply, that the meaning of a word or idea or symbol is the effect it has in the world. One of the most lucid discussions of this philosophy is James's own. See William James, *Pragmatism* (1908; Reprint: Prometheus Books, 1991).

69–70   **I felt quite at home."** Charles Johnston, "Three Came Back," in *Captured by the Indians: 15 Firsthand Accounts, 1750–1870,* ed. Frederick Drimmer (Dover Publications, 1985), pp. 183–215. Johnston's story was originally published in 1827.

70   **veterans, or vice versa."** Peter Binzen, *Whitetown, U.S.A.* (Vintage Books, 1970), p. 215.

70   **I'm their advocate."** Quoted in Barbara Ferguson, "A POW Translator Talks," *Arab News,* April 4, 2003. Available online at <www.arabnews.com>.

71   **rather than to his occupation.** L. Sinclair and Z. Kunda, "Reactions to a Black Professional: Motivated Inhibition and Activation of Conflicting Stereotypes," *Journal of Personality and Social Psychology* 77, no. 5 (1999): 885.

71   **think of me as police."** Quoted in Jodi Wilgoren, "Michigan Officers Fear Pressure of U.S. Plan," *New York Times,* November 17, 2001.

71   **Bureau of the Census.** Clara E. Rodriguez, *Changing Race: Latinos, the Census, and the History of Ethnicity in the United States* (New York University Press, 2 72), p. 162.

72   **information in a smart way."** Alfonso Renart, personal communication, 2004.

74   **to name two.** See D. M. Behar et al., "Contrasting Patterns of Y Chromosome Variation in Ashkenazi Jewish and Host Non-Jewish European Populations," *Human Genetics* 114 (2004): 354–65.

75   **of sophistication and urbanity.** Gaye Tuchman and Harry G. Levine, "New York Jews and Chinese Food: The Social Construction of an Ethnic Pattern," *Contemporary Ethnography* 22, no. 3 (1992): 382–407.

76   **had plaid to sell.** Hugh Trevor-Roper, "The Invention of Tradition: The Highland Tradition of Scotland," in *The Invention of Tradition,* ed. Eric Hobsbawm and Terence Ranger, pp. 15–43 (Cambridge University Press, 1983).

76   **Hutu and Tutsi spheres.** Mahmood Mamdani, *When Victims Become Killers: Colonialism, Nativism, and the Genocide in Rwanda* (Princeton University Press, 2001); see especially chaps. 2 and 3.

77   **Middle Eastern political Islam."** Thomas Hylland Eriksen, "Ethnic Identity, National Identity, and Intergroup Conflict," talk delivered at the Rutgers Symposium on Social Identity, Intergroup Conflict, and Conflict Reduction, New Brunswick, N.J., April 23, 1999.

78   **is monstrous and meaningless."** Francis Galton, *Inquiries into Human Faculty* (Macmillan, 1883), p. 230.

78   **half to another mark."** Francis Galton, *Hereditary Genius* (Macmillan, 1892), p. 29.

79   **with objective, valid *measurements.*** For examples of this argument, see Vincent Sarich and Frank Miele, *Race: The Reality of Human Differences* (Westview Press, 2004); J. Philippe Rushton, *Race, Evolution, and Behavior: A Life History Perspective,* 3rd ed. (Charles Darwin Research Institute Press, 2000); and Jon Entine, *Taboo: Why Black Athletes Dominate Sports and Why We're Afraid to Talk about It* (Public Affairs, 2000).

79   **the Japanese and the Native Americans.** Jared Diamond, "Race without Color," *Discover* (November 1994): 83–89.

81   **about these alternate universes?** J. Philippe Rushton, "Statement on Race as a Biological Concept," *American Renaissance,* November 4, 1996. Available online at <http://www.amren.com/rushton.htm>.

81   **a bleeding stomach ulcer.** Ritchie Witzig, "The Medicalization of Race: Scientific Legitimization of a Flawed Social Construct," *Annals of Internal Medicine* 125 (1996): 675–79.

82   **Irish names began with one.** Henry Louis Gates, talk delivered at the Rutgers Symposium on Social Identity, Intergroup Conflict, and Conflict Reduction, New Brunswick, N.J., April 23, 1999.

83   **different kinds of people.** Described by Ian Hacking, "The Looping Effects of Human Kinds," in *Causal Cognition: A Multidisciplinary Debate,* ed. Dan Sperber, David Premack, and Ann James Premack, pp. 350–94 (Clarendon Press, 1995).

83   **historians don't agree.** For different theories about the origin of today's idea of "race," see Michael Banton, *Racial Theories* (Cambridge University Press, 1998); and Ivan Hannaford, *Race: The History of an Idea in the West* (Johns Hopkins University Press, 1996). See Lawrence Hirschfeld, *Race in the Making* (MIT Press, 1996), pp. 33–34, for a brief rundown of historical race theories.

84   **racial categories don't line up.** Rodriguez, *Changing Race.*

84   **the documents after death.** R. A. Hahn, "Why Race Is Differentially Classified on U.S. Birth and Infant Death Certificates: An Examination of Two Hypotheses [see comments]," *Epidemiology* 10 (1999): 108–111. See also R. A. Hahn, *Sickness and Healing: An Anthropological Perspective* (Yale University Press, 1995), p. 113.

86   **Jewish, Italian, or Irish.** This development is described in Thomas Hylland Eriksen, "Ethnicity, Race and Nation," in *The Ethnicity Reader: Nationalism, Multiculturalism and Migration,* ed. Montserrat Guibernau and John Rex (Polity Press, 1997), pp. 33–41.

86   **that it be *believed*.** Max Weber, "What Is an Ethnic Group," ibid., pp. 15–26.

87   **men in the other tribes.** R. Chaix et al., "The Genetic or Mythical Ancestry of Descent Groups: Lessons from the Y Chromosome," *American Journal of Human Genetics* 75 (2004): 1113. Where stories of common descent *did* match the genetics was at the smaller-scale level of clans and lineages, the authors of this paper report. Members of a particular clan who say they're kin are in line with the genetic markers, but Kazakhs who say this about their entire ethnic group are not, literally, correct.

87   **on ethnic conflict.** Donald L. Horowitz, *Ethnic Groups in Conflict* (University of California Press, 1985), p. 53.

87   **van den Berghe's term, *ethny*.** Pierre L. van den Berghe, *The Ethnic Phenomenon* (Praeger Paperbacks, 1987), p. 22.

89   **class lines.** Michael Marmot, *The Status Syndrome: How Social Standing Affects Our Health and Longevity* (Times Books, 2004), p. 30.

90   **as a branch of zoology.** Terry Eagleton, *Ideology: An Introduction* (Verso, 1991), pp. 66–67.

90   **of race and ethnicity.** Rodriguez, *Changing Race,* p. 80.

91   **from marrying a white person.** Ibid.

FIVE: MIND SIGHT AND KIND SIGHT

93   **signs of other things.** St. Augustine quoted in Michel Pastoureau, *Une histoire symbolique du Moyen Âge occidental* (Seuil, 2004), p. 9.

93   **"person construal."** See Malia F. Mason and C. Neil Macrae, "Categorizing and Individuating Others: The Neural Substrates of Person Perception," *Journal of Cognitive Neuroscience* 16 (2004): 1785–1795.

95   **about kinds of people).** This definition of a code as the link between one realm and another is that of Marcello Barbieri, a theoretical biologist. See Marcello Barbieri, *The Organic Codes: The Birth of Semantic Biology* (Casa Editrice Pequod, 2001), pp. 89–95.

96   **a person in motion.** This phenomenon is discussed in Ralph Adolphs, "Cognitive Neuroscience of Human Social Behaviour," *Nature Reviews Neuroscience* 4 (March 2003): 165–78.

97   **look for an action.** Roger Brown, "Linguistic Determinism and the Parts of Speech," *Journal of Abnormal and Social Psychology* 55 (1957): 1–5. I was led to this study by the discussion of it in Gary Marcus, *The Birth of the Mind: How a Tiny Number of Genes Creates the Complexities of Human Thought* (Basic Books, 2004), p. 29.

98   **that were completely random.** Ibid., p. 29.

100   **Chomsky has said.** Noam Chomsky, interview with the author, 1992.

100   **when nobody is doing it.** Paul Bloom, interview with the author, 2002.

100   **except for some trivialities."** Chomsky, interview, 1992.

101   **ignore evidence from the other.** For the "shaped by experience" argument, see Steven R. Quartz and Terrence J. Sejnowski, *Liars, Lovers, and Heroes: What the New Brain Science Reveals about How We Become Who We Are* (William Morrow, 2002). For the opposite, "it's all built in" case, see Michael S. Gazzaniga, *The Mind's Past* (University of California Press, 2000).

102 **each dedicated to its particular job.** See Steven Pinker, *How the Mind Works* (Norton, 1997).

102 **he told a reporter.** C. J. Sullivan, "Lifesaver: Save the Jumpers," *New York Press,* January 1, 2003.

104 **received a particular kind of information.** D. H. Hubel and T. N. Wiesel, "Receptive Fields of Single Neurones in the Cat's Striate Cortex," *Journal of Physiology* 148 (1959): 574.

107 **than do ordinary people.** This finding is described in Eric R. Kandel and S. Mack, "A Parallel between Radical Reductionism in Science and in Art," in *The Self: From Soul to Brain,* ed. Joseph Ledoux, Jacek Debiec, and Henry Moss, pp. 272–94, *Annals of the New York Academy of Sciences,* vol. 1001 (2003).

107 **actually shrink.** Ibid.

107 **genitalia on the sensory map.)** V. S. Ramachandran and Sandra Blakeslee, *Phantoms in the Brain* (William Morrow, 1998), p. 35.

108 **into a new signal.** Antonio R. Damasio, "The Brain Binds Entities and Events by Multiregional Activation from Convergence Zones," *Neural Computation* 1 (1990): 123–32.

108 **kind of information: flavor.** As described in Edmund T. Rolls, "The Orbitofrontal Cortex," in *The Prefrontal Cortex: Executive and Cognitive Functions,* ed. A. C. T. Roberts, W. Robbins, and L. Weiskrantz (Oxford University Press, 1998), pp. 67–86.

108 **Sir Frederic Charles Bartlett.** See F. C. Bartlett, *Remembering: A Study in Experimental and Social Psychology* (Cambridge, 1932). My account of Bartlett's work and impact draws largely on William F. Brewer, "Bartlett's Concept of the Schema and Its Impact on Theories of Knowledge Representation in Contemporary Cognitive Psychology," in Akiki Saito, ed., *Bartlett, Culture and Cognition* (Psychology Press, 2000), pp. 69–89.

112 **converged on the little group's.** Muzafer Sherif, *The Psychology of Social Norms* (Octagon Books, 1936), pp. 93–106.

112 **They changed their estimates.** Solomon Asch, "Effects of Group Pressure on the Modification and Distortion of Judgments," in *Readings in Social Psychology,* ed. E. E. Maccoby, T. M. Newcomb, and E. L. Hartley (Holt, Rinehart and Winston, 1958).

112 **where he's not alone.)** This study is briefly described in Cass Sunstein, "Hoover's Court Rides Again," *Washington Monthly,* September 2004.

113 **communicating with the other.** Paul Rozin et al., "Disgust," in *Handbook of the Emotions,* ed. Michael Lewis and Jeannettte Haviland-Jones, pp. 637–53 (Guilford, 2000).

113 **over into their scribbling.** C. Neil Macrae, talk presented at UCLA Symposium on Social Cognitive Neuroscience, Los Angeles, April 26, 2001.

114 **there at all.** Archie Thomas, "Reel Nemo Spurs Run on Real Fish," *Variety,* December 8, 2003.

116 **scores of people as fakes.** D. L. Rosenhan, "On Being Sane in Insane Places," *Science* 179, no. 70 (1973): 250–58.

SIX: LOOKING FOR THE CODES

117 **confirm that he is there.** Charles Sherrington, "The Wisdom of the Body," in *Man on His Nature* (Cambridge University Press, 1951), pp. 92–118.

117 **even miracles in obscurity.** Michel de Montaigne, "Of the Resemblance of Children to Fathers," in *The Complete Essays of Montaigne,* trans. Donald M. Frame (Stanford University Press, 1965), pp. 574–98; these lines are on p. 578.

117 **other sights don't.** See Gary Marcus, *The Birth of the Mind: How a Tiny Number of Genes Creates the Complexities of Human Thought* (Basic Books, 2004), pp. 19–20; and Jonathan Cole, *About Face* (MIT Press, 1997), pp. 109–10.

118 **their playmate's *face.*** This experiment, by Charman et al., is described in Jay Schulkin, *Roots of Social Sensibility and Neural Function* (MIT Press, 2000), p. 101.

119 **happily ever after.** Fritz Heider and Mary-Ann Simmel, "An Experimental Study of Apparent Behavior," *American Journal of Psychology* 57 (1944): 243–59.

119 **"get" this kind of movie.** G. Gergely et al., "Taking the Intentional Stance at 12 Months of Age," *Cognition* 56 (1995): 165–93.

119 **had cartoon faces on them.** These findings by Valerie Kuhlmeier, a psychologist, are reported in Alexandra Galin, "Babies and Emotional Intelligence," *Yale Alumni Magzine,* January-February 2004, p. 8.

121 **other people having minds.** Mark Haddon, *The Curious Incident of the Dog in the Night-time* (Doubleday, 2002), p. 116.

122 **it sounded like gibberish."** Temple Grandin, "My Experiences with Visual Thinking Sensory Problems and Communication Difficulties," 2000. Available from autism.org. at <http://www.autism.org/temple/visual.html>.

122 **hanging in the air."** Oliver Sacks, "An Anthropologist on Mars," *New Yorker* (December 27, 2003).

122 **"'foreigners' in any society."** Jim Sinclair, "Don't Mourn for Us." Available from ani.autistics.org. <http://www.ani.autistics.org/dont_mourn.html>.

123 **dent their feelings."** Donna Williams quoted in Jonathan Cole, *About Face* (MIT Press, 1997), p. 97.

123 **the language of expressions.)** For more on this software, called MindReading, see this Web site: <http://www.jkp.com/mindreading/>.

123 *"What is this person?"* This distinction was pointed out by the Dartmouth social psychologist C. Neil Macrae, talk delivered at UCLA Symposium on Social Cognitive Neuroscience, Los Angeles, April 26, 2001.

124 **scripts like that."** Lawrence Hirschfeld, telephone interview, July 18, 1999.

126 **They must be fakes.** See Leslie Brothers, *Friday's Footprint: How Society Shapes the Human Mind* (Oxford University Press, 1997), chap. 1.

127 **has called a "module":** Jerry A. Fodor, *The Modularity of Mind* (MIT Press, 1983), pp. 44–100.

127 **woorngly palced lteters.** This phenomenon was first described by Graham Rawlinson in "The Significance of Letter Position in Word Recognition," Ph.D. diss., University of Nottingham, 1976.

    A Cambridge researcher, Matt Davis, tracks research on the idea on his Web site: <http://www.mrc-cbu.cam.ac.uk/personal/matt.davis/Cambridge/>.

128 **objects that moved together.** Paul Bloom and Csaba Veres, "The perceived intentionality of groups," *Cognition* 71 (1999): B1–B9.

130 **the late Donald T. Campbell.** The list of features that Campbell worked out is summarized in Robert Alan LeVine and Donald T. Campbell, *Ethnocentrism* (John Wiley and Sons, 1971), p. 105.

131 **they are all One.** William H. McNeill, *Keeping Together in Time: Dance and Drill in Human History* (Harvard University Press, 1997).

132 **human-kind codes.** Jesse Jackson said, "Let's talk black talk" to a group of African Americans, one of whom was the reporter Milton Coleman. Coleman wrote up Jackson's "Hymietown" remark. The story of both Jackson's remark and Coleman's reporting of it is recounted in Philip Weiss, "Hazy, Brilliant Hitchens Strokes Anti-Clinton Sword," *New York Observer,* May 3, 1999.

132 **for psychological research today.** For example, see Brian Lickel, David L. Hamilton, Amy Lewis, Steven J. Sherman, Grazyna Wieczorkowska, and A. Neville Uhles, "Varieties of Groups and the Perception of Group Entativity," *Journal of Personality and Social Psychology* 78 (2000): 223–246.

133 **a claim to my compassion."** See, for example, the argument against economic protectionism made by the economist Steve Landsburg in his Web log, available at http://www. marginalrevolution.com/marginalrevolution/2004/10/protectionism_r.html: "[David] Duke thinks it's imperative to protect white jobs from black competition. [Senator John] Edwards thinks it's imperative to protect American jobs from foreign competition. There's not a dime's worth of moral difference there."

134 **in Michigan, Korea, and France.** These experiments are described in Lawrence A. Hirschfeld, *Race in the Making: Cognition, Culture and the Child's Construction of Human Kinds* (MIT Press, 1996).

135 **cues that represent class.** Lawrence A. Hirschfeld, "Is the Acquisition of Social Categories Based on Domain-Specific Competence or on Knowledge Transfer?" In *Mapping the Mind: Domain Specificity in Cognition and Culture,* ed. Lawrence A. Hirschfeld and Susan Gelman, pp. 201–33 (Cambridge University Press, 1994).

135   **'He is a Yale man.'"**) Walter Lippmann, *Public Opinion* (Macmillan, 1922), p. 89.

136   **and see it whole."** Ibid., p. 114.

136   **such as psychologists.** For the history of stereotype research, I relied on two articles: David J. Schneider, "Modern Stereotype Research: Unfinished Business," in *Stereotypes and Stereotyping,* ed. C. Neil Macrae, Charles Stangor, and Miles Hewstone, pp. 419–54 (Guilford Press, 1996); Wolfgang Stroebe and Chester A. Insko, "Stereotype, Prejudice and Discrimination: Changing Conceptions in Theory and Research," in *Stereotyping and Prejudice: Changing Conceptions,* ed. Daniel Bar-Tal, Carl F. Graumann, Arie W. Kruglanski, and Wolfgang Stroebe, pp. 3–37 (Springer-Verlag, 1989).

136   **declared at mid-century.** Gordon W. Allport. *The Nature of Prejudice* (1954; Reprint: Addison Wesley, 1979), p. 191.

136   **a sluggard's best friend."** Quoted in C. Neil Macrae and Galen V. Bodenhausen, "Social Cognition: Categorical Person Perception," *British Journal of Psychology* 92 (2001): 239–55.

137   **most perturbed,"** Banaji says. Personal communication, August 2000.

138   **other elderly people.** T. M. Hess et al., "The Impact of Stereotype Threat on Age Differences in Memory Performance," *Journals of Gerontology, Series B,* 58, no. 1 (2003): 3–11.

138   **on a subsequent test.** Claude Steele and J. Aronson, "Stereotype Threat and the Intellectual Test Performance of African-Americans," *Journal of Personality and Social Psychology* 69 (1995): 797–811.

138   **stereotype is even greater.** C. Neil Macrae, talk delivered at Conference on Social Cognitive Neuroscience, Los Angeles, April 26, 2001.

139   **my truck!" he cried.** Paul Moore, *Presences: A Bishop's Life in the City* (Farrar, Straus and Giroux, 1998), p. 124.

139   **our conscious minds.** A controversy in social psychology centers on what it means to say stereotypes are "automatic." John Bargh, a psychologist at Yale, argues that stereotype use is highly automatic, like a lot of other mental processes. See J. A. Bargh and T. L. Chartrand, "The Unbearable Automaticity of Being," *American Psychologist* 54 (1999): 462–79.

SEVEN: HOW MIND MAKES WORLD

141   **Bertrand Russell.** Bertrand Russell, *An Inquiry into Meaning and Truth* (G. Allen and Unwin, 1948), p. 15.

143   **were still with him.** Glenn Prusky, neuroscientist at the University of Lethbridge, Alberta, explained H.M.'s different memories in a conversation in August 2002.

144   **depression makes its home.** For example, two researchers recently warned: "With the advent of human neuroimaging over the last 15–20 years, there have been some who use this technique with its pretty pictures of coloured blobs on brain slices almost as a modern-day phrenology." Morten L. Kringelbach and Edmund T. Rolls, "The Functional Neuroanatomy of the Human Orbitofrontal Cortex: Evidence from Neuroimaging and Neuropsychology," *Progress in Neurobiology* 72 (2004): 341–72.

144   **seat of emotions.** See Paul D. MacLean, *The Triune Brain in Evolution: Role in Paleocerebral Functions* (Kluwer Academic Publishers, 1990).

145   **pointed out its flaws.** Joseph LeDoux, *Synaptic Self: How Our Brains Become Who We Are* (Penguin Books, 2002), pp. 220–30.

145   **noticed and the second."** Paul Whalen, interview, July 2001.

146   **in nature from the body.)** Antonio R. Damasio, *Descartes' Error: Emotion, Reason, and the Human Brain* (Quill, 1995). On the need to put Descartes behind us and understand the mind as "embodied," see Francisco J. Varela et al., *The Embodied Mind: Cognitive Science and Human Experience* (MIT Press, 1992); and George Lakoff and Mark Johnson, *Philosophy in the Flesh: The Embodied Mind and Its Challenge to Western Thought* (Basic Books, 1999).

146   **than merely retentive."** John McCrone, "Reasons to Forget," *Times Literary Supplement,* January 30, 2004, p. 3.

147   **given a different name.** This debate is discussed in Morten L. Kringelbach and Edmund T. Rolls, "The Functional Neuroanatomy of the Human Orbitofrontal Cortex: Evidence from Neuroimaging and Neuropsychology," *Progress in Neurobiology* 72 (2004): 341–72.

147   **medial temporal lobe?"** Elizabeth Murray, "What, If Anything, Is the Medial Temporal Lobe?" Talk delivered at the 2003 annual meeting of the Society for Neuroscience, New Orleans, November 12, 2003.

147   **what it should be."** Lawrence Swanson, talk given at meeting on the Human Brain Project, Society for Neuroscience, New Orleans, November 12, 2003.

147   **mental life, either.** See Leslie Brothers, *Friday's Footprint: How Society Shapes the Human Mind* (Oxford University Press, 1997), pp. 113–15.

147   **that underlie them."** Ralph Adolphs, "Cognitive Neuroscience of Human Social Behaviour," *Nature Reviews Neuroscience* 4 (March 2003): 165–78.

148   **Dabbs and his colleagues).** Paul C. Bernhardt et al., "Testosterone Changes during Vicarious Experiences of Winning and Losing among Fans at Sporting Events," *Physiology and Behavior* 65, no. 1 (1998): 59–62.

148   **other strategy was better.** A. Bechara et al., "Insensitivity to Future Consequences Following Damage to Human Prefrontal Cortex," *Cognition* 50 (1994): 7–15.

149   **back to A.** Francisco Varela, *Ethical Know-How: Action, Wisdom and Cognition* (Stanford University Press, 1999), pp. 46–47.

151   **part of the orbitofrontal cortex.)** Edmund T. Rolls, "The Orbitofrontal Cortex," in *The Prefrontal Cortex: Executive and Cognitive Functions,* eds. A. C. Roberts, T. W. Robbins, and L. Weiskrantz (Oxford University Press, 1998), pp. 67–86.

151   **in for brain surgery.** Hiroto Kawasaki et al., "Single-neuron Responses to Emotional Visual Stimuli Recorded in Human Ventral Prefrontal Cortex," *Nature Neuroscience* 4, no. 1 (January 1, 2001): 15–16.

151-2 **his orbitofrontal cortex.** H. Damasio et al., "The Return of Phineas Gage: Clues about the Brain from the Skull of a Famous Patient," *Science* 264 (1994): 1102–5.

152   **basically, a myth.** Malcolm Macmillan, *An Odd Kind of Fame: Stories of Phineas Gage* (MIT Press, 2002). Macmillan fires skepticism in all directions. His doubts about Damasio's story are described on pp. 80–85.

152   **have social-rule troubles.** S. W. Anderson et al. "Impairment of Social and Moral Behavior Related to Early Damage in Human Prefrontal Cortex," *Nature Neuroscience* 2 (1999): 1032–37.

152   **others of the same tribe.** For a description of frontal-brain structures apparently required to learn social rules, see Antonio R. Damasio, *Descartes' Error: Emotion, Reason, and the Human Brain* (Quill, 1995), pp. 20–33.

152   **showed no preference.** Elizabeth Milne and Jordan Grafman, "Ventromedial Prefrontal Cortex Lesions in Humans Eliminate Implicit Gender Stereotyping," *Journal of Neuroscience* 21, RC150 (2001): 1–6.

153   **group of other people.** N. I. Eisenberger and M. D. Lieberman, "Why Rejection Hurts: A Common Neural Alarm System for Physical and Social Pain," *Trends in Cognitive Sciences* 8 (2004): 294–300.

153   **in an MRI scan.** Wemara Lichty, a psychologist at Stanford, described this work to me in a conversation in November 2003, and in e-mails in April 2005.

153   **region to "burn out."** H. Yamasue et al., "Voxel-based Analysis of MRI Reveals Anterior Cingulate Gray-matter Volume Reduction in Posttraumatic Stress Disorder due to Terrorism," *Proceedings of the National Academy of Sciences of the United States of America* 100 (2003): 9039–43.

153   **had been blanked out.** R. Adolphs et al., "Recognition of Facial Emotion in Nine Individuals with Bilateral Amygdala Damage," *Neuropsychologia* 37 (1999): 1111–17.

153   **guilt about misdeeds).** This list is based on Sec. F60.2 of the ICD-10 Classification of Mental and Behavioural Disorders, World Health Organization, 1992.

155   **it active in people listening to music.** Anne J. Blood and Robert J. Zatorre, "Intensely Pleasurable Responses to Music Correlate with Activity in Brain Regions Implicated in Reward and Emotion," *Proceedings of the National Academy of Sciences of the United States of America* 98, no. 20 (September 25, 2001): 11818–23.

156   **paintings were lovely.** Camilo J. Cela-Conde et al., "Activation of the Prefrontal Cortex in the Human Visual Aesthetic Perception," *Proceedings of the National Academy of Sciences of the United States of America* (April 20, 2004): 6321–25.

156   **religious practice: meditation.** Andrew Newberg et al., "Cerebral Blood Flow during Meditation," *European Journal of Nuclear Medicine* (2000).

156 **important or comforting activities.** Noted in Pascal Boyer, "Religious Thought and Behaviour as By-products of Brain Function," *Trends in Cognitive Sciences* 7, no. 3 (2003): 119.

157 **Saul Bellow.** Saul Bellow, "'I Got a Scheme!': The Words of Saul Bellow," *New Yorker,* April 25, 2005, p. 82. Bellow here is recalling his childhood move from Canada to Chicago.

158 **"experimental anthropology."** Donald T. Campbell, "Introduction," in Muzafer Sherif, O. J. Harvey, B. Jack White, William R. Hood, and Carolyn W. Sherif, *The Robbers Cave Experiment: Intergroup Conflict and Cooperation* (Wesleyan University Press, 1961), p. xx.

158 **he turned away.** This account of Sherif's early life is from Robert J. Trotter, "Muzafer Sherif: A Life of Conflict and Goals," *Psychology Today,* September 1985, pp. 55–59.

158 **less German than they had before.** Described in Marion A. Kaplan, *Between Dignity and Despair: Jewish Life in Nazi Germany* (Oxford University Press, 1998).

158 **not the case in the 1990s.** Andrea Elliott, "Study Finds City's Muslims Growing Closer since 9/11," *New York Times,* October 5, 2004.

159 **primitives, and children.** Gustave Le Bon, *The Crowd* (1896; Reprint: Viking Press, 1960), pp. 19, 23, and 25.

159 **Wednesday luncheons.** See Stephen Reicher, "The 'Crowd' Century: Reconciling Practical Success with Theoretical Failure," *British Journal of Social Psychology* 35 (1996): 535–53.

159 **of Le Bon's work.** Sigmund Freud, *Group Psychology and the Analysis of the Ego,* trans. James Strachey (1921; Reprint: Norton, 1980), chap. 2.

159 **contained as a pre-disposition."** Sigmund Freud, "Why War? A Correspondence between Sigmund Freud and Albert Einstein," International Institute of Intellectual Cooperation, 1933. Reprinted in the "Standard Edition" of *Freud's Works in English,* volume 22, p. 203.

160 **threatened with disintegration."** Sigmund Freud, *Civilization and Its Discontents,* trans. James Strachey (1930; Reprint: Norton, 1989), p. 69.

160 **to be authoritarian traits.** Theodor Adorno et al., *The Authoritarian Personality,* abridged ed. (1950; Reprint: Norton, 1982). See Adorno's chapter, "Types and Syndromes," pp. 346–85. With characteristic lucidity, Adorno saw the same problems with coining human kinds that Hume had noticed. Here, he acknowledges that human categories are probability judgments, not essences; that people are individuals who change over time; that categories make no sense unless one accounts for the categorizer as well as the categorized. Nonetheless, he argues, society is organized into human kinds — he calls them typologies and classes — and so "the marks of social repression are left within the individual soul" (p. 349). In other words, human kinds aren't stable or logical, but people can still be split into authoritarians and nonauthoritarians, because that describes the effects of human-kind arrangements on their psychology. Ingenious.

161 **church fathers had said.** Frederick Crews, "Freudian Suspicion versus Suspicion of Freud," in *The Flight from Science and Reason,* eds. Paul R. Gross, Norman Levitt, and Martin W. Lewis (New York Academy of Sciences, 1996), pp. 470–82. According to Crews's notes, Freud made these remarks in letters to his friend Wilhelm Fliess.

161 **Le Bon was wrong.** As described in Stephen Reicher, "The 'Crowd' Century: Reconciling Practical Success with Theoretical Failure," *British Journal of Social Psychology* 35 (1996): 535–53.

161 **pictures taken for posterity.** Enough people did this to furnish an entire book of lynching photography, accompanied by this essay on the phenomenon: James Allen, "Notes on the Plates," in *Without Sanctuary: Lynching Photography in America* (Twin Palms Publishers, 2000), pp. 165–209.

161 **a lid on things.** The account of Adang's work in this paragraph is based on (1) Otto M. J. Adang, "Systematic Observations of Violent Interactions between Football Hooligans," in *In-group/Out-group Behaviour in Modern Societies: An Evolutionary Perspective,* ed. K. Thienpont and R. Cliquet (Vlaamse Gemeenschap, 1999); and (2) Otto Adang, interview, July 1997.

162 **watched the body burn.** Described in James Allen, "Notes on the Plates."

162   **outlet, then exploded.** See Konrad Lorenz, *On Aggression* (Harvest Books, 1974), chap. 11.

162   **far more frustrated?** Sherif and his colleague and wife, Carol, enumerated and anato-mized various flaws in conventional wisdom, including the frustration-aggression idea, in Muzafer and Carol Sherif, *In Common Predicament: Social Psychology of Intergroup Conflict and Cooperation* (Houghton Mifflin, 1966). See especially chap. 3.

163   **more touchy-feely.** See Rupert Brown, "Authoritarianism," in *The Blackwell Encyclope-dia of Social Psychology,* ed. Antony S. R. Manstead and Miles Hewstone (Blackwell Pub-lishers, 1995), pp. 76–8.

163   **conceited in 1948.** All the studies mentioned in this paragraph are described in Penel-ope J. Oakes et al., *Stereotyping and Social Reality* (Blackwell, 1994), pp. 14–16.

163   **"war-monger," and "cruel."** Ibid., p. 17.

164   **Americans with positive words.** L. N. Diab, "Factors Affecting Studies of National Stereotypes," *Journal of Social Psychology* 59 (1963): 29–40.

164   **artistic, cultured, and democratic.** L. N. Diab, "Factors Determining Group Stereo-types," *Journal of Social Psychology* 61 (1963): 3–10.

165   **the Greeks as slaves.** Orlando Patterson, *Slavery and Social Death: A Comparative Study* (Harvard University Press, 1982), p. 90.

166   **outgoing types, or Republicans.** Alan P. Fiske and Nick Haslam, "Social Cognition Is Thinking about Relationships," *Current Directions in Psychological Science* 5 (1996): 131–48.

167   **or even cultural values."** Konner here is quoting Willard Gaylin, *Hatred: The Psycho-logical Descent into Violence.* (Public Affairs, 2003).

167   **beyond religion and politics."** Melvin Konner, "'Hatred': When Bad People Do Bad Things," *New York Times Book Review,* August 3, 2003, p. 12.

168   **and 'challenge' them,"** Muzafer Sherif, O. J. Harvey, B. Jack White, William R. Hood, and Carolyn W. Sherif, *The Robbers Cave Experiment: Intergroup Conflict and Cooperation* (Wesleyan University Press, 1961), p. 94.

169   **but not see?** Ibid., p. 84.

169   **Communists because they had been killed.** Leslie Dwyer and Santikarma Degung, "'When the World Turned to Chaos': 1965 and Its Aftermath in Bali, Indonesia," in *The Specter of Genocide: Mass Murder in Historical Perspective,* ed. Robert Gellately and Ben Kiernan, pp. 289–305 (Cambridge University Press, 2003); see especially p. 294.

170   **the Eagle way.** Sherif et al., *Robbers Cave Experiment,* p. 83.

170   **a Rattler custom.** Ibid., p. 70.

170   **southsider clique dissolved.** Ibid., p. 71.

171   **the group average.** Muzafer Sherif, *The Psychology of Social Norms* (Octagon Books, 1936), pp. 93–106. The following discussion of Sherif's experiment is drawn from pp. 77, 85, 100, 101, 109, 115, and 151.

173   **"a nasty business."** Steven Pinker, *How the Mind Works* (W. W. Norton, 1997), p. 524.

173   **also stresses tribal violence.** Judith Rich Harris, *The Nurture Assumption* (Free Press, 1998), p. 127.

174   **recognize this affinity.** For Conservative Christian praise of Darwinian pessimism about human nature, see John O. McGinnis, "The Origin of Conservatism," *National Review,* December 22, 1997, pp. 31–36.

175   **unblock the spigot.** Sherif et al., *Robbers Cave Experiment,* p. 163.

175   **with the Rattlers?"** Ibid., p. 166.

175   **not each camper.** Ibid., p. 167.

176   **The other boy just laughed.** Ibid., p. 180.

176   **They had to choose.** Ibid., p. 180.

176   **Eagle songs and Rattler songs.** Ibid., p. 181.

177   **ignored Rattler-Eagle lines completely.** Ibid., pp. 194–95.

178   **Ghost versus Genie.** Lutfy N. Diab, "A Study of Intragroup and Intergroup Relations among Experimentally Produced Small Groups," *Genetic Psychology Monographs* 82 (1970): 49–82.

178   **over the political ally.** Jacob M. Rabbie and Karel Huygen, "Internal Disagreements and Their Effect on Attitudes Toward In- and Outgroups," *International Journal of Group Tensions* 4 (1974): 222–46.

179   **change their attitude."** Quoted in Elkan Nathan Adler, ed., *Jewish Travellers: A Treasury of Travelogues from Nine Centuries* (Hermon Press, 1966), p. 215, emphasis added.

179 **religious ceremonies and processions."** David Nirenberg, *Communities of Violence* (Princeton University Press, 1996), p. 157. For the following discussion, see also pp. 35, 37, and 39.

180 **at least three hundred years.** Peter Sahlins, *Boundaries: The Making of France and Spain in the Pyrenees* (University of California Press, 1989), p. 112.

180 **"fairly recent inventions."** David D. Laitin, "Comment on 'Are Ethnic Groups Biological Species in the Human Brain?'" *Current Anthropology* 42 (2001): 542–43.

180 **position in the caste system.** Nancy E. Levine, "Caste, State, and Ethnic Boundaries in Nepal," *Journal of Asian Studies* 46, no. 1 (1987): 71–88.

180 **for different purposes.** Marilynn B. Brewer, "Ethnocentrism and Its Role in Interpersonal Trust," in *Scientific Inquiry and the Social Sciences: A Volume in Honor of Donald T. Campbell,* ed. Marilynn B. Brewer and Barry E. Collins, pp. 345–60 (Jossey-Bass Publishers, 1981), p. 350.

180 **"Ibo folkways."** See Abner Cohen, *Custom and Politics in Urban Africa* (University of California Press, 1969).

180 **ethnic identity.** Edmund R. Leach, *Political Systems of Highland Burma* (London School of Economics and Political Science, 1954).

181 **by Pathan rules.** See Fredrik Barth, introduction to *Ethnic Groups and Boundaries,* ed. Barth, pp. 9–38 (1969; Reprint: Waveland Press, 1998).

181 **Culture through Choosing Heritage."** Mark P. Leone, "Creating Culture through Choosing Heritage," *Current Anthropology* 42 (2001): 582.

NINE: THEM, WE BURN

182 **Michael Oakeshott.** English philosopher and historian. This quotation is from his essay "On the Human Condition," in *Rationalism in Politics and Other Essays* (Liberty Fund, 1991), pp. 465–87.

182 **James Morone.** Professor of political science at Brown University. This quotation is from his book *Hellfire Nation: The Politics of Sin in American History* (Yale University Press, 2003).

183 **canceling his subscription.** Alan Lindsey, "Eddylines" (letters column), *Paddler,* March–April 2003.

184 **ill-suited to perform."** Naomi Quinn, "Cultural Selves," in *The Self: From Soul to Brain,* ed. Joseph LeDoux, Jacek Debiec, and Henry Moss, pp. 145–76, *Annals of the New York Academy of Sciences,* vol. 1001 (2003).

186 **right and obvious.** Ibid.

187 **to wait for the light?"** Quoted in Quinn, "Cultural Selves," p. 174, fn. 7.

187 **to the next page."** "Eddylines" (letters column), *Paddler,* July–August 2003.

188 **there are no offspring?** See Jonathan Haidt, "The Emotional Dog and Its Rational Tail: A Social Intuitionist Approach to Moral Judgment," *Psychological Review* 108 (2001): 814–34.

189 **admit a new member.** Jonathan Haidt et al., "Differentiating Diversities: Moral Diversity Is Not Like Other Kinds," *Journal of Applied Social Psychology* 33 (2003): 1–36.

189 **He's Lerian.** Peter Jay, trans., "Phokylides," in *The Greek Anthology,* ed. Jay, pp. 36–37 (Penguin Books, 1981).

190 **opposition — from the law.** Gordon W. Allport, *The Nature of Prejudice* (1954; Reprint: Addison Wesley, 1979), pp. 261–82.

190 **of Michigan Law School.** Allport's argument for promoting diversity was colloquially summed up by Justice Ruth Bader Ginsburg when this case was argued before the U.S. Supreme Court, in her questions for the U.S. Solicitor General, Theodore Olson.

Referring to an affirmative-action approach to admissions, Justice Ginsburg said: "The reasons for it is they want to produce a diverse class and the reason they want to do that, using it as a plus, they say, is they think it breaks down stereotypes within the class. They think it's educationally beneficial. They think it supplies a legal profession that will be diverse and they think a legal profession like business and the military that is diverse is good for America from a civics point of view, et cetera, breaks the cycle." *Detroit News,* "Law School Case: Argument in Support of Petitioners," April 1, 2003.

This transcript, as recorded by the *Detroit News,* is also available online at <http://www.detnews.com/2003/schools/0304/01/schools-125391.htm>.

190   **is a muddle.** See H. D. Forbes, *Ethnic Conflict: Commerce, Culture and the Contact Hypothesis* (Yale University Press, 1997), chap. 3.

191   **warm, funny and clever."** Elliot Aronson quoted in Susan Gilbert, "A Conversation With/Elliot Aronson; No One Left to Hate: Averting Columbines," *New York Times,* March 27, 2001. More on the jigsaw classroom can be found on Aronson's Web site: <http://www.jigsaw.org/overview.htm>.

192   **them, we burn."** Stanley Fish, "'Them We Burn': Violence and Conviction in the English Department," in *English as a Discipline or, Is There a Plot in This Play?,* ed. James C. Raymond, pp. 160–73 (University of Alabama Press, 1996).

192   **a Bugatti.** See Peter K. Unger, *Living High and Letting Die: Our Illusion of Innocence* (Oxford, 1996). Bob's Bugatti is succinctly described in Peter Singer, "The Singer Solution to World Poverty," *New York Times Magazine,* September 5, 1999.

193   **increment of distance.** For example, see Frans de Waal, *Good Natured: The Origins of Right and Wrong in Humans and Other Animals* (Harvard University Press, 1996), p. 213.

193   **during the Christmas season.** Stephen J. Dubner and Steven D. Levitt, "What the Bagel Man Saw," *New York Times Magazine,* June 6, 2004.

195   **don't touch you directly.** See Jonathan Haidt, "Emotional Dog."

195   **as a progression.** See Jean Piaget, *The Moral Judgement of the Child* (Free Press, 1997; originally 1932).

196   **universality, and consistency."** Lawrence Kohlberg, "The Child as Moral Philosopher," *Psychology Today,* September 1968, pp. 24–30.

196   **masquerading as the high priest."** Jonathan Haidt, "Emotional Dog."

196   **sometimes guiding the emotions.** David A. Pizarro and Paul Bloom, "The Intelligence of the Moral Intuitions: Comment on Haidt (2001)," *Psychological Review* 110, no. 1 (2003): 193–96.

196   **psychologist at Harvard.** Marc D. Hauser, interview, August 26, 2003.

196   **patterns of brain activation.** Specifically, they found that the personal dilemmas caused significantly more activity in regions of the cortex called the medial frontal gyrus, the posterior cingulate gyrus, and the angular gyrus. These are regions that are more active in emotionally charged situations than they are when a person's attention is focused on something neutral. Joshua Greene et al., "An fMRI Investigation of Emotional Engagement in Moral Judgment," *Science* 293 (2001): 2105–8.

197   **any particular human kind.** See Michael Specter, "The Dangerous Philosopher," *New Yorker,* September 6, 1999.

197   **his aged mother.** Ibid.

197   **could think it was fun."** Quoted in Sylvia Nasar, "Princeton's New Philosopher Draws a Stir," *New York Times,* April 10, 1999, p. A1.

198   **lobsters feel pain."** Quoted in "New Animal Rights Cause Urges, 'Free the Lobsters!'" *New York Times,* December 31, 1995, p. A25.

TEN: "OUR COMMON HUMANITY MAKES US WEEP"

202   **the rest of our time together."** Patrick Leigh Fermor, *A Time of Gifts* (Penguin USA, 1988), p. 87.

202   **commemorative banquet in Crete.** The story is recounted in Janice Benario, "Horace, Humanitas and Crete," *Amphora* (American Philological Association) 2, no. 1 (Spring 2003). For more on Kreipe, who returned to Germany from a POW camp in 1947 and died in 1976, see the entry on this Web site on German POWs: <http://www.specialcamp11.fsnet.co.uk/Generalmajor%20Heinrich%20Kreipe.htm>.

203   **hated being shut out of."** Janice Page, "Sometimes, It's the Good News That Makes the Patient Feel So Bad," *New York Times,* August 7, 2001.

203   **than to her childless neighbors.** This mother is quoted in Suzannah Lessard, "The Split," *New Yorker,* December 8, 1997, p. 80.

203   **happened to be a fellow Marine.** Paul Moore, *Presences* (Farrar, Straus and Giroux, 1998), p. 86.

203   **makes us weep sometimes."** Quoted in Paul Fregosi, *Dreams of Empire: Napoleon and the First World War, 1792–1815* (Hutchinson, 1989), p. 216.

203   **their own kind.** Canon 68, Fourth Lateran Council, trans. Paul Halsall. Available online at <http://www.fordham.edu/halsall/basis/lateran4.html>.

204   **kinds of idiotic sentimentality."** Joseph Goebbels quoted in Christopher Browning, *The Origins of the Final Solution* (University of Nebraska Press and Yad Vashem, 2004), p. 390.

204   **other than the native bestial hordes."** Wilhelm Kube quoted ibid., p. 394.

204   **Nation expects of you.** Curtis Le May quoted in Peter Novick, *The Holocaust in American Life* (Houghton Mifflin, 1999), p. 25.

205   **in an upcoming election.** James Astill, "The Truth behind the Miss World Riots," *The Guardian,* November 30, 2002. Available online at <http://www.guardian.co.uk/ international/story/0,3604,850959,00.html>.

206   **sent into the Holocaust.** This sketch is drawn from John C. Turner, "Henri Tajfel: An Introduction," in *Social Groups and Identities,* ed. W. Peter Robinson, pp. 1–23 (Butterworth Heinemann, 1996).

206   **was left alive."** Henri Tajfel, *Human Groups and Social Categories* (Cambridge University Press, 1981), p. 2.

206   **to know what I was talking about."** Ibid.

206   **assigned at random.)** Michael Billig and Henri Tajfel, "Social Categorization and Similarity in Intergroup Behavior," *European Journal of Social Psychology* 3 (1973): 27–52.

207   **no gender difference).** These studies are summarized in Penelope Oakes, S. Alexander Haslam, and John C. Turner, *Stereotyping and Social Reality* (Blackwell, 1994), pp. 15–16.

207   **made less money.** Henri Tajfel, "Experiments in Intergroup Discrimination," *Scientific American* 223, no. 5 (November 1970): 96–102.

207   **over the other team's.** Ibid.

207   **"they" words.** Charles W. Perdue et al., "Us and Them: Social Categorization and the Process of Intergroup Bias," *Journal of Personality and Social Psychology* 59 (1990): 475–86.

208   **"our kind of person."** Don Beck, interview with author, August 1999.

210   **powers human-kind perceptions.** See, for example, the discussion of "self-categorization theory" in John C. Turner, "Henri Tajfel: An Introduction," in *Social Groups and Identities,* ed. W. Peter Robinson, pp. 1–23 (Butterworth Heinemann, 1996).

210   **another in various ways.** Among Tajfel's critics along these lines in the 1980s was Jacob M. Rabbie. See, for example, Jacob M. Rabbie and M. Horwitz, "Categories versus groups as explanatory concepts in intergroup relations," *European Journal of Social Psychology,* 18 (1988), 117–23. A more recent attack on Tajfel's work is in Francisco Gil-White, "Are Ethnic Groups Biological 'Species' in the Human Brain?" *Current Anthropology* 42 (2001): 515–54. In Gil-White's view, Tajfel's "minimal groups" seem relevant to "ethnic groups" or "religious groups" only if "group" is defined so vaguely as to be meaningless. On the general problem of definitions, see Gil-White's "The Study of Ethnicity Needs Better Categories" (2005), an unpublished paper available on Gil-White's Web site: <http://www.psych.upenn.edu/~fjgil/Connor.pdf>.

210   **the experiments do not capture."** Donald L. Horowitz, *Ethnic Groups in Conflict* (University of California Press, 1985), p. 147.

211   **survived their usefulness."** William Graham Sumner, *Social Darwinism: Selected Essays of William Graham Sumner* (Prentice-Hall, 1963), p. 122.

211   **products of the same situation."** Both quotations in this paragraph are from William Graham Sumner, *Folkways: A Study of the Sociological Importance of Usages, Manners, Customs, Mores, and Morals* (Ginn and Company, 1906), pp. 12–13.

212   **toward each other.** Elizabeth Cashdan, "Ethnocentrism and Xenophobia: A Cross-Cultural Study," *Current Anthropology* 42 (2001): 760–65.

212   *all* **their relationships.** Otto Adang, interview with the author, July 1997.

212   **contemptuous of other human kinds.** Marilynn B. Brewer and Donald T. Campbell, *Ethnocentrism and Intergroup Attitudes: East African Evidence* (John Wiley and Sons, 1976).

212   **at any time."** Lawrence Hirschfeld, telephone interview, July 18, 1999.

213   **back and forth with ease."** Edward O. Wilson, *On Human Nature* (Harvard University Press, 1988), p. 169.

215   **that life-warmth of the tribe."** Tayeb Salih, *Season of Migration to the North,* trans. Denys Johnson-Davies (Heinemann, 1969), p. 1.

215   **Woolf once described it.** Virginia Woolf, "The Russian Point of View," in *The Common Reader: First Series* (1925; Reprint: Harvest Books, 1984), p. 173.

216   **"playing the same game."** Fredrik Barth, introduction to *Ethnic Groups and Boundaries,* ed. Barth, pp. 9–38 (Waveland Press, 1969).

216   **the Ivy League.)** See Eric Hobsbawm, "Mass Producing Traditions: Europe, 1870–1914," in *The Invention of Tradition,* ed. Eric Hobsbawm and Terence Ranger (Cambridge University Press, 1983), p. 297.

217   **a hero's grave.** V. A. C. Gattrell, *The Hanging Tree: Execution and the English People, 1770–1868* (Oxford University Press, 1994), p. 33.

217   **the most unsupportable."** Adam Smith, *The Theory of Moral Sentiments* (1759; Reprint: Liberty Fund, 1982), pp. 60–61. I was led to this passage by Gattrell, *Hanging Tree.*

217   **on a buggy for the photographer.** The incident is described in James Allen, "Notes on the Plates," in *Without Sanctuary: Lynching Photography in America* (Twin Palms Publishers, 2000), pp. 165–209.

218   **mailing the card to his parents.** Ibid.

218   **much more apt to fail."** Smith, *Theory of Moral Sentiments,* p. 61.

219   **about 150 individuals.** See Robin Dunbar, *Grooming, Gossip, and the Origin of Language* (Harvard University Press, 1996).

220   **injuries, and perhaps deaths).** Peter J. Richerson, interview. June 10, 2004.

220   ***what* is this?** C. Neil Macrae, talk delivered at Conference on Social-Cognitive Neuroscience, Los Angeles, April 2001.

221   **altruism and niceness."** Jonathan Haidt, "The Emotional Dog and Its Rational Tail: A Social Intuitionist Approach to Moral Judgment," *Psychological Review* 108 (2001): 814–34.

221   **followed for centuries.** For an African example of this pattern, see Marilynn B. Brewer and Donald T. Campbell, *Ethnocentrism and Intergroup Attitudes: East African Evidence* (John Wiley and Sons, 1976), p. 135. For Europe's royal houses, see Lawrence H. Keeley, *War before Civilization* (Oxford University Press, 1997), pp. 121–22.

221   **"We marry them."** Quoted in David Nirenberg, *Communities of Violence* (Princeton University Press, 1996), p. 10.

221   **"We marry the people we fight."** Quoted in Keeley, *War before Civilization,* p. 122.

221   **a single process.** Ibid., pp. 120–26.

222   **Taliban stuff, whatever it is."** Barry Bearak, "With Relief and Sarcasm, Soldiers Recall Whizzing Bullets Fired by 'Wimps,'" *New York Times,* March 12, 2002.

222–3 **American South in 1959.** John Howard Griffin, *Black Like Me* (Houghton Mifflin, 1977), p. 111.

223   **I never heard anything crazier in my life!** Gregory Howard Williams, *Life on the Color Line* (Plume, 1996), pp. 33–34.

ELEVEN: NO HUMANS INVOLVED

224   **against other prisoners.** See David Grann, "The Brand," *New Yorker* (February 16 and 23, 2004), pp. 157–71. NHI is also used by law enforcement as a code for crimes against prostitutes, homeless people, and other stigmatized human kinds. See, e.g., this Web page: <http://crca.ucsd.edu/~esisco/nhi/>.

224   **he was a "foreigner."** Tété-Michel Kpomassie, *An African in Greenland* (New York Review of Books, 2001), p. 13.

224   **get reports from them.** These lines from Ludwig Wittgenstein's *Remarks on the Philosophy of Psychology* are quoted in Hilary Putnam, *The Threefold Cord: Mind, Body and World* (Columbia University Press, 1999), p. 89.

226   **only fifty miles apart).** Such fine linguistic discriminations between one village and another are described in James B. Given, *Inquisition and Medieval Society* (Cornell University Press, 1997), p. 27.

226   **idols of the tribe."** See Harold R. Isaacs, *Idols of the Tribe: Group Identity and Political Change* (Harvard University Press, 1989).

228   **quit the job.** This story is told in Ellen Walterscheid, "Getting to Know You: The Year 2000 Census Could Make All Americans Count," *The Sciences* (1998): 20–25.

228   **eating it right then and there."** Herbert Passin, "The Paekchong of Korea," *Monumenta Nipponica* 12 (1956), pp. 27-72; see especially pages 45 and 64.

228   **a theory to explain it.** See Paul Rozin, Jonathan Haidt, Clark McCauley, and Sumio Imada, "Disgust: Preadaptation and the Cultural Evolution of a Food-Based Emotion." *Food Preferences and Taste,* ed. Helen Macbeth (Berghahn Books, 1997), pp 65–82.

229   **unworthy of our kind.** See Paul Rozin, "Moralization." *Morality and Health,* eds. Brandt, Allan M., and Paul Rozin (Routledge, 1997), pp. 379–401.

230   **proper behavior and right order."** Given, *Inquisition and Medieval Society,* p. 220.

231   **making way for them?** Cathy Yarbrough, interview, July 1996.

231   **against the mind's natural fluidity.** A good discussion of stigmatizing rhetoric is in William Brennan, *Dehumanizing the Vulnerable: When Word Games Take Lives* (Loyola University Press, 1995). Brennan classifies all fetuses as part of humanity, so he cites pro-choice language as dehumanizing. What is, to me, reasonable language to describe an embryo is, to him, Fascist-style rhetoric. It's an illustration of how much moral judgment depends on a map of human kinds.

      An account that touches on emblems of human kinds is Isaacs, *Idols of the Tribe,* with its chapters on how languages, bodies, and cultures are used as codes for Us and Them.

232   **fine in another.** Erving Goffman, *Stigma: Notes on the Management of Spoiled Identity* (Touchstone, 1986), p. 3: "An attribute that stigmatizes one type of possessor can confirm the usualness of another, and therefore is neither creditable nor discreditable as a thing in itself."

232   **"spoiled identity."** Ibid., p. 3. I'm not describing exactly the same idea as Goffman is. He defines stigma as a damaged version of a normal identity. It might be better viewed as mental representation that prevents normal identities from seeming relevant.

232   **similar results.)** Jamie Arndt et al., "Subliminal Exposure to Death-Related Stimuli Increases Defense of the Cultural Worldview," *Psychological Science* 8 (1977): 379–85.

233   **horses at state funerals.** Herbert Passin, "The Paekchong of Korea," *Monumenta Nipponica* 12 (1956), pp. 27–72; see especially p. 45.

233   **especially love murder."** Andrea Dworkin, in *Take Back the Night: Women on Pornography,* ed. Laura Lederer (William Morrow, 1980), p. 148.

233   **and Bennett recanted.** See Andrew Sullivan, "False Bennett: Gay-Bashing by the Numbers," *New Republic,* January 5 and 12, 1998.

234   **about his gay son.)** In an interview with the religiously oriented Web site Beliefnet in April 2004, Terry said: "The average death age of a male homosexual is forty-two years old because of disease, because of suicide, because of alcoholism, because of drugs, because of violence. It's just not a good world. It's a self-abusive, self-destructive sexual addiction." Available online at <http://www.beliefnet.com/story/144/story_14449_3.html>.

234   **executed a death sentence."** Ralph Blumenthal and Judith Miller, "Japan Rebuffs Requests for Information about Its Germ-Warfare Atrocities," *New York Times,* March 4, 1999, p. A12.

235   **"human-footed stock."** Orlando Patterson, *Slavery and Social Death* (Harvard University Press), 1982, p. 88.

235   **as in four-legged.** George De Vos and Hiroshi Wagatsuma, *Japan's Invisible Race* (University of California Press, 1966), p. 4.

235   **vermin to be destroyed."** John Beeson, *A Plea for the Indians* (1857; Reprint: Ye Galleon Press, 1982), p. 24.

235   **you've lost control of them."** General Karpinski was quoted in BBC News, "Iraq abuse 'ordered from the top,' " June 15, 2004. This report is available online at <http://news.bbc.co.uk/1/hi/world/americas/3806713.stm>.

236   **But you can exterminate it."** Quoted in Peter Edgerly Firchow, *The Death of the German Cousin: Variations on a Literary Stereotype* (Associated University Presses, 1986), p. 40.

236   **a beast or a god."** Aristotle, *Politics,* in *The Basic Works of Aristotle,* ed. Richard McKeon (Random House, 1941), p. 1130 (1253a, lines 27–29).

236   **march under a yoke.** For example, see Caesar, *Gallic Wars,* I, 7.

236   **eat grass.** Stéphane Courtois et al., *Le Livre Noir du communisme* (Robert Laffont, 1997), p. 569.

236   **men, women, and children.** Jean-Pierre Liégeois, "Governments and Gypsies: From Rejection to Assimilation," in *The Other Nomads,* ed. Aparna Rao, pp. 357–72 (Böhlau Verlag, 1987).

237   **pygmy chimps."** Sarah Lyall, "For Blair's Cabinet, These Outings Are Not Picnics," *New York Times,* November 12, 1998, p. A4.

237   **Korea in the thirteenth century.** Herbert Passin, "The Paekchong of Korea," *Monumenta Nipponica* 12 (1956): 27–72.

237   **previous dynasty was collapsing.** Anders Hansson, *Chinese Outcasts: Discrimination and Emancipation in Late Imperial China* (E. J. Brill, 1996), p. 135.

237 **converted to Islam.** David Nirenberg, *Communities of Violence* (Princeton University Press, 1996), p. 15.

237 **among the transgressions.)** Michael J. Casimir, "In Search of Guilt: Legends on the Origin of the Peripatetic Niche," in *The Other Nomads,* ed. Aparna Rao, pp. 373–90 (Böhlau Verlag, 1987).

238 **painful state in which they find themselves.** Ibid.

238 **to Korean ears.** Passin, "The Paekchong of Korea."

238 **pejorative connotations.)** Recounted in Peter Balakian, *Black Dog of Fate* (Broadway, 1998).

238 **"These Aren't Savages?"** The post is on the Web at <http://littlegreenfootballs. com/weblog/?entry=7041&only=yes>.

239 **not our prison guards."** Quoted in Stephen Kinzer and Jim Rutenberg, "The Struggle for Iraq: American Voices," *New York Times,* May 13, 2004.

239 **amounted to work clothes.** Passin, "The Paekchong of Korea."

239 **older men "boy."** Described in Patterson, *Slavery,* pp. 83, 88, and 350.

240 **even to punks like me."** Passin, "The Paekchong of Korea."

240 **vulgar, unrefined."** Ibid.

241 **not a proper person to associate with.** Ibid., p. 46.

241 **social or political position."** Claude Meillassoux, *The Anthropology of Slavery: The Womb of Iron and Gold* (University of Chicago Press, 1992), p. 318.

242 **(Yes, he asked.)** Paul Rozin, M. Markwith, and Clark McCauley, "The Nature of Aversion to Indirect Contacts with Other Persons: AIDS Aversion as a Composite of Aversion to Strangers, Infection, Moral Taint, and Misfortune," *Journal of Abnormal Psychology* 103 (1994): 495–504.

242 **to spit and to speak Breton."** R. B. Le Page and Andrée Tabouret-Keller, *Acts of Identity: Creole-based Approaches to Language and Identity* (Cambridge University Press, 1985), p. 236.

242 **from a clean environment.** Described in Leslie Dwyer and Degung Santikarma, "'When the World Turned to Chaos': 1965 and Its Aftermath in Bali, Indonesia," in *The Specter of Genocide: Mass Murder in Historical Perspective,* ed. Robert Gellately and Ben Kiernan, pp. 289–305 (Cambridge University Press, 2003).

243 **catch from me."** Charles L. Mee, *A Nearly Normal Life,* Little, Brown, 1999, p. 83.

244 **that of lepers.** Quoted in Vincent Raymond Rivière-Chalan, *La Marque infâme des lépreux et des Christians sous l'ancien regime* (La Pensée Universelle, 1978), pp. 11–13; translation mine.

244 **husband of a dying woman.** Howard Markel, *Quarantine!* (Johns Hopkins University Press, 1997), p. xi.

245 **"a communicable disease."** Quoted in Barry Werth, "Father's Helper," *New Yorker,* June 9, 2003, pp. 61–67.

245 **pellagra of the soul."** Wallace Stegner, *Where the Bluebird Sings to the Lemonade Springs: Living and Writing in the West* (Penguin, 1993), p. 200.

246 **real or perceived, has not."** Markel, *Quarantine!* p. 5.

246 **shaving the head.** Hansson, *Chinese Outcasts,* p. 26.

247 **barbers, and bathhouse attendants."** Emily Honig, *Creating Chinese Ethnicity* (Yale University Press, 1992), p. 40.

248 **status "native" for themselves.** Ibid., p. 40.

248 **their own traditions."** Ibid., p. 56.

248 **these kinds of problems."** Ibid., p. 17.

249 **from Subei, of course."** Ibid.

249 **wawawawawa."** Ibid., p. 83.

249 **common Shanghai phrase.** Ibid., p. 2.

249 **Japanese during World War II.** Ibid., p. 98.

249 **gray colored garments."** Ibid., p. 56.

249 **of Subei origins."** Ibid., p. 4.

249 **on the forms people turn in.** Ibid., p. 113.

250 **the mayor is from Subei?!' "** Ibid., p. 117.

TWELVE: DON'T BE A STRANGER

253 **started to walk.** Primo Levi, *The Reawakening,* trans. Stuart Woolf (Collier Books, 1986), p. 143.

253 **almost as satisfactory."** Clifford Geertz, *Interpretation of Cultures* (Basic Books Classics/Basic Books, 1977), pp. 412–13.

254 **into the nineteenth century.** Orlando Patterson, *Slavery and Social Death* (Harvard University Press, 1982), p. 41.

255 **of this great body."** David Grossman, "Fifty Is a Dangerous Age," *New Yorker,* April 20, 1998.

255 **as American citizens."** Testimony of James Zogby, "The Status of Aviation Security Efforts with a Focus on the National Safe Skies Alliance and Passenger Profiling Criteria": Hearings before the Subcommittee on Aviation of the House Committee on Transportation and Infrastructure, 105th Cong., 2d Sess., pp. 12–87 (May 12, 1998).

255 **and we play ours."** Selma Fraiberg, "Blind Infants and Their Mothers: An Examination of the Sign System," in *The Effect of the Infant on Its Caregiver,* ed. Michael Lewis and Leonard A. Rosenblum, pp. 215–32 (John Wiley and Sons, 1974).

256 **and correctly interpreted.** Ibid.

256 **in the Gobi Desert."** Paul Moore, *Presences: A Bishop's Life in the City* (Farrar, Straus and Giroux, 1998), p. 86.

257 **how *Negroes* feel."** Charles L. Mee, *A Nearly Normal Life* (Little, Brown, 1999), p. 131.

258 **his human capacity and merit.** Homer, *Odyssey,* bk. 17, about line 320 (depending on translator).

258 **into a brute!"** Frederick Douglass, *Narrative of the Life of Frederick Douglass, An American Slave* (Barnes and Noble, 2003), p. 75.

259 **from a salmon's.** Bruce McEwen with Elizabeth Norton Lasley, *The End of Stress as We Know It* (Joseph Henry Press, 2002), pp. 29–31.

260 **victimized or preyed upon."** Richard Wilkinson, *Mind the Gap: Hierarchies, Health and Human Evolution* (Yale University Press, 2001), p. 33.

260 **ready to run or fight.** McEwen, *End of Stress,* p. 21.

260 **kidneys, and genitals.** Ibid., p. 70.

261 **sad story much better.** Larry Cahill, B. Prins, and James McGaugh, "Beta-adrenergic Activation and Memory for Emotional Events," 371 *Nature* (1994): 702–4.

261 **saw more clearly.** L. Cahill and M. T. Alkire, "Epinephrine Enhancement of Human Memory Consolidation: Interaction with Arousal at Encoding," *Neurobiology of Learning and Memory* 79 (2003): 194–98.

261 **"stress induced trafficking.")** McEwen, *End of Stress,* p. 95.

261 **minerals from bone.** Ibid., p. 24.

262 **digestion moving, and relax.** Ibid., p. 71.

262 **than their fellow citizens.** Eleanor Maguire, David G. Gadian, Ingrid S. Johnsrude, Catriona D. Good, John Ashburner, Richard S. J. Frackowiak, and Christopher Frith. "Navigation-related structural change in the hippocampi of taxi drivers." *Proceedings of the National Academy of the United States.* 97:8 (2000): 4398–03.

262 **who did not suffer.** See Robert M. Sapolsky, "The possibility of neurotoxicity in the hippocampus in major depression: a primer on neuron death." *Biological Psychiatry* 48 (2000): 755–65. A crucial issue about the connection between trauma and a smaller hippocampus is: Which comes first? Does trauma make the hippocampus smaller, or does a small hippocampus predispose a person to be vulnerable to the effects of trauma? One study of twin pairs, in which only one twin had been traumatized, found that *both* had relatively small hippocampi — which means the small size could not have been caused by suffering alone. M. W. Gilbertson, M. E. Shenton, A. Ciszewski, K. Kasai, N. B. Lasko, S. P. Orr, and R. K. Pitman, "Smaller hippocampal volume predicts pathologic vulnerability to psychological trauma." *Nature Neuroscience* 5 (2002): 1242–47.

262 **fight another day."** McEwen, *End of Stress,* p. 127.

263 **relations between people and people.** Richard Wilkinson, *Mind the Gap: Hierarchies, Health and Human Evolution* (Yale University Press, 2001), p. 7.

263 **these extremely important risk factors."** Ibid., p. 17.

263   **stress-related health problems.** See Michael Marmot, *The Status Syndrome: How Social Standing Affects Our Health and Longevity* (Times Books, 2004).

264   **what Fisher believed.)** See David Salsburg, *The Lady Tasting Tea: How Statistics Revolutionized Science in the Twentieth Century* (W. H. Freeman, 2001), pp. 181–94.

264   **pecking order.** Marmot, *The Status Syndrome*, p. 39.

265   **life expectancies than Americans.** Marmot, *The Status Syndrome*, p. 65.

265   **study of public health.** See Nancy E. Adler and Joan M. Ostrove, "Socioeconomic Status and Health: What We Know and What We Don't." in *Socioeconomic Status and Health in Industrial Nations: Social, Psychological, and Biological Pathways.* Eds. Nancy E. Adler, Michael Marmot, Bruce S. McEwen, and Judith Stewart. *Annals of the New York Academy of Sciences* (vol. 896), 1999, pp. 3–15.

265   **results were clear.** Nancy E. Adler, interview with author, August 6, 1998, and correspondence, March 17, 2005. On the MacArthur Scale of Subjective Social Status, see Elizabeth Goodman, Nancy E. Adler, Ichiro Kawachi, A. Lindsay Frazier, Bin Huang, and Graham A. Colditz, "Adolescents' Perceptions of Social Status: Development and Evaluation of a New Indicator," *Pediatrics* 108 (2001): 31–39.

266   **facing them head-on.** Adler, Ibid.

267   **too full of himself.** See Christopher Boehm, *Hierarchy in the Forest: The Evolution of Egalitarian Behavior* (Harvard University Press, 2000).

267   **the alien and the slave."** Quoted in Meillasoux, p. 1.

267   **the most extreme humiliation."** Victor Klemperer, *I Will Bear Witness: A Diary of the Nazi Years, Volume 1: 1933–1941* (Random House, 1998), p. 395.

268   **tied to a tree.** Terry Alford, *Prince among Slaves: The True Story of an African Prince Sold into Slavery in the American South* (Oxford University Press, 1977), p. 44.

268   **in the master's hands.** Patterson, *Slavery*, p. 72.

268   **of slaveholding societies,"** Ibid., p. 60.

268   **cannot compose myself."** Klemperer, *I Will Bear Witness*, p. 429.

268   **as we were, still remains."** Primo Levi, *Survival in Auschwitz* (Collier Books, 1961), p. 20.

269   **competing attempts to enslave."** Jonathan Shay, *Achilles in Vietnam: Combat Trauma and the Undoing of Character* (Touchstone, 1995), p. 36.

269   **two prisons,"** Ibid., p. 36.

THIRTEEN: HAZINGS AND CONVERSIONS

271   **Tupinamban slave.** Quoted in Orlando Patterson, *Slavery and Social Death* (Harvard University Press, 1982), p. 81.

271   **replaced his name.** Pierre L. van den Berghe, *Stranger in Their Midst* (University Press of Colorado, 1989), p. 104.

272   **their strongest motivation.)** See William Darryl Henderson, *Cohesion, the Human Element in Combat* (National Defense University Press, 1985), pp. 5–6.

273   **medieval inquisitors.** See James B. Given, *Inquisition and Medieval Society* (Cornell University Press, 1997), pp. 55–56.

274   **Germany became Nazis."** Paul Moore, *Presences: A Bishop's Life in the City* (Farrar, Straus and Giroux, 1998), p. 60.

274   **value their membership.** A famous and rare demonstration of this principle in lab psychology is E. Aronson and J. Mills, "The Effect of Severity of Initiation on Liking for a Group," *Journal of Abnormal and Social Psychology* 5, 1959, pp. 177–81.

        The experimenters compared college women who had to read a statement aloud to take part in a roundtable discussion. The session was designed to be very dull, and women who read an untroublesome statement said so. But women who had to read an embarrassing passage about sex (this was the 1950s) rated the meeting much more highly.

274   **sensitive, protected preppy."** Paul Moore, *Presences*, p. 60.

275   **regardless of the needs of others."** Richard Wilkinson, *Mind the Gap: Hierarchies, Health and Human Evolution* (Yale University Press, 2001), p. 17.

275   **beards stopped growing.)** P. K. Opstad, "Androgenic hormones during prolonged physical stress, sleep, and energy deficiency," *Journal of Clinical Endocrinology and Metabolism* 74 (1992): 1176–83.

275   **experience a drop.** Paul C. Bernhardt et al., "Testosterone Changes during Vicarious Experiences of Winning and Losing among Fans at Sporting Events," *Physiology and Behavior* 65, no. 1 (1998): 59–62.

276   **get the rule quashed.** Robert M. Sapolsky, *Why Zebras Don't Get Ulcers: A Guide to Stress, Stress-Related Diseases, and Coping* (W. H. Freeman, 1994), p. 328n.

276   **control over life circumstances"** Marmot, *Status Syndrome*, p. 30.

276   **they were helpless.** Bruce McEwen with Elizabeth Norton Lasley, *The End of Stress as We Know It* (Joseph Henry Press, 2002), p. 53.

277   **and self-hatred."** Charles L. Mee, *A Nearly Normal Life* (Little, Brown, 1999), p. 127.

277   **wicked pied piper.)** Ruth Mellinkoff, *Outcasts: Signs of Otherness in Northern European Art of the Late Middle Ages* (University of California Press, 1993), p. 15.

277   **image of infamy."** Ibid., p. 39.

277   **of other women.** This opinion from 1930s Shanghai is quoted in Emily Honig, *Creating Chinese Ethnicity* (Yale University Press, 1992), p. 56.

278   **into trouble anyway."** Quoted in William L. Hamilton, "Cracking the Dress Code: How a School Uniform Becomes a Fashion Statement," *New York Times,* February 19, 1998.

278   **you must try it!"** Quoted in Mellinkoff, *Outcasts,* p. 10.

279   **is the same.** These statistics are reported in Michael Marmot, *The Status Syndrome: How Social Standing Affects Our Health and Longevity* (Times Books, 2004), p. 51.

280   **authorities to reimpose them.** For example, multicolored, dagged clothes, the "gangsta" style of medieval Europe, were banned in France by Philip the Bold in 1279 and by Philip the Fair in 1294. Yet in the 1300s, these kinds of clothes — supposedly fit only for soldiers and thugs — were still in fashion among young men. See Mellinkoff, *Outcasts,* pp. 4–5. One reason the boundaries kept slipping was that wealthy "marked" people could sometimes *pay* the authorities to exempt them from the clothing rules. See Ulysse Robert, *Les signes d'infamie au Moyen Age: Juifs, Sarrasins, heretiques, lepreux, cagots et filles publiques* (H. Champion, 1891), pp. 56–57.

281   **thicker the mask."** James C. Scott, *Domination and the Arts of Resistance: Hidden Transcripts* (Yale University Press, 1990), p. 3.

281   **personal advantage."** Ibid., p. 33.

281   **bows and farts."** Ibid.

283   **rather difficult times.** The full text of this remarkable speech is in Arthur M. Schlesinger, Jr., *Robert Kennedy and His Times* (Houghton Mifflin, 1978), p. 875.

FOURTEEN: THE HEADS ON THE POLES

284   **David Sloan Wilson.** David Sloan Wilson, "Nonzero and Nonsense: Group Selection, Nonzerosumness, and the Human Gaia Hypothesis," *Skeptic* 8:1 (January 2000). Available online at <http://www.skeptic.com/review10.html>.

284   **Elias Canetti.** Elias Canetti (trans. Carol Stewart), *Crowds and Power* (Farrar, Straus and Giroux, 1984), p. 22.

285   **the particulars are accidents.** See Stephen Jay Gould, *Wonderful Life: The Burgess Shale and the Nature of History* (W. W. Norton & Company, 1990).

285   **windy steppes of Asia.** For example, Stephen Pinker calls the epicanthic fold "goggles for the tundra." Stephen Pinker, *The Blank Slate: The Modern Denial of Human Nature* (Viking, 2002), p. 143.

285   **often disappears later.** Steve Olson, *Mapping Human History: Genes, Race and Our Common Origins* (Houghton Mifflin, 2002), p. 133. Whether the epicanthic fold is an instance of natural selection (an adaptation to the environment) or sexual selection (a consequence of tastes in partners) is not settled, as Olson explains. That sexual selection is an important aspect of skin, hair, and eye appearance in humans was something Darwin took for granted, as do population geneticists today. See Luigi Cavalli-Sforza, Luigi Luca, Paolo Menozzi, and Alberto Piazza, *The History and Geography of Human Genes (Abridged)* (Princeton University Press, 1996), p. 267.

286   **shape of arches.** Stephen Jay Gould and Richard C. Lewontin, "The Spandrels of San Marco and the Panglossian Paradigm: A Critique of the Adaptationist Programme." *Proceedings of the Royal Society B (Biological Sciences)* 205 (1979): pp. 581–98.

286   **"What is grief for?"** Steven Pinker asks this question with a slight hedge — "What, if anything, is grief for?" — in Pinker, *How the Mind Works* (W. W. Norton, 1997), p. 430.

286 **of non-evolutionary biologists."** John Tooby, "View from the President's Window: The Most Testable Concept in Biology," *Human Behavior and Evolution Society Newsletter* (Fall 1999).

287 **emotional high point" of the meeting.** "Comments on the Conference," *Human Behavior and Evolution Society Newsletter* (Fall 1997).

287 **and it is. Sociobiology."** Clifford Geertz, "Sociosexology," *New York Review of Books,* January 24, 1980.

288 **undermine evolutionary science.** Robert Wright, "The Accidental Creationist: Why Stephen Jay Gould Is Bad for Evolution," *New Yorker,* December 13, 1999.

288 **and who is with Them.** The novelist and critic David Lodge thinks idea waving is particularly common among American academics, who compete hard for allies, money, and publicity. Professors in the United States, he says, often are not people who took up ideas and then divided into enemy camps and factions; rather, they're already going to divide into camps and factions and take up ideas to map the territory of their dog-eat-dog world. In the humanities, he writes, "The very difficulty and esotericism of theory make it all the more effective for the purposes of professional identification, apprenticeship, and assessment." Lodge, *After Bakhtin: Essays on Fiction and Criticism* (Routledge, 1990), p. 181.

291 **"word blindness."** This point, and the rest of this description of dyslexia, are drawn from Simon E. Fisher and John C. DeFries, "Developmental Dyslexia: Genetic Dissection of a Complex Cognitive Trait," *Nature Reviews Neuroscience* 3 (2002): 767–80.

293 **Darwinism to work."** The quotation is from Frank Miele, "Darwin's Dangerous Disciple: An Interview with Richard Dawkins," *Skeptic* 3, no. 4 (1995): 80–85. It's available online at <http://www.skeptic.com/03.4.miele-dawkins-iv.html>.

293 **physicists can pursue.** Still, the physicists who worked out the properties of the quark in 1964, Murray Gell-Mann and George Zweig, wavered over whether the concept belonged on more than one level of analysis. According to Gell-Mann's biographer, he hedged for years on the question of whether quarks were real or simply a convenient "notion" that made the equations work. George Johnson, *Strange Beauty: Murray Gell-Mann and the Revolution in Twentieth-Century Physics* (Knopf, 1999), p. 262.

  Noam Chomsky has pointed out how often, in the history of science, this pattern occurs. So, for example, Ludwig Boltzmann described his molecular theory of gases as a convenient analogy only. Most nineteenth-century chemists considered the atom a handy fiction that made chemistry easier. And Friedrich Kekulé, who established the principles of structural chemistry, refused to commit to the idea that his "rational formulae" reflected the actual arrangement of real atoms in a molecule. See Noam Chomsky, "Language and Nature," *Mind* 104 (1995): 1–61.

  Then, too, the Danish scientist who coined the term *gene,* W. L. Johannsen, sought to "urgently warn against" the idea that the gene was a physical object. It was, he wrote, "to be used as a kind of accounting or calculating unit." See Ernst Mayr, *The Growth of Biological Thought* (Harvard University Press, 1982), p. 737.

294 **all the levels of description.** Wilson describes his philosophy in E. O. Wilson, *Consilience: The Unity of Knowledge* (Knopf, 1998).

296 **a gale of laughter.** Recounted in Niles Eldredge, *The Triumph of Evolution and the Failure of Creationism* (Owl Books, 2001), p. 193.

296 **unimaginably distant past."** Peter Galison, *Image and Logic: A Material Culture of Microphysics* (University of Chicago Press, 1997), p. 805.

296 **I had ever met."** Edward O. Wilson, *Naturalist* (Warner Books, 1994), p. 219.

298 **how much it gets bent."** John Gribbin, *The Scientists: A History of Science Told through the Lives of Its Greatest Inventors* (Random House, 2002), p. 615.

298 **how physics proceeds from there."** Rob Myers quoted in Ivan Semeniuk, "No Going Back," *New Scientist,* September 20, 2003, p. 28.

298 **asks miasmal questions.** James F. Jekel et al., *Epidemiology, Biostatistics, and Preventive Medicine* (W. B. Saunders Company, 1996), p. 59.

299 **talking about.** Putnam is quoted in Peter Galison, *Image and Logic* (University of Chicago Press, 1999).

300 **a valid connection.** The meta-analysis that found no certain links between genes and novelty-seeking personality traits is A. N. Kluger et al., "A Meta-analysis of the Associ-

ation between DRD4 Polymorphism and Novelty Seeking," *Molecular Psychiatry* 7 (2002): 712–17.

The negative meta-analysis of a broad swatch of gene-personality studies is M. R. Munafo et al., "Genetic Polymorphisms and Personality in Healthy Adults: A Systematic Review and Meta-analysis," *Molecular Psychiatry* 8 (2003): 471–84.

300 **populations don't have.** A. Nebel et al., "Y Chromosome Evidence for a Founder Effect in Ashkenazi Jews," *European Journal of Human Genetics* (2004).

300 **in other populations.** K. Skorecki et al., "Y Chromosomes of Jewish Priests," *Nature* 385 (1997): 32.

300 **contributed by non-Jews.** D. M. Behar et al., "Multiple Origins of Ashkenazi Levites: Y Chromosome Evidence for Both Near Eastern and European Ancestries," *American Journal of Human Genetics* 73 (2003): 768–79.

FIFTEEN: SPECIES OF DARWINISM

302 **Emile Durkheim.** Quoted in Howard L. Kaye, *The Social Meaning of Modern Biology* (Yale University Press, 1986), p. 1.

303 **would be natural selection."** Charles Darwin, *The Descent of Man* (1871; Reprint: Modern Library, 1958), p. 500.

303 **woolly-headed field.** George C. Williams, introduction to *Adaptation and Natural Selection* (Princeton University Press, 1996), p. ix.

304 **temporary and ill-defined."** George C. Williams, telephone interview, October 1996.

304 **watch a hypocrite bleed."** Quoted in Elliott Sober et al., *Unto Others: The Evolution and Psychology of Unselfish Behavior* (Harvard University Press, 1999), p. 5.

305 **shared "inclusive fitness."** William D. Hamilton, "The Genetical Evolution of Social Behaviour," *Journal of Theoretical Biology* 7 (1964): 1–16. This paper is reprinted, with a fascinating introduction, in William D. Hamilton, *Narrow Roads of Gene Land, Volume 1* (W. H. Freeman, 1996), pp. 11–46.

306 **than by genetic kin.** Martin Daly and Margo Wilson, *Homicide* (Aldine de Gruyter, 1988).

306 **with a cat.)** John Archer, "Why Do People Love Their Pets?" *Evolution and Human Behavior* 18:4 (1997): 237–60.

306 **nonrelated comrades.** Robert Wright, *The Moral Animal: Why We Are the Way We Are: The New Science of Evolutionary Psychology* (Vintage, 1995), p. 390.

306 **watch one another's backs.** Lee Dugatkin, *Cheating Monkeys and Citizen Bees: The Nature of Cooperation in Animals and Humans* (Free Press, 1999), p. 73.

306 **University of Western Ontario.** Vincent Sarich and Frank Miele, *Race: The Reality of Human Differences* (Westview Press, 2004); J. Philippe Rushton, *Race, Evolution, and Behavior: A Life History Perspective,* 3rd ed. (Charles Darwin Research Institute Press, 2000).

307 **equal to those of Japanese.** Described in Steve Olson, *Mapping Human History: Genes, Race and Our Common Origins* (Houghton Mifflin, 2002), p. 62.

308 **achieving their goals."** Kevin MacDonald, *Separation and Its Discontents: Toward an Evolutionary Theory of Anti-Semitism* (Praeger, 1998), p. 9.

309 **feats of running.** Jon Entine, *Taboo: Why Black Athletes Dominate Sports and Why We're Afraid to Talk about It* (Public Affairs, 2000), pp. 285–88.

309 **from white ancestors.** For example, according to Rick Kittles, codirector for Molecular Genetics at the National Human Genome Center at Howard University, 30 percent of African American men carry Y-chromosome genetic markers that come from Europe. Kittles is one of them. See Rick Kittles, remarks at the conference "African Genealogy and Genetics," University of Minnesota, June 21–22, 2002. Available online at <http://www.bioethics.umn.edu/afrgen/html/ Geneticsandgenealogy.html>.

A survey of ten African-descended populations in the United States and Jamaica used different genetic markers and found that the presence of European genes in the groups ranged from 6.8 percent in Jamaica to 22.5 percent in New Orleans. E. J. Parra et al., "Estimating African American Admixture Proportions by Use of Population-specific Alleles," *American Journal of Human Genetics* 63 (1998): 1839–51.

309 **physics journal of our time."** John Tooby, comments in "How to Deal with Fringe Academics," *Slate* magazine, available online at <http://www.slate.com/id/74139/entry/74141/>.

310 **dishonoring their family.** Accounts of this sort of decision are recounted in Souad, *Burned Alive: A Victim of the Law of Men* (Warner Books, 2004).

310 **stopped speaking to him.** For teenagers, this change in the family's human-kind map often leads to abuse or even to abandonment. See R. C. Savin-Williams, "Verbal and Physical Abuse as Stressors in the Lives of Lesbian, Gay Male, and Bisexual Youths: Associations with School Problems, Running Away, Substance Abuse, Prostitution, and Suicide," *Journal of Consultative and Clinical Psychology* 62 (1994): 261–69.

311 **to whom I am useful."** Muhammad ben Sulaïman Al Sudaïs, *A Selection of Current Najdi-Arabic Proverbs* (Librairie du Liban, 1993), p. 93.

311 **for number one.** For experiments that show how humans don't just go after profit for themselves, see Joseph Henrich, Robert Boyd, Samuel Bowles, Colin Camerer, Ernst Fehr, and Herbert Gintis, *Foundations of Human Sociality: Economic Experiments and Ethnographic Evidence from Fifteen Small-Scale Societies* (Oxford University Press, 2004). For an idea of how economics has moved away from "rational economic man" models, see Paul Seabright, *The Company of Strangers: A Natural History of Economic Life* (Princeton University Press, 2004).

311 **I'll scratch yours.** Robert Trivers, "The Evolution of Reciprocal Altruism," *Quarterly Review of Biology* 46 (1971): 35–57.

312 **the exchange organ."** Matt Ridley, *The Origins of Virtue: Human Instincts and the Evolution of Cooperation* (Viking Press, 1996), p. 130.

312 **rules for people's conduct.** For example, here is a logical problem: You're an administrator organizing records at the local high school. The way the system works is that each student in category D should have his or her folder coded with a 3. (To solve the problem, you don't need to know what D and 3 mean.) Take a look at these four folders; which ones do you need to check to make sure they have been coded properly? They're labeled first, D; second, F; third, 3; and fourth, 7. The correct answer isn't obvious to most people: You need to check folder D (to make sure it has been assigned a 3), and you need to check folder 7 (to make sure it has not been assigned a D by mistake). That's it; you're done.

Peter Wason, the psychologist who devised this kind of scenario in the 1960s, found that three quarters of the people he tested went wrong. They might think they needed to check both D and 3, for instance, or that they needed to check all. The problem is not easy for most people.

Now we're going to change the terms. You're a bar bouncer, and you want to make sure your establishment is not serving alcohol to people below the legal drinking age (twenty-one in most parts of the United States). You see four people. Which ones do you need to check to make sure they're legal? The four are a person drinking a beer, someone else drinking a Coke, a forty-five-year-old, and a sixteen-year-old. This is easier; at least, most people think so. Three quarters of the people who take this version get it right. You check the beer drinker and you check the sixteen-year-old. You don't care what the forty-five-year-old does, and people can drink Coke no matter their age.

Logically, these two setups are exactly the same. But Leda Cosmides and John Tooby found that the Wason test is easy *only* when it is framed as a search for people who might be cheating on a rule — which the bar problem is, and the file folder problem is not. This is evidence, Tooby and Cosmides argue, for the "cheat detector" mental code that you would expect to find in a species that depends on reciprocal altruism. See Leda Cosmides and John Tooby, "Cognitive Adaptation for Social Exchange," in *The Adapted Mind: Evolutionary Psychology and the Generation of Culture,* ed. Jerome H. Barkow, Leda Cosmides, and John Tooby, pp. 163–228 (Oxford University Press, 1992).

312 **someone else will give to you."** Ron Bluntschli, interview.

313 **demands for reciprocity.** Patrick Geary, "The Humiliation of Saints," in *Saints and Their Cults: Studies in Religious Sociology, Folklore and History,* ed. Stephen Wilson, pp. 123–40 (Cambridge University Press, 1983).

313 **his genetic stake.** See Richard D. Alexander, *The Biology of Moral Systems* (Aldine de Gruyter, 1987), chap. 2.

313 **"tribal social instincts."** Peter J. Richerson and Robert Boyd, "The Evolution of Subjective Commitment to Groups: A Tribal Instincts Hypothesis," in *Evolution and the Capacity for Commitment,* ed. Randolph Nesse (Russell Sage Foundation Publications,

2001), pp. 186–220. Also see Peter J. Richerson, Robert T. Boyd, and Joseph Henrich, "The Cultural Evolution of Human Cooperation," in *The Genetic and Cultural Evolution of Cooperation,* ed. P. Hammerstein (MIT Press, 2003), pp. 357–88.

314   **large-scale cooperation.** Peter J. Richerson, telephone interview with the author, July 2004.

315   **about ethnic groups.** Francisco Gil-White, "Are Ethnic Groups Biological 'Species' in the Human Brain?" *Current Anthropology* 42 (2001): 515–54.

317   **categorize by race."** Robert Kurzban et al., "Can Race Be Erased? Coalitional Computation and Social Categorization," *Proceedings of the National Academy of Sciences* 98 (2001): 15387–92.

319   **Celts and Saxons."** William D. Hamilton, "Extraordinary Sex Ratios," in *The Narrow Roads of Gene Land: The Collected Papers of William Hamilton,* vol. 1, pp. 131–69 (W. H. Freeman, 1995), p. 135.

CONCLUSION

321   **conduct and cognition are racialized."** Lawrence A. Hirchsfeld, *Race in the Making* (MIT Press, 1996), p. 7n.

323   **But that's changing.** For example, see Rogers Brubaker, *Ethnicity Without Groups* (Harvard University Press, 2004), and Rogers Brubaker, Mara Loveman, and Peter Stamatov, "Ethnicity as Cognition," *Theory and Society* 33 (2004): 31.

326   **crime to the world.** For example, see Dan M. Kahan and Eric A. Posner, "Shaming White Collar Criminals: A Proposal for Reform of the Federal Sentencing Guidelines," *Journal of Law and Economics* 41, no. 2 (1998).

326   **unconscious parts of the mind.** See Martha C. Nussbaum, *Hiding from Humanity: Disgust, Shame, and the Law* (Princeton University Press, 2004).

327   **which is criminality.** Probably the most ferocious version of this argument is Michelle Malkin, *In Defense of Internment: The Case for 'Racial Profiling' in World War II and the War on Terror* (Regnery Publishing, 2004).

327   **as well as other techniques.** See David A. Harris, *Profiles in Injustice: Why Racial Profiling Cannot Work* (W. W. Norton & Company, 2003).

327   **the entire human race.** Peter Singer, *The Expanding Circle: Ethics and Sociobiology* (Farrar, Straus and Giroux, 1981), pp. 25–53.

329   **(In fact, somebody did.)** Psychological profiles supposedly reveal that sport-utility buyers tend to be more restless, more sybaritic, less social, and more self-oriented; minivan buyers tend to be more self-confident and more involved with family, friends, and communities. See Keith Bradsher, "Was Freud a Minivan or S.U.V. Kind of Guy?," *New York Times,* July 17, 2000.

Index

ABOUT THE AUTHOR

David Berreby was born in France, raised in the
United States, and educated at Yale. He has
written on scientific and cultural issues for the
*New York Times, The New Republic, Slate, Lingua
Franca, The Sciences,* and *Discover,* among
other publications.
He lives in Brooklyn, New York.